To John & family
with all best wishes

Tony Carruthers

KERRY: A NATURAL HISTORY

KERRY:

A
NATURAL HISTORY

TERRY CARRUTHERS

THE COLLINS PRESS

Published by The Collins Press, Carey's Lane, The Huguenot Quarter, Cork, 1998
© Terry Carruthers

Printed in Ireland by Colour Books Ltd., Dublin

Jacket design by Upper Case Ltd., Cornmarket Street, Cork

ISBN: 1-898256-45-4

CONTENTS

For Niamh,
Fiona and Ciara
with love

PREFACE

THE COUNTY of Kerry covers nearly 5,000 square kilometres of the south-west corner of Ireland. It is well known at home and abroad for its dramatic scenery and for many years has been Ireland's premier visitor destination. Less well known is the attraction the region holds for biologists, geologists and all those interested in the natural history of the region.

The southwest differs from the rest of Ireland in its geology, history of glaciation, climate, flora and fauna and these differences are part of the reason for its attraction to naturalists from a wide range of disciplines. Due to its geographical location, broad mix of habitats and a mild, oceanic climate, Kerry is biologically the most interesting county in Ireland. Its habitats include the highest mountains in the country, a variety of lakes, the largest tracts of native woodland still surviving in Ireland, precipitous marine islands with important seabird colonies, several large estuaries, extensive sand dune systems and a variety of farmland types. The oceanic influence penetrates all these habitats, allowing the development of some of the finest oceanic plant communities in Europe. The county's species diversity is enhanced by a southern component of Mediterranean and Pyrenean species, a northern component of Arctic and sub-Arctic species, for which Kerry is the southern limit of their distribution, as well as an interesting North American group.

In this book I describe the geological developments which provided the basic rock framework of the county, the action of the various erosive agents which continue to operate on the landscape, and the influence which people have had on it. I then describe some of the animal and plant communities to be found from the highest peaks to the oceans which virtually surround the county. In each chapter I choose a sample of the common and rarer plants and animals to be found in these communities, enlarging on some specific aspects of their lives. By doing so I hope to stimulate greater interest and enthusiasm for all aspects of the region's natural history. Throughout the book I use the current common plant and animal names where possible. Where no common names exist I have used the scientific names in the text. The English names of species mentioned are listed in Appendix 1 along with their scientific names.

An enormous volume of literature has been published on the natural history of Kerry. The majority of this lies in scientific journals which are often difficult for the general reader to procure. I have made use of many such journals, books and other sources of information, which are listed in the Bibliography. In reading through these one begins to appreciate the amount of work which is undertaken every year. I pay tribute to all those fieldworkers without whom this book could not have been written. However, it is also apparent that the region has not been covered evenly. In the botanical and zoological spheres, much of the work has been concentrated on the Killarney district, due to the particular set of circumstances which make this region so special. Unfortunately, much of the north Kerry area appears to have been largely ignored. Except for the coastal fringe, we know little about the distribution of many species north of a line from Killarney to Tralee. Even distinctive and widespread groups such as dragonflies have hardly been touched, as a look at any distribution map will show. This alone would make a very suitable project for any aspiring naturalist or school group.

I am exceedingly grateful to a number of different people who gave me their unstinting help and co-operation while researching and writing this book: Simon Berrow, Hugh Brazier, Tim Burkitt, Alan Craig, Aidan Forde, Irish Meteorological Service, Andy Gosler, Jane Keane, Gabriel King, Jim Larner, Kate McAney, Peter McDermot, Ede Ní Thuama, Tommy O'Connor and Peter O'Toole. I would particularly like to thank those whose company I enjoyed on various field trips that were such an interesting part of the learning experience which this undertaking gave me: Chris Barron, Cathriona Douglas, Rose Fitzgerald, Kieran Griffin, Toby Hodd, Tim Lavery, John O'Connor, Jim O'Malley, and Martin Speight. Some of the above-mentioned also read various drafts of the book, as did Vivien O'Shea – a special thanks goes to those who did so – any errors, omissions or inaccuracies are entirely mine.

I would also like to thank those who have encouraged and supported me in many ways from the very outset: Ann and Michael Crowley, Michael Miller and Liam Lysaght. Here I would also like to pay a special tribute to the late Tony Whilde and his wife Marianne, whose work I have long admired and who provided me with many hints and tips about approaching this project. I wish that

Tony was still around to see it coming to fruition.

The book is enlivened by the work of a number of photographers, whose input I value enormously – Paudie O'Leary, Billy Clarke, Kieran Griffin, Kevin Tarrant, Evelyn Moorken, John Cronin, Kevin Dwyer, John Earley, Eddie Dunne and Michael Diggin.

Last but by no means least I must thank Niamh FitzGerald for her assistance with typing, finding references and for her general support, understanding and patience, without which I could not have completed *Kerry: A Natural History.*

Map 1: Location map of Kerry

10

Chapter 1

THE LANDSCAPE OF KERRY

GEOGRAPHICALLY AND politically, Kerry can be divided into two broad regions; the mountainous areas of the Beara, Iveragh and Dingle peninsulas and the low-lying plains and rolling hills of north Kerry. The county is famous for its scenic beauty – high mountains mirrored in lakes, estuaries and sea inlets, dense stands of forests; all combine to provide the necessary scenic ingredients. The presence of the ocean, which virtually surrounds the county, provides a moisture-laden atmosphere which softens our perception of the landscape and creates dramatic lighting effects.

The influence of the sea is felt everywhere. The county's peninsular form and mountainous nature provides one with many vantage points from which to view its remarkable coastline. The numerous gales which occur throughout the year leave plants salt-burned many miles inland. And the ocean influences the climate of Kerry and thus its flora, fauna and the moods of its people.

The Kerry we see today has been changed in many ways over the millions of years since the dawn of time. As far as the beginning is concerned, the oldest rock on earth so far dated has an age of 4,500 million years, but it is believed the earth is considerably older. The oldest Irish rocks, from Co. Wexford, are 2,400 million years old.

Of the first two-thirds of the earth's history, little is known. What crust the earth had was thin and subjected to enormously violent disturbance. There appears to have been repeated cycles of extreme rock deformation. However, by 600 million years ago, the intensity of these disturbances declined and with the aid of fossils and other methods of dating, we are able to follow geological events more closely.

PLATE TECTONICS

The Earth's outer shell or lithosphere is composed of at least 12 large rigid areas known as tectonic plates, which are continually moving against or away from each other. The lithosphere averages approximately 100 kilometres in thickness and rests upon the asthenosphere, the semi-liquid upper layer of the mantle. Scientists do not as yet fully understand the detailed mechanism of plate movement, but believe it is related to the transfer of heat energy deep within the earth.

---

600 million years ago the sea covered the area we call Wales, which the Romans had earlier called Cambria. In that early sea there were many forms of animal life, and these left fossils in the local rocks, which are known as *Cambrian*. The vast period of time before this, from which little dateable material survives, is known as the Precambrian Era.

The time from 600 million years ago to the present is divided into a number of periods of geological time, called Eras. These are further sub-divided into Periods and Epochs. The earth's rocks can be broadly divided into three different types. Sedimentary rocks, such as limestones and sandstones are created from the deposition of other materials. Igneous rocks, such as granite and basalt, result from the cooling of molten rock at different rates. Metamorphic rocks, such as slates and marbles, have been changed from either sedimentary or igneous rocks by the tremendous pressures and intense heat of earth movements.

The time from 600 million years ago to the present is divided into a number of periods of geological time, called Eras. These are further sub-divided into Periods and Epochs. The earth's rocks can be broadly divided into three different types. Sedimentary rocks, such as limestones and sandstones are created from the deposition of other materials. Igneous rocks, such as granite and basalt, result from the cooling of molten rock at different rates. Metamorphic rocks, such as slates and marbles, have been changed from either sedimentary or igneous rocks by the tremendous pressures and intense heat of earth movements.

The oldest visible rocks in Kerry are on the Dingle peninsula. Gneiss and schist, both igneous rocks, found as pebbles in younger conglomerate near Inch, are believed to be of Precambrian age. Somewhat younger are the rocks of Ordovician age to be found between Annascaul and Slieve Mish. Further west in the region of Ballydavid the lowlands are composed of flagstones and slates of Silurian age, believed to be some 2,000 metres (6,000 feet) deep. Fossils of shellfish such as brachiopods are found in these Silurian rocks, while the stones of Sybil Head contain amongst others, fossils of coral. Volcanic rocks of Silurian age occur in the area between Inishvickillaun, Beginish and Clogher Head, but due to

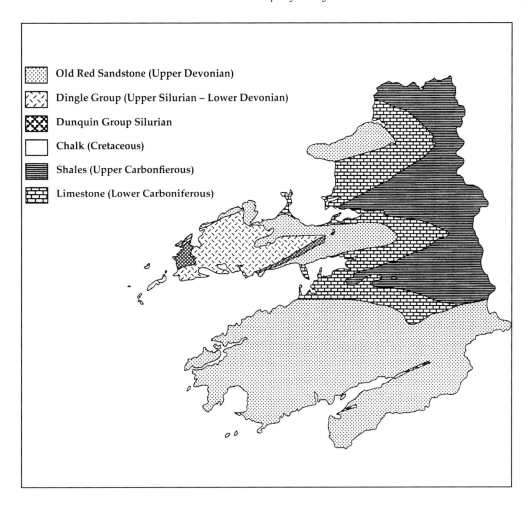

Map 2: The geology of Kerry

erosion very little of this volcanic material now remains. But the bulk of the county's rock framework was laid down in a period between 400 and 250 million years ago. As this is one of the more important periods in the formation of Kerry, I will cover it in some detail.

Sometime before 500 million years ago the two great landmasses of the then North American and European continents started to move towards one another. As they collided, some 450 million years ago, great mountains running northeast/southwest were formed in what is now Newfoundland, north west Ireland, Scotland and Scandinavia. This folding is known as the Caledonian folding after the old name for Scotland. The new super-continent thus formed is known as the 'Old Red Continent'.

Era	Period	Epoch	Ages Millions of years before present	Events in Kerry
Cenozoic	Quarternary	Holocene	0.01	Bogs forming
		Pleistocene	2	Glaciation
		Pliocene	13	
	Tertiary	Miocene	25	
		Oligocene	36	
		Eocene	58	
		Palaeocene	70	
Mesozoic	Cretaceous		135	Chalk formed in Kerry
	Jurassic		180	
	Triassic		225	
	Permian		270	
Palaeozoic	Carboniferous		350	Limestone laid down
	Devonian	Caledonian	400	Old red sandstones
	Silurian		430	Ballydavid siltstones
	Ordiovician		500	
Precambrian	Cambrian	Dalradian	600	

Figure 2: Geological timescale

From the rugged Caledonian highlands to the north, numerous rivers flowed south, carrying with them vast amounts of eroded rock. This material was deposited in a large landlocked basin called the South Munster Basin. Most of the rocks of Kerry were deposited in this basin during the latter part of the Devonian Period, which lasted over 50 million years. The oldest Devonian rocks in Ireland, termed the Dingle Beds, form Brandon mountain on the Dingle peninsula.

Conditions changed towards the end of the Devonian Period. Grey shales and yellow sandstone, referred to as the Kiltorcan Beds, were laid down on top of the red formations. The Kiltorcan Beds are renowned for their fossil plant remains, which are the earliest record of land vegetation in Ireland. A narrow band of these Kiltorcan Beds girdle the eastern end of the Dingle peninsula and Kerry Head.

As the Devonian period drew to a close, volcanic activity increased, resulting in the presence of volcanic rocks near Lough Guitane, south-east of Killarney. Volcanic ash ejected during this period hardened into felsite, pale grey in colour with whitish crystals of feldspar in it. It can be found in the area from the Devil's Punchbowl on Mangerton mountain as far as Glenflesk.

EARLY LIFE IN KERRY

Rocks of Silurian age outcrop in a number of locations on the Dingle peninsula. These occur in the Dunquin area, in Derrymore glen, at Bull's head and between Annascaul and Caherconree mountain. These are mostly of shallow marine origin, and contain a rich fossil fauna including brachiopods, bryozoans, bivalves, corals and trilobites. The latter are an extinct group of arthropods which first appeared during the Early Cambrian, were particularly common during the Late Cambrian, but became extinct by the end of the Permian. Caherconree mountain contains the finest Silurian trilobites in Ireland. They occur in hard limestone, with at least 16 species present.

Some 345 million years ago there occurred further tectonic disturbances, when north-west Europe, including Ireland, was engulfed by a shallow, warm and calcium rich sea. The calcium was used by animals and plants to form skeletons of calcium carbonate. When these died, their calcareous skeletons built up in tremendous thicknesses, and consolidated to form limestone.

At a later stage sand and clay began to be carried in, which hardened into sandstone and shale, lying on top of the limestone. Over time, the water became so shallow that tropical swamp forests developed, and vegetable debris accumulated in backwaters and swamps. This debris gradually transformed into coal. Because of the presence of this coal, this sedimentary cycle is called the

---

VALENTIA'S SLATE QUARRY

On the north-eastern end of Valentia island, beneath the ridge of Geokaun mountain, lies the slate quarry of Dohilla. The slates are composed of fine, purple-coloured siltstones, formed during the middle-upper Devonian Period, which were compressed and folded by Earth pressures. Because it developed a good cleavage, Valentia slate could be split into large, thin slabs. The quarry was opened in 1816, and production continued until 1911. The slate had many uses, including the manufacture of billiard tables, shelving, seating, headstones, paving and roofing.

Carboniferous period. Virtually all the coal which once covered Ireland has long since been eroded away. Early geologists however, finding very small quantities of poor quality coal in the north Kerry plateau, called these rocks Coal Measures. This north Kerry plateau, extending into Limerick and Clare, is now the alrgest area of Upper Carboniferous of 'Namurian' rocks in Ireland.

About 300 million years ago, dramatic tectonic movements brought the Carboniferous cycle to an end. At this time the 'Old Red Continent' collided with the super-continent of Gondwanaland, which contained the future continents of Africa, South America, Australasia and Antarctica. This collision folded the tremendous layers of sandstones, shales, limestones and coal, formed during the

AGEING ROCKS

There are a number of ways in which geologists attempt to understand the Earth's geological history, some physical, some biological. One method used is radiometry. When molten material solidifies into rock, it will contain small quantities of radioactive elements which proceed to break down into simpler materials at a constant rate, e.g., uranium breaks down into lead. By determining the amount of uranium originally present, the rate of breakdown, and the amount of lead formed, geologists can calculate how long the process has been going on, and hence the age of the rock.

The Earth has a powerful magnetic field, with north and south poles. The field is not constant, but varies over time. During the process of rock formation, minerals such as oxides of iron are influenced by the magnetic field and align themselves with it. These minerals are locked in position, and so record the direction of the field at the time of rock formation. Studies of this fossil magnetism in rocks have enabled the former positions of magnetic poles at various geological times to be located. The study of magnetism in rocks is called palaeomagnetism.

With the passage of time animals and plants evolved and their hard parts changed and developed. As successive rocks were deposited, some of these hard parts were preserved in them as fossils. If the fossils in the different layers of rock can be placed in an evolutionary sequence, their relative ages will become apparent. This gives us a biological method of dating, which is of the greatest importance.

Caherconree Mountain on the Dingle Peninsula

Devonian and Carboniferous periods, into great mountain ranges. The ripple effect of this disturbance lost force as it approached Ireland, but still caused extensive rock deformation in Kerry and Cork. Geological features created at this time are known as Armorican or Hercynian, named after European sites where this folding was first described.

The mountain ranges of Kerry were thrust up during this period. Because the direction of thrust was from the south, our mountains run in an east-west direction.

During this folding episode the top layers of rock stretched and cracked, and the forces of erosion proceeded to attack the weakened rocks. Firstly the coal deposits disappeared, then much of the sandstone, shale and limestone was eroded. In Kerry, the underlying Old Red Sandstone was widely exposed. Being more resistant to erosion than the limestone, the ORS survives to this day to form the bulk of the county's high ground.

The less resistant limestone was eroded to a greater extent than the ORS or the Namurian shales of the north Kerry plateau. The remaining limestone now

DEVONIAN ROCKS

Three main types of Devonian rocks are found in Kerry. Sandstones consist of grains of sand which are deposited in areas such as river floodplains. This rock varies in colour from green to red and purple, depending on the binding agent. Chlorite, silica and oxides of iron are all important natural cements. The deep red colour of much of Kerry's sandstone is caused by the presence of the red oxide called red ochre or haematite. This rock has long been known as Old Red Sandstone, or ORS for short. As quartz is the principal component of Devonian rocks, these rocks are therefore extremely hard and resistant to erosion. Although the Old Red Sandstone outcrops over less than 10% of Ireland's surface, it forms almost 50% of the 190 or so Irish peaks that rise over 600 metres (2,000 feet), over 90 of them in Kerry. In the county, there are 88 peaks in the 600-900 metre range (2,000-3,000 feet), and over 190 peaks above 450 metres (1,500 feet).

Shales are composed of particles of silt and mud laid down in calmer waters of lakes and estuaries. Conglomerates are composed of coarser pebbles, often of quartz, deposited in fast-flowing rivers or as shingle-beach deposits, and subsequently cemented together with different binding materials.

Mist over the Upper Lake of Killarney

17

occupies an agriculturally and ecologically important band between ORS mountains and the shales of north Kerry.

Where intense deformation of this sort occurs, the enormous pressures generated can cause the rock strata to fracture, and then move relative to one another. This is called a fault line, and one such fault line occurs at Clogher Head, where the older Silurian rocks were forced above the younger ORS.

The heat and pressure caused by this mountain building episode caused the rock strata and water trapped deep within the rock to heat up enormously. Minute concentrations of minerals such as copper, zinc and lead within the rock were dissolved by these fluids, which migrated towards the earth's surface. On cooling, the minerals were redeposited as concentrated veins of ore. Copper lodes occur at Killarney, Coad mountain near Caherdaniel, Valentia and Ardtully, near Kenmare, while lead lodes also occur at the latter site. Some sites have been worked by man since the Bronze age.

Little evidence remains in Ireland of the vast period from 270 to 65 million years ago. By about 220 million years ago, the south Atlantic began to open up between South America and Africa. By 180 million years ago, at the beginning of the Jurassic Period, the central Atlantic began to open up, separating North America from Africa. This was the beginning of the Age of Dinosaurs, but of this whole period little material has been found in Ireland. All during this time, a vast amount of rock was gradually being eroded away.

About 70 million years ago, during the Cretaceous period, sea levels rose again, flooding all of Europe, including Ireland. Tiny floating organisms with calcareous shells drifted in this sea and when they died and sank to the sea floor, a fine oozy sediment accumulated there. This was later consolidated and uplifted as a fine-grained white limestone, chalk. Although this chalk probably covered almost the whole of Ireland – in places to a depth of more than 100 metres – it was nearly all stripped away by later erosion. Outside of north-east Ireland, where extensive areas of chalk were buried and subsequently protected from further erosion by outpourings of basaltic lava, the only place in Ireland where chalk still survives is in County Kerry, near the Killarney/Farranfore road.

The period from 65 to 2 million years ago is known as the Tertiary Period, and is characterised by the appearance of modern flora and fauna. Due to massive erosion, little material of Tertiary age has survived in Ireland today. At the beginning of this period, 65 million years ago, the modern Atlantic was taking shape, with Greenland parting company from Europe. Some 5 million years later, with Greenland still moving steadily northwards, a further split occurred. Some geologists argue that this deprived the west side of Ireland of support, causing it to sag oceanwards. This sagging allowed the ocean to flood the valleys of Kerry, giving us the rias or drowned valleys, such as Kenmare bay, of today. Other geologists argue that rias are principally products of rising sea levels after the last ice age, but more of this later.

These stresses in the earth's crust caused volcanic activity throughout Ireland. Volcanic activity does not just mean the classic massive explosions of volcanoes such as Mount St Helens in the American state of Washington, but also includes the steady extrusion of lava over long periods. All rocks which owe their origin to the solidification of molten rock, or magma, are described as igneous. If the molten lava should solidify in underground fissures before it reaches the surface, it becomes a dyke. Dolerite dykes of presumed Tertiary age traverse the Beara, Iveragh and Dingle peninsulas. Some of these dykes have been dated to 42 – 25 million years ago.

Other material of presumed Tertiary age occurs in the Gweestin river valley, near Listry Bridge, where a number of outliers of breccia occur. Breccia is a rock composed of angular fragments greater than two millimetres and cemented in a fine matrix. These rocks are regarded as terrestrial deposits formed by the collapse of the roofs of former limestone caverns.

THE AGE OF ICE

The Pleistocene Epoch, characterised by the alternate waxing and waning of Arctic ice sheets, started about 2 million years ago. The world climate gradually cooled, and polar icecaps began to spread. Intense periods of cold occurred in Europe, cold polar currents lapped the shores of Ireland, and ice began to form. Continuous Arctic conditions did not occur, however, throughout this whole period. Kerry was affected by a number of cold stages, separated by warm periods called *interglacials*. The immense weight of ice-sheets caused the earth's crust to sag; when this ice melted during interglacial periods, the crust gradually returned to its 'normal' position. This upwarping of the ground often left former beaches raised above sea-level. Pre-glacial raised beaches are to be seen on the Dingle peninsula at Ballydavid, just south of the slip-way, at the western tip of Ventry harbour, and the eastern side of Dingle harbour, almost to the lighthouse.

Pollen analysis has been invaluable in identifying the pollen trapped in organic deposits left behind after different interstadials or interglacial periods. On the beach near Spa, on the north side of Tralee bay, deposits of peat and silts of interstadial or interglacial age are to be seen in low cliffs. These deposits vary from 2 to 30 centimetres in thickness. Dr Frank Mitchell examined pollen from this deposit and found that it included some pollen grains of fir and rhododendron.

This deposit was subsequently re-examined by Dr Pete Coxon and his colleagues of Trinity College, Dublin. Using a very advanced method of dating, the uranium-thorium disequalibrium method, it was found that these peat deposits were laid down between 123,000 and 114,000 years ago. In the lowest peat layers,

A GLOSSARY OF GEOLOGICAL TERMS NOT EXPLAINED IN THE TEXT

CRETACEOUS PERIOD — The major chalk-forming period. From Latin *creta*, chalk.

DOLERITE — A dark, medium grained igneous rock.

DYKE — Dykes are sheets of molten rock, more or less parallel-sided and usually not much more than 3 metres in width.

INLIERS — An inlier is an outcrop of older rocks surrounded by younger rocks.

INTERGLACIAL PERIOD — A major warm phase between Ice Ages when closed canopy woodland developed.

INTERSTADIAL — A minor period of climatic warming, many of which can be identified in the Ice Age record, which was too short for closed canopy woodland to have developed.

OUTLIERS — An outlier is any outcrop of younger rock surrounded by older rocks.

ORDOVICIAN PERIOD — A period characterised by the appearance of primitive types of fish, named after the Ordovices, an ancient Celtic tribe in North Wales where Ordivician rocks were first described.

SILURIAN PERIOD — A period characterised by the appearance of land plants, named after the Silures, an ancient Celtic tribe of Wales, where Silurian rocks were first described.

POLLEN ANALYSIS

Analysis of pollen trapped in peat deposits and lake sediments gives us some idea of the plant communities that occurred while these were being formed. This branch of science is called palynology and is of relatively recent origin. Pollen and the spores of ferns, mosses etc. are very resistant to decay and many are sufficiently different from each other to be identifiable to particular species. So by taking a vertical core down through this peaty sediment and examining the pollen grains and spores trapped within, it is possible for scientists to construct a pollen diagram. The material can be dated using the radiocarbon or C14 technique to within a narrow time frame, thus giving us a fairly accurate idea of the different plant communities which were present in the area at various periods.

dating from the earlier phase, pollen of pine and heath species predominated, indicating a cool, temperate climate with open, sparsely wooded terrain. In the uppermost layers, an increase in the pollen of oak, holly, alder and hazel possibly indicate a slightly warmer period than before.

These pollen assemblages were unlike any others recorded in Ireland. They appear to represent a cool temperate phase towards the end of the last interglacial period, or an interstadial early in the last glaciation. After being wiped out by the last period of glaciation, rhododendron and firs were re-introduced into Ireland by man in the past 200 years.

The last great cold stage, called the 'Midlandian Glaciation', ran from 120,000-10,000 years ago. During the earlier phase of this cold stage, the higher peaks had a covering of snow for much of the year. Nearby lowlands may have looked like the sub-Arctic tundra of today, with areas of polar desert, interspersed with richer oases of grasses, herbs and low shrubs. From fossil remains found in a cove near Doneraile, Co. Cork, dating to 34,000 years ago, we know that the fauna was basically an Arctic one. Arctic hares, Norway and Arctic lemmings, wolf, brown bear, spotted hyena, woolly mammoth, reindeer and the giant Irish deer roamed this landscape.

As the climate deteriorated, a large ice-cap developed, centred over the Templenoe area near Kenmare. As this sheet of ice built up to perhaps 1,000 metres (3,000 feet) in thickness, the force of gravity caused it to send tongues of ice in all directions. The westward flowing tongue gouged through Ballaghbeama Pass, excavating Caragh Lake to finish at Castlemaine harbour. Other tongues, diverted by the Macgillycuddy Reeks, made breaches at Moll's Gap, the Windy Gap and the Gap of Dunloe, Kerry's most spectacular and famous 'glacial breach'.

Apart from the Templenoe ice-cap, smaller glaciers formed in many of the higher mountain areas such as Mangerton, Brandon and the MacGillicuddy's Reeks. The weight and action of the ice gouged out deep bowl-shaped hollows at the head of valleys called 'corries' or 'cooms'. Where two corries formed back to back, they are separated by a sharp-edged ridge called an 'arete', such as the ridge between the Devil's Punchbowl and the Horse's Glen on Mangerton mountain. Not all the peaks were covered by ice. The MacGillicuddy's Reeks stood above the ice-flow as 'nunataks', developing their jagged appearance from the freeze-thaw process to which they

Cnoc an Capeen near Kenmare, an enormous glacial erratic

were subject.

As ice moves, it picks up rocks and boulders, which act as scouring pads on the surface of the land. Just as scouring pads leave scratches on pots and pans, so these boulders left scratches, called 'striae', on the rock surface below. These can still be seen clearly, indicating the direction of flow of the ice. As the ice flows over the rock surface below, it exerts a plucking action on it. Typically the upstream side of exposed rock is worn smooth by abrasion, while the downstream side has a short, steep face from this plucking action. These are called 'roche moutonnee', meaning a sheep-like rock. All these features can be seen in Kerry's glaciated areas.

As the climate warmed again, the ice-cap finally melted, depositing huge quantities of eroded material in its wake. This material is called 'glacial till'. The melting process occurred in stages, leaving much of this till as mounds or moraines. It is moraines which impounded Lough Leane and Caragh Lake, as well as many of our smaller mountain lakes. The town of Waterville is built upon a long moraine which impounds Lough Currane.

When the ice sheets melted worldwide, large volumes of water were released into the oceans. Sea levels rose, low coastal areas were flooded and the coastal sections of rivers were drowned. No better examples of a drowned river valley, called a ria, exist than the long inlets of the south-west coast, which area has long been regarded as one of the classic drowned landscapes of Europe. The peninsulas of Kerry and Cork were once ridges separating west flowing rivers. The valleys were so deeply drowned that the short rivers which enter the sea at the heads of the inlets today are merely the upper sections of the lengthier rivers of the past.

By about 15,000 years ago, the ice-sheets finally started to retreat, and had virtually disappeared after about 2,000 years. Those Arctic plants which had survived in Kerry or nearby during the Ice Age began the process of recolonising the newly exposed ground. Lichens and mosses would have been first on the scene, quickly followed by arctic/alpine flowers, juniper, willow and birch scrub. Low-lying marshy areas on base rich soils would have quickly developed into extensive fens. By 13,000 years ago the climate was gradually warming, and animals and plants were re-invading Ireland across a land-bridge from Britain.

It was at this stage that the giant Irish deer reached its zenith in Ireland. This enormous deer, with an antler spread of some 3 metres and up to 2 metres high at the shoulders, was widely distributed throughout the country, and well preserved skeletal remains have been found across the Kerry border in Co. Limerick. With such a large body and antlers, it would have required lush, calcium-rich grazing. While no finds have occurred in Kerry, it is hard to believe that it did not penetrate to the county's rich limestone vales. From this same period comes a record of the presence of reindeer from near Ballylongford, on the Shannon estuary.

However, a short, severe cold spell returned from 10,900 to 10,200 years ago.

Corrie glaciers again developed, and Arctic/Alpine plants were growing on low-lands around Killarney. It was during this period that the giant Irish deer became extinct in Ireland.

AFTER THE ICE AGE

By 10,000 years ago the climate had improved, and the permanent ice finally disappeared from Kerry's high mountains. Sea-level was still very much lower than today, perhaps by as much as 90 metres, and it is believed that a continuous land-bridge existed from Ireland, through Britain to France, along which plants and animals invaded Ireland. The Arctic/Alpine plants, unable to survive the increasing temperatures and strong competition, either became extinct or retreated to refuges in the high mountains.

Many interesting pollen studies have been carried out in County Kerry, and four of the more detailed works have been drawn on to highlight the modifications to our environment since the Ice Age. At Ballinlohig, not far from the town of Dingle, the peat core examined covered a period going back 13,800 years BP (before the present). This and other cores examined showed that following on from the last glaciation, juniper spread widely, followed and later replaced by hazel and birch woods. Then, from about 9,800 years BP, pine appeared, with smaller amounts of elm, oak and birch. By 7,500 years BP, oak and elm, along with birch and hazel dominated the woodland scene. Between 7,000 and 5,000 years ago the climate was warmer and more moist than today. Alder arrived to Killarney by 7,000 years BP, and quickly spread throughout the wetter sites, forming extensive fen woods. Today we think of alder as a small tree with a relatively short life-span, but in some of Killarney's older woods, ancient alders with circumferences in excess of 6 metres survive. By 5,500 years BP pine pollen had increased, and pine-dominated mixed woodlands formed much of the landscape for many thousands of years.

THE ARRIVAL OF MAN

For about 3,000 years after the Ice Age, life in Kerry went about its own way, without any major external influences. Then humans appeared on the scene, arriving to fish and hunt along the bountiful coastline. Estuaries like those of the rivers Cashen, Laune and Inny would have been attractive sites seasonally for people to catch fish, shellfish and birds. Our earliest records of human influence come from Ferriter's Cove, west of Dingle, where material dated to the late Mesolithic (*circa* 7,000 years ago) has been identified. The settlement evidence shows that Mesolithic groups preferred to settle near water, either along the coast, on islands, or along the banks of lakes and rivers. Mesolithic sites have produced the remains of migratory fish such as eels and salmon, various shellfish and sea mammals, as well as ducks, divers and other birds. Forest material such as fruit, nuts, tubers, fungi, grubs and birds eggs are assumed to also have been on the Mesolithic menu.

These small roving parties of people would not have had a significant impact on the flora and fauna. When humans later introduced livestock and started clearing trees for agriculture, a change began which continues to the present. The archaeological evidence shows that by the Late Bronze Age a human-adapted landscape had evolved in many parts of the southwest. Kerry is rich in antiquities, particularly from the Bronze Age period, when deposits of copper were quarried on the Iveragh and Bearagh peninsulas. The Copper Age mines at Ross island near Killarney, have been dated to 2,200 years BC, the oldest known mines of this type in north-west Europe.

The pollen evidence suggests that it was into the pine-dominated mixed woodland of the late Stone Age that possible human-related disturbance enters. At Cashelkeelty, on the Beara peninsula, a pollen grain of triticum (a primitive type of wheat) was found dating to 5845 years BP. From this period onwards there is increasing evidence of woodland interference, with falling tree pollen values, the presence of weeds of agricultural importance such as dandelions, thistles and plantains, and increasing quantities of charcoal, indicating that people were using fire to clear patches of woodland. The long process of man-made modifications had begun, leading to the environment we see today.

DECAY, EROSION AND DEPOSITION – THE BREAKDOWN OF KERRY CONTINUES

Because of its geology and climate, Kerry is an excellent region to observe first-hand the continuing processes of erosion, both natural and due to human activities. Let us follow the course of a river from its source to the sea, to observe these processes in action. Our chosen watercourse, the Gearhameen river, rises beneath the southern face of Carrauntoohil, Ireland's highest peak, which reaches a height of nearly 1,040 metres at the western end of the MacGillycuddy's Reeks. This is an area where rainfall exceeds 2,000 millimetres annually, and frost and snow are common on the high peaks from October onwards. High above the river, and on the steep slopes along its earlier course, a variety of forces act on the rocks and soils which make up and clothe these mountains.

One such force is weathering. Weathering may be defined as the mechanical or physical disintegration and chemical decomposition of rocks by natural agents at the surface of the earth. Physical weathering is the breakdown of rocks into smaller fragments by changes in temperature and other factors. The most marked effects are produced by frost, especially when there is alternate freezing by night and thawing by day. Water enters the pores and fissures of rock and on freezing to ice expands by 9%, exerting powerful bursting pressure on the rock. By this process, which may be called freeze thaw, angular pieces of rock are wedged from the mountain tops, tumbled down-slope, and build a steep thalus or scree that is banked against the mountainside. The action of frost is most marked in cold climates and at high altitude in the more temperate regions. Continuous splitting off of rock fragments keeps peaks angular and it is this which produces the serrated skyline of many of Kerry's mountains. The saw edge outline of the MacGillycuddy's Reeks has its origin in freeze thaw at the end of the Ice Age. This process still continues. Further down slope, ice formation in soils, supported by the action of rain, reduces the sizes of stones, breaks up hard lumps of earth, and separates the particles to give a good tilth.

CHEMICAL WEATHERING

Break-up of rock by chemical reactions is all important in the production of soil and soluble substances. Quartz and muscovite are the only abundant minerals which strongly resist chemical decay. When rain combines with carbon dioxide, which makes up about 0.03% of air, a weak carbonic acid is formed. On penetration of the soil the water also absorbs acids of organic origin (humic acids). Rain is therefore a dilute chemical reagent, capable of acting slowly on most minerals.

Hydration involves chemical combination with water, while oxidation is the formation of oxides. Both processes take place in the rusting of iron when it is damp. In moist temperate regions such as Kerry, the subsoil is generally stained by yellow ochre or limonite, as is the broken rock beneath the soil. In many boggy areas along the banks of the Gearhameen and elsewhere, a brown staining is visible. This is brown ochre, a form of ferric oxide which has been converted by a bacteria called *Thiobacillus ferrooxidans* from ferrous iron. Another by-product of bacterial activity in boggy conditions is ferric hydroxide, which is the oily film often visible on the surface of bog pools or drains. Hydration is accompanied by an increase in volume due to the absorption of water by minerals. The growth of expanded new minerals within rock exerts pressures which cause the rock to shatter. Therefore chemical changes promote physical changes – decomposition and disintegration work together.

GRAVITY, RAINWASH AND RIVERS

Gravity is a powerful agent of erosion in its own right, particularly in a hilly area such as Kerry. Loose materials on slopes move downhill under the influence of gravity. In Kerry the most striking effects of gravity are landslides, which generally occur in conjunction with heavy rainfall. Bogflows, which are patches of sliding peat, are well known in the county. The effects of some which occurred in the Rathmore region are described by that great Irish naturalist, Robert Lloyd Praeger, in his classic book, *The Way That I Went*.

On a sloping field, particularly one that has been tilled over the years, soil will gradually creep downhill to form a lynchet or low ridge across the base of the field. On steep peaty hillsides, particularly if grazing is heavy, a series of ridges will form running parallel to the contours of the hill. In time, these will cause more serious landslides, often denuding the hillside of soil and exposing the bare rock. Examples of this process can be seen on the slopes above the Gearhameen river.

Running water is one of the most potent agents of erosion and transportation of all, both as rainwash, which is water washing down hillsides and as streams upon the valley floor. More destructive work is accomplished by running water during a storm of exceptional severity, than under many years of normal rainfall. In many areas the natural vegetation has been denuded by fires, overgrazing and soil compaction caused by excessive trampling. Water flows quickly across such surfaces rather than being slowed down by vegetation and seeping in. Gullying also occurs on a major scale over extensive areas where the natural vegetation has been destroyed. Rainwash and gravity co-operate in removing soil and bringing it eventually to the valleys, where it is picked up by streams for further transport. These agents work in conjunction with weathering, for it is only through the removal of the blanketing soil that fresh rock is brought within reach of the weathering process.

Rivers, like humans, go through a life cycle. Full of erosive energy in youth, they pass onto a mature stage during which they lack energy for much down-cutting, but instead broaden their courses and 'put on weight' by increasing their load. Finally in old age, they are unable to cut, make a feeble effort to carry, and resort to flooding, shedding their muddy loads on land or in estuaries. In the case of lengthy rivers, the different stages of their life cycle are all present at the same time. A river system reduces the land by erosion in two directions. In the first place it deepens its valley by downward erosion, or down-cutting. Secondly, a river is continually growing longer, because its headwater or source erodes back in the upstream direction. Such extension inland is called head-ward erosion. In youth, rivers cut steep, V-shaped valleys into rock. They flow rapidly, carrying sand and mud, and roll along rock fragments which act like cutting tools. Softer rocks are abraded more easily than harder ones, which protrude above the average level of the river bed to form rapids and waterfalls. Many waterfalls are cut back rapidly, retreating upstream and leaving steep-sided gorges in their wake. Small examples of these gorges are visible above you on the sides of Brassel mountain and above Lough Reagh, where side tributaries enter the Gearhameen. During dry weather a mountain stream may reduce to a mere trickle, wending its way around rocks and boulders. After heavy rain, it becomes a raging torrent, with the strength to move large stones. A stream which is just able to shift pebbles of 28 grams weight can move boulders of 7 kilos or more if its velocity is trebled.

The Gearhameen passes through a series of attractive lakes in the bottom of the Black valley, before entering the Upper Lake of Killarney, the valley of which was originally formed by glaciation. This region is surrounded by extensive oak-woods, and large amounts of organic matter are picked up by the water, particularly in the autumn during leaf fall. As we leave the Upper Lake, we enter Muckross Lake, where carboniferous limestone butts up against the Old Red Sandstone and it is here that another process called solution comes into play. The effects of solution are most pronounced in the case of the carbonate rocks, limestone and dolomite. Carbon dioxide from the air mixed with rain or groundwater forms carbonic acid, (H_2CO_3) a weak acid which converts limestone into calcium bicarbonate. The bicarbonate is carried away in solution. Limestone is readily dissolved and only the insoluble substances it contains are left to form soil. Solution is concentrated along planes of weaknesses called joints. This process of solution, combined with the effects of wave action, have helped to form the series of caves and fantastically-shaped rocks which are to be seen along the shores of the Muckross peninsula. Other unique features of limestone also owe their origins to solution. Streams often enter large vertical pipes called swallow holes, and disappear underground. A swallow hole can be seen beside the entrance to Muckross House near Killarney. The streams then follow subterranean passages for some distance, and emerge at the surface once more. The underground passages are here and there enlarged to form large caverns, such as the spectacular examples at Crag Cave near Castleisland.

From the lakes of Killarney, the water which started its journey on the southern slopes of the Reeks has changed direction and is now flowing westward as part of the River Laune. Before the river was dredged and partly embanked many years ago, it would have poured out over its flood-plain west of Ballymalis after periods of heavy rain, to enrich the soil with its load of organic material and nutrients. After flowing through the market town of Killorglin, perched above its banks, the river finally begins to deposit the bulk of its load over its estuary. The river is laden with organic material, which eventually settles out to provide the basis for the rich food chain of the estuary.

Inchiquin Waterfall, Beara peninsula

WEATHER AND CLIMATE

Weather and climate are subjects of special interest to naturalists, farmers and others whose livelihoods and interests take them outdoors. By weather we mean the state of the atmosphere at a given time, described by variables such as temperature, wind speed and precipitation. A day of rain in Valentia, the strong gusts of wind at Ballyheigue, the sunny day in June are all weather events.

Climate is the sum of many factors including rainfall, temperature, wind speed and the number of hours of sunshine. Climate is one of the limiting factors in the distribution of plants and animals, while weather affects them on a daily basis. More than that, there are many climates, for the climate in the shelter of a wood is different from outside, while the climate at ground level is different to that of two metres above ground. These are called microclimates and are of very great importance to many animals and plants.

Using daily observations of many weather variables from a number of weather stations, meteorologists can provide average values for periods of specified lengths. Because of the presence of the Atlantic ocean and our abundant rainfall, Kerry is described as having a moist, oceanic climate. Within the county, however, there is quite a variation in climate, which is influenced by such factors as distance from the sea, altitude and local geography. We shall now go on to have a closer

Clouds build up over Muckross Lake

VALENTIA OBSERVATORY

In 1860 Vice-Admiral Robert FitzRoy set up the first organised system for collating weather data in these islands. Forty stations around the coasts of Britain and Ireland sent him daily weather reports by electric telegraph, of which Valentia observatory was the first Irish station to submit data on 8 October of that year.

Originally situated actually on Valentia island, in 1892 the observatory was moved across the channel to Westwood house near Caherciveen, then owned by Trinity College. It remains on this site to the present, recording hourly and daily data on barometric pressure, temperature, wind speed, humidity, rainfall, sunshine and more. Now one of Europe's most important meteorological and geophysical observatories, Valentia also monitors radiation coming from the sun, variations in the Earth's magnetic field, and operates a seismograph which can detect earthquake activity many thousands of miles away.

---

look at some details of the climate of Kerry.

The most obvious features of Kerry's climate are its cloudiness, the high rainfall and year-round mildness. The presence of the surrounding relatively warm ocean, and the vast area of high mountains, account for many of these climatic features. Kerry lies in the path of the moist humid air streaming continually off the Atlantic. With the prevailing winds coming from the south and southwest, this moisture-laden air rises when it meets the bulk of the great mountain ranges of the Beara, Iveragh and Dingle peninsulas. As it rises, the air condenses to form clouds. This is often graphically seen by visitors to offshore islands such as the Blaskets and Skelligs. In summer, these islands may be basking in bright sunshine, while cloud forms over the hills on the nearby mainland, thus reducing sunshine levels there.

The extent of cloud cover can be measured by judging what proportion of the sky, in eights or oktas, is covered by cloud. The mean monthly values for cloud cover at Caherciveen weather station vary from 5.7 in March, April and May to 6.3 in July, the cloudiest month. These figures are based on observations made at each hour of the day. The county's mountainous areas probably produce somewhat higher average cloud cover values. The increased cloudiness of late summer is due to pressure rising over the ocean and falling generally over Europe, resulting in a westerly flow of air off the ocean, causing increased cloudiness and humidity. It may come as a surprise to learn that July is the cloudiest month of the year, but this does not mean it is the wettest month. Much of our cloud in summer is of the cumulus type, which may produce showers but rarely heavy continuous rain.

Humidity is defined as the amount of water vapour or moisture in the air, and is normally quantified as a percentage known as the relative humidity. The amount of moisture which air can hold varies with temperature; warm air can hold more moisture than cold air. If the relative humidity of air at a particular temperature reaches 100%, we say the air is saturated. Because our air has generally spent a long time over the ocean, the humidity in Kerry is invariably quite high. Depending upon the time of day and month, our relative humidity averages from 70-90%. Humidity is normally at its highest overnight and lowest around midday. The lowest monthly figures for relative humidity occur from March to June.

When the relative humidity of the air is low, surface water from soil and plants is evaporated. The annual mean rate of evaporation at Caherciveen weather station is about 700 millimetres, with the greatest evaporation occurring from May to August. The evaporation rate is a measure of the drying power of the wind. Apart from affecting people trying to dry clothes, evaporation also affects plants, particularly more delicate types such as ferns, mosses and lichens. The polypody ferns which live perched high on the branches of many Kerry trees, depend on the fact that rainfall exceeds evaporation by at least 700-800 millimetres per year.

SUNSHINE

The amount of sunshine is measured as the number of hours of bright sunshine per day, and varies considerably about the county. Coastal and lowland areas away from high ground receive considerably more sunshine than mountainous regions, where cloud cover is normally more prevalent. While the weather station at Caherciveen averages about 75 days per year without sunshine, mountainous areas must have even more sunless days. At Caherciveen, the 30 year mean for the period 1961-1990 shows that May is the sunniest month, averaging about six hours sunshine per day, with only two days without sunshine. December is the dullest month, with only one hour of sunshine per day and an average of 13 days without sunshine.

TEMPERATURE

Temperature plays a very important part in the ecology and distribution of plant and animal species in Kerry. A glance at the figures for Caherciveen shows us that the annual average air temperature is 10.5^0C. Moreover, the mean temperature range is quite small, from 6.6^0C in February to 15^0C in August. Extremes are few and far between; the hottest day in the 30 year period from 1961-1990 was 29.7^0C in July, the coldest -7.3^0C in February. Again, there is a fair amount of variation about the county, even within the narrow range of temperatures we experience. Eastern, inland areas such as Rathmore experience more extreme conditions, especially in winter, than coastal zones.

Altitude also has a pronounced effect on temperature. For every 150 metres of ascent, the air temperature drops by 1^0C, so the temperature on the summit of Carrauntoohil (1039 metres) will average 7^0C cooler than lowland areas only five kilometres away. Wind has a further cooling effect (the wind chill factor), so a hiker climbing Carrauntoohil on a breezy April day may go from 10^{0}C on the lowland to sub-zero conditions on the summit. The low summer temperatures on the mountains in Kerry are one of the primary obstacles to plant growth, restricting the tree-line to below 600 metres, even for the hardier conifers.

WATER TEMPERATURE

The average temperature of the sea waters off the Kerry coast ranges from 10^{0}C in winter to 15^{0}C in summer. These temperatures are remarkably warm for our latitude, and are due to the influence of the North Atlantic drift, which brings warmer water to us from the Caribbean. These relatively high temperatures are also the reason for the presence of many southern species of seaweeds, fish and other marine creatures off our coast. These sea water temperatures will vary somewhat from place to place about the coastline, more sheltered spots experiencing a greater range of temperatures than the open ocean.

The waters of inland loughs, rivers and streams show wider annual variations in temperatures, subject as they are to influences such as water source, depth, altitude and aspect, as well as their lower volume. Temperature is of critical importance to fish growth and the oxygen carrying capacity of water. Freshwater temperatures in Kerry average 8-10^{0}C over the year, ranging from a low of 4^{0}C to a high of 18^{0}C. High level mountain lakes frequently freeze over for extended periods during cold weather in winter.

RAINFALL

Many people would say that Kerry's most memorable climatic feature is its rainfall. The county does, however, show a remarkable local variation in rainfall levels. The driest area is the north Kerry coastal strip from Ardfert to Ballylongford, and inland to Listowel, with annual averages of 1,000-1,100 millimetres. Further south, the lowlands from Killorglin and Tralee to Castleisland receive about 1,250 millimetres annually, while the hills about Lyreacrompane and Brosna average 1,350 millimetres annually. As you approach the mountains, rainfall levels climb dramatically. This is best seen by examining the figures for the Killarney area. The town receives an average of 1,250 millimetres annually, while the station at Muckross House, at a height of 58 metres, averages 1,585 millimetres annually. Climbing the Old Kenmare road, the former station below Torc mountain, at 223 metres, averaged 1,995 millimetres. One kilometre away, the station at 808 metres on the summit of Mangerton mountain experiences an average of 3,184 millimetres annually!

These figures also show the influence of local topography. With the prevailing winds from the south and south-west, the rain-bearing clouds tend to be funnelled around the eastern shoulders of the MacGillycuddy's Reeks and down the valley of Killarney's famous Upper Lake. This is part of the reason why the northern side of the 'Reeks' have a much lower rainfall than the southern and eastern side. This local variation in rainfall levels can be experienced in all the mountainous areas of the county.

Although the months of April to July are the driest months, this period still receives an average of 73-89 millimetres per month. Long dry spells are rare and most parts of the county experience 220-250 rain-days per year. Any day receiving more than 0.2 millimetres of precipitation (a light shower) is classed officially as a 'Rain Day'. A 'Wet Day' is any day with more than 1.0 millimetres of rain. One of the reasons why areas like Killarney have such an incredibly rich bryophyte flora (mosses and liverworts) is because of the high number of rain days per year, allowing the delicate surfaces of these plants to remain moist. The high rainfall also has an effect on Kerry's fauna. Continually wet weather makes life difficult for invertebrates, birds and even larger animals such as deer.

SNOW AND FROST

Snow on low ground in Kerry is an infrequent sight, but the higher mountains on all three peninsulas are often snow covered in winter, if only for short periods. This severe weather is often associated with cold northerly or easterly winds. Lowland areas in east Kerry often receive falls of snow in winter, suffictrees and shrubs in spring.

The mean annual wind speed at Caherciveen weather station is about 11 knots, ient to make driving difficult.

Ground frosts occur principally between December and March on about 40 days a year, again more often in inland sites. Days of air frost are a much less frequent occurrence, averaging only 10 days a year in coastal areas. While prolonged cold spells do have an effect on animal populations, they are thankfully infrequent. An indication of severe weather in Europe is the sight of large numbers ofbirds such as lapwings, golden plover, thrushes and starlings, which may move many hundreds of miles in the hope of finding better conditions in the west and south-west of Ireland.

WIND

Wind is a major ecological factor in the climate of Kerry. Wind makes life difficult for plant growth in exposed sites and causes damage to trees. It sends animals seeking shelter, shakes insects and other creatures off trees, and especially in combination with rain, can be lethal to many living organisms.

Wind speed is influenced by factors such as altitude and local topography. A stiff breeze in an open area may come roaring through a narrow valley. Amongst tall herbage at ground level, where many animals live, that same wind speed will

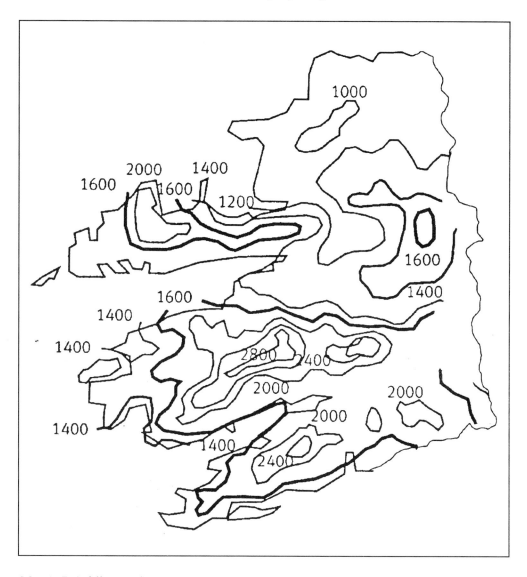

Map 3: Rainfall map of Kerry

be reduced considerably. The wind shapes and re-shapes the sand dunes along our coast and carries salt many kilometres inland, often burning the new leaves of trees and shrubs in spring.

The mean annual wind speed at Caherciveen weather station is about 11 knots, or 20 kilometres per hour. January is the windiest month, averaging 13.4 knots or 25 kilometres per hour, with an average of 2.5 days with gales. Caherciveen has an average of 12 gale days per year, not too bad when compared to Malin Head, Donegal, which has 42 gale days per annum!

A very useful skill for any naturalist is to be able to estimate wind speed by its effect on common surface features. This one can do by using the Beaufort scale of wind force, introduced by a Meath man, Admiral Beaufort, in the early 1900's. Originally designed for ship-borne weather observations, it is equally useful for judging wind speed on land. The scale, which ranges from 0, calm to 12, hurricane, is recognised and used internationally.

THE BEAUFORT SCALE

Beaufort Number	Short Description	Wind Velocity at 10 m above ground (m/sec.)*	Specification for use on land	Specification for use at sea or large lakes
0	Calm	<0.3	Smoke rises vertically	Sea mirror smooth
1	Light Air	0.3-1.5	Direction shown by smoke, but not by windvanes	Small wavelets like scales, no crests
2	Light Breeze	1.6-3.3	Wind felt on face: leaves rustle; ordinary vanes move	Small wavelets short but more pronouced; crest glassy and do not break
3	Gentle Breeze	3.4-5.4	Leaves and small twigs in constant motion; wind extends light flag	Large wavelets. Crests begin to break; foam is glassy
4	Moderate Breeze	5.5-7.9	Raises dust and loose paper; small branches move	Small waves growing longer; frequent white horses
5	Fresh Breeze	8.0-10.7	Small leafy trees begin to sway; crested wavelets on inland waters	Moderate waves and longer; many white horses
6	Strong Breeze	10.8-13.8	Large branches in motion; whistling heard in wires; umbrellas used with difficulty	Large waves begin to form; white crests more extensive
7	Near Gale	13.9-17.1	Large trees in motion; difficulty when walking against the wind	Sea heaps up; white foam blown in streaks
8	Gale	17.2-20.7	Twigs break off trees; generally impedes progress	Moderately high waves of greater strength; crests begin to form spindrift; foam blown in well marked streaks
9	Strong Gale	20.8-24.4	Slight structural damage (slates, chimney pots,)	High waves; dense streaks of foam; crests begin to roll over
10	Storm	24.5-28.4	Seldom experienced inland; trees uprooted; considerable structural damage	Very high waves with long overhanging crests surface becomes white with large patches of foam; visibility affected
11	Violent Storm	28.5-32.6	Very rarely experienced; widespread damage	exceptionally high waves sea completely coverd with foam
12	Hurricane	32.7 and over		The air filled with spray and visibility seriously affected

*Multiply by 3.6 to give km/hr; multiply by 2.2 to give m/hr.

Kerry: A Natural History

TABLE 1
WEATHER STATISTICS FOR VALENTIA OBSERVATORY, CAHERCIVEEN, CO.KERRY
AVERAGES FOR PERIOD 1961-1990 (30 YEARS)

Total/average	Jan	Feb	Mar	Apr	May	Jun	Jul	Aug	Sep	Oct	Nov	Dec	Yearly
Daily mean air temp (C)	6.8	6.6	7.6	9.0	11.0	13.4	14.9	15.0	13.7	11.6	8.7	7.6	10.5
Daily max air temp (C)	9.4	9.3	10.5	12.3	14.4	16.5	17.9	18.0	16.7	14.3	11.4	10.1	13.4
Daily min air temp (C)	4.2	3.9	4.7	5.8	7.8	10.3	12.0	12.0	10.7	8.8	6.1	5.1	7.6
Sunshine hours daily	1.4	2.2	3.0	5.0	5.8	5.1	4.5	4.5	3.6	2.5	1.7	1.1	3.4
Rainfall (mm)	167	123	122	77	89	80	73	111	125	157	147	159	1430
Number of wet days (> 0.2mm)	23	19	21	17	18	17	17	20	19	22	22	23	239
Number of rain days (> 1.0mm)	20	15	17	12	14	13	12	15	15	19	19	19	188
Monthly wind speed (kph)	24.8	23.3	22.4	18.9	19.1	16.8	15.7	16.5	18.5	21.1	21.8	23.3	20.2
Max gust (kph)	161	146	124	117	113	107	98	111	163	139	129	152	163

TABLE 2

MONTHLY AND AVERAGE RAINFALL (MM) AT SELECTED STATIONS THROUGHOUT KERRY, 1951-1980 (30 YEARS).

Station name	Ht (m)	Jan	Feb	Mar	Apr	May	Jun	Jul	Aug	Sep	Oct	Nov	Dec	Yearly
Ardfert	23	113	76	70	56	60	57	69	78	94	101	114	120	1009
Ballylongford	9	113	78	72	63	63	61	79	87	103	107	129	134	1090
Brosna	134	156	106	99	82	82	72	88	99	118	127	153	173	1356
Castleisland	41	137	94	86	74	77	69	88	97	113	121	143	152	1250
Dingle	6	147	109	100	82	82	82	97	105	126	135	154	164	1383
Glenbeigh	23	187	130	121	91	91	79	91	97	136	164	174	191	1552
Kenmare	9	175	125	123	95	90	80	103	108	137	160	169	191	1555
Kilgarvan	44	209	149	147	96	105	76	91	103	145	170	180	200	1671
Muckross	58	207	137	133	91	98	73	88	94	136	159	173	197	1585
Killarney	55	153	105	96	72	76	62	78	85	111	123	142	152	1253
Killorglin	28	150	105	91	73	74	65	86	87	110	128	146	159	1273
Knocknagoshel	152	158	106	98	84	87	77	97	103	126	139	163	170	1408
Lauragh	8	246	179	191	109	126	93	106	120	170	205	191	228	1965
Listowel (Inch)	15	105	74	65	59	60	59	73	81	94	100	122	119	1012
Portmagee	6	163	122	122	79	86	78	91	104	130	148	153	162	1440
Rathmore	168	169	114	111	85	85	70	84	95	120	130	153	168	1383
Tralee (Clash)	15	137	95	87	66	72	65	83	84	105	120	135	151	1201
Valentia Observ	11	162	118	115	79	85	76	86	98	128	142	151	159	1400
Ballaghbeama Gap	311	355	245	251	172	489	180	204	243	287	337	319	372	3153
Mangerton Mt	808	383	266	253	184	201	169	197	222	288	314	331	375	3184

Chapter 2

KERRY'S GREEN MANTLE

K ERRY HAS been a mecca for botanists for many generations. The reasons for this will become apparent later. Of the many botanists who have visited the county, the person who has probably left the greatest mark is Dr Reginald Scully (1858-1935). Though a qualified doctor, Scully had independent means and did not practice his profession. He lived in Dublin, where his first love was plants. He spent most of his summers on botanical excursions around the country, particularly to Kerry. On these visits he explored virtually every nook and cranny and in 1916 published *The Flora of Kerry*, still regarded as one of the finest works on Irish botany. This was a comprehensive list of the Kerry flora, with detailed notes on their distribution throughout the county, resulting from his own work and that of earlier botanists.

Robert Lloyd Praeger, another eminent naturalist, advised visiting Kerry in May and early June to see the flora at its best. This is when the large-flowered butterwort, which Dr Scully considered to be 'the most beautiful member of the Irish flora', is in flower. Others in full bloom are the Irish spurge, with its soft buttery-yellow flowers and both of the saxifrage specialties; St Patrick's-cabbage and the kidney saxifrage, with their star-shaped flowers. In the field drains and wet areas the majestic royal fern is in full growth, reaching up to nearly two metres in places, while more common species such as gorse and broom provide splashes of colour everywhere. For most visitors, however, the strongest impression tends to be made by the introduced species such as the rhododendrons, whether the 'wild' *Rhododendron ponticum*, which grows in such profusion, or the numerous cultivated varieties they see on visits to various ornamental gardens. Many visitors find it hard to believe how much time, money and effort is put into trying to eradicate *R*.

ponticum in parts of Kerry, when they may spend a small fortune trying to raise much poorer specimens in their own gardens. Another introduced species coming into bloom at this time is the fuchsia, which brightens the hedgerows of the three peninsulas with its red and purple flowers.

Against a background of common European species are to be found representatives of the 'Lusitanian', Mediterranean, North American and arctic / alpine flora. In the mild humid climate of Kerry the 'Atlantic' flora of the Irish west coast reaches its finest development. Probably the best known members of this Atlantic or oceanic flora is that group of plants whose main centre of distribution is the Mediterranean region and north-west Spain and Portugal – the so-called 'Lusitanian' flora. Included among this group are such well known plants as the strawberry tree, greater or large-flowered butterwort and St Patrick's-cabbage. While some of these are found as far north as Donegal, the majority have their centre of distribution in Kerry and west Cork. The current thinking as to how the 'Lusitanian' flora came to reach Kerry is that these species migrated along a landbridge which formerly existed between south-west Europe, Britain and Ireland, when sea level may have been up to 90 metres lower than today. Some scientists argue, however, that these species were introduced by the activities of early man.

Kerry has also the richest 'Atlantic' bryophyte flora (mosses and liverworts) of anywhere in these islands, with 129 out of a total of 162 species. This includes a large proportion of both southern and northern elements in the bryophyte flora. The presence of these elements is considered to be due to our cool summers and mild winters, as our temperatures lie within the tolerance range of both groups. Many species which are common in Kerry are found in few locations elsewhere in Ireland or Britain, and many species which are relatively widespread are more abundant here than elsewhere. The county is also a rich area for many of the 'Atlantic' lichens, which again achieve a luxuriance rarely seen elsewhere.

One of the major influences on our mountain flora is climate. The chief characteristics of our climate are cool summers, mild winters and high rainfall, evenly spread throughout the year. It is the frequency of rain-days and the high humidity that are significant in Kerry, not the inordinate precipitation. Sunshine levels are also low. Wind is also a major climatic factor, which is shown by the distribution of various plant communities in relation to aspect and the degree of exposure they experience. While gales are infrequent, an examination of the wind speeds recorded at Valentia show that more than 50% of the westerly and south-westerly winds were force 4-6 in strength. A second major factor has been the influence of humans through woodland clearances, burning and grazing of stock. These activities have influenced soil fertility and the composition of montane communities.

MONTANE HABITATS

Because of their dramatic influence on the landscape of Kerry, the high peaks make an excellent starting point for our survey of Kerry's flora. Dr Caroline Mhic Daeid, in her comprehensive survey of the flora of peatlands and heaths in the Killarney valley, divided the vegetation into four main groups. The most wide-spread vegetation types are heaths and ombrotrophic mires (bogs and wet heaths whose only source of water and nutrients is from rainfall). Heath communities were usually dominant on ground with slopes of greater than 15^0, whereas deep peatbogs dominate on less steep slopes. Both these community types are found at all altitudes from the valley bottoms to the mountain tops. The two other main community types are rheotrophic mires (plant communities on peaty soils subject to flooding or seepage by waters from outside the mire itself – these include fens and swamps), and other aquatic communities (plant communities associated with streams and springs with a faster flow of water).

On the wind-swept summits above 500 metres exists a low-growing community dominated by plants such as heather. This is also called ling; a name which is derived from the Anglo-Saxon *lig*, a 'fire', referring to its importance as fuel in early times. Bilberry makes an attractive show among heathers with its lighter green, deciduous foliage, and on drier ground is sometimes the dominant species.

Broaghnabinnia and the Black Valley

Its flowers are attractive to many insects, and its purplish-black fruits are important for birds and animals in the autumn. The fruits were once used as a source of a purple dye to colour cloth and paper and are still appreciated for their delicious flavour. Crowberry is similar in appearance to heather, but produces black fruits. Intermingled with these are mosses, the dominant species being *Rhacomitrium lanuginosum*, brownish with a silvery tinge, which is also to be found on some bogs lower down, and *Sphagnum rubellum*, which grows to about 15 centimetres, with crimson or pinkish stems. It often forms a carpet beneath heather or on the drier hummocks of bogs. The bryophyte layer also includes other common heath species such as *Hypnum cupressiforme,*

Hylocomium splendens and *Rhytidiadelphus loreus*. Fir clubmosses, with their tuft of stiff, erect branches, are widespread on bare patches of soil. The clubmosses belong to an ancient group of plants which appeared over 250 million years ago, and once included giant trees. Though moss-like in appearance, they are structurally more similar to ferns, having a vascular system for the transportation of water and minerals through their system. They are hardy plants, being found on our highest and most exposed peaks.

The most common lichen is *Cladonia arbuscula*. This is a species of mountains, sandy and stony heaths, forming bushy yellow-tinged erect tufts. It can be distinguished by its multi-branched stems all bent in one direction. It contains an antibiotic, usnic acid, which gives the plant its yellow colour. Another interesting lichen which occurs locally in mountainous areas is the Iceland moss, a brownish, edible species with forked branches up to six centimetres long, edged with tiny spines.

Lichens

Lichens are a combination of organisms. They consist of a fungus, which provides the plant with its shape and form, living in a close association with an alga, which like other green plants, can manufacture its own food from simple materials using the sun's energy. The algal partner is either a green alga, often a species of Trebouxia, *or a blue-green alga, usually* Nostoc. *The two are sandwiched together – the fungus forms the outer layer or cortex, while the inner layer – the medulla – contains algal cells interwoven with fungal threads. This type of mutually beneficial association is called symbiosis. Lichens may be crust-like, leafy or shrubby structures depending on the species, and show a tremendous range of colours. The shrubbier species generally grow in wetter habitats. Lichens are slow growing and long-lived; some tundra species may have lived for more than 10,000 years.*

Lichens are generally light demanding plants; woodland species grow most actively when the trees are not in leaf. Other factors which affect lichens are temperature, the availability of water, whether the substrate is acidic, neutral or alkaline, the degree of exposure to drying winds and the amount of air pollution. For lichens growing on trees factors such as the age, extent of corrugation, degree of flakiness, the pH and nutrient status of the bark surface all affect which species can colonise particular trees.

Also present are the heath rush and grasses such as wavy hair-grass, common bent and viviparous fescue. Viviparous fescue is one of the easiest grasses to identify. Rather than producing flowers and seeds, it grows miniature plants at the end of its stems. When these fall to the ground they are ready to root and develop immediately – a good competitive advantage.

In more sheltered habitats on north and north-east facing slopes, or among boulders in scree, a somewhat different community exists. This is particularly rich in 'Atlantic' bryophytes which often occur in great abundance. *Herberta adunca*, a brownish, erect liverwort, often with rust-coloured tips to its stems, forms large cushions especially on moist mountain ledges. The distinctive *Pleurozia purpurea* is a purplish-red coloured liverwort with branched shoots up to 14 centimetres long. The tiny leaves are designed in such a way as to hold water, which is believed to help provide nutrients by trapping microscopic animals. Steep, damp, north-facing cliffs such as those in the Horse's Glen, on Mangerton mountain, where grazing animals are few or absent and nutrients are washed down the slopes, provide a particularly rich habitat for many species. Among the flowering plants are the yellow-flowered autumn hawkbit, goldenrod and roseroot, with its fleshy leaves, the purple/blue devil's-bit scabious, harebell and wild thyme, and rarer plants such as alpine saw-wort and alpine hair-grass. The latter is a montane subspecies of the more common tufted hair-grass, which outside of Kerry is known only from Mayo.

HEATHER

Heather plays a major role in the structure and dynamics of the moorland community. The lifespan of a normal plant averages 30-40 years, during which time the plant goes through a number of different phases. In the pioneer phase, during the first ten years of life, the shape of each plant is more or less pyramidal. During the building phase, covering the next five years or so, the heather plants completely close in to form a dense canopy, little light penetrates, and most other species are excluded. Individual plants produce a proliferation of green shoots and flower profusely. Towards the end of this period, the central branches begin to separate and gaps appear in the canopy. This is the start of the mature phase, when a central gap opens up in the plant allowing increased illumination to ground level and air circulation within the bush. By the time the plant reaches about thirty years of age, it enters the degenerative phase, when the central branches have collapsed further and are progressively dying from the middle of the bush outwards.

As any one area of heather passes through its sequence of phases, there are accompanying changes in species diversity. Diversity is usually highest during the pioneer phase, where there are bare patches for colonisation by other species. These species will be pushed out during the building phase. As the canopy begins to open up during the mature phase, shade tolerant species such as mosses will increase, and once the degenerative phase is reached, flowering plants such as tormentil and heath milkwort increase.

Lower down the slopes of Mangerton heather is the dominant plant, but where fires have been frequent or on wetter, shallow slopes, purple moor-grass becomes dominant. This grass gets its name from its purplish-coloured flowers and is a very common species along the western seaboard of Ireland and Britain, preferring areas of damp and sometimes waterlogged peat. On bog habitats it occurs in a non-tufted form, but in very wet areas large tufts up to a metre across may develop. When the grass on these tufts die back in the autumn, they form a wet, inhospitable layer which prevents other plants from growing there, thus creating a virtual monoculture. It is taken as food by livestock and deer in spring when the leaves are soft and nutritious. On relatively well-drained soils small areas of grassy 'lawns' occur, generally consisting of a mixture of common and velvet bent, viviparous fescue and sweet vernal grass. When dry, sweet vernal grass has a strong hay scent. These grasses are favoured by and can withstand heavy grazing.

Most of the steeper mountains in Kerry such as those in the MacGillycuddy's Reeks are dominated by the grass species already mentioned, due largely to overburning and grazing. Considering the extent of suitable terrain in the Reeks, their alpine flora is poor, but they are rich in bryophytes. The only alpine species to occur here which is not found elsewhere in Kerry is hoary whitlowgrass, an erect perennial herb with small, white flowers. It is found on the cliffs about Carrauntoohil. Other alpines found at the highest levels include alpine scurvygrass, with fleshy leaves and white flowers, the creeping stems of the dwarf willow, and mountain sorrel.

The best area in Kerry for alpines is undoubtedly the Brandon range. This area is renowned for its wealth of arctic and arctic/alpine plants which occur on the cliffs. The richest areas are found between Gearhane and Brandon Peak, on the cliffs above Lough Duff and between Lough Nalacken and Brandon mountain.

Three major communities are present on Brandon, and at several places a very rich bryophyte flora is associated with them. One such community is to be found in wet rivulets, as are found at the base of sheer cliff faces with water dripping from above. Such sites are dominated by the starry saxifrage, whose white flowers have two yellow spots at the base of each sepal, blinks or water chickweed, with its minute white flowers, and the moss, *Philonotis fontana*.

The second community occupies wet gullies and ledges on Brandon. The dominant vascular plant of this community is creeping bent grass, along with the very rare alpine lady's-mantle, found at only three sites in Ireland, including cliffs near Moll's Gap. This rarity grows 15-20 centimetres tall, has palmate leaves which are silky-white beneath, and clustered yellow-green flowers. Irish saxifrage, mountain sorrel, alpine scurvygrass and roseroot also accompany these. The 'Atlantic' bryophytes are well represented. The bryophyte flora of the Lough Duff area in particular compares well with that of the MacGillycuddy's Reeks. Interesting ferns include the green spleenwort, brittle bladder-fern, Wilson's filmy fern and the holly fern. The last-named species, whose spine-edged leaves bear only a passing resemblance to those of holly, is a montane plant of scree habitats in mountainous areas along the west coast, and is one of the rarest ferns in Ireland. Apart from

Brandon it also occurs on Mullaghanattin mountain on the Iveragh peninsula. Another rare species, the Killarney fern, was discovered on Brandon in 1988 at a new site for this plant.

On and around the summit of Brandon mountain occurs a dwarf alpine heath community. This consists mainly of common bent, crested hair-grass and wild thyme. The presence of crested hair-grass at this height is an altitude record for this species in Ireland or Britain. The most interesting plant of this community is alpine bistort, a small montane perennial with pink or white flowers, which occurs at only six sites in Ireland.

Lower down the slopes along the fringes of the Atlantic may be found patches of dry, maritime heath, normally dominated by heather and autumn gorse, a combination of which provides a lovely splash of colour from mid-July onwards. The scarcest plant of this community, confined to about twenty square kilometres around Derrynane, is the Kerry lily. It has rather few, white flowers, is up to thirty centimetres tall and generally grows among short vegetation on rocky knolls.

BRYOPHYTES — THE MOSSES AND LIVERWORTS

The bryophytes are a well-defined group of plants of which over 1,000 species have been recorded in Ireland and Britain. This is over 60% of the total number of species recorded in Europe, compared to an equivalent figure for vascular plants of less than 20%. Dr Derek Ratcliffe, a noted ecologist, remarking upon the Irish and British flora, stated that, 'in its Atlantic bryophyte element, it is not only the richest part of the whole continent, but it is also one of the richest areas of the world'. This richness is primarily due to our mild wet climate with prevailing westerly winds, which gives rise to a number of unique communities, especially in the western woodlands, bogs and mountain tops. Over 75% of the whole Irish and British bryophyte flora is found in Kerry, which highlights the importance of the county for these plants. The oceanic woodlands of Kerry support a very rich byrophyte flora, and are one of the most important Irish or British habitats in international terms. An internationally important liverwort community exists on the north and east-facing slopes of Brandon at altitudes between 300-600 metres.

A KERRY BRYOLOGIST

Arnold Patrick Fanning (1905-1980) was born in Offaly, but taught science and mathematics in Tralee, where he continued to live after his retirement. His interest in bryology began in 1948, when he began collecting specimens in Tralee, and continued on and off until 1971, when he was forced to stop due to ill health. His collection of over 2,000 specimens, mainly from Kerry and Offaly, was presented to the National Herbarium in 1981.

Some bryophytes have a peculiar disjunct world distribution. The purplish-red liverwort, *Pleurozia purpurea* is restricted in Europe to Ireland, Britain, Norway, the Faeroes and Jan Mayan island, then reappears in China, the Himalayas, Alaska, Guadeloupe and Hawaii. Another liverwort, *Plagiochila carringtonii,* which is ecologically more demanding, has only been found in Ireland, Britain, the Faeroes and the Himalayas.

The bryophyte community which may be expected in any one area varies depending on such factors as rainfall, aspect, and substrate. Derrycunnihy, in the Killarney valley, has typical sessile-oakwoods with an understory of holly. The ground is strewn with boulders up to a metre across, covered in a mantle of greenery. The rainfall is high, averaging 2,000 millimetres per year and evenly distributed throughout the seasons, so conditions are generally humid.

A luxuriant brypohyte community thrives here. In areas of lower rainfall, the pioneering species of bare boulders consist mainly of small liverworts such as *Diplophyllum albicans* and *Frullania tamarisci.* These are two of the commonest liverworts of non-calcareous soils and are more resistant to drying out than others. They have numerous thread-like growths called rhizoids which enable them to colonise even steep boulders. In higher rainfall areas where the boulder surfaces rarely dry out, the pioneers include *Harpanthus scutatus, Marsupella emarginata* and *Scapania umbrosa.* These are eventually succeeded by taller mosses such as *Thuidium tamariscinum,* with a bright green, feathery appearance, and *Polytrichum formosum,* dark green with erect stems like miniature palm trees. These eventually form large, heavy mats which may be dislodged by heavy rain, animals or even their own weight, leaving a bare area of boulder to be re-colonised.

On fallen logs a parallel succession occurs, but generally encompassing different species. Logs which have reached a certain stage of decay may have liverwort species such as *Nowellia curvifolia,* which is never found on boulders. This is an oceanic species which forms extensive patches and normally has a characteristic tinge of dull purplish-red. On the trunks of living trees, species which can grow on the vertical trunks such as the yellowish-green moss *Isothecium myosuroides* will be found, extending onto the larger branches. In the higher, more exposed branches, grow species which are more light demanding and relatively resistant to drying such as the moss *Ulota crispa* and the *Frullania* liverworts.

Less common species in Kerry include the liverwort *Plagiochila atlantica,* which is almost endemic to Ireland and Britain, as there is only one other known site at Finistere in France. It is a pale, brown-green colour, forming large, pure patches with downward-pointing shoots up to nine centimetres long. It is only known from two locations in Ireland, both in Kerry, in humid, deciduous woodland, where it grows on east-facing acid boulders close to streams. At one of these it is threatened by rhododendron encroachment. *Lejeunea flava* is another scarce,

TABLE 3

RED DATA SPECIES OF LIVERWORTS FOUND IN KERRY

Acrobolbus wilsonii	Shaded ravines near water	*Marsupella adusta*	Unshaded screes, cliffs
Barbilophozia barbata	Rock outcrops, walls scree	*Marsupella sprucei*	Montane, sheltered gullies and scree
Bazzania pearsonii	Moist, peaty soils	*Mastigophora woodsii*	Oceanic: cool, humid north-facing slopes
Cephalozia hibernica	Humid woodlands and ravines	*Pallavicinia lyellii*	Lowland bogs, carrs, woodlands
Cephaloziella turneri	Crumbly banks and cliffs	*Pedinophyllum interruptum*	On limestone; damp ledges. Extinct in Kerry?
Cladopodiella francisci	Damp heath and bogs	*Plagiochila atlantica*	Humid, deciduous wood
Dumortiera hirsuta	Damp, wooded ravines	*Plagiochila carringtonii*	Heaths, boulder scree
Eremonotus myriocarpus	Montane, damp outcrops	*Petalophyllum ralfsii*	Damp calcareous dunes
Fossombronia incurva	Damp, gravelly sites	*Radula carringtonii*	Humid, wooded glens
Geocalyx graveolens	Humid, sheltered banks	*Radula holtii*	Shaded sites in ravines
Gymnomitrion corallioides	Montane outcrops boulders	*Radula voluta*	On boulders in shaded, very humid sites
Haplomitrium hookeri	Montane gravelly or sandy soils	*Riccia cavernosa*	Exposed, base-rich muddy sites
Lejeunea flava moorei	Oceanic: wooded ravines	*Scapania nimbosa*	Montane: heaths, screes
Lejeunea hibernica	Dark, sheltered ravines	*Sphenolobopsis pearsonii*	Oceanic: sheltered, ravines, screes and cliffs
Lejeunea holtii	Waterfall spray zones	*Telaranea nematodes*	Oceanic: humid, shaded sites
Lejeunea mandonii	Oceanic: woods and ravines	*Tritomaria exsecta*	On rotting wood in sheltered woodlands

strongly oceanic liverwort known from about 50 sites in Ireland. In Kerry it occurs near Killarney, around Lough Currane, in Uragh Wood and on Mount Brandon, by waterfalls, shady streams and in wooded ravines, usually below the 100 metre contour. It is not found in Britain and is rare in Europe. Threats include localised tree-felling, which would reduce humidity and rhododendron encroachment.

Ephemerum stellatum is a minute, rosette-like moss, found at only three British sites and two sites in Kerry, both near Derrynane. It is thought to require open, semi-disturbed habitats, as competition from other vegetation may be a problem for it. An even smaller moss (less than three millimetres in height) with similar problems of competition is *Fissidens algarvicus*. This is known in Ireland from only two Kerry sites at West Cove and Glenbeigh, but has not been recorded since 1951. It requires open soils on steep, sheltered banks or beside tracks. A species new to Ireland, *Fissidens rivularis*, was discovered near Ross Castle, Killarney in 1983. This is a typical oceanic species, occurring in southern England, Wales, and from Belgium to Spain. On Ross island it was found on damp, limestone rocks close to the water level, where it was shaded by trees. The rocks where it grew were subject to periodic inundation by water and it was found in association with two other liverworts, *Lejeunea lamacerina* and *Lejeunea holtii*. Like *Fissidens rivularis*, the latter is a *Red Data Book* species.

PEATBOGS AND WET HEATHS

On the Mangerton plateau and some summit plateaus on the Dingle and Beara peninsulas, blanket bog with peat up to two metres deep covers many square kilometres. Numerous small pools, lakes and boot-sucking quaking bogs are interspersed and criss-crossed by drainage gullies and erosion channels. Due to severe erosion in some areas, all that remains are peat hags, upstanding blocks of peat left as islands among the surrounding mineral soil. Heather, crowberry, bilberry, hare's-tail cottongrass and heath rush are all equally prominent, but in particularly wet areas heather and bilberry are confined to low hummocks of peat mosses. These areas are rich in *Sphagnum* species, which play an important part in peat-building. *Sphagnum rubellum*, previously mentioned, grows in drier areas. In wetter areas *Sphagnum papillosum* forms yellow-green or ochre tussocks, with individual stems up to 25 centimetres long. *Sphagnum tenellum* may be recognised by its small size and pale green colouration, while in the wettest parts of all *Sphagnum cuspidatum* flourishes. It has long stems up to 40 centimetres in length, is usually a light green colour, and tolerates a wide range of acidity. One variety of this moss grows submerged in pools, and can be recognised by its 'drowned cat' appearance.

Despite the wet climate and the 'boggy' nature of the terrain, relatively little intact lowland blanket bog survives in Kerry. Less than 2,500 hectares of intact bog exist throughout the county, compared to areas of Mayo and Galway where single sites can extend over 2,000 hectares. While the lack of lowland blanket bogs is mainly due to the mountainous terrain of Kerry, much of what was present has been lost to piecemeal forestry development and mechanised turf-cutting, particularly on the Iveragh peninsula where much of the turf is cut for sale to the electricity generating station at Caherciveen. Many of the remaining sites are threatened by these same factors, as well as suffering from the impact of overgrazing by sheep, and in some cases, deer, which reduces their botanical interest.

To safely explore a quaking lowland blanket bog requires waterproof boots and a nimble-footed nature. Once you progress from the firm edge of the roadside,you enter an area which consists mainly of water, covered with a thin skim of vegetation. The bog surface quakes and trembles at each step, and except for

---

BOG PLANT ADAPTATIONS

Peat consists of partly decomposed organic matter principally of plant and, to a lesser extent, animal origin. This organic matter consists of the partly-rotted remains of leaves, stems, roots, seeds, etc. These remains are only semi-decayed because the soil they are in is waterlogged — peat consists of over 90% water. This soil water is virtually stagnant, so oxygen cannot be mixed in. Without oxygen, the aerobic bacteria which are so important in the decomposition of organic material are absent. So, rather than decomposing as normal, the organic remains build up over thousands of years to form peat.

The anaerobic, waterlogged medium of peat is a very difficult and hostile environment for plants to live in and plants have developed many adaptations to enable them to survive. One structural adaptation which most bog plants have in common is that their bulk is composed of special tissue called aerenchyma – a meshwork of living cells separated by special airspaces for transporting oxygen. This meshwork is visible to the naked eye if one slices across the stem of a bog cotton plant. This gives the plants maximum strength with minimum weight, so reducing the need for excess cells. One problem which bog plants face, paradoxically, is that of drying out during summer weather and also of being unable to take up water through their roots when the bog surface is frozen during Winter. If they could not control their water loss at such times, they would be placed under severe stress. Thus some, like heathers, have small waxy leaves, others needle-like leaves, while more are low-growing, creeping species which hug the bog surface; all designed to reduce the loss of precious water vapour.

Nutrients in a bog system are very scarce, so many species recycle what nutrients they have obtained during the year and store them overwinter in underground bulbs and rhizomes. Others supplement the nutrients taken in through their roots by trapping and digesting insects in various ways. Kerry is the only county in which all eleven species of insectivorous plants found on Irish bogs occur. Probably the most successful colonisers of this environment are the peat mosses (Sphagnum species) which have a competitive edge by actively increasing the acidity of their surroundings. They exchange hydrogen ions, one of their main waste products, for minerals such as potassium and calcium present in the water. The hydrogen ions thus released increase the acidity of the water, so making it even more difficult for other species.

TABLE 4

RED DATA SPECIES OF MOSS FOUND IN KERRY

Acaulon muticum	Disturbed soil patches	*Hedwigia integrifolia*	On boulders in moorland and screes
Aloina ambigua	Dry calcareous soils	*Isopterygiopsis muellerana*	Montane: Shaded soils in rock crevices
Antitrichia curtipendula	On dry rocks in sheltered situations	*Mnium marginatum*	On rocks by streams in wooded glens
Arctoa fulvella	Dry shaded sites	*Orthotrichum rivulare*	Tree trunks overhanging streams
Bartramia hallerana	Shaded rock ledges in wooded valleys	*Orthotrichum sprucei*	Low on tree trunks overhanging water
Byrum donianum	Sheltered sites on walls and banks	*Orthotrichum stramineum*	Tree trunks in hedgerows and woodland
Byrum marratii	Coastal: Dune slacks and saltmarsh edges	*Oxystregus hibernicus*	Oceanic: Wooded ravines, boulder screes
Campylopus saxicola	Damp rocks in wooded humid ravines	*Philonotis cernua*	Peaty soils among heather
Campylopus schimperi	Montane: stream banks and sheltered valleys	*Philonotis rigida*	Loose cliff-faces in wooded valleys
Cyclodictyon laetivirens	Oceanic: wet, shaded rocks and caves	*Plagiopus oederiana*	Moist crevices in woodland, overhangs
Daltonia splachnoides	Sloping, sheltered rocks by streams	*Plagoiothecium cavifolium*	Montane: damp, calcareous ledges
Dicranella crispa	Damp, sandy/gravelly sites	*Pottia crinita*	Thin soils among rocks: extinct?
Dicranella subulata	Montane: disturbed, acid ground	*Pottia recta*	Disturbed, base-rich sites
Dicranodontium uncinatum	Montane: among boulders and rocks	*Rhabdoweisia fugax*	Dry rocks in shaded sites
Ephemerum stellatum	Sparsley vegetated sites	*Rhynchostegiella curviseta*	Wooded ravines, cuttings, coastal rocks
Fissidens algarvicus	Sheltered banks in woods, lanes, cliffs	*Scleropodium tourettii*	Coastal
Fissidens polyphyllus	Sheltered wooded valleys	*Sematophyllum demissum*	Shaded rocks in humid sites
Fissidens rivularis	On rocks by rivers and lakes	*Tortula atrovirens*	Dry, sandy soils on walls and cliffs
Grimmia torquata	Montane: Damp, rock ledges	*Tortula cuneifolia*	Bare patches close to sea
Hamatocaulis vernicosus	Calcereous fens and flushes	*Ulota coarctata*	On trees in wooded ravines

during very dry weather, the pools and muddy areas between the mounds of veg-etation are traps for the unwary. The first feature you may notice are the mounds of multi-coloured peat mosses, varying from the lightest yellow through a range of greens, pinks and red, to dark brown and black species. Some of those species we have already met with on the mountain blanket bogs occur in this habitat, along with others such as the golden-coloured *Sphagnum auriculatum*, nor-mally, found inpools,*Sphagnum compactum*, which forms dense, golden mounds and the rare *Sphagnum pulchrum*, found on only two Kerry bogs. This is a bright orange colour with large tufts at the tops of its stems.

The white-beak sedge is an important component of peat bogs. This prefers the margins of pools and muddy areas, where it can form quite dense stands, with individual plants growing to 20 centimetres tall. It has small white flowers which-brighten the bog surface in summer, and like many bog plants produces under-ground bulbs which overwinter in the peat surface. These bulbs are one of the pre-ferred foods of the Greenland white-fronted goose, some small flocks of which occur in Kerry. A close relative, but scarcer, is the taller, brown-beak sedge, which prefers wetter sites. As its name indicates it has brown flower spikelets. The yel-low-orange flowers of the bog asphodel are common everywhere. Even when they die off in autumn their orange seed heads remain visible standing erect above the surface for many months.

Purple moor grass, deergrass, bog cotton and cross-leaved heath, which prefers wetter conditions than ling, protrude through the *Sphagnum* carpet. Bog myrtle, with its aromatic deciduous leaves occurs frequently and can form exten-sive stands in wet sites where minerals are more plentiful. One of the most obvious flowering plants of the bog pools is the bogbean, with its large, oval leaves and pinkish-white flowers. In ancient times it was considered to be good for puri-fying the blood and curing boils.

INSECTIVORES

As bogs are very low in nutrients, a number of plant species augment their nutri-ent supply by trapping and digesting insects. Scattered around the bog pools will be the sundews; small, reddish insectivorous plants. All three species occur in Kerry, separated by the shape of their leaves and their habitat preferences. The round-leaved sundew is the most widespread species. It has one centimetre diam-eter leaves on the end of short stems. Each of the leaves is covered by an arrange-ment of fine hairs tipped with a clear, sticky globule. This catches any small insect which settles on it. They are then digested by enzymes produced by the leaves. It has been estimated that a single sundew may catch up to 2,000 small insects every year. The great sundew has long, strap-shaped leaves on stems which may be up to 12 centimetres in length. The oblong-leaved sundew has leaves intermediate in shape between the other two species which taper to a shorter stalk. It is normally found on very wet peat or in groups floating on the water surface of pools. These little flotillas drift from one side of the pool to the other, depending on wind direction. All three species produce small, white flowers on the ends of short stalks.

A large-flowered butterwort

The bladderworts are underwater insectivores. Four species occur in Kerry, of which the lesser and the intermediate bladderwort are the most widespread, although the latter is rare in north Kerry. In summer their delicate yellow flowers rise above the surface of pools and drains. Beneath the waters, however, the plants are actively working to trap unwary insects. Bladderworts are rootless plants and the small underwater leaves bear tiny, translucent bladders with sensitive bristles at one end. Water is pumped out of these bladders, creating a partial vacuum. When the bristles are brushed by an insect such as a water flea, a trap-door is triggered and the insect is sucked in with the inward rush of water. Because it would be energetically expensive for the plant to produce digestive enzymes for each occupied bladder, as they would be diluted by the water in the trap, the animal is left imprisoned and alive. Its faeces and finally its dead body decompose and the soluble products are absorbed by the plant.

Another insectivore, found on only one bog near Listowel, is the pitcher plant. A native of North America, it was first successfully introduced into Ireland in 1906. In 1988 it was discovered to have been introduced to Kerry. The leaves are fleshy

---

'KERRY' BUTTERWORT

Our most renowned insectivorous plant is the large-flowered butterwort, which only occurs in Kerry and parts of west Cork. This attractive plant, with its two centimetre wide, purple flowers can be found on hillsides, the slopes of wet banks and the margins of bogs all over the mountainous parts of Kerry, but is scarcer in the north. Clumps of up to twenty plants are frequently encountered, producing an attractive splash of yellowy-green and purple colour. The butterworts have a linear arrangement of glands along the length of their fleshy leaves which attract and stick their victims. Other glands emit digestive enzymes which finish off the job. All three Irish species occur in Kerry, the others being the pale butterwort and the common butterwort. Paradoxically, the latter is the rarest in the county.

---

and very hairy, forming a hollow cone with a lid-like flap at the mouth, which is often purplish-red in colour. The flowers are produced on the end of a tall, stiff stem. The inside of the leaves have downward pointing hairs, so designed to trap

The introduced pitcher plant on a bog near Listowel

insects which may enter or fall in. Like the bladderworts, the hapless insects are left to die and decompose at their own pace, when their nutrients are absorbed by the plant. The introduction of any foreign species is to be deplored, particularly one such as the pitcher plant which has the potential to quite drastically change the ecology of its new environment. It has already been noticed on other bogs that its large leaves shade out many native species, thus reducing the floral diversity of a site.

The white, fluffy fruiting heads of the cottongrasses are a well-known sign of boggy ground. The hare's-tail cottongrass, with its single white-topped stem and the common cottongrass, with its multiple stems, are the most widespread species. The broad-leaved cottongrass has wider, more flattened leaves than its more common relatives, and is localised about the county, seldom oc-curring in abundance. Our rarest species is the slender cottongrass, known from only two localities near Killarney and in the Black Valley. It was first recorded in Ireland from Connemara in 1966.

Another rare bog-dweller, known from only six localities on the Iveragh and Beara peninsulas is the bog orchid. This is a tiny, twelve centimetre high plant, which bears inconspicuous green flowers. It normally grows among clumps of *Sphagnum,* making it even more difficult to find.

Large areas of cut-over bog exist around the county, many of which are interesting in their own right. Some of these sites, not yet developed for forestry or too heavily grazed, possess interesting pool systems. These are slowly being recolonised by colourful peat mosses and other bog plants, recreating the early stages of blanket bog conditions. Many are studded with the gaunt remains of ancient tree roots, while patches of white-headed bog cotton shine like snow in summer. These bogs make excellent natural laboratories for the study of colonisation processes, and many are hauntingly beautiful, wild places. Most are threatened, however, by forestry, dumping and drainage. There is a strong case to be made for actively protecting and conserving a good selection of these wonderful areas, before they are lost forever. We lack a sense of local and national pride in our boglands. In many areas of Kerry they are the main landscape feature, and worthy of our appreciation. We should value

A mass of bog cotton in cutaway bog near Cromane

their beauty, importance and sense of wildness and do far more to conserve and protect those that remain.

GLOSSARY OF TERMS NOT EXPLAINED IN THE TEXT

BRYOPHYTE — Any plant of the major botanical division Bryophyta, which includes the mosses and liverworts. They have stems and leaves but lack true roots and vascular tissue.

PINNA (PLURAL PINNAE) — One of the primary divisions into which the leaves of most ferns are divided.

PROTHALLUS — Tiny heart-shaped plates of tissue which develop from fern spores. They contain male and female reproductive structures. New fern plants develop from the fertilised eggs.

WHERE MOUNTAIN MEETS FARMLAND

The interface between moorland and farmland tends to be quite sharply defined. At one moment you may be walking along a track edged with heather and low gorse, the next moment you pass through a gate or negotiate a wall and are crossing farmland. The upper limit of these fields is normally about 200-250 metres. Just above the fields you may meet an area with scattered shrubs of rowan, hawthornand holly, often overhanging a low cliff or stream gully out of the reach of grazers. These may be the remnants of former woodland, or have been bird-sown in more recent times. In some areas the transition is more gradual and this is often a sign of farm abandonment. Many of the old fields are dominated by bracken or heather, with patches of both the tall, spring-flowering gorse or the low-growing western gorse intermixed. Larger shrubs are frequent and given time and a bit of encouragement, extensive areas of woodland could develop.

These overgrown areas are well worth closer botanical examination. Toby Hodd, a Killarney-based naturalist, spent some time exploring one such area. Within a kilometre of his home he found such scarce species as lemon-scented fern, beech fern and ivy-leaved bellflower, a small, delicate perennial with light blue flowers. These were all new records for the area, and help extend our knowledge of these species' distribution.

FERNS

At least 52 species and hybrids of ferns have been recorded in Kerry, or approximately two-thirds of the native species and hybrids which occur in Ireland. Thus the county, and in particular the area around the Killarney and Kenmare valleys, ranks among the richest fern sites in Europe.

This species richness is due to the same combination of geographic and climatic factors which suits the bryophytes – principally to Kerry being a mountainous area on the mild, western seaboard of Europe. Thus the region satisfies the requirement of a broad suite of species, including those of montane habitats and species of more southern and 'Atlantic' affinities. Species within the latter group contribute more to the species richness of the locality than montane species and are also more abundant overall.

Bracken is our most abundant fern species and is especially common on abandoned hill fields, where it thrives on the more acid mineral soils. Bracken was originally a woodland species, where its distribution was limited by shading. However, with deforestation, bracken has become a widespread and a serious pest species. It is a highly successful coloniser, being generally toxic to livestock as well as many herbivorous invertebrates. However, this toxicity to livestock varies from plant to plant and throughout its life cycle, so some bracken plants are grazed occasionally. It has also been found that phytotoxins leached by rain from dead, standing bracken fronds suppress the growth of herbs and other plants, thus further enhancing its competitiveness.

Bracken was once used by people for many purposes. Its biochemical properties repelled insects, reduced the attack of moulds and slowed the rate of decay, so it was used as a bedding for humans and livestock, as packaging for fruit, fish and other foods, as well as fragile materials such as slates. Its rhizomes and fronds were used for dyes. The ash from burnt bracken has a high potash content, so was valuable as a top-dressing for plants, for making soap and washing soda, and in the leather-tanning and glass-making industries. In more recent times, the change in hill grazing regimes from cattle to sheep and consequent reduction in trampling of fronds, as well as a complete cessation in its use for animal bedding and other purposes, has allowed bracken to maximise its spread.

One of the most majestic species is the aptly named royal fern. It normally occurs in ditches, old peat workings and along lakeshores. It is a particularly striking feature of coastal areas where drains border fields rather than hedgerows. Large stands can reach over two metres in height, making it Europe's tallest fern. Within lowland deciduous wooded areas, male ferns are common. These have long, graceful fronds growing from a central crown, and may be up to a metre high. A distinctive species with two different types of fronds is the hard fern, which occurs on acid soils up to quite high altitudes. Its sterile, evergreen fronds lie flat against the ground in a rosette shape, while its fertile fronds, 15-75 centimetres in height, stand erect. The lemon-scented fern is another tall species, with a yellow-green colour and a strong lemony scent when crushed. It is widespread but local throughout, occurring on rocks by rivers, preferring to have moist, aerated, acidic conditions around its roots. The beech fern is a much rarer species,

---

THE KILLARNEY FERN

Kerry's most famous fern species is the Killarney fern, which has been recorded at 43 sites in Ireland, of which eighteen are in Kerry. It has dark green, translucent leaves and grows in shady sites beneath boulders and near waterfalls, though rarely in their splash zone as has been often quoted. While prothalli are often found in the leaf litter close to these ferns, for some unknown reason these rarely mature into adult plants. Probably not all sites have been recorded, as a new one in the Killarney valley was discovered in 1994. The Killarney fern is a Red Data Book *species protected under the Wildlife Act.*

---

recorded mainly from around the Killarney valley. It can be distinguished by its lowest pinnae being held out and downward at a different angle to the rest and the lack of pinnae on the lower half of the stem. Another rarity, recorded from only four sites in Ireland, is the mountain male-fern, which in Kerry has only been found on moorland around Mangerton mountain.

The marsh fern is a delicate species growing in damp areas on the Muckross peninsula and Ross island near Killarney, where it is locally common, though rare elsewhere in Kerry. Two types of fronds are produced annually. The shorter sterile fronds are produced about a month before the thicker, fertile fronds.

The spleenworts are small, close-growing ferns of walls, rock outcrops and hedgebanks. The rusty-back fern has the undersides of its fronds covered with silvery scales which turn rust-coloured with age. The black spleenwort has green fronds with brittle, dark stems and prefers well lit situations. The rare Irish spleenwort, with its finely-dissected leaves, is found at about six localities from Glenflesk to Glencar as well as in five other counties. It is not known to occur in Britain. A species with an interesting distribution is the sea spleenwort, which is normally only found in the spray zone on rocky sea shores and cliffs. However, it had one inland station in Ireland, along the rocky shores of the Upper Lake of Killarney, but this population may now be extinct. It is now generally accepted that its distribution is due to its intolerance of frost, so the

Sea spleenwort

mild climate of the Killarney area may have allowed it to grow further inland than usual.

Two of our smallest species, with 10 centimetre long fronds, are Tunbridge filmy-fern and Wilson's filmy-fern. Both could easily be confused initially as mosses, growing as they generally do in dense mats on damp, shaded boulders or as epiphytes on trees. The two species are distinguished by differences in their sori –

the spore-bearing structures of ferns – and in their leaf venation. The sori of Wilson's have a smooth-edged, oval profile, while the leaf veins nearly always reach the margin, while the sori of the Tunbridge filmy-fern have a circular, jagged profile and the veins end short of the leaf margin. Although the latter is generally more abundant at lower altitudes, Wilson's is the more widespread of the two species.

A species with unusual fronds is the hart's tongue fern, with its strap-shaped, undivided fronds. It prefers a calcareous substrate on shady walls and rocks. The adder's tongue does not show the usual fern shape either. Its single, bright green

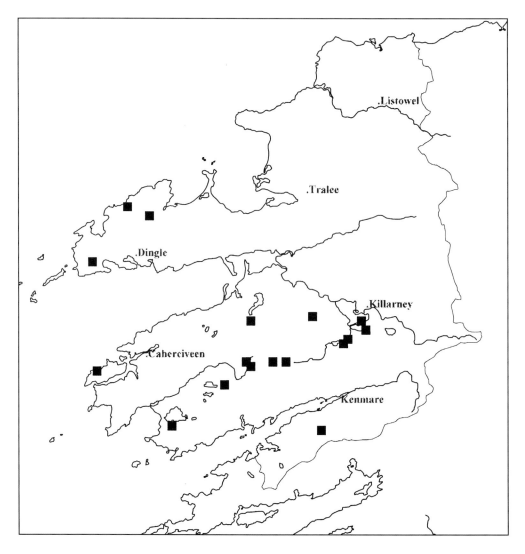

Map 4: Distribution of the Killarney Fern in Kerry

waxy-looking leaf partly encloses a tongue-like fertile shoot. It grows in woods and grasslands at a few localities, the most unusual of which is a turlough-type sink-hole hidden within the woods near Muckross house. This floods in winter to a depth of nearly ten metres, yet in summhas produced up to 90 plants of the adder's-tongue. Another protected species of unusual form is the pillwort, which has narrow, grass-like leaves. The young fronds, how-

The tiny curved fronds of the pillwort

ever, have the characteristic curled, watchspring-like tips of unfurling ferns. Its preferred habitat is the muddy shores of lakes and ponds, which are submerged in winter and generally exposed in summer. Pillwort's Irish distribution includes counties Galway, Mayo and Donegal, as well as Kerry, where it occurs only in the Killarney valley, primarily on muddy banks along the edge of the Upper Lake. Although it was also once found at a site on Lough Leane, it appears to have become extinct at that location, possibly due to pollution. It is threatened throughout its European range by pollution and drainage of its habitat.

TABLE 5
KERRY FLORA REGARDED AS 'THREATENED'

Alder buckthorn	Hoary whitlowgrass
Allwort	Holly fern
Alpine lady's mantle	Irish spleenwort
Alpine meadow-grass	Ivy-leaved bellflower
Alpine saw-wort	Marsh clubmoss
Moonwort	Narrow-leaved helleborine
Cornish moneywort	Sea kale
Dwarf spike rush	Slender cicendia
Henbane	Smooth brome
Whorled caraway	

WOODLANDS

One of the features which makes the Killarney area so scenically attractive is its rich variety of woodlands. Other areas have lakes, mountains and moorlands, but it is the added texture and character of the woodlands in combination with these ingredients which makes this region so outstanding. It is also arguably the main feature which makes the area so important for naturalists of all sorts.

Apart from being of interest in their own right, trees bestow many other benefits upon their surroundings. They soften the effect of climate, creating their own micro-climate beneath their sheltering canopy. Sunlight is filtered, wind speed reduced and the earth protected from the worst effects of frost. Trees provide a vertical element to the habitat, both on their living roots, trunk, boughs and leaves as well as on their dead skeletons. Also, by bringing up nutrients from deep within the earth and by their leaf-fall, they play a vital part in enriching the soil surface annually.

Despite the best attempts of people over the past few hundred years, we are fortunate in Kerry in having the largest area of native forest cover remaining in

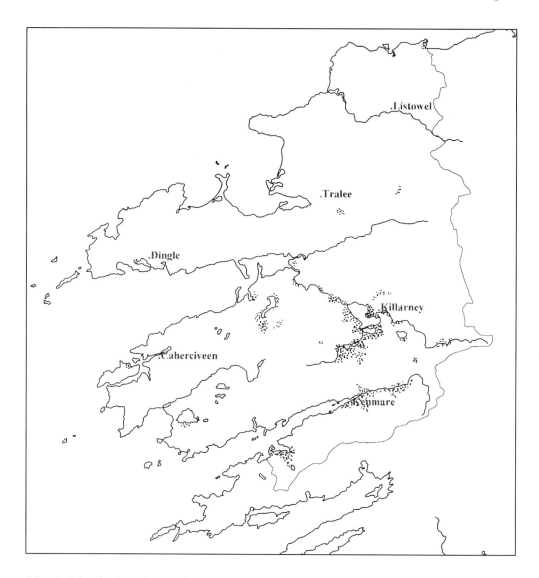

Map 5: Distribution of natural and semi-natural woodlands throughout Kerry

Ireland. While most of this forest is concentrated in the Killarney valley, important patches of predominantly native woodland are found elsewhere in the county. The principal species concerned is sessile oak, but there are also interesting stands of birch and hazel, particularly in the Roughty river valley, while the Lough Leane area has some of the largest Irish concentrations of alder woods, as well as a yew wood of international importance.

Because of the presence of the gulf stream offshore, with prevailing westerly winds providing abundant rainfall and high humidity, our woodlands are described as oceanic. They are of international importance for bryophytes, ferns and lichens, and have been described as being the nearest approach in Britain or Ireland to temperate evergreen rainforest.

A typical natural forest is composed of various layers. The canopy layer consists of the larger tree species such as oak, ash and beech. They absorb and filter out much of the incoming sunlight, reducing the amount available to plants growing beneath the canopy. Species such as holly and hazel make up the shrub layer, although in certain areas, where the overall canopy height may be quite low, these shrub species may be sufficiently tall to break through and form part of the canopy layer. Beneath the shrubs, the field layer consists of plants such as wood-rush, bluebells and wild garlic. Most of these flowering species must complete their flowering season before the deciduous trees put on their new leaves in spring. Many woodland plants have bulbs, corms, tubers or rhizomes as food stores to see them through the long dormant period when there is insufficient light for them to photosynthesise. The ground layer consists of the mosses and liverworts, many of which can tolerate very low light levels.

Let us examine some of the different types of woods more closely. On the acidic soils which predominate in Kerry the principal canopy-forming tree is the sessile oak. This is the tree of rocky ground, as its specific name *petraea* (of the rock) indicates. Its English name, sessile, refers to the fact that its acorns are unstalked, i.e., attached directly to the twigs, which distinguishes it in autumn from the pedunculate oak. Sessile oaks occur on well-drained sloping hillsides up to an altitude of nearly 300 metres. Its hard, heavy

A good fall of acorns

wood has made it attractive to man for many thousands of years and it was one of the principal species which was devastated during recent historical times. While archaeologists have found straight oak trunks of over 22 metres in length, very few if any such trees exist in Kerry today, having been preferentially selected by wood-cutters for generations. One of the finest oaks remaining is the so-called 'royal oak' on the shores of Lough Leane in Killarney. In 1901 it measured 4.15 metres in circumference at a height of one metre above ground, and in 1997 measured 5.69 metres.

Oaks play host to a wealth of invertebrates and flora. The polypody fern is one of the most obvious epiphytic plants on oaks. Epiphytes are plants which grow on other plants, depending on them for support but not for their nutrients. Its 30-40 centimetre-long fronds are common on the boughs of oaks up to 15 metres or more off the ground. All their nourishment is obtained from rainfall, and the fronds become brown and crinkled during dry spells. Wherever leaf litter has built up in damp tree holes, or at the junction of limbs and trunk, seedlings of rowan, holly and rhododendron may be seen. Table 6 lists the more common epiphytes on oak trees.

TABLE 6

THE MORE COMMON EPIPHYTES ON OAK TREES IN DERRYCUNNIHY WOOD. FROM KELLY (1981).

EPIPHYTES ON TRUNKS AND LARGER BRANCHES

FERNS	BRYOPHYTES	LICHENS
Wilson's filmy fern	*Dicranum scoparium*	*Lepraria incana* (drier sides)
Polypody fern	*Frullania tamarisci*	*Lobaria laetevirens*
Intermediate polypody	*Hypnum cupressiforme*	*Thelotrema lepadinum*
	Isothecium myosuriodes	
	Metzgeria Furcata	
	Plagiochila punctata (higher rainfall areas)	
	Plagiochila spinulo	
	Zygodon viridissimus	

EPIPHYTES ON SMALLER BRANCHES

	BRYOPHYTES	LICHENS
	Drepanolejeunea hamatifolia	*Cladonia coniocraea*
	Frullania dilitata	*Lobaria pulmonaria*
	Frullania germana	*Normandina pulchella*
	Frullania tamarisci	*Ochrolechia androgyna*
	Harpalejeunea ovata	*Parmelia trichotera*
	Hypnum cupresssiforme	
	Isothecium myosuriodes	
	Lejeunea ulicina	
	Metzgeria furcata	
	Ulota crispa	

One of the attractions of our oakwoods, rarely seen elsewhere, is the abundance of holly as the chief understory species and the green mantle of bryophytes covering the lower trunks, rocks and soil. This gives a year-round evergreen appearance. Hollies are either male or female and only females bear the bright red berries. In many areas quite old hollies survive, some with diameters in excess of 60 centimetres, their trunks and limbs gnarled from the effects of age, fires, browsing and disease. Because of the heavy shade which they cast, and the twice-yearly leaf-fall in oak/holly woods (oak leaves drop in autumn, old holly leaves in mid-summer), the ground flora of these woods tends to be very poor, composed principally of bryophytes.

In wetter areas such as by streams and in swampy ground, alders may be found. Alders are normally regarded as lowland trees, where they prefer such mineral-rich sites as lakeshores and river valleys, but they occur quite high up stream valleys. They have an average life-span of about 80 years and very few develop to a diameter of more than half a metre or so. Archaeological evidence shows that much bigger alders were once more common, as shields have been found made from a single slice of alder nearly a metre in diameter. Two of the oldest and largest alders to be found in Kerry, and possibly in Ireland, occur in a small wooded valley called Glasheenamarbh in the Killarney valley. The largest of these alders measures six metres in circumference at a height of 1.5 metres from the ground, and the other measures five metres. They would not be much use for shields, though; being so old the roots of their boughs are growing down through the heart of the main trunks.

THE SCOURGE OF RHODODENDRON

The evergreen appearance of these woods is added to by another introduced species, *Rhododendron ponticum*. Of many hundred rhododendron species and hybrid varieties which are planted in Kerry, only *Rhododendron ponticum* has spread from its original planting sites to become the major pest it now is. A native of the Black Sea region and parts of the Iberian peninsula, it was introduced into Ireland and Britain from the eighteenth century onwards, being used as an ornamental plant and for game cover. In Kerry it was often used as a shelter belt around various houses and lodges. The origin of most badly infested areas can be traced back to such plantings. Each of the attractive mauve-coloured flower-heads may hold up to 5,000 tiny seeds, which are easily disseminated by the wind. It grows vigorously on the acid soils, reaching heights of over six metres and forming dense, impenetrable thickets, replacing the holly understory. Because it casts a very dense shade, the ground flora is eliminated, tree regeneration is impossible and only mosses such as *Hypnum* and *Leucobryum* can survive.

The most infested areas are the slopes of Glena and Torc mountain in the

Killarney valley, the woods around Blackwater Bridge and Tousist overlooking Kenmare bay, and ornamental gardens such as Glanleam on Valentia island. Unfortunately, one still meets with misguided people who plant *Rhododendron ponticum* as a hedge or windbreak, something which is not to be recommended if one lives on acidic soil. If you really want a rhododendron hedge, do choose one of the non-invasive varieties.

Apart from clumps of bilberry and great wood-rush, often much depleted by

Wood sorrel cloaks a tree stump

grazing, flowering plants are scarce in Kerry's oakwoods. Wood sorrel, with its bright green, clover-like leaves, is common on moss-covered rocks and fallen trees. It flowers quite early from March onwards. The leaves have the peculiar characteristic of folding downwards when sunlight falls on them. Wood sorrel has a curious system of reproduction. It produces two sorts of flowers; the first is the familiar lilac-veined flower of spring, which droops at night or in rain to protect the pollen. Though rich with nectar and a strong attraction for early bees and insects, these produce very little seed. A second type of flower, which seldom opens and is self-pollinating, is produced in summer on short stalks close to the ground. These flowers produce most of the seed for the next generation.

The two 'Lusitanian' saxifrages, St Patrick's cabbage and the kidney saxifrage, are characteristic of sandstone areas. In Ireland, the kidney saxifrage, with its hairy-stemmed, kidney-shaped leaves, is the rarer of the two species, being confined to Kerry and west Cork. Outside Ireland it is only found in the Pyrenees, northern Spain and Portugal. St Patrick's cabbage, which has longer, spoon-shaped leaves, is distributed more widely in Ireland. Where the two species meet they hybridise freely, producing fertile offspring, resulting in plants showing a wide variety of leaf shapes. Both saxifrages grow best in areas of higher rainfall, on cliff ledges, large boulders or moss-covered trees, wherever they can escape the attentions of grazers. Their white, star-shaped flowers brighten such locations in early summer.

Another interesting species is Irish spurge, also a member of the 'Lusitanian' flora. It is common only in south-west Ireland, but is surprisingly absent from much of the Dingle peninsula and around the Shannon estuary. Its bright yellow-green tufts are a special feature of spring and early summer. The rare lesser tway-blade, a delicate little orchid, was recently discovered in some of these woods. Its two tiny leaves and brownish flowers make it very difficult to find among the mosses of the woodland floor. This is an unusual habitat for this species, as in

Ireland it is usually found beneath the sheltering canopy of heather on moorlands. Later in summer, the tall, stately flowers of foxgloves add a dash of purple colour to the woodland scene.

The dearth of flowering plants is made up by the wealth of bryophytes. In Derrycunnihy wood beside the Upper Lake of Killarney there are at least 90 species, or three times the number found in a mature English oakwood. At least 71 species have been recorded on living oak bark in Kerry. On the woodland floor and the lower half of the oaks, mosses and liverworts predominate, but as one ascends the trunk into the branches, numerous species of lichens occur. *Frullania dilitata* is a common, purple-red liverwort. Its leaves have tiny lobes formed into helmet-shaped pitchers, which contain water. These are commonly occupied by microscopic animals called *Callidina symbiotica*. It is believed that the 'pitchers' have the same food-trapping function as those of *Pleurozia purpurea* appear to have.

The tree lungwort is a common lichen of these wet western woods; green and leathery when moist, becoming pale and papery when dry. *Cladonia coniocraea* is a grey-green lichen, with what appear to be small horns growing from it. The tips of these erect, slender stalks, which are hollow inside and usually curved, are covered with powdery reproductive structures called soredia. Many older tree trunks will be covered with striking, large patches of the yellow-green lichen, *Parmelia caperata*. Its vertical distribution on tree trunks is determined by water availability rather than light. Some rarer or locally important species which have been found here include the blue-green *Parmeliella atlantica*, the somewhat jelly-like *Leptogium burgessii* and the green-grey, leathery *Lobaria amplissima*.

TABLE 7
PROTECTED SPECIES OF FLOWERS FOUND IN KERRY

Alpine bistort	Penny royal
Betony	Pillwort
Bog orchid	Recurved sandwort
Heath cudweed	Sea pea
Irish lady's tresses	Slender bog-cotton
Kerry lily	Slender naiad
Killarney fern	small cudweed
Lanceolate spleenwort	Small white orchid
Opposite-leaved pondweed	Three-lobed water crowfoot
Oysterplant	Traingular clubrush
Pale dog violet	

WOODS ON LIMESTONE

On lowland, limestone soils a more varied woodland develops. One of the most interesting woods on limestone is to be found on Ross island, near Killarney. Formerly a true island, it is now easily accessible by crossing an old stone bridge beneath the towering parapets of Ross castle. If one has recently come from the relatively uniform oakwoods, one is immediately struck by the variety of tree species here. Although many foreign species were planted here in the past hundred years, the area is still rich in native species.

The pedunculate oak is commoner in lowland areas, and can be distinguished from sessile oak by its stalked acorns, different shaped leaves and short petioles, or leaf stalks, which are rarely over five millimetres long. Those of the sessile oak are normally from 12 to 18 millimetres in length. The two species appear to hybridise freely, which has caused some concern among ecologists. The beige-coloured bark of ash is a common sight. Because of the arrangements of its leaves, ash casts a comparatively light shade, and a good ground flora normally develops beneath it. Due to its base-rich bark, a rich lichen flora tends to develop on ash trees, especially older specimens in well-lit areas such as woodland edges or in hedgerows. Scattered yew trees appear on outcrops of rock, while in marshy sites alders and willows are common, but we shall travel elsewhere to examine these. At one time, wych elms would have been frequent here, but now only their decaying skeletons remain. Elms predominated on rich, limestone soils, and were one of the principal trees of Kerry's lowland landscape, but are now a rare sight due to the depredation of Dutch elm disease. Young elms still survive in hedgerows, developing from suckers and the herring-bone pattern of their winter branches can still be seen. These young trees are invariably hit by the disease as soon as they reach a certain stage of development.

DUTCH ELM DISEASE

Accidentally introduced from north America in the 1960's, Dutch elm disease is caused by a fungus, Ceratocystis ulmi. *This is carried by an elm-bark beetle of the genus* Scolytus, *after the adult hatches from the pupa and moves to a new tree to feed and lay its eggs. The fungus clogs the vascular system of the tree, preventing the passage of sap and thus killing the tree. The term 'Dutch elm disease ' was coined because the Dutch studied it in an effort to breed resistant trees. It is probably not the first time that elms have been destroyed en masse. The archaeological records show that about 5,100 years ago, elms virtually vanished from the Irish and European landscape over a very short period. Originally it was believed that this decimation was climate-related or caused by large-scale woodland clearances by people, but it is now believed to have been a naturally occurring phenomenon similar to that which has occurred recently.*

Beech was introduced into Ireland in 1642. Its leaves cast a dense shade, thus reducing the ground flora which exists beneath it. However, old, decaying beech trees are good sites for invertebrates. Sycamore is also an introduced species, and like beech is valued for its timber. Despite being introduced, (native tree species normally support a richer invertebrate fauna than introduced species) sycamore supports a surprisingly rich invertebrate fauna, and due to its base-rich bark, is also good for lichens. Both horse chestnut and sweet chestnut are common in this area. If you snap off a leaf-stalk from a horse chestnut twig you will notice the horseshoe-shaped scar on the twig, hence its name. Although its nuts are inedible, those of the sweet chestnut are particularly delicious, either raw or roasted. They are avidly eaten by many birds, animals and humans in the autumn. Along with these deciduous introductions, there is a large variety of mature coniferous trees here, including fine specimens of silver fir, Monterey pine and Scots pine.

The Scots pine was once native to Ireland, but became extinct by about 1,000 years ago, although some evidence suggests that scattered individuals may have survived into recent historical times. We do know, however, that due to its absence or scarcity, large quantities of seed were being brought in from Britain for planting from the first half of the eighteenth century. On Ross island it now grows mainly along the shoreline, where seedlings germinate from water-drifted seeds. Pollen analysis has shown that several thousand years ago Scots pine was an important component of Derrycunnihy wood, where it was part of a mosaic of pine/oak/birch woodland. Pine had vanished from the Muckross peninsula by 3,500 years ago, and from Derrycunnihy wood by 1,100 years ago. It has been suggested that its earlier disappearance from Camillan wood was due to an inability to compete with other species on the richer lowland soils.

Birch can tolerate a wide variety of soil types, including acid soils. It is a fast growing, relatively short-lived coloniser of cut-over bogs, abandoned fields and woodland edges and clearings. It is also valuable as a soil improver, being able to 'fix' atmospheric nitrogen through its symbiotic relationship with special bacteria found in nodules on its roots. This, coupled with the fact that birch does not cast a dense shade, generally allows a diverse flora to develop beneath it. Aspens occur locally throughout the county alongside streams and in damp places in woods, but are nowhere common. The leaves are borne on long flattened stems, allowing them to flutter in the slightest breeze, hence the tree's Latin name *Populus tremula*. Aspens turns a lovely yellow colour in autumn; a large specimen produces a beautiful autumn display.

Ross island is renowned in botanical circles as an excellent location for many calcicole (lime-loving) plants of interest. A visit to the area in mid-May before the trees come into full leaf is probably best, but any time of summer has its attractions. As you cross onto the island branch off into the woods, where the delicate

A woodland pool, Ross island

flowerheads of sanicle and pignut are visible everywhere on drier ground. Occasional patches of the vanilla-scented woodruff can also be seen. Woodruff has small, funnel-shaped white flowers which are especially visible against the darker background of the soil. It has a very limited distribution in Kerry, being fairly common around Killarney but rare elsewhere. Other white-flowered plants to be found here are the northern bedstraw, a scarce plant in the south of Ireland and the straggly three-nerved sandwort, which has three conspicuous veins or nerves beneath each leaf. This is the only sandwort to grow in woodlands. The tiny seeds of this plant have an oily appendage that is attractive to ants, which thus play an important part in dispersing the seeds about the woodland floor.

Orchids such as the early purple and the common twayblade abound, and the scarcer bird's-nest orchid can also be seen here. The latter is a strange-looking orchid, being totally devoid of leaves and chlorophyll. Its name is derived from the tangled mass of short, fleshy roots, which look like a badly-made bird's nest. It normally flowers in the shadiest parts of a woodland floor, where it is often the only flower among the carpets of dead leaves. The single flowering spike carries 50 to 100 creamy-brown coloured flowers. The old spikes are quite long-lasting, often remaining visible into the following year. Like most orchids, they are slow to reach maturity from seed, taking about nine years. A plant which looks superficially similar to the bird's-nest orchid is the rare toothwort, which like the latter lacks chlorophyll. The whole plant is a creamy-pink colour, with flowers drooping to one side of the thick stem. Tooth-wort is a parasite, attaching small pad-like suckers to the roots of its host plant, usually a hazel. It dissolves its way through to the main feeding area of the root, then diverts some of the sap from the root to itself. Other rarities found on Ross island include stone bramble, betony, wood vetch and marsh hawk's-beard, the latter at its only Kerry site.

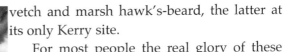

The parasitic toothwort

For most people the real glory of these woods are the swathes of bluebells and the white-flowered ramsons or wild garlic which abound here in the month before leaf growth is complete on the trees. The two species appear to be mutually exclusive, forming extensive single-species stands. The bulbs of the ramsons are shallow-rooted, so crowding

---

BETONY — A WINNING PLANT

With its large, purplish red coloured flowers and rarity status, betony is a worthy subject for study. For David Curran of Killorglin, a detailed study of the ecology of this plant in Kerry and west Cork scooped him three awards at the 1995 Aer Lingus Young Scientist Exhibition. David carried out his research while a student at the Intermediate School in Killorglin, where he was encouraged by his teachers Jim O'Malley and Kieran Griffin, both active botanists and naturalists in their own right. With the support of his parents, David travelled to west Cork, Muckross and near his own home at Knockawaddra to study three different populations of the plant. His efforts won him second prize in the senior Ecological and Biological Sciences section, a National Heritage Council award for promoting awareness of the country's flora, and a new award sponsored by Aer Lingus and the Swiss Youth Council – a visit to represent Ireland in the Sixth International Wildlife Conference in Switzerland.

---

out other species at the soil surface or sub-surface, and they may also use chemical inhibitors to restrict competition from other plants.

Betony

Interesting plants found along the limestone shores of Ross island are thrift and sea campion. These are mainly coastal plants, so their occurrence inland is unusual. While thrift grows on the summit of some hills as far inland as Mangerton mountain, Ross island is its only lowland, inland station in Ireland. In its usual coastal habitat it can tolerate a lot of salt in the soil, and its appearance on Ross island, where it grows around the abandoned copper mines, may be due to an ability to tolerate a high mineral content in the soil.

Mixed woodlands are particularly good for fungi. A number of edible species occur. The wood blewit has a large smooth brownish cap and lilac coloured gills and stem. The gills are closely spaced and the whole fungus has a strong pleasant scent. Chanterelles are funnel-shaped and the colour of egg-yolk. They have a faint but characteristic smell of apricots. Puffballs are whitish-grey when young, becoming yellow-brown with age. Its scientific name, *Lycoperdon,* comes from the Greek *lucos,* the wolf and *perdon,* its dung, possibly because it was thought to grow on wolf dung or to resemble its dung. Puffballs are quite edible, especially when young. When mature, plumes of brown spores are ejected through a hole on top of the fungus, particularly if it is hit by drops of water. A common fungus of dead trees, found all year round, is *Trametes versicolor.* It is found most commonly on dead birches, growing in tiered clusters. The velvet-like upper surface is marked with alternating bands of grey, yellow and brown.

FUNGI

Fungi are the natural recycling agents of your garden and the countryside in general. They come in a wide variety of forms and include moulds, rusts, mildews, smuts, toadstools and mushrooms. They range in size from small, microscopic forms to bracket fungi the thickness of a person's waist. The essential characteristic of all fungi is that they lack chlorophyll, the green colouring matter of plants which enables them to photosynthesise. Lacking this substance, fungi must obtain their organic food already prepared.

Many are parasitic, obtaining their food from other living organisms. Some are specific to certain hosts, others attack a wide variety of hosts. Most fungi grow on the ground, obtaining their food from decaying plant and animal matter. These are called saprophytes. Their active growing and feeding parts are multi-branched fine threads called hyphae, which spread throughout the soil. Many woodland species have formed a symbiotic relationship with certain tree species, penetrating their roots and forming a dense covering over them. The modified root with its layer of fungal hyphae is called a mycorrhiza. One such fungus which grows on birch is the well known fly agaric, with its white-spotted red cap. Both tree and fungus benefit – the tree absorbs water and mineral salts taken in by the fungus, while the fungus obtains foods such as sugars from the roots.

Bracket fungus on a decaying tree

When walking through a woodland in summer or autumn your senses may be assailed by the smell of putrefying flesh. Closer inspection will probably reveal the presence of the stinkhorn fungus. Within the conical cap is a thick layer of green jelly, which contains the plant's spores. Sub-stances in the jelly break down rapidly on exposure to air, producing the powerful, fetid smell. This attracts flies, particularly blowflies, to feed on the jelly, thus distributing the spores. Dr Paddy Sleeman and his colleagues at University College Cork have shown that the distribution of stinkhorns in their study area in Cork was clearly associated with badger setts. This is believed to be linked to the presence of numerous blowflies near setts, attracted by the presence of dung, decaying bedding and badger carcases.

THE YEW FOREST

South of the town of Killarney, washed by the waters of Lough Leane and Muckross Lake, lies the rocky tongue of land that is the Muckross peninsula. Covering the eastern end of the peninsula, where the carboniferous limestone lies exposed as raised ridges of rock, is the Reenadinna yew wood. Approximately 28 hectares in extent, it is the only large yew forest in Ireland. Reenadinna is one of only a handful of yew woods in Europe, where they also occur on exposed limestone or chalk.

Yew forests were once more common throughout Ireland than they are today. This is evidenced by the occurrence of yew in place-names such as Mayo, from *Mhaigh-Eo*, the 'Plains of the Yew', and in early Irish literature. Yew pollen has also

---

SOME USES OF YEW

The timber of yew is one of the hardest European woods, and has always been highly prized. Until late mediaeval times it was the principal raw material for the longbow, but its use for bow-making goes back nearly 5,000 years. Other uses have been for mill cogs, skewers, axles, drinking vessels and furniture. In the eroded peat bogs near Connor's Pass on the Dingle peninsula, hundreds of short, sharpened sticks of yew lie scattered about. It is believed that these were part of a deer trap, dating to the early Bronze Age. The surviving floors of Dunloe Castle near Killarney are made of yew wood.

---

appeared in many recently published pollen diagrams from the west of Ireland. Although scattered yews do grow in sandstone areas on well-drained sites, yew is predominately a tree of limestone areas. It is probable that wherever limestone occurred on the surface, as in the Burren, Co. Clare, that yew may once have been the dominant tree species.

Yew is a slow-growing tree, often living to 500 years or more, with some specimens in Britain reaching ages of 4,000 years. Its bark is purplish brown, scaling and stripping away to expose bright reddish-coloured patches. It is a primitive conifer, with separate male and female trees. In the autumn the females produce masses of small dark seeds surrounded by a deep succulent cup called an aril. The dark green foliage is poisonous to livestock, especially when drying out, due to the presence of the alkaloid, taxine. Yew also has very few insect herbivores. Only about six species of insect are known to feed on yew, partly due to the presence of another chemical, ecdysone, which causes premature moult in insect larvae. However, it does not appear to be so toxic to deer or rabbits, which can prevent the regeneration of yew by their grazing. This is evident on some of the Killarney lake islands where yew is busily regenerating in the absence of grazing. Also, pollen diagrams taken on the Muckross peninsula show how yew played an important role in woodland dynamics when grazing was restricted.

The floristic composition of the yew woodland has been described in detail by Dr Daniel Kelly, one of the botanists most closely linked with the woodlands of Killarney. The yew canopy varies from 6 to 14 metres in height, substantially lower than nearby oakwoods, with the largest tree having a diameter at breast height of 125 centimetres. In contrast to the nearby oakwoods, little or no understory is present beneath the yew canopy, although wherever a thin layer of soil occurs tall hazels replace yew as the canopy species. While pollen diagrams show that yew has been present on the peninsula for the past 5,000 years, none of the 20 or so dead yews which have been aged were older than 200 years. This suggests that the larger specimens have been selectively cut over the years. The large yew growing in the cloisters of the nearby Muckross abbey is much older. In 1780 it measured 60 centimetres in diameter (1.88 metres in circumference) and when measured in 1904 was 2.84 metres in circumference at a height of 60 centimetres above the ground. By 1994 it had a girth of 3.33 metres at 60 centimetres. Going by these measurements, it was probably planted in the late fifteenth or early sixteenth century around the time of the Abbey's foundation.

The dense evergreen canopy buffers the effect of wind and maintains a constantly cool and even temperature below, even on the hottest days. Because of the dense shade, humid atmosphere and lack of leaf litter, the limestone rock is nearly entirely enveloped by a thick layer of moss. Growing directly on the rock surface is a layer of almost pure *Thamnium alopecurum*, with a mixture of other species such as *Eurhynchium striatum* and *Thuidium tamariscinum* growing where a thin layer of humus has developed. Despite its apparent luxuriance, the bryophyte fauna of the yew wood is species-poor compared to Killarney's oakwoods. Epiphytes are also scarce. The smooth, flaking bark of yew makes it an inhospitable substrate for these and the principal colonists are close-growing, leafy liverworts such as *Marchesinia mackaii, Frullania dilatata* and *Frullania microphylla*. A common sight where water trickles down scarred trunks are the black, spongy growths of the fungus *Peniophora laevigata*. The most regular species of the scanty field layer are false brome grass, wild strawberry, barren strawberry, sanicle, wood sorrel and the lime-loving soft-shield and hart's tongue ferns.

Along the edge of the yew wood, where the limestone cliffs overhang the lakes on either side of the Muckross peninsula, grows the strawberry tree, *Arbutus unedo*, one of Kerry's botanical curiosities. A member of the 'Lusitanian' flora, it is found from Lough Currane to Killarney and as far east as Glengariff, but it is in the Killarney valley that it reaches its full splendour. Arbutus has a distinctive, flaking bark, a twisting trunk and evergreen leaves. It is very intolerant of shade, growing at the edges of woods. The tree's boughs arise from a lignotuber, a woody structure usually buried below ground. These have numerous dormant buds on them, ready to sprout should the tree be badly burned by fire. In its Mediterranean haunts it occurs as a shrub of three to five metres in height, in dry, sandy or acid soils. In Kerry, however, freed from the constraints of long, dry summers, it reaches the size and form of a small tree of ten to twelve metres in height. It does not appear to be fussy in its soil preferences once the site is well drained, large specimens being found on both the sandstone and limestone formations.

The strawberry tree has an interesting manner of reproduction. It produces masses of pinkish-cream, bell-shaped flowers in October, when very little else is in flower. It thus provides a welcome late flush for bees and other insects. The fruits then develop slowly over winter, but do not fully ripen until the following autumn, when they swell and change through orange to bright red in colour. Their surface has a rough, grainy texture to it. Thus it carries its current year's flowers and the previous years ripe fruit at the same time. Its specific name *unedo* is derived from the Latin *unum edo* – I eat only one – referring to the insipid taste of its fruit.

Along the limestone fringes of the Muckross peninsula and at a few other locations elsewhere, grow two rare varieties of rock whitebeam. Both are somewhat similar in appearance, with silvery-white underleaves. *Sorbus rupicola* is found at a number of locations mainly on the west and north coast, but *Sorbus anglica*, which has slightly different-shaped leaves, is found only in Killarney.

CONIFEROUS PLANTATIONS

The current rush to plant land with trees is not a new phenomenen. As early as the end of the eighteenth century, landowners were reafforesting their land with trees. The great oakwood of Tomies in the Killarney valley was clear-felled in 1802 and replanted with more oaks, as is evidenced by the straight rows of trees still noticable today. Large quantities of Scots pine seed was brought in from Britain for planting and smaller amounts of more exotic trees from North America and further afield were introduced. Many of our specimen trees of Monterey pine, Monterey cypress, silver fir, Douglas fir, Chilean pine and others date from the mid-nineteenth century, when the introduction of exotic species was at its height.

TABLE 8

BREAKDOWN OF TREE SPECIES PLANTED BY COILLTE IN CO. KERRY

(DETAILS COURTESY OF COILLTE TEO)

SPECIES	%
Sitka spruce	78.0
Lodgepole pine	12.0
Scots pine	2.0
Corsican pine	0.5
Monterey pine	0.1
Douglas fir	0.4
Japanese larch	2.0
European larch	0.1
Noble fir	0.7
Hardwoods	3.5
Others	0.7

When the government forestry service started to plant trees on a large scale, their experiments showed that the quickest growing trees under Irish conditions were conifers from the western United States. These include Douglas fir, sitka spruce and lodgepole pine. The latter two species have become the most popular for planting. Sitka does best on poor rush-covered, mineral soils and provides the pale timber sold as white deal, as well as our sharp-needled Christmas trees. Lodgepole pine can tolerate the wetter conditions of blanket peat and is nick-named 'the pump' by foresters. Its softer, non-shed foliage has become more pop-ular for Christmas trees, while most of its timber is sold for pulp-making. However, ecologically speaking they are not as welcome as native hardwood species. As of the end of 1994, the total area of land under forestry in Kerry was 33,813 hectares, 21,159 hectares of which was Coillte property. The balance was on private land. A breakdown of the species mix on Coillte land is given in Table 8.

After the initial drainage, fencing and planting operations, the original bog-land plants are replaced by dense stands of heather and purple moor-grass. Densities of wood mice and bank voles increase, sometimes causing considerable damage to the young trees as their bark is stripped off. In the first decade or so, the young forests can also support high densities of birds, but after this period the branches of the closely-spaced trees close in, thus preventing any light from reach-ing the forest floor. The flora is greatly diminished, except at woodland edges or along tracks, the diversity of insect species is reduced, and only a few specialised species can thrive. If allowed to reach maturity, though, and particularly if some native hardwood species are allowed to develop with them, these woods can regain some of their lost ecological interest, as is witnessed by the mature stands of mixed forests in the Killarney area. Some of the finest specimen conifers in the country are to be found in Killarney, some of which were planted as far back as the late 1800s. Details of some of these specimens are found in Table 9.

TABLE 9
SOME SPECIMEN CONIFERS IN KILLARNEY, MEASURED IN SPRING 1995
(COURTESY T. HODD)

SPECIES	LOCATION	HEIGHT (METRES)
Douglas fir	Torc Waterfall	47.7
Monterey pine	Muckross peninsula	36.9
Sequioa	Muckross abbey	34.5
European larch	Torc	33.0
Maritime pine	Torc	31.0
Scots pine	Muckross peninsula	28.0

With the more generous grants now available for planting of deciduous species, it is hoped that we will see more native species planted in our countryside. Nationally, this trend is already occurring, and at an accelerating rate. Over the last few years the level of broadleaf planting in the country as a whole doubled annually from 385 hectares in 1991 to 2974 hectares in 1994 – an encouraging sign. Both the state and private sector are increasingly planting broadleafs – in the latter year 23% of private planting was of deciduous species.

WET WOODLANDS

Before the advent of river drainage schemes, large areas of swamp woodlands would have bordered our major rivers and lakeshores. Despite extensive clearances, Kerry still has the largest remaining tracts of such woods in the country, the majority of which border the Killarney lakes and river Laune. On the south-east shore of this river, just east of Killorglin lies a small but interesting wet woodland. It stretches for some hundreds of metres between the river bank and a nearby road and is fed by mineral-rich springs. Though similar in some ways to the larger areas of wet woodland upstream around Lough Leane, it has a richer ground flora due to a lack of grazing. The trees present are mainly alder and some grey willows, all with a rich covering of lichens. The lush vegetation includes water dropwort, two metre high clumps of greater tussock-sedge, gypsywort, horsetails, common valerian and meadowsweet, with its deli-

American skunk cabbage

cious, heady scent. The aptly-named common scurvy-grass, once used by sailors as a preventative against the dreaded disease of scurvy, is indicative of a brackish influence locally. Curled dock and marsh ragweed overhang the stream, while beds of the reed canary-grass stand at the water's edge. The brilliant yellow flowers of marsh marigold are one of the earliest to appear in spring, a welcome sign that winter is truly over.

Two 'escapes' are widespread throughout the wood. Krauss' clubmoss is a small moss-like plant, frequently used in flower arranging, and originally introduced from the Azores. Much more obvious are the large, yellow-green leaves of American skunk cabbage, a very invasive plant of American wet woodlands, which probably drifted here

A flooded alder wood, early spring, Killarney

from the ornamental gardens at Muckross or Dunloe castle.

The rich bryophyte flora of these swamp woodlands include distinctive species such as *Climacium dendroides,* a bushy moss which looks like miniature trees, *Eurhynchium speciosum* and the liverwort, *Chiloscyphus polyanthus.* Older trees carry a particularly rich lichen flora. Due to the high, constant humidity, Atlantic species such as the blue-green *Parmeliella plumbea* and the grey-blue *Lobaria scrobiculata* and *Pannaria rubiginosa* are abundant.

PLANTS OF LOW-LYING FARMLAND

Although most of the county is farmed in some way, I would define low-lying farmland as agricultural land below the 250 metre contour and bounded by hedgerows and/or stone walls. This habitat has seen enormous changes in the past twenty years. The area of land in Kerry under cultivation has declined to virtually zero and intensively managed grassland dominated by one or two fast-growing grass species has become the norm. Instead of taking a single cut of hay most farmers now take two or three cuts of silage, using large amounts of artificial fertilisers and animal manures to increase productivity. Many hedgerows have been grubbed out to create larger fields and marshy areas drained. In a few areas, traditional farming methods still survive, but these are the exception rather than the rule. All this activity has served to reduce plant species diversity and many of the flowers of cultivated land in particular have become virtually extinct. Species such as corncockle, cornflower, darnel and shepherd's needle, all once common species, have followed the corncrake, the premier bird of farmland, into extinction in Kerry.

Many of the flowering plants of farmland are opportunists. Most produce masses of light, easily dispersed seed, ready to take advantage of any open ground. Thistles, dandelions and ragweed fall into this category. Others such as the creeping buttercup hug the ground, sending out trailing stems to avail of any gaps in the plant cover, while some like the broad-leaved dock have deep tap roots to sustain the plant should the tops be cut. Many of the common meadow plants which are classed as farm weeds are noxious or unpalatable to grazing animals, so have an immediate competitive advantage over edible species.

Often the best places to see a good floral display in these areas are roadside verges. Stretches of roads which have been recently widened or improved often have a wide strip of rough land left on either side which can prove particularly good. The species mix will vary depending on season and soil types, but apart from the above mentioned plants, ubiquitous species include umbellifers such as cow parsley, wild carrot and wild angelica, white and gold splashes of oxeye daisy, the yellow of hawkbits and the purple of common knapweed and foxgloves.

Although hedgerows have only been part of our scenery for the past 200 years or less, they are now an important habitat in their own right, especially as woodland is so scarce. While in some areas hedgerows consist only of a few straggly gorse bushes, in others a good mix of species occurs. The principal hedging species are hawthorn, elder, gorse, blackthorn, hazel and holly, intertwined with brambles. If the hedge has not been severely cut back each year, mature specimens of birch, ash and other tree species may have developed, adding enormously to the ecological

Common knapweed

GORSE

Three species of gorse are found in Ireland, of which two occur in Kerry. The spring-flowering gorse or furze is the taller of the two species, standing up to two metres in height. It grows on well-drained stony soils. In autumn the yellow flowers of the low-growing, western gorse are normally seen mixed in with the purple flowers of heather, providing a lovely splash of colour on bogs and moorlands.

Gorse had many uses in older times. Being evergreen, it was an important source of winter fodder for all livestock, as it is today for sheep and deer. It was also planted to provide cover for game. Gorse is highly flammable and was used for home heating and the firing of bricks, while its potash was used in the manufacture of soap. It also produced a yellow dye. So important was the plant that seeds were brought from Ireland into Scotland and Wales, principally to provide plants for cattle fodder. Even today, resourceful people harvest the attractive, coconut-scented flowers to make an excellent home-brewed wine; probably one of its better uses!

---

interest and importance of the hedge. Apart from providing shelter to farm livestock and crops, a good hedge gives shelter to many animals and birds, as well as lesser plants. Insects abound around a mature hedgerow, badgers dig their setts at its base, voles and other rodents live within its cover, bats hunt along its fringes, birds nest in its thickets and feed on its berry crop in winter. Where farmland has been neglected, or on steep, unworkable ground, hedges spread out to gradually become woods. Dense stands of gorse interspersed with odd hawthorn bushes and birches can be seen on many such sites, providing an attractive show of yellow when the gorse is in flower.

For many visitors to Kerry their most cherished memory is of the miles of fuchsia hedgerows in coastal areas, particularly on the Dingle peninsula. Its attractive purple and crimson flowers are on display from May to early October. Originally a native of Chile and Argentina, the seed was sold widely in Kerry during the last century as being ideal for planting in coastal areas. Unlike another introduction, rhododendron, fuchsia is not as invasive, as it rarely fruits or has suckers. Beneath the fuchsia hedges one often sees the sword-like leaves and orange flowers of montbretia, another introduced plant. This is a garden hybrid of two South African species. Now naturalised, it seems to find the mild climate of Kerry to its liking.

Marsh and water plants

Despite the ravages caused by land drainage, Kerry is fortunate to have some large tracts of marshlands in relatively good condition, with a rich and interesting flora. The best such areas fringe the lower reaches of our major rivers, including the Shannon, but interesting plants are also to be found in marshes fringing some lakeshores, valley bottoms and even in wet ditches. Late summer is a good time to look for marsh and water plants. Wetlands can still be blooming at this time, and lower water levels in drains and streams makes access generally easier; an important practical advantage!

You don't have to wait until late summer however, to start visiting these sites. One of the earliest leaves to appear in spring are the strong spikes of yellow iris or yellow flag, which later produces its showy yellow flowers. Another yellow-flowered plant is the lesser spearwort, an easily identified member of the buttercup family, with spearhead-shaped leaves and the typical yellow flowers. Its bitter,

View across the Caragh Valley

acrid sap can readily cause skin blisters, containing as it does a greater concentration of the poisons common to all the buttercup family. The lilac flowers of the cuckoo flower or lady's smock are also readily identifiable. This is an important foodplant of the orange-tip butterfly, which is often seen on it. The divided, reddish flowers of ragged robins add a splash of colour to many wet meadows from May to June, and are also a popular flower for many insects.

Horsetails are found in marshy areas and the margins of lakes. At least seven species occur in Kerry. They have erect, hollow stems with whorls of short branches. These grow from smooth, blackish, creeping stems buried in the mud of the marsh or lakeshore. The stems of horsetails have a very rough texture, due to the presence of a high density of silica grains embedded therein – an anti-grazing measure. This imparts to the stem a texture of fine-grade sandpaper, and there exists a long tradition of using horsetails for this very purpose. Before the advent of 'brillo' pads, horsetails were used as scouring pads, for finishing and polishing wood in furniture making, putting a fine edge on blades and as files for enlarging and rounding holes. All horsetails are poisonous to livestock.

The largest species is the great horsetail, which may reach two metres in height and grows in base-rich, marshy soils. It is more common in the north of the county, quite rare and local elsewhere. The field horsetail, which grows to 80 centimetres, is widespread in fields, waste ground, roadsides and gardens, and is sometimes a troublesome weed. The wood horsetail has graceful, drooping branches, and reaches about 60 centimetres in height. It is locally common, but generally scarce throughout the county.

A number of species of mint are associated with marshy habitats. One of the most widespread is the water mint, which has bluish mauve flowers in compact, fluffy heads, and emits a sweet, minty smell when crushed. Much scarcer is penny royal, a *Red Data Book* species protected under the Wildlife Act. This is an herb of damp, sandy areas, with trailing, reddish stems, small rounded leaves and mauve flowers in dense whorls around the stem. It has strongly aromatic leaves, and was commonly used by herbalists in former times. Penny royal has been recorded from about 50 locations in Ireland, the majority of which are in Kerry and

The great willow herb adds shades of pink to the summer palette

Cork. It has declined due to drainage and disturbance of its habitats.

A non-aromatic relative of the mints is gipsywort, locally common in wet areas, which reaches a metre in height. It has small whitish whorls of flowers about its stiff stem, with large, distinctive coarsely-toothed leaves. It was formerly used to obtain a black dye, once used by fortune-tellers to dye their skin a dark colour to pass themselves off as mysterious foreigners or gypsies, hence its name. In late summer the heavy scent and fluffy, creamy-white flowerheads of meadowsweet are evident in marshy sites and drains. Its common name derives from an old English name, *mede sweete*, as the plant was once used to sweeten mead. It was also strewn on the floors of houses as a primitive but effective air freshener. Meadowsweet had other important uses in easing pains, inducing sweating and reducing fevers, as its sap contains chemicals of the same group as salicylic acid, an ingredient of aspirin. Purple loosestrife often accompanies meadowsweet in wet drains and marshy areas. Its graceful, purplish-red flowers are very attractive to pollinating insects, although its tannin-rich leaves are a good defence against herbivorous insects.

The giant rhubarb, *Gunnera manicata*, is a rather dramatic and eye-catching plant. In sheltered sites it grows up to two metres tall, with large leaves of a metre or more in width. The stems and leaf ribs are armed with nasty spines. Originally a native of South America, it was probably introduced into Ireland around the middle of the last century.

A number of rarities are confined to damp meadows and marshes. Whorled caraway is an erect, slender perennial with whorls of bristle-like linear leaflets running the full length of the stem. Its flowers are small and whitish in colour. It is relatively common in Kerry and west Cork, but known elsewhere from only a few locations in Mayo, Donegal, Derry, Antrim and Down. It is an Atlantic coast species, occurring in western Britain and the west coast of Europe. The water-dropworts have the characteristic umbrella-shaped flowers of the parsley family. Hemlock water dropwort grows in slightly acidic conditions in ditches and streams throughout Kerry. It is one of our most poisonous plants, and has been mistaken by a few unwary people for other, more harmless, members of the parsley family. A similar plant, corky-fruited water-dropwort is a very rare species, confined to a small area of wet meadows in Co. Clare and only recently discovered in Kerry near Caherciveen.

Blue-eyed grass

The delightful blue-eyed grass is one of a number of North American species to occur in Kerry, growing in damp meadows and the fringes of cut-over bogs. It reaches a height of 30 centimetres and has two centimetre-wide blue flowers which open only in bright sunshine, making it a difficult plant to find at other times. Blue-eyed grass is a native of North America and Ireland, where it has been recorded in eleven counties, but was introduced to Britain and Europe. In Kerry it is found around the Clonee lakes, near Sneem, Caherciveen and Boolteens, and around Caragh Lake, Lough Yganavan and the Killarney lakes. Another North American species which has its Irish head-quarters in south Kerry and west Cork is Irish lady's-tresses, an orchid of damp meadows, seasonally flooded pastures and lake shores. It has a rosette of lanceolate leaves around the stem, with cream-coloured hawthorn-scented flowers arranged in three spirally-twisted rows. Its distribution in Kerry is shown in map 6. Outside of Ireland it is found in western Scotland and the Hebrides, but does not occcur in Europe.

Another *Red Data Book* species is Cornish moneywort, a small, creeping perennial with lobed, kidney-shaped leaves and tiny, pinkish-purple flowers. Its only Irish location is on the Dingle peninsula from Tralee to Connor's Pass, in damp, grassy fields, along streamsides and in wet ditches. It is another Atlantic coast species, occurring elsewhere in the Outer Hebrides, south west England and Wales, and the west European coast to the Iberian peninsula. It appears to be under threat from the aggressive spread of the introduced New Zealand willow-herb, which competes for the same habitat. Finally, *Carex punctata*, a very rare sedge of coastal marshes is found from Kerry head around to Ballycotton in Co. Cork, as well as in Galway.

One of the more obvious plants of the water's edge is the common reed, which grows in dense stands in water up to a metre deep along the muddy edges of more productive lakes and marshes. It is our tallest grass, producing a mass of purplish flowers on top of stems up to three metres in height. The seeds are an important food for wintering wildfowl. In deeper water the water lilies spread their leaves over the surface. Two species occur in Kerry. The white water-lily has circular leaves and flowers of ten to twelve centimetres in diameter, occurring in lakes, pools and slow-flowing streams. The fleshy, edible rhizome may be up to two metres below the surface. The white flowers open only towards midday, and close and partly sink below water at the approach of evening. The yellow water-lily has smaller flowers measuring five centimetres across and larger, oval leaves up to forty centimetres in length, the largest of all our water plants. The flowers emit an aroma of stale alcohol.

Another widespread and conspicuous water plant is common water-crowfoot, with its white and yellow flowers. It is found in rivers, ponds, lakes and ditches throughout the county. It has two different type of leaves; large ones which float on the surface, and streamlined, feathery ones which are submerged. A much scarcer species in the same genus is the three-lobed crowfoot, a semi-terrestrial herb with small, white flowers less than one centimetre across and round or kidney-shaped floating leaves. It is a plant of nutrient-poor, temporary pools, ditches and ponds, which has only been recorded from five sites in Ireland, all in Kerry or

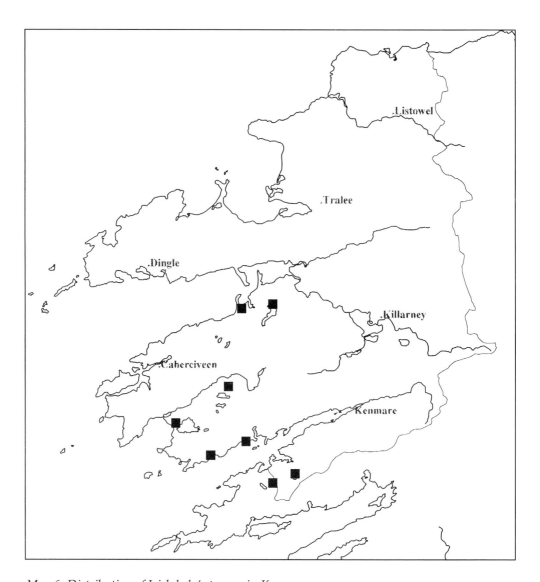

Map 6: Distribution of Irish lady's tresses in Kerry

west Cork. Two of the Kerry sites are in the area of Sneem, the other to the west of Killarney. It is thought that as its preferred habitat is very common throughout the region, this species may be more widespread than records indicate. As it flowers early in the season when few botanists are about, it may have been overlooked.

The many oligotrophic or nutrient-poor lakes of our mountainous areas contain few plant species. Quillwort is an unusual fern which is an aquatic plant of upland lakes. Each plant has a tuft of long, stiff leaves arising from thick, white roots. Unlike most other ferns, which normally bear their spore-bearing structures on the undersides of their leaves, those of quillwort are contained in a recess at the base of the leaves. The pipewort is a submerged perennial with basal rosette of soft, linear leaves, which grows in the shallow, muddy margins of some lakes and larger bog pools. In late summer the plants produce whitish-grey button shaped flowers about twelve millimetres across. In Europe, it occurs in only a few locations from west Kerry to Donegal and on the Scottish west coast. Like the blue-eyed grass, it is a botanical curiosity, one of a few species which has a restricted distribution in Europe but is widely distributed in North America. It was originally speculated that these plants were introduced by human agency, but recent pollen studies have shown that pipewort was present in Ireland nearly 6,000 years ago, long before humans could have influenced its distribution. The question of how these species originally arrived here has still not been satisfactorily answered. Another 'American' species with a restricted European distribution is the slender naiad. In Ireland it is only found in Galway, Mayo, Leitrim, Donegal and Kerry, where it is found in the Killarney lakes and Caragh lake. It is rarely seen when growing as it is confined to deep water, where it produces its tiny green flowers on slender stems. It is generally only noticed when fragments of the plant are washed up onshore.

COASTAL FLOWERS

Kerry is well-endowed with numerous sand dune systems, some of which rank among the largest on the west coast. Due partly to natural reasons many are suffering from extensive erosion, a situation which is aggravated by over-grazing and recreational use by people. One of the most interesting sand dune systems for botanists is that which links Castlegregory to some of the Magharee islands – a classical tombolo (see chapter 1). Some of the species which can be seen on the sand dunes at Castlegregory are listed in Table 10. The main stabilising plant of dunes is marram grass, which is often the only species along the windward edge of the dunes. Marram comes from two Norse words, *marr* and *halmr*, meaning 'sea reed'. Its coarse greyish-green stems and leaves, combined with its long roots, help to bind the dunes and prevent wind erosion. In the marram zone one finds sea holly, with its prickly leaves and powder-blue flower heads. Its leaves and stems have a thick cuticle or outer skin, which is an adaptation to seashore life, protecting the plant from salt spray and excessive water loss. The roots of sea holly were once candied and sold as a delicacy under the name of 'eringoes'. They were believed to have aphrodisiacal properties.

Behind the marram zone grasses such as creeping bent and crested dog's-tail occur, particularly in the wetter dune slacks. These areas can be remarkably rich in flowers. Chaffweed is one of the smallest European plants, rarely growing more than five centimetres high. It has alternate leaves with tiny stalkless flowers.

TABLE 10
SOME FLOWERS OF SAND DUNES AND GRASSLANDS AT CASTLEGREGORY

Autumn lady's tresses	Dove's-foot cranes-bill
Beaked tasselweed	Fragrant orchid
Bee orchid	Fringed rock-cress
Biting stonecrop	Kidney vetch
Blunt-flowered rush	Lady's bedstraw
Bog pimpernel	Sand cat's-tail
Common bird's-foot trefoil	Squinancywort
Common centaury	Wild pansy
Chaffweed	Wild thyme
Dodder	Yellow bartsia

Where it occurs, chaffweed is often found in association with two other species; allseed, a diminutive plant which somewhat resembles chaffweed, and yellow centaury, a small, slender annual with a profusion of yellow flowers. The latter is unknown in Ireland outside of Kerry, where its headquarters is around Kenmare bay, and an adjoining part of west Cork. Squinancywort is another small, white flowered plant with tiny, funnel-shaped flowers. It occurs locally in rocky pastures and sandhills from Kerry to east Galway, but is unknown elsewhere.

Sea spurge thrives among sand dunes

The colourful scarlet pimpernel is widespread among sand dunes, although to see its five-petalled red flowers at their best you must look for them on sunny days, as they close in dull or wet weather. Another common seaside plant is wild pansy, which grows in profusion among sand dunes. Its scientific name, *tricolor,* means three-coloured, and refers to the fact that the flowers may be violet-blue, yellow, or more rarely, pink. By hybridising the naturally occurring species, horticulturalists have produced the large-flowered garden pansies in a wide range of colours.

The purplish flowers of wild thyme abound in these coastal areas. Long used as a herb, its leaves contain thymol, an aromatic oil with antiseptic and preservative properties. Dodder is an unusual parasitic plant of wild thyme which occurs in the Castlegregory area. It has long, reddish thread-like stems which produce suckers to penetrate the stem of the host plant, from which it obtains all its nutrients. It produces miniature, bell-shaped pinkish flowers grouped into dense, globular heads. One of the rarest species of Kerry's sand dunes is the sea pea, a prostrate, grey-green herb with stems up to a metre long. It has large purple flowers up to two centimetres in length, which fade to a bluish colour. Its seeds are a dark colour and quite buoyant. A survey by Dan and Caroline Minchin in the early 1990s found seeds stranded on the high shore along many west and south coast beaches. Some of these were sent to Dr Charles Nelson at the National Botanic Gardens, Dublin and found to be viable. In Kerry, sea pea plants were found only at Inch

The fine threads of the parasitic dodder trail over wild thyme

and Kells and there are recent records from Rossbeigh and Inch. Elsewhere it has occured in Donegal, Cork and Wexford. Another coastal site in Mayo was washed

---

THE FORMATION OF SALT MARSHES

Salt marshes are areas of low-lying coastal grasslands frequently inudated by the tide, which contain a distinct plant community. They are of particular interest to ecologists for a number of reasons, but before we look at them more closely we should look at how salt marshes are formed. A salt marsh will only form where there is a source of sand or silt such as from river-borne sediments or from offshore islands, and where there is some form of shelter such as a protruding spit of land, which slows down the water speed and protects the embryo marsh from being washed away. Such conditions exist in Castlemaine harbour, and this area contains some of the finest salt marshes in the county. The most important factor controlling the extent and longevity of salt marshes is vegetation. The above-ground parts of the plants attract and hold sediment, while the roots bind the material together, preventing easy erosion.

From a plant ecologists viewpoint they are remarkable for two reasons. Firstly, they comprise large areas of natural vegetation undergoing primary succession and containing relatively few species. Thus they provide an opportunity to examine the conditions under which communities develop largely without human interference. Secondly, salt marshes frequently show strong parallel zonation, that is the plant communities change with increasing distance from the seashore. There is a successional sequence of plants from pioneering species at the tide's edge to 'dry-land' species higher up the shore.

---

away during storms shortly after the plant had been discovered there. Because of the large numbers of seeds involved and their pattern of distribution, Dr Nelson has suggested that they may originate from North America, where they are common on the Canadian east coast.

Some of the most interesting plants of mudflats are the eel-grasses. They are the only group of flowering plants which have become fully marine and can survive, even flower, beneath sea water. Eel-grass grows in sheltered estuaries in water less than three metres deep – at greater depths there is insufficient light for it to photosynthesise properly. Its deep roots, creeping underground stems and strap-shaped leaves help stabilise the mud. All three Irish species occur in Kerry. The leaves of *Zostera marina*, the most widespread species, grow up to 50 centimetres long, lying flat on the mud surface when the tide is out, giving a green tinge to the mudflats. The inconspicuous flowers grow from the leaf bases during summer when the water temperature has reached 15⁰C. The seeds are heavier than water and are dispersed by the currents and perhaps on the feet of birds. Eel grass is an important food plant for a number of birds, particularly brent geese and wigeon, which concentrate on this plant in the autumn on their return from their Arctic breeding ground.

Another factor assisting accretion of mud below the vegetated zone on the saltmarsh is the presence of various species of diatoms and bacteria. These actively secrete mucus and polysaccharides (starch-like chemicals), so sticking the mud and silt particles together. Research has shown that where the density of snails which graze these is artificially increased, higher rates of soil erosion occur.

Cord grass is also a major pioneer plant of mudflats and salt marshes. Until the beginning of the nineteenth century only one species, the small cord grass, *Spartina maritima*, was known from the east coast of Ireland. Then in 1829 an American species, *Spartina alterniflora* was noticed in a British estuary, which subsequently hybridised with *Spartina maritima*. The hybrids thus produced were known as Townsend's cord-grass, and proved, like many hybrids, to be very vigorous, establishing themselves by fragments or whole plants being uprooted by storms and washed along the coast. It was also deliberately planted in many estuaries to reclaim land. It occurs in most Kerry estuaries where it seems to be spreading steadily. This is a matter of concern as it reduces the area of mud available for small waders to feed in, as well as probably upsetting the ecology of these areas in ways we as yet do not fully appreciate.

Glasswort is one of the major pioneering species of mudflats. It has distinctive, jointed stems up to 30 centimetres long. The annual species of glasswort can establish roots from seed in three days, so it only needs a very short period of exposure to establish itself. The plants were once collected, dried and burned to obtain a poor quality soda from its ash. This was then mixed with sand to make a low grade glass, hence its name. In autumn its leaves turn a bronze-red colour, enhancing the attraction of such areas at this time. Higher up the salt marsh plants spend less time inundated by the tide, salinity decreases, and drainage improves. Plants with a lower ability to tolerate salt invade, and species diversity increases. The most common salt marsh species above the glasswort/cord grass zone are common saltmarsh-grass, sea plantain, annual sea-blite, sea arrowgrass and sea aster.

On shingle beaches, rocky seashores and cliff edges, above the tidal zone, sea campion often grows in profusion. The white petals are backed by a deep, bladder like tube, and the whole flower emits a clove-like scent in the evening. Because of the depth of the flowers, its nectar is not easy for even long-tongued bees and night-flying moths to reach. Some bumble-bees have learned an easier way to get at the nectar; they bite their way through the base of the flower, leaving a characteristic small hole. The pink-flowered thrift and the yellow-flowered sea radish also thrive in this habitat, along with sea beet, with its large leathery leaves and small, greenish flowers. Scarcer plants include the edible sea kale, which has large, blue-green leaves and white flowers. One of the few native forebears of our common garden vegetables, sea kale has a thick, fleshy rootstock which acts like a tap root, allowing it to obtain water from deep within the shingle. It is known from only three sites in Kerry. It has been found at only one of these since 1970.

ISLAND PLANTS

The islands off Kerry provide a wide range of habitats, from the storm-washed, precipitous slopes of the Skelligs to the gentle, flat-topped islands of the Magharees. Some such as the Little Skellig are virtually devoid of vegetation, due mainly to the presence of the large gannet colony, while others such as Inisnabro in the Blasket group are covered with large, soft mounds of thrift, due to the absence of grazing.

Their flora is generally a continuation of that which is found on the nearby mainland; maritime species such as common scurvygrass, thrift, sea campion, rock sea-spurrey and rock samphire dominate the lower slopes, with heather and bracken on the higher slopes. This situation varies greatly between the islands, and is influenced by factors such as slope, exposure, grazing history and the presence of digging animals such as rabbits and puffins.

Common scurvygrass

Interesting flowering plants include tree mallow on the Skelligs, sea beet on the Tearaght, and field mouse-ear, St Patrick's cabbage, lesser twayblade, and the fern, adder's tongue on Great Blasket.

The lichen flora of some islands have been examined in detail. Inishvickillane has the richest lichen flora of all, with at least 160 species on the island, more than almost any other treeless island of similar size in Britain or Ireland. This is probably due to its complex geological make-up in which volcanic rocks such as agglomerates and lavas play an important part. One of the peculiar features of the island's lichen flora is the occurrence of a number of species normally found in old, oceanic woodlands. These include tree lungwort, *Lobaria laetevirens, Nephroma laevigatum, Parmeliella atlantica, Heterodermia obscurata* and *Pseudocyphellaria crocata*. Another peculiarity is the number of normally epiphytic species present including *Sticta canariensis, Sticta sylvatica, Usnea rubicunda, Menegazzia terebrata* and *Parmelia laevigata*.

Chapter 3

THE FAUNA OF KERRY

BIRDS OF THE MOUNTAINS, MOORLANDS AND LOWLAND BOGS

THE MORNING is dry and cool, with the promise of a fine day ahead. Below spreads the green floor of the valley, with the twin black eyes of Lough Gouragh and Lough Callee shining from the head of the glen. Above Lough Gouragh rise a series of broken cliffs. Further down the valley a jagged spike of rock pushes skyward – the Hag's Teeth. To the north the rugged valley gives way to fertile fields, to the south the broad mass of the MacGillycuddy's Reeks curves around on three sides. Carrauntoohil, Ireland's highest peak, slopes away upwards into the morning mist.

Across the glen comes the croaking voice of ravens, followed shortly by the ringing call of choughs. Sounds travel well in this natural amphitheatre, and there is no wind yet. Mornings such as these are a rarity among these high peaks. After an hour of waiting and quiet listening you finally hear your quarry, giving its long, piping song; a ring ouzel, one of Kerry's special breeding birds. Your early start has been well rewarded.

Because of the large area of mountainous terrain in the county, Kerry is relatively well endowed with mountain and moorland birds, but it takes an effort to find them. The ring ouzel is one of the most elusive of our montane birds. This relative of the blackbird, which it replaces at higher altitudes, is a migrant. Similar in size to the blackbird, the male has a distinctive white crescent on its breast, the female's is less obvious. The first feature which normally attracts your attention

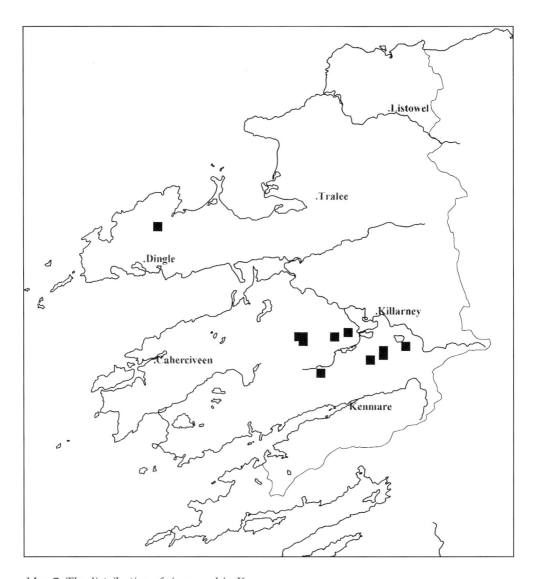

Map 7: The distribution of ring ouzel in Kerry

is the loud 'chack-chack' of their warning call, or the male's far-carrying song. Probably no more than 10 to 15 pairs nest in Kerry, but some of these sites are readily accessible, including the Gap of Dunloe and the Hags Glen, below Carrauntouhil. Ouzels are notoriously difficult to observe and are very wary. I visited a known breeding glen on three occasions in one year, always drawing a blank, but eventually saw fledged juveniles on the fourth visit. The Irish population is estimated to be less than 100 pairs and the ring ouzel has been included in the *Irish Vertebrate Red Data Book*.

The twite is another scarce mountain breeder, now much less common than before. Small numbers of these streaky brown finches occur on some of our peninsulas, particularly around Sybil Head on the Dingle peninsula, on Valentia island and the Great Blasket. They prefer heather and bracken-dominated moorlands – one of the habitats in Kerry which has undergone severe reduction in the past 20 years. It is another very rare breeding bird in Ireland, probably numbering less than 1,000 pairs.

Lake Callee, MacGillycuddy's Reeks

The classic bird of heather-dominated moorland is the red grouse. Grouse need a mixture of tall mature heather for nesting cover and short young heather to provide nutritious shoots for the chicks. Their numbers have suffered largely due to a decline in heather cover caused by overgrazing and uncontrolled burning. Densities of this lovely bird are as low as one pair per 100 hectares in the Killarney valley area. The male has a loud 'go back, go back' call and birds rising suddenly and explosively from nearby cover have startled many a walker.

The commonest bird of the mountains is the meadow pipit – a small streaked bird with orange-red legs. You are sure to notice one if you rest awhile on any hillside during summer. Pipits are noisy, active birds and highly territorial, continually scolding any intruders near their nest. Meadow pipits seem to prefer areas of longer grass for nesting than skylarks, another streaked brown bird of mountains and bogs. Meadow pipits are the preferred host of cuckoos, which lay their eggs in pipits' nests and three or four will normally be seen mobbing any cuckoo in the vicinity. In winter, our population of meadow pipits in Kerry is augmented by Icelandic pipits which overwinter on our lowland areas, sharing pastures with their Irish cousins. Skylarks are somewhat larger and chunkier than meadow pipits. Their beautiful song, poured forth by the male while on the wing, is one of the first harbingers of spring on the moorlands. Skylarks prefer to winter on stubble fields, feeding on old corn and weed seeds. However, this has become a scarce habitat in Kerry.

Another winter visitor to hill areas is the snow bunting – a chunky black and white finch – small parties of which may seem like a flock of snowflakes. I once saw a pair in full breeding plumage on the summit of Carrauntouhil on St Patrick's Day, a truly memorable sight. High peaks can hold wonderful surprises for those bird watchers willing to make the effort to reach them. Birds such as dotterel, a very rare wader which breed on high mountains in Scotland, are reported to be an annual visitor to, and have even bred on, high plateaus in Kerry. Another wader of the summits is golden plover. Small parties of up to 100 winter on high plateaus such as Mangerton, feeding on overwintering invertebrates. A few have been seen on mountaintops in summer, but breeding has never been proven – their nearest regular breeding site is Connemara.

The raven is our largest crow, and quite unmistakable. Its large size, all black plumage and distinctive croaking call readily identify it at a distance. They nest all over the county, even using tall trees in lowland areas. Their rolling, tumbling display flight is a treat to watch in spring. They are one of the earliest nesting birds, laying four or five eggs in February or March. They build a large untidy nest, normally on the most inaccessible ledges. Their diet is varied, ranging from soil-dwelling invertebrates to carrion. Raven numbers have probably been boosted by the large amounts of sheep carrion to be found on hills. This is a consequence of the serious overstocking which has occurred in recent years. Hooded crows are also a frequent sight in hill areas, though they tend to be tree-nesters, often using stunted rowans and birches. They are more frequent in lowland areas, and in winter form quite large roosts of over 150 birds. Their summer diet includes large numbers of eggs and chicks of various species, a fact which does not make them popular with gun clubs. Hooded crows cache food, a habit which is common to the crow family. Coastal dwelling crows regularly cache mussels and other intertidal food items. The birds recover them within two to three days, normally during high tide. This behaviour is a response to daily, short-term fluctuations in food availability.

Our scarcest mountain crow is the chough. This all black bird, with its bright red legs and decurved bill, is a welcome sight on a hill or coastal walk. Choughs are a delight to watch, being wonderfully acrobatic flyers. Kerry is the most important county in Ireland for them. 315 pairs were recorded in a 1992 survey and another 122 non-breeders. This is about 28% of the Irish population, an increase of 33% since the last survey in 1982. The tips of Kerry's peninsulas hold nationally important numbers, and islands are also popular breeding sites for choughs. Valentia is the most important island for choughs in the county, with up to 40 pairs present. Choughs also breed up to 20km inland in Kerry although there appears to have been a decline in numbers of inland nesters in recent years. As their nesting locations are well known, this is a situation which should be monitored in future years. In autumn, large flocks gather, some spending the winter months among the sand dunes along Dingle and Tralee bays. A flock of 213, the largest ever seen in Ireland, was recorded in Kerry in 1968!

Peregrines are the most majestic bird of prey still breeding in Co. Kerry. Peregrines suffered enormously in the 1960s due to pesticide poisoning. This caused thinning of the eggshells; the eggs were then easily damaged in the nest by the incubating parents. Their population declined to very low levels, but since the offending pesticides were withdrawn, the peregrine population has recovered. It now stands at over 300 pairs. The recovery in Kerry, however, and other western counties, appears to be slower than expected. The Kerry population is probably less than 20 pairs. Elsewhere, particularly in eastern counties, nesting sites are now at such a premium for the birds that many have taken to nesting on buildings and in quarries, some of which are still in use! In Kerry, many suitable crags still remain unoccupied, and peregrine productivity (the number of young produced to fledging stage every year) is lower than elsewhere. There are indications that the severe exposure which western crags suffer from wind and rain is a major factor affecting breeding birds and their chicks. Many of our recent springs have been particularly wet and cold, which leads to a higher risk of chilling for the eggs and chicks.

Peregrines take a wide range of prey; at one nest site in the Killarney area the remains included woodpigeon, common gull, oystercatcher and redshank. The latter three species do not breed near Killarney, but use the Killarney valley as a convenient route from Kenmare bay to the western estuaries.

The merlin is our smallest falcon and is typically a bird of moorlands, where it preys on small birds like meadow pipits. They normally fly fast and low, making them a difficult species to observe. In Britain they are usually ground nesters, hiding their nest among tall heather, whereas in Ireland many pairs are tree nesters, using old crow and woodpigeon nests. Our merlins often migrate to coastal areas in winter, where they are joined by others from Iceland and Scandinavia.

A sight which has become increasingly rare is that of a hen harrier drifting its way across bogs and fields, quartering the ground for its quarry of rodents and large invertebrates. The male is a handsome bird, a crisp grey colour with black wing tips and white rump patch. The females are brownish, also with a white rump. They nest in tall heather or young plantations, generally on relatively low level bogs. Central and north Kerry is their stronghold in the county. Hen harriers are undergoing a decline due to loss of habitat, disturbance (linked to the increased mechanisation of turf-cutting) and direct human persecution. There are probably less than 15 pairs now nesting in Kerry.

One distinctive moorland bird is the stonechat. The male has a black head, white neck and wing flashes. The female is duller but has the same bold behaviour. Stonechats normally scold people passing through their territories and have a distinct 'chat-tsack-tsack' call, like hitting two stones together. They are residents, sometimes staying on their territories throughout the year during mild winters. Many, however, move to lowland and coastal areas. Mortality increases sharply during harsh winters, causing their numbers to decline. They are insectivorous, feeding on caterpillars, large flies and spiders, using taller gorse bushes as vantage points to watch for food or intruders. Some gorse bushes are nearly always present in their territories. When the chicks are on the wing, the whole brood often gets involved in scolding a passer-by.

Curlews nest on many of the lowland bogs about the county, but are absent from west Kerry and appear to be declining overall. Their lovely bubbling call makes them relatively easy to locate. Although they invariably nest in heather- or rush-dominated areas, they make a lot of use of nearby fields for feeding, preferring soft damp ground, where they probe for worms and grubs. One 10 kilometre square which I surveyed north of Killarney held nine territories. This is a low density compared with the 40-70 pairs per ten kilometres found at some Northern Ireland sites.

Snipe are another breeding bird of bogs which are notoriously difficult to survey. They are particularly fond of lowland bogs and wet grassland areas, but can be found at altitudes up to 300 metres in suitable habitat. Snipe are fairly catholic in their diet, feeding on worms and insect larvae, even seeds. Most feeding takes place during the first half of the night and at dawn, with non-nesting birds retiring to preferred roost sites. During a recent survey of wintering wildfowl, the two best snipe haunts in the country were in Kerry, where over 200 birds were regularly counted each winter. Wintering birds seem to prefer to congregate at these traditional sites; apparently suitable bogs nearby may have only a handful of snipe.

A close cousin of the common snipe which is to be found in small numbers in winter is the jack snipe, which breed in Scandinavia and the Baltic countries. About five centimetres smaller than the snipe, jack snipe can be relatively easily identified by their size and shorter bill. They also have a habit of rising quietly when disturbed and flying only a short distance before landing. Snipe invariably give a rasping call when flushed, and zigzag vigorously out of sight. I have flushed up to four jack snipe on particularly good snipe bogs.

A flock of Greenland white-fronted geese take to the air

The classic wintering bird on boglands, now regrettably scarce, is the Greenland white-fronted goose. This handsome dark grey bird, with its yellow bill and orange legs, used to frequent a number of bogland sites in Kerry. Due partly to habitat loss and disturbance, they now occur regularly only on the Dingle peninsula and in the Killarney valley, where the largest flock of 20-30 birds winter. They feed on the underground bulbils of various bog plants, in particular the white-beak sedge and bog cotton, flying to roost on nearby lakes in the evening. Like most geese, they are very wary birds and prone to disturbance. Their digestive system is rather inefficient – much of what they eat passes through their system relatively undigested. Thus they need to feed virtually continuously throughout the short winter days to maintain their energy requirements. Excessive disturbance from people or other sources reduces the amount of time available to the geese for feeding, and may affect their survival or reproductive chances. The National Park authorities in Killarney have taken steps to reduce the amount of disturbance the geese experience, but if you are a walker you can help by avoiding all the lowland bog areas in the Killarney valley during the winter months.

WETLAND BIRDS

The small moorland lakes which are frequent in the Kerry hills are relatively poor bird habitats. In summer, a few pairs of teal and tufted duck may breed on some, and the larger ones will often have a pair of common sandpipers holding territory. The latter are summer visitors. They nest in the undergrowth close to lake or river edges and can be recognised at a distance by their colouration and tail bobbing behaviour.

Apart from mountain lakes and streams, Kerry has few large expanses of freshwater lakes or marshes. Because of the underlying nature of the rock, many are poor in insect and plant life and thus poor also for birds. The best freshwater habitats tend to be on the limestone areas of mid-Kerry. In these richer areas such as the northern and eastern shores of Lough Leane, up to 9 species of waterfowl regularly breed. The largest of these are the mute swans, of which an average of six to ten pairs breed on Lough Leane every summer. By late June, the population of nesting swans is augmented by an influx of non-breeders or failed breeders. These move onto the lakes to moult. Up to 90 may be present

Tufted ducks breed on a number of Kerry lakes

then. Most wildfowl species moult their flight feathers simultaneously and are thus flightless for a number of weeks. They often become very secretive at this time. The males of many duck species assume a much drabber, 'eclipse' plumage, more similar to the females, before acquiring their breeding colours again in late autumn.

The most numerous nesting duck species in Kerry are mallard and tufted duck. Mallard begin breeding early in the year. By January, drakes have staked out territories along the shores of lakes and rivers and will chase and mate with any females in their territory. The females lay up to 14 eggs in a down-lined nest, generally under old bracken clumps or brambles. If they survive the attention of rats, hooded crows and mink, broods of chicks can be seen scurrying after the duck, picking instinctively at anything moving within their range. Large numbers of mallard are attracted during good acorn years to the Killarney lakes, where they will forage along the shorelines beneath the oaks. Up to 570 have been counted on the lakes at this time.

Dr Aine Ní Shuilleabháin carried out her Ph.D. studies on the ecology of waterfowl on Lough Leane. She found that Inisfallen island was the most important breeding area for mallard. The smaller islands were more important for tufted duck. Common rats were a major problem on the larger islands, predating many nests.

Tufted duck are divers, feeding on small molluscs, crustaceans and insect larvae. They nest later than Mallard but are less well-adapted than the latter for walking on land. They normally nest closer to the shoreline, sometimes nesting in old trees overhanging water. Tufted ducks sometimes combine their broods into creches; one female was observed with 23 chicks trailing along behind her.

Two of the most interesting regular breeding waterfowl in Kerry are great-crested grebe and the red-breasted merganser. Great-crested grebes have undergone a range expansion in the last 30 years. They were first proven to breed in

---

MOULT IN BIRDS

Moulting is a very important but stressful physiological process in birds. All birds moult to replace their feathers which suffer from wear and tear over a season. Every year, most species undergo at least one full moult, with some species going through a secondary partial moult. The principal moult normally takes place after the breeding season, when food is plentiful and there is ample cover, as during moult a bird's ability to fly and possibly escape predators is impaired. Those birds about to undertake a long migratory flight also need to have their plumage in good condition for the journey.

Different species employ a variety of moulting strategies. Most species moult over a period of some months, so they are able to fly at all times, even if not as well as usual. Migratory species may undergo a partial moult after the breeding season, then renew or complete the process at some staging area en route, or at the end of their journey. Most wildfowl, however, which are relatively safe from predators on the open water, moult their flight feathers all at once, renewing them over a period of three to four weeks. Thus they remain flightless until their wing-feathers have regrown. Their body feathers are moulted more gradually.

Bird ringers who catch and mark birds for various studies use their knowledge of moult and feather wear to age many species of birds.

Kerry at Lough Currane, near Waterville in 1972. Breeding was not recorded again until 1980 and 1981, in Lough Gill and Lough Leane respectively. The adults have an attractive frill of rufous and black feathers around the head which is used during their elaborate courtship display, when the male brings gifts of waterplants to the female. They are diving birds, like all grebes, feeding on fish, insects and aquatic invertebrates. The attractive, striped chicks are often carried by the adults on their backs when very young. In winter, they abandon the freshwater lakes and move to coastal areas.

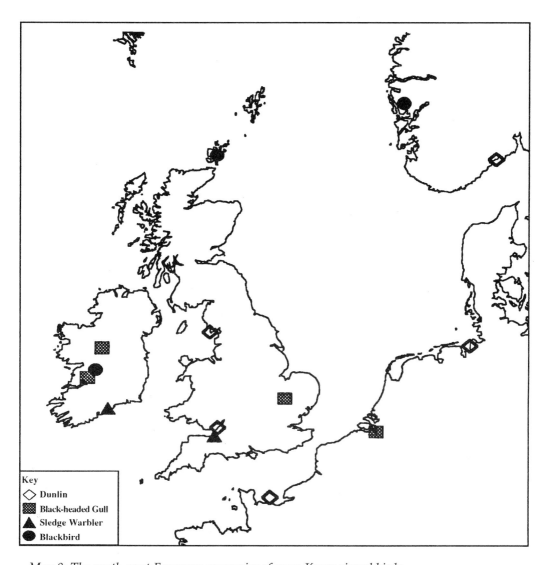

Map 8: The north-west European recoveries of some Kerry-ringed birds

Red-breasted mergansers are also diving birds, found on most of the larger rivers and lakes in the county. They are slender, thin necked ducks, the male with a dark greenish head and black and white back pattern. Both sexes have red bills with serrated edges. These give them a better grip on the small fish and eels which form their principal prey. They are very wary birds, particularly during the nesting season. Outside of the breeding season they winter on estuaries and the quieter bays. The larger and rarer goosander is a striking bird which sometimes turns up on freshwater loughs in Kerry during winter. They breed in very small numbers in Co. Donegal. Unlike other wintering ducks, they are most likely to occur on larger oligotrophic lakes in winter where they feed on small fish. During the cold winter of February 1982, two females occurred on Cumeendubh Lough in the Black Valley and a third the same day on Muckross Lake, Killarney. Two handsome males, with their pink-tinged, white bodies and bottle green heads found their way to Muckross Lake in January 1990, again during cold weather.

In winter, our richer freshwater lakes prove attractive to numbers of pochard, goldeneye, wigeon and other wildfowl which migrate to Ireland to escape the harsh winters of their northern breeding grounds.

Small numbers of whooper and bewick swans also occur in winter. The sight and sound of a flock of whooper swans on a crisp winter evening, winging their way steadily to their destination, is truly one of the magical experiences of nature. Our wintering whooper swans breed in Iceland. With their black and yellow bills and straight necks, they are readily distinguished from our resident mute swan.

Male teal at water's edge

They can, however, be confused with their smaller cousins, the bewick swan. The latter are much scarcer in Kerry. Whooper swans tend to be more grassland feeders than mute swans and can sometimes be seen feeding in fields along the banks of our larger rivers. In recent years a flock of up to 400 has taken to feeding along the banks of the river Cashen in north Kerry and commuting as far as Lough Gill on the Magharee peninsula.

Pochard are another widespread wintering duck, occurring in small numbers, even on oligotrophic lakes. The males have a uniform, chestnut-coloured head and neck, with black breast and a pale grey body. The female has a brown head and breast and a less clean-cut grey body. Both sexes have a distinct head profile, with a high crown and long sloping forehead and bill. They are active divers, feeding on aquatic invertebrates and plant material.

Teal are our smallest duck. A handful of pairs breed on lakes, small ponds and lochans throughout the county, wherever there is reasonable nesting cover close to shore. Their numbers are increased by a substantial influx of immigrants in the autumn, and small parties of 10 to 20 teal are frequently seen on lakes, large rivers and around our estuaries. The male's piping, 'prrip' call is quite distinctive, which, combined with their small size, make them easily identifiable. A lone male in summer, calling nervously, skulking around the edge of a moorland lake or pond is a good indication of a female on eggs nearby.

COASTAL BIRDS
WINTERING BIRDS OF ESTUARIES

Kerry is fortunate in having a long and varied coastline, from the Shannon estuary in the north to Kenmare bay in the south. Many of these sites are of national and international importance as refuges for vast numbers of wintering wildfowl and waders. Some of these species just 'stop in' during autumn and spring, to refuel on their way to and from their Arctic breeding grounds. Others stay with us throughout the winter, providing some of our best wildlife spectacles.

Our most important areas are the estuaries of the rivers Shannon, Laune, Maine and Lee which between them form one of the most important wetland clusters in the country. In summer these sites are very quiet and almost devoid of birds. Ringed plover nest along the shoreline in low densities, generally on shingle beaches. In some areas lapwings nest among dune systems and on nearby farmland. By August, however, the first of the Arctic breeding birds start to trickle south, the earliest birds being non-breeders or failed breeders.

During September, numbers increase dramatically as the juvenile birds of the year return. Then the shores of these estuaries come alive with ducks, geese, swans and waders. As the tides come in, depositing a fresh load of nutrient rich organic silt on the mudflats, the birds move upshore to roost on small islets, at the edge of beaches or on the open water. Once the tides recede, small parties, then larger flocks, start to move onto the first areas of exposed mud. Each species has its own preferred feeding habitat. Some waders feed on the open

Overlooking Blennerville and Tralee Bay

mud, others on sandy shores. Brent geese and wigeon graze on the extensive beds of eel grass, other ducks dabble in the shallow waters at the tide's edge or in creeks, while mergansers and scaup dive in the deeper waters of the estuaries. Some 17 species of wildfowl and 14 species of waders winter regularly on our estuaries. These are joined by other wetland species such as cormorants, shags, divers and grey herons. Table 11 lists some recent data for Castlemaine harbour and Tralee bay.

Although these two estuaries are only 20 kilometres apart and appear superficially to be much the same, the difference in the species mix and their numbers is quite striking. Factors such as substrate type and food available must partly account for this difference, but other factors such as competition, disturbance and the availability of safe roost sites may be also involved. It is a subject worthy of further study.

Kerry is one of the first counties to receive returning brent geese, small parties

Male pintail can be seen at Inch

of which arrive by September. Brent are our smallest goose, being only slightly larger than mallard, but have the distinction of being one of the most easily observed, as well as the noisiest. They have black heads, necks and breasts, a narrow white collar, dark upperparts and pale underparts. The race which winters in Ireland is the pale-bellied brent, all of which nest in Arctic Canada. The dark-bellied brent nest in Arctic Siberia, wintering in Britain and the Low countries and only rarely occur in Ireland. Brent, like most geese, are very sociable birds, except during the breeding season. In Arctic Canada they nest on low-lying marshy tundra or lake shores. The males spend most of their time watching out for predators such as Arctic foxes and wolves. They are one of the northernmost nesting geese on earth, and as such have to contend with a very short nesting season. The female lays her eggs within 48 hours of the snow thawing off her chosen nesting area. From then on it is a race against time and predators to hatch the eggs and rear the young to fledging stage before the first autumnal snows in August. When they arrive back in Ireland, the young are easily distinguished by the white bars on their wings. A count of the number of young in a flock will indicate how successful the breeding season was.

The other coastal goose is the barnacle goose. They are a small handsome bird, with dark grey upperparts, white underparts, black head and breast and a white face patch. A flock of about 270 winter on the Magharee islands in Tralee bay. Our barnacles breed in Greenland, nesting on high cliffs and winter along the west coast of Ireland and Scotland. They graze on grasses and other plant material.

TABLE 11
PEAK COUNTS OF WILDFOWL AND WADERS WINTERING ON SOME KERRY ESTUARIES
WINTER 1995/96*

SPECIES	CASTLEMAINE HARBOUR	TRALEE BAY
Brent geese	1062	400
Wigeon	4093	150
Teal	48	180
Mallard	602	110
Pintail	150	58
Scaup	210	1310
Red-breasted merganser	31	18
Common scoter**	7070	160
Oystercatcher	1115	80
Ringed plover	120	213
Grey plover	27	674
Golden plover	2200	4000
Lapwing	1766	3730
Knot	309	90
Dunlin	1100	4122
Bar-tailed godwit	967	903
Curlew	632	826
Redshank	144	352
Turnstone	250	197

* From Delaney 1997
** Off Rosbeigh Strand

Most flocks in Ireland occur on small offshore islands.

One of the commonest waders is the dunlin. In winter their drab grey upperparts and white underparts allow dunlin to blend in well with their background, protecting them from predators. Having short bills and legs they feed on surface-dwelling invertebrates in or on the mud. Dunlin numbers have declined on many estuaries partly due to the spread of the introduced cord-grass. As dunlin feed at higher levels on mudflats than most other species, encroachment of cord grass into this zone reduces the availability of their preferred feeding area.

Redshank are somewhat larger than dunlin, with long reddish legs and bills and white

Dunlin in winter plumage

patterning on their rump and wings. They are wary birds, flying off with loud, yelping calls if disturbed. Redshanks probe slightly deeper than dunlin, and often wade in shallow water. Oystercatchers space themselves out over mudflats, keeping an eye open for the telltale movements of sub-surface worms. Some oyster-catchers spend most of their time on mudflats, while others specialise in preying on mussels and other shellfish on rocky shores. Curlews have their own feeding preferences too. Males to hunt small crabs on the mud surface, while the longer-billed females probe more for worms. At high tide, both curlew and oystercatch-

---

THE CASE OF OBR

Brent geese move around a lot after their arrival into Ireland and not all come directly to Kerry. One goose, identified by its ring colour ring as OBR, was ringed on Bathhurst Island in arctic Canada during 1984 as a yearling. It was first seen at Rossbeigh in winter 1984/5. The next winter Dr Micheál O'Briain, who originally ringed the bird in Canada, observed it at Strangford Lough, Co. Down on 6 October, 1985. A few days later on 10 and 11 October, it was seen again by Micheál at Sandymount Strand, Co. Dublin. Micheál then drove to Kerry that evening and to our astonishment we observed OBR on 12 October at Rossbeigh! It was the first case of a brent having been recorded at three major wintering sites in Ireland and all within a week. OBR probably used the sites to feed and replace energy lost on migration. It was subsequently see during winter in Tralee Bay as well.

---

ers often move inland to continue feeding on earthworms in soft fields.

Knot are another medium sized greyish wader, with short black bill, greenish legs and white rump. They feed in closely knit flocks, which when disturbed form a dense mist-like flock, wheeling about the sky. Larger still, but true loners, are grey plover. They have stout dark bills, dark legs and distinctive black axillaries (underwing feathers) when seen in flight. Grey plovers stalk slowly about the mudflats, stopping frequently to watch or search a particular patch of mud.

PLOVERS AND GULLS: A COMPLEX RELATIONSHIP

Lapwings preferentially feed in pastures with high densities of earthworms, and golden plover choose fields on the basis of the presence of lapwings, which they use as food finders. If you ever watch a flock of lapwing and golden plovers feeding in a field, you will normally see some black-headed gulls among the flock. The gulls will usually be well spaced out among the plovers, often perched on any raised mound of earth or vegetation. Black-headed gulls are kleptoparisitic, stealing worms from the plovers and lapwings. It is a common sight to see a gull chasing after one of the plovers or lapwings, trying to force it to drop its wriggly prey. The gulls, however, provide some benefits by providing early warning of predators.

When scanning the mudflats, your attention may be caught by a closely-packed mass of yellowish-coloured birds. The combination of colour and their habit of forming large flocks readily identifies them as golden plover, which feed both on mudflats and soft fields. They have a plaintive whistling 'too-lee' call, uttered on the ground and in flight. They often form flocks of over 1,000 birds and occur in Castlemaine harbour, Tralee bay, Carrahane sands and the mouth of the Shannon. During cold spells other golden plover and lapwings from further east migrate in their thousands westwards to the milder conditions of Kerry. Sometimes, however, even the fields of Kerry are frozen over, and many die of starvation. As soon as the cold spell is over, the survivors return eastwards, leaving the 'resident' plovers behind.

A NEW IRISH BREEDING SPECIES

Little egrets are distinctive, all white members of the Heron family. Over recent decades, little egrets have expanded their range northwards in Europe. Numbers of birds summered and wintered in Ireland, some turning up in Tralee Bay, Castlemaine and Kenmare harbours throughout the 1980s and 1990s. In 1997, breeding was first proven in Co. Cork when 12 pairs were discovered nesting among a colony of herons. It is quite likely that little egrets will nest in Kerry before too long – keep your eyes open for them!

Two species of waders prefer rocky shores, the turnstone and the scarcer purple sandpiper. Turnstones are dumpy brown and white waders with stout orange legs and slightly upturned bill. They can be quite tame and often allow close approach. As their name suggests they find their food by turning over small stones and seaweed, taking insects and small worms. Turnstones can often be seen searching the mounds of discarded waste at shellfish-processing plants such as that at Cromane Point. Purple sandpipers are the other birds of rocky winter shores. With their dark grey heads and upperparts, they are probably even more difficult to see than turnstones, probing among seaweed-covered rocks, often on the tips of rocky peninsulas. The best mainland site in the county is probably the tip of the Magharee peninsula, but small numbers do occur elsewhere. These species are often missed during regular estuary counts, as they occupy a different habitat. A 1987 survey of non-estuarine birds covered counties Kerry, Clare, Galway, Donegal, Leitrim and Sligo. In Kerry, a total of 941 turnstones and 110 purple sandpipers were counted. These figures were 37% and 20% respectively of the total counted, indicating the importance of the county for these species.

If you scan the water off most Kerry beaches in winter, you may see small flocks of black seaducks. These are common scoter, a large, black duck which feed by diving for cockles, crustaceans and other marine prey. Up to 5,000 occur off some beaches, with Rossbeigh, Ballinskelligs bay and Banna being the best localities. If you are lucky and patient, you may spot the rarer velvet scoter, with their white wing patches. A regular visitor to Ballinskelligs bay for many winters has been a striking male surf scoter, a very rare visitor to Irish waters. The male has two white patches on its head and a large multi-coloured bill of red, orange, white and black.

Mixed with the scoter flocks one will often see small numbers of divers, or loons as they are evocatively called in North America. The great northern diver is the larger and bulkier of the two common species, dark grey black above with a heavy looking, dagger-shaped bill. They feed principally on small fish, staying submerged for quite long periods when fishing. Sometimes they occur inland on lakes. One of my most pleasant memories of them is of a single bird on Lough Barfinnihy near Moll's Gap, wailing plaintively – a wild, ethereal sound. One or two great northern divers have appeared on the Killarney lakes in summer. The other diver is the red-throated, small numbers of which breed in Co. Donegal. They are slimmer than the great northern and paler in colour.

Long-tailed skuas turn up on autumn passage

Due to its location and rich feeding grounds, Kerry also attracts many rarer waders, gulls, and ducks, particularly of American origin, blown in on westerly gales. Tralee bay and Akeragh Lough in particular have a long list of rarities to their credit. This is partly due to the fact that they are close to centres of population and regularly watched. An active branch of Birdwatch Ireland is centred on Tralee and they offer regular outings to many sites in the area. New members are always welcome to join any of the outings.

BIRDS OF OFFSHORE ISLANDS

It is a fine July day and the party on board our launch are all visibly excited. The sea is relatively calm and landing should be straightforward. As we leave the shelter of the Portmagee channel and round the headland, our destination, Puffin island, comes into view. About 53 hectares in extent, the island slopes up steeply from a low-lying area on its landward side to a rugged peak 159 metres above sea level. The cliffs we are to visit look terrifyingly steep, cast as they are in deep shadow. As we approach closer, we can see the 45^0 slope falling away below the summit, before plunging the final 70 metres vertically to the sea below. Our landing site comes into view. After some hairy moments our group of four lands with tents, food, water and other equipment onto Puffin island. For most of us it is our first visit. Not as well known as its distant cousins, the Skellig islands, Puffin island lies a kilometre off the tip of the Iveragh peninsula and is a bird reserve owned by Birdwatch Ireland. Hugh Brazier, a long-time member and officer of that body has, for many years, visited Puffin island to catch and ring its namesake, puffins. About 4,000 pairs nest here, along with many other seabird species.

The Kerry islands are one of the most important island groups in Ireland or Britain for seabirds. Twenty-two seabird species nest on our islands, from the islets in Kenmare bay to the Magharee islands in Tralee bay. The best-known seabird is the puffin, which delights visitors from all over the world on their Skellig visit. These sea clowns or sea parrots as they are sometimes called, nest in their thousands on Skellig Michael, Puffin island, the Tearaght and other islands. To avoid predation they nest underground, often using rabbit burrows but also digging their own nest sites, generally on a steep slope. The sight of hundreds of these birds flying past in

The Blasket Islands hold important colonies of petrels and shearwaters

waves as they circle the nest slope is an exciting spectacle.

On steep, vertical cliffs you will find guillemots, with their long pointed beaks, hugging the cliff face and carefully brooding their single, pear-shaped egg. This shape has evolved to prevent the egg from rolling off the nesting ledge. Lower down among loose boulders nest razorbills. Along the cliff ledges you will also see and hear kittiwakes, wheeling and circling, flying to and from their nest sites, giving their onomatopoeic call of 'kitti-waakk, kitti-waakk'. Great black-backed gulls regularly patrol seabird cliffs searching for unwary auks, young chicks and rabbits. The numerous skins of these birds and mammals, turned inside out, are a sure sign of the gulls' activities.

From Puffin island we can see the two Skellig islands, as well as the Bull and The Cow rocks to the south. These are good seabird islands as well. The Little Skellig is another Birdwatch Ireland reserve, hosting 22,000 pairs of gannets, our largest seabird. These regularly patrol the seas around our island. If a shoal of fish is sighted, a large party of gannets will soon arrive. From 50-70 metres overhead, some of the circling birds will close their wings and

Kittiwakes preening

plummet into the sea below, like a squadron of dive bombers. They soon bob up again not far away, generally with a fish caught in their beaks.

TABLE 12
SEABIRD POPULATIONS OF THE MAJOR KERRY ISLAND GROUPS

	GREAT SKELLIG	PUFFIN ISLAND	BLASKET ISLANDS
Manx shearwater	*c.*5,000	5,500	10-15,000
Storm petrel	*c.* 10,000	5,500	< 150,000
Fulmar	857	2,100	2,200
Herring gull	18	?	130
Lesser black-backed gull	54**	?	425
Great black-backed gull	4	63	400
Kittiwake	961	?	800
Razorbill	335**	500**	420
Guillemot	1,176**	?	360
Puffin	5,432**	5,400	5,100**

Data from Great Skellig is for 1994, courtesy of O. Merne, N.P.W.S.

Data from Puffin island is from Way et al. (1993).

Data from Blasket islands is from Brazier and Merne (1989).

** Indicates count is of individual birds, not pairs.

Gannets have specially reinforced skulls to cushion the tremendous impact of such dives.

Darkness settles over the island and the uninitiated might expect a quiet night of inactivity. However, this is the time when the other subterranean dwellers of these islands return from their foraging trips at sea. At first you might hear the banshee-like wails of the manx shearwaters – crow-sized black and white birds with long wings. They return to their colony after dark to avoid predators such as the large gulls. As they come in to land, some thump off the sides of our tent, before scurrying away into their nearby burrows. Manx shearwaters are long-lived birds and prodigious travellers; Irish-ringed birds have been recovered as far away as Brazil. After the breeding season, their migrations take them into the south Atlantic, returning in spring along the eastern seaboard of America.

From within old stone walls and beneath loose rocks can be heard the churring of storm petrels; dainty, dark birds with white rumps.

Feeding time for a cormorant chick

These are also active travellers. Non-breeding birds frequently spend time visiting other colonies around the Irish and Scottish coasts. Somewhere on the Kerry islands there is probably a small colony of the rarer Leach's petrel, which have been caught and ringed on at least three of the Kerry islands. These have the wierdest call of all, sounding like somebody having a fit of hysterical laughing.

These three species belong to a group called the tubenoses, so called because of the tube-shaped aperture above the beak, believed to be used for discharging excess salt from their system. Recent work has shown that some of the tubenoses have a very highly developed sense of smell and use this to locate their food across many kilometres of ocean. Another tubenose is the fulmar, a relatively recent colonist of the Irish coastline and one of the few seabirds which can still be seen when all the other species have abandoned their cliffs and islands by mid-August. Since they first nested in Ireland in 1911, after expanding from their Arctic nesting areas, they have successfully colonised the whole coast of Ireland. Breeding was first proven in Kerry in 1913. Fulmars now occupy most islands and coastal cliffs, even the low cliffs near Inch Strand. They defend themselves by discharging a vile mix of stomach fluids and fish oil at any would be attacker. Masters of the air, they are a delight to watch cruising the updraughts along the top of coastal cliffs.

Common guillemot

On some of the smaller coastal islands one can find colonies of terns. The very similar common and Arctic terns nest in Tralee bay and Kenmare bay. Arctic terns have a dark red bill, tail streamers which project beyond their wings when at rest, and a dark trailing edge to their white wings, visible when in flight overhead. Common terns have an orange-red bill with black tip, relatively shorter tails and lack the distinct wing pattern of the Arctic tern. The smaller and rarer little tern nests on one of the Magheree islands, where they are very prone to disturbance from sailors and day-trippers. It has a white forehead to its black crown and a yellow and black bill. The largest tern is the sandwich tern, which looks bulkier and shorter tailed in flight than the others. They are generally the first terns to return to our islands in spring, the earliest birds being recorded in late March. All the terns nest on smaller, lowlying islands and apart from suffering the attentions of aerial and mammalian predators, are prone to disturbance from human visitors. If you do visit any potential tern islands, be aware of the possibility of them being present

Razorbills

and avoid any colonies you might encounter.

Birds of Woodland, Forest and Farmland

Kerry has the largest area of native woodlands in the country, as well as extensive areas of coniferous plantations. The native woodlands include our well-known oakwoods of the Killarney valley and Beara peninsula, the wet alder woods around Lough Leane, and the dark and mysterious yew wood of the Muckross peninsula. A few other patches of woodland are to be found, generally on steep, rocky slopes throughout the county, but deciduous woods are particularly scarce on the shales of north Kerry.

The breeding birds of our deciduous woods have been relatively well studied compared with elsewhere in the country. A wide range of woodland types were first censused in 1973, when they were visited by a joint Anglo-Irish expedition led by Dr Leo Batten of the British Trust for Ornithology (BTO). Since then some of these woods have been re-surveyed, in particular the Muckross yew wood, which I have censused every year since 1982. (See Table 13). The bird communities of these woods vary somewhat, depending on what the principal tree species are. In oak-dominated woods, robins, blue tits and chaffinches tend to be the most common species.

In Ireland we have only four tit species, compared to seven species found in Britain. The coal tit is our smallest species, with a black crown and bib and white nape patch. In winter they cache large amounts of seeds and other food to see them through periods when food is scarce or unobtainable. In Britain both male and female coal tits have the same bill size, and feed in the same part of a tree. Kerry coal tits, however, have different sized bills. Females have deeper beaks than males, allowing them to feed more on hard-shelled seeds and forage lower in trees or on the ground, thus reducing competition between themselves. This is an example of competitive release, where a species expands its niche in the absence

---

Caterpillars, blue tits and oaks

Blue tits are primarily oakwood birds, reaching their highest density in this habitat. The nesting season of blue tits is highly correlated with the life cycle of various defoliating species of moths, which in turn is closely tied to the timing of leaf bud. This is all ultimately controlled by spring temperatures. There is a complex relationship between blue tits, their caterpillar prey, and oak leaves. As the young oak leaves develop and mature, they produce increasing amounts of tannin, which renders them more unpalatable to the caterpillars. Caterpillars grow quicker and mature earlier on a diet of tannin-free leaves. Young, tannin-free caterpillars are more digestible to tit chicks; tits which hatch later grow more slowly and fledge at lighter weights than earlier broods, a significant disadvantage, so timing of nesting is crucial.

of competing species. Coal Tits are more common in conifer plantations than in deciduous woods, but even in conifers they are usually outnumbered by gold-crests, our smallest bird. The male goldcrest has a fiery orange streak on his crown, hence the name. Their thin 'see-see-see' call can be easily distinguished from all others.One of the least often observed birds is the treecreeper, a small speckled brown bird with thin, decurved bill for probing cracks and crevices. They are well camouflaged, and are best located initially by their thin high-pitched call. They nest behind loose bark, and in winter often roost in a hollowed-out scrape on the trunks of giant sequoias. The scrapes can be easily spotted on these soft-barked trees. If you examine such a tree after dark in winter, you can sometimes spot a treecreeper roosting in whichever scrape is out of the wind. The bird's fluffed up plumage gives the appearance of a pine cone wedged into a crack.

GREAT TITS — THE WOODLAND COBBLERS?

The great tit is the largest European tit, with a strong bill very suited for hammering open tough nuts and seeds. In winter they spend more time than any other tit species foraging on the ground for seeds of beech and yew in particular. When they find a suitable nut they will carry it up to a nearby branch and proceed to hammer it open to get at the kernel. This hammering sound carries quite far on a still day, yet can be difficult to locate the source of. In the depths of a quiet wood it can almost be eerie hearing these steady 'tap, tap, tap' sounds — perhaps these are the source of legends about 'little people' hammering at tiny shoes?

Jays are more often heard than seen, although they are now a well established part of the woodland scene in Kerry since they were first recorded in the county in 1966. Breeding was first proved in Killarney in 1978. Their call has been described as like somebody tearing a brown paper bag!

In areas of scrub woodland a different community exists. Here robins are still com-mon, but wrens become more frequent, their loud vigorous song belying their small size. The male wren builds up to eight nests each winter, using them to roost in. The female chooses one for her summer nest. Willow warblers are more common in scrub habitat, singing their jingly tune all summer long. Another warbler which prefers scrub, mixed with some taller trees, is the blackcap, a species which has undergone a range expansion in Ireland in recent years. They are now common in many wooded areas of Kerry. A much scarcer cousin of the blackcap is the garden warbler, which has been recently

A brood of great tits in a nestbox

TABLE 13

DENSITY OF BIRD SPECIES IN THE MUCKROSS YEW WOOD (TERRITORIES/10 HA.)

Species	'82	'83	'84	'85	'86	'87	'88	'89	'90	'91	'92	'93	'94
Woodpigeon	9.6	5.6	6.4	8.0	10.4	7.2	9.6	5.6	8.8	7.2	4.8	4.8	5.6
Wren	5.6	1.6	2.4	4.0	1.6	1.6	2.4	4.8	0.0	2.4	0.8	7.2	6.4
Robin	19.2	19.2	13.6	12.8	13.6	16.0	14.4	13.6	16.0	16.0	12.0	15.2	12.
Blackbird	10.4	7.2	6.4	5.6	4.8	8.0	6.4	8.0	10.4	6.4	6.4	8.0	5.6
Song thrush	3.2	2.4	2.4	0.8	0.8	0.8	1.6	3.2	2.4	1.6	2.4	3.2	3.2
Goldcrest	6.4	10.4	8.8	7.2	4.0	13.6	10.4	12.0	13.6	4.0	5.6	17.6	12.
Coal tit	5.6	7.2	6.4	6.4	6.4	12.8	8.8	15.2	10.4	12.8	9.6	20.0	18.
Blue tit	4.0	4.0	3.0	4.8	4.0	6.4	3.2	6.4	3.2	8.8	4.8	8.0	7.2
Great tit	5.6	4.8	1.6	3.2	4.0	8.0	4.0	10.4	5.6	11.2	7.2	9.6	10.
Treecreeper	1.6	1.6	1.6	2.4	2.4	2.4	1.6	2.4	1.6	1.6	3.2	3.2	3.2
Chaffinch	5.6	2.4	3.2	2.4	3.2	3.2	4.0	4.8	4.0	4.8	3.2	4.0	4.0

BIRD RINGING

The catching and ringing of birds is an important research tool, widely used throughout the world. Birds are usually caught in mist nets, which were originally developed in Japan to catch birds for food. Mist nets look like huge hairnets stretched between two tall canes and can be up to 20 metres in length and 3 metres high. When a bird is caught, a small, lightweight ring is applied to a leg with special pliers. Rings are normally made from magnesium/aluminium or other alloy and stamped with an individual number and a return address. Both the ringer and the finder receive a note giving details of the bird's place and date of capture and recovery. Ringing birds on a large scale allows us to study many aspects of birds' lives. These include:

* *timing and duration of migration*
* *routes taken and the resting points used en route*
* *average life expectancy and life span*
* *principal causes of death*
* *monitoring population changes*

---

recorded nesting in the Killarney valley. Their habitat requirements overlap with blackcaps. The two species compete for territory, although the garden warbler generally prefers sites near water.

Ringing a female blackcap

In the early stages of growth, conifer plantations can hold high densities of birds, especially willow warblers, wrens and other scrub dwellers. As they mature and reach thicket stage, they loose their attraction for many species. Studies have found, however, that even the presence of a few deciduous trees within the plantation, particularly mature oaks, enhance the nature conservation value of plantations enormously. In mature stands of conifers, old pigeon or crow nests may be occupied by kestrels, which will hunt over open fields nearby, or even by a pair of long-eared owls. These shy retiring birds are best located by their hooting calls in February, or by the sound of the hungry chicks calling for food on a June evening. The chicks have a call that is best described as being like a squeaking gate hinge!

Another conifer-nesting bird is the siskin, a small green and yellow finch. Siskins are widely distributed throughout the county, particularly in mature plantations. In winter our breeding population is augmented by many migrants from Scotland and Scandinavia.

BIRDS OF FARMLAND

What Kerry lacks in woodlands, it makes up for in farmland. With its fields, hedges and copses, farmland is one of the single largest habitats in the county, but

its attractiveness to birds depends largely on the underlying soil type and its overall management. The best hedgerows for birds are to be found on the limestone soils, where tall hedges of hawthorn and elderberry are common. Both are very important species to birds for food, shelter and nest sites. In west Kerry, fuchsia is the most important hedgerow species and provides good shelter for birds. Its long-lasting flowers are attractive to many insects,

Spotted flycatcher at its nest

which in turn provide feeding for birds. On the shales of north Kerry, hedges, if present at all, tend to be low, scrappy and often of gorse and other species, which are relatively poor habitats for birds.

The county has lost many of its hedgerows to farm development and much of its mixed farming of hay and tillage, which provided rich stocks of food for birds and other creatures. With the switch to silage making, Kerry has lost most of its hay meadows, which were important for nesting corncrakes, now extinct in the county, as well as pheasants, skylarks, yellowhammers and other birds. The rich seed supply to be found in these meadows in late summer is important for finches in particular. A good hay meadow will attract greenfinches, chaffinches, linnets and goldfinches in summer, before and after harvesting.

Farmyard areas themselves can be good for birds. Silage clamps and slurry pits often attract many insects, food for pied wagtails and other species. Pied wagtails are particularly fond of man-made habitats and are frequent farmyard visitors. Old sheds house nesting swallows and perhaps a pair of barn owls, now becoming a rare species nationally. Barn owls in particular are susceptible to

ingesting poisons from contaminated rats, one of their main prey items. Nesting sites for barn owls are also scarcer these days as new prefabricated haysheds replace older stone barns, but they will readily accept on old box or barrel hung in a dark corner of a shed as an alternative nest-site. The farmhouse itself sometimes provides shelter for house martins, which build their mud nests under the eaves.

A barn owl found roosting in a tree near the centre of Killarney

Farmyard areas can be made more attractive

for birds by farmers not being too scrupulous in 'tidying up' corners with nettles and other plants, leaving old apple trees, if present and allowing scrubby species such as bramble to develop beneath stands of taller trees.

One species associated with farmyards and old buildings are tree sparrows. Similar to the familiar house sparrow, but with a smaller black bib, a chestnut-coloured crown and 'ear patch', tree sparrows have become quite rare throughout the country. A small population still exists in coastal areas of Kerry centred on the district from Tralee to Ballyheigue. Changes in farming practice and eradication of weed seeds have been the main causes of their decline.

Farmers, as individuals or as a group, have the greatest capacity to improve our countryside for the benefit of birds and other wild creatures, without necessarily impacting upon the economics of running a farm.

BIRDS OF TOWNS AND VILLAGES

One of the pleasures of walking around a town or village on a summer's evening is observing the swifts wheeling and screeching high overhead. Sometimes they appear to dice with death as three or four birds race in pursuit of one another low down a street at car height. Swifts are true summer birds, arriving in early May and departing by early August. When the weather is inclement and insect food scarce, the chicks can lapse into a torpor and survive long periods with little or no food. They will resume their rapid rate of growth when supplies start rolling in again. The only time swifts come to earth is during the nesting season, otherwise they eat and sleep on the wing.

Collared doves are common around some towns and villages, as well as farms, generally wherever there is grain stored. These handsome doves with their black neck collar were originally birds of the Indian subcontinent, which expanded from Asia across Europe in the early 1900s. They first nested in Ireland in 1959. Nowadays they can be seen throughout the country, even on off-shore islands.

Changing patterns of land use in Ireland are making urban and suburban areas increasingly important as habitats for wildlife. Towns provide important roost sites, particularly in severe cold weather, when the temperature

A winter flock of starlings circles a roost near Killarney

will be a crucial few degrees warmer than the surrounding countryside. Rooks and jackdaws make use of town parks as nest and roost sites, with some winter roosts totalling over 5,000 birds. A spectacular sight to see is a big winter roost of starlings. One such roost uses a forestry plantation near Castleisland every winter.

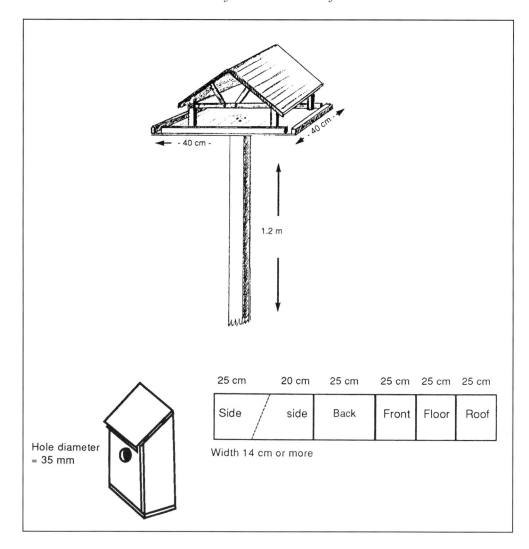

Figure 2: Sketch of Bird Table and Nest Box Design

Roosts of over 10,000 starlings occur in other areas when immigrants are driven westwards by cold weather off the Continent. Such flocks perform dramatic aerial manoeuvres just before plunging en masse earthwards into their chosen roost site.

Apart from a warmer microclimate, towns offer good stocks of berried trees and shrubs, bird tables and plentiful nest sites in summer, including man-made nest boxes. One important feature of suburban ecology is that many people provide food for wildlife, particularly birds. A well stocked bird table is a pleasure to have outside one's house, allowing good views of many bird species. Recent research has shown that birds can be fed throughout the year. Few species, however, are generally attracted during the height of the breeding season, when most passerines feed insects to their young. From August onwards, though, the provision of bread, fat, seeds and nuts, especially peanuts, is beneficial to a wide range of species.

While our summering blackcaps depart for Mediterranean countries in the autumn, their place is taken by northern European blackcaps which come to Britain and Ireland to overwinter. They feed in particular on the berries in gardens and food scraps at bird tables. One Tralee bird table had seven blackcaps coming to it at the same time! Siskins are an increasingly frequent bird table feeder, being particularly fond of peanuts. Gerry Murphy, a Killarney-based forester, erected a bird table in the garden of his new house one winter's day, hanging 4 peanut feeders from it. The next day 4 siskins were at the feeders, and inside a week he had no less than 30 queuing up to feed.

RARE BIRDS

Due to its location and good bird habitats, Kerry is an ornithological hotspot for rarities. American migrants in particular turn up every autumn on our shores, tired and bedraggled after the long trans-Atlantic journey. North-west winds push passing seabirds onto our north-facing shores, southerlies drop tired continental migrants into bushes and gardens. Tralee bay in particular attracts many rarities – its list rivals anywhere in the country. The bay area from Kerry Head in the north to Brandon mountain in the west has seen some of the rarest Irish avian visitors. Many other sites are probably as good, particularly Castlemaine harbour, but the dearth of birdwatchers in the area means these sites are underwatched.

One of the most famous bird-watching sites in Irish ornithology is Akeragh Lough, near Ballyheigue. This is a small brackish lake situated between the sand dunes of Banna and the Ballyheigue-Ardfert road. In its hey-day it consisted of three large ponds with surrounding vegetation of reeds and marsh plants. Apart from holding large numbers of wintering wildfowl and waders, with up to 3,500 teal and 10,000 lapwing, its main claim to fame was as an attraction to tired North American vagrants. Rare American species used to arrive here in greater numbers than virtually anywhere else in Europe. Birds attracted include pectoral sandpipers, lesser yellowlegs, Wilson's phalarope and white-rumped sandpipers, as well as many 'lesser' rarities.

These days the ponds are silting up, the water is badly polluted from raw sewage entering it, and the area is heavily shot over. These sort of problems are guaranteed to reduce the avian interest of a site, and bird numbers are much reduced. Akeragh Lough is exactly the sort of site which could be returned to its former glory if enough local interest was present to tackle the jobs which need doing.

TABLE 14

BIRD SPECIES FOUND IN KERRY WHICH ARE LISTED IN THE *IRISH RED DATA BOOK*

Barn owl	Merlin	Tree sparrow
Hen harrier	Pochard	Twite
Little tern	Ring ouzel	Wood warbler
Nightjar	Short-eared owl	

MAMMALS

It is an October morning, clear, cold and still. There is a chill in the air, almost a touch of frost, that makes you want to move around to warm yourself. To do so would break the magic and you stand still, waiting, listening, whispering quietly. Sounds are plentiful, for the rut of the deer is well underway and four or five stags are in full throat; their deep roars echoing across the glen.

The red deer of the Killarney valley have been roaming these hills for thousands of years. They are descendants of red deer which re-entered the country

Young red deer sparring

after the last great ice age. Bones from red deer dating to 3985 ± 60 years before present were excavated from an archaeological site at Ventry, their earliest recorded occurrence in Kerry. Venison has long been on the human menu, and outside of Kerry red deer were harried and hunted to extinction by the end of the last century. Elsewhere in Ireland they were reintroduced by landlords with animals brought in from England and Scotland. Kerry almost lost its red deer too. Thanks to protection measures, particularly over the past 30 years, their population in the Killarney area has built up from a low of about 170 animals to their 1997 level of approximately 650.

A big red stag is an impressive sight, particularly in the autumn after a summer of good feeding and antler development. Large stags weigh up to 150 kilograms and may have sixteen or more points to their antlers. Eighteen pointers are not unknown in Killarney. The effect of broad heavy forequarters, thick necks and slimmer hindquarters give the stags the appearance of prizefighters. In a sense that is what they are, for the prize is the privilege of mating with many hinds and passing their genes on to the next generation. Despite their impressive size, strength and armoury, stags do not often fight. Instead they mix a range of threat displays and other gestures to intimidate their opponents and reduce the need for actual combat.

Outside of the rut, stags tend to form small bachelor groups. Hinds and calves travel as sub-units within the overall herd, each sub-unit led by a matriarchal hind. Calves are born from early to mid June, losing their spotted coats after about two months. Killarney has two populations of red deer. Tagging has shown they inter-mix to some extent, but in general can be treated as two separate populations. The lowland herd frequents the area between the River Laune and Muckross. The upland herd, which is about three times as large, populates the highlands from Mangerton mountain to Derrycunnihy. These are the core areas for red deer in Kerry. Smaller numbers exist in the Roughty valley, south to Caherdaniel and west to Glencar. Another herd is to be found on Inisvickillaun, one of the Blasket island group, owned by former Taoiseach Charles Haughey. They were first brought to the island in 1980.

The second deer species in Kerry is the smaller Japanese sika deer. They were introduced to Killarney in 1865 from the Powerscourt estate in Co. Wicklow. From an initial introduction of two hinds and one stag, sika numbers have grown dramatically. They once substantially outnumbered the red deer. In the late 1970s, the sika population in the Killarney valley was estimated to be between 1,000 and 1,500 animals. These numbers were causing serious problems of overgrazing to their habitat. With heavy culling during the 1980s, their population has been reduced to about 700 animals.

Sika change from having a light red coat, spotted with cream in summer, to a thick dark grey or black winter coat. In all seasons they have a white rump patch, trimmed with black. Stags weigh up to 65 kilograms and have up to eight points on their antlers, while females weigh about 34 kilograms. Being smaller and more skulking than red deer, their total population in any area is difficult to assess. They are widespread and increasing through central Kerry from Glencar and Killorglin to the Cork/Kerry border. They are probably also spreading northwards, making use of the extensive conifer plantations across the hills north of Killarney.

The vexed question of whether sika x red hybrids occur in Kerry pops up frequently when deer matters arise in con-

A red hind lies snagged in a waterfall

Yew trees with trunks scored by sika stags

versation. As far as we know, no hybrids have been confirmed in the county yet, despite their presence in Co. Wicklow and elsewhere in Ireland. The Wicklow hybrids originated from captive breeding programmes on the Powerscourt estate in the late 1800s. One suggested reason for the lack of hybrids in Kerry is that it may initially require crossing in captivity to begin the hybridisation process. Recent evidence has shown that the original introduction of sika to Killarney was made before hybridisation experiments were begun at Powerscourt. Worldwide, Japanese sika are on the I.U.C.N. Endangered Species list, and Kerry sika are important internationally as one of the purest strains of Japanese sika in the world.

With the introduction of Continental red deer and fallow deer for deer farming, it seems inevitable that other regions in Kerry will develop deer herds from animals escaping from these population centres. Deer can be viewed as either a game animal, a nuisance or an attraction in their own right. Large numbers of wild deer can, however, be a serious nuisance to farmers, gardeners and foresters, as well as competitors and a threat to the purity of our native red deer. As such we should be aware that these threats exist and should be addressed before deer in Kerry become as big a problem as in many parts of Britain.

JAPANESE SIKA AND GREENLAND WHITE-FRONTS

In parts of the Killarney valley, where sika deer feed over the same bogs as overwintering Greenland white-fronted geese, the deer have developed some peculiar dietary habits. Like all geese, white-fronts have very inefficient digestive systems, and must eat a large volume of green material each day. On bogland their principal foods are the underground storage organs of white-beak sedge and bog cotton. They produce numerous droppings quite frequently, at the rate of one dropping every 3-4 minutes. So a flock of 30 geese will produce from 400 to 600 droppings every hour they are feeding. These are the length and thickness of a finger, and still rich in semi-digested, nutrient rich green matter.

Sika deer have discovered this fact and have taken to eating these droppings whenever they can get them. They will actively approach a flock of geese on a bog and forage among the birds exclusively for droppings; the ultimate hot snack! They do a very thorough job in finding them; after deer have been feeding among geese virtually the only droppings left are those in bog-pools, which are inaccessible to the deer. I have watched up to 19 sika feeding among a flock of only 30 geese. Unfortunately, the close attention of so many deer sometimes causes the birds to take flight and leave the site. This is an energetically expensive activity which the geese can do without. Interestingly, our native red deer do not seem to have discovered this unique snack food, as no instance of red deer foraging among geese has been recorded.

Some large herds of feral goats roam the mountains of Kerry. Most are probably descended from animals kept in captivity during pre-famine times. Their numbers, however, are augmented by the callous habit of goat owners dropping off unwanted animals 'into the wild'. Even quite small numbers of goats can have a significant damaging impact on shrubs and bushes. They will often browse these severely and even de-bark them, thus killing many already hard-pressed shrubs. Kerry has a special link with its feral goats, symbolised by the 'crowning' every year of a large billy goat at Killorglin's Puck Fair.

Foxes are widespread throughout the county, from the highest mountain summits to the centre of towns and villages. They are only absent from the offshore islands. Though normally nocturnal, foxes can frequently be seen on their rounds in daytime, particularly when adults have hungry cubs to feed. Evidence of their passing can be found by finding their distinctive pointed droppings and the unforgettable musky smell which foxes leave behind them. This is produced from the subcaudal gland at the root of the tail.

Despite being persecuted for centuries for their fur and as 'pests', foxes are doing quite well, partly due to their undoubted intelligence and resourcefulness. They are omnivorous, eating a wide range of foods from beetles and mice to fruit, rabbits and carrion. Hill foxes probably depend to a large extent on carrion, and with the frequent overstocking of hills with sheep in many places, carrion is rarely in short supply. Most outdoor people have had some encounter with these animals. My own memories of foxes include coming across one which lay fast asleep on a rock, of another trailing a hare across the snow-covered summit of Mangerton mountain, and of watching two cubs at play outside their den.

Badgers are less often encountered, even by the most active outdoor people. They are highly social animals, living in groups of up to a dozen animals. Badgers occur where the soil is fertile and fairly deep, up to an altitude of 300 metres. Though generally thought of as woodland animals, they are commonly found on farmland and overgrown scrubby areas. They dig long underground tunnels or setts, which can be quite complex, with many exits. Some may have been in continuous occupation for hundreds of years. Old, well established setts invariably have a large soil mound at the entrance, which the badgers regularly keep clear of loose earth, leaves, etc. The remains of old bedding will often be found near the entrance. Badgers are quite fastidious about their hygiene, changing their bedding frequently. There will normally be one or more secondary setts in each territory, often used as a bolt-hole in times of emergency.

The badger's principal food is earthworms, but they also eat fruit, carrion, eggs and chicks of birds, as well as small mammals and various invertebrates. When digging for food they leave distinctive shallow scrapes in the soil, a good indication of their presence in an area.

Pine martens often use sheds and old buildings

The rarest mammal in the county is the pine marten. Small numbers occur in the Killarney and Kenmare valleys, but are rarely seen. They are similar in shape to stoats or mink, but are larger and have bushy tails. The cream-coloured throat and inner ears, set against a rich chocolate-brown fur, are distinctive. Often the only clue to their presence is their spiral-shaped droppings. These are normally deposited on a raised feature such as a crossing point on a wall or fallen log, and are used as territorial markers. Territories cover up to 13 hectares in extent, the owners using a regular system of pathways every night to hunt. Like badgers and foxes, they have a wide and varied diet, including carrion, birds, field mice and ground beetles. Bees, honey and wax are taken in summer and a variety of fruits in the autumn. Pine martens take readily to trees, often using old holes to lie up in, and will take squirrels when possible. Dry, dark corners of old buildings and attics are also used as dens.

A close relative of the pine marten is the American mink. Originally introduced in 1951 from North America into Ireland for fur-breeding, mink have since escaped into the countryside. They are now well established over much of the county. It was originally believed that the presence of these aggressive, alien predators would cause havoc among Irish wildlife, particularly wildfowl and game populations. It was also felt that they would be a threat to otter populations. However, studies in Ireland and abroad have shown that, apart from certain situations such as among tern colonies on offshore islands, mink have had no major impact on our wildbird or otter populations. It is now believed that they have taken up a niche which was vacant in these islands in the absence of the European mink.

The majority of mink are black in colour, with a small white throat patch, but a proportion of silver-grey animals occur. They prefer to hunt along waterways, and dominant males will hold a territory along a stretch of river up to two kilometres in length. They are excellent swimmers and are regularly encountered by boating anglers on our larger lakes. While they will take fish, small mammals, frogs, birds and invertebrates are more commonly eaten. Like many of their tribe, they are curious and quite fearless, sometimes entering farmyards to raid hen runs, a habit which does not endear them to humans.

An otter devours an eel

The Irish stoat is the smallest member in Ireland of the Mustelid family. Our stoat is an endemic subspecies, found only in Ireland and the Isle of Man, and differs from the British stoat in size and colour. Within Ireland there is a cline in size from north to south, northern animals being smaller and lighter than southern animals. There are no weasels in Ireland, but the stoat is often erroneously referred to as a weasel. Irish stoats have a reddish-brown coats, white undersides, and a black tip to their tail; an obvious distinguishing character. With sinuous, tapering bodies, they are capable of squeezing through very narrow crevices and will raid the nest holes of tits and other birds. Other food includes mammals up to the size of rabbits, as well as various invertebrates.

Stoats are widespread if thinly distributed in Kerry. Although one study in the early 1970s found no stoats in the Muckross area near Killarney, they certainly occur there now but are by no means common. Most people's experience of stoats is of one darting across a road, its bounding gait and supple undulating outline quickly distinguishing it from the scurrying form of a rat. They are known to form packs of up to ten or more animals, which probably comprise more than one family. In particularly severe winters, stoats will turn almost entirely white, although I have only seen this phenomenon once in Kerry.

One of our least observed mammals is the otter, partly because they are nocturnal, aquatic and generally wary of man. To come across one quietly swimming along a river or lakeshore is a real delight. Otters are widely distributed about the county, particularly along the more productive rivers and lakes and can also be found along the seashore. They are best seen early in the morning, when careful scanning of a suitable stretch of river or lake will often prove fruitful. They also leave distinctive droppings or 'spraints' on exposed boulders in rivers. This is a useful indicator of their presence in the vicinity.

Studies of their diet have shown that they normally take whatever is most common in local waters; eels, crayfish, fish of various species and waterbirds up to the size of cormorants. Examination of otter spraints from the lakes of Killarney showed that eels occurred in 76-85% of spraints, with shad and salmonids (salmon and trout) occurring in lesser quantities. Shad occurred more frequently in spraints collected along the Tomies shoreline, where these fish are believed to be more common. Frogs were frequently taken during their spawning season. Coastal otters eat a wide variety of fish from butterfish to conger eels. Cubs may be born in all seasons and the breeding dens or 'holts' are invariably only approachable from underwater. Litter sizes vary from one to three, but litters of up to five cubs have been recorded.

Rabbits were introduced into Ireland in late Norman times, rabbit warrens being first mentioned in the time of Edward I, between 1274 and 1301. In Kerry they are now abundant in most places outside the mountainous and boggy parts of the county. They are particularly numerous in coastal sand dunes. Their numbers fluctuate dramatically over a period of years particularly when colonies are devastated by an outbreak of myxomatosis, spread by the rabbit flea. Rabbits are found on most of our offshore islands, having been introduced by man. They are frequently preyed upon by the larger gulls and ravens.

The Irish hare, a subspecies of the mountain hare, is to be found throughout the mainland parts of Kerry and on one or two offshore islands where it was introduced. Good views of them feeding in fields are rare. One's normal experience of a hare is of an animal exploding from the vegetation underfoot, racing off for 50 or 60 metres before stopping to look back at you. They are found at all altitudes – I have seen partially white hares on high Kerry peaks in winter – and have a wide diet from grasses and herbs to heather and cotton-grass. Hares are not always animals of open spaces either, being frequently seen well within wooded areas in the Killarney Valley. They have a long breeding season from February to October, the young being born well developed and fully furred.

Beyond the Killarney and Kenmare Valleys, little is known of the distribution of red squirrels throughout the county. They are animals of coniferous and mixed woodlands and are less common in pure deciduous woods. Red squirrels are incredibly agile within the treetops, leaping from the smallest of twigs on one tree across to the canopy of others. Stephen Mills, wildlife film producer, took some excellent footage once of a red squirrel feeding quite happily in the crown of a spindly oak tree, which was being whipped about in a force seven gale. They are most active and easily seen in autumn, when they spend time gathering nuts, acorns and other woodland. They can even be seen out and about on mild winter days.

The least popular member of our mammalian fauna is the common rat. They are widely distributed and common throughout the county except in bogland areas and at altitude. Rats are closely associated with human habitations, farms and waste disposal sites. Their diet is varied, including meat, fish, cereals, young birds and eggs, and more. They are excellent swimmers and found on many lake and offshore islands. Rats can cause considerable damage among seabird colonies and to nesting ducks.

Another serious pest and disease carrier is the house mouse. Their usual colour is greyish-brown but variants occur. In summer they can be found around gardens, farms and cultivated grounds, but in autumn they prefer to move indoors into human habitations. Like most of their fellow rodents, they are prolific breeders.

Far more attractive than the house mouse is the wood mouse. They are slightly bigger, with marginally larger eyes, ears and hind feet. Wood mice are a tawny colour above, white beneath, with a small yellow-brown throat patch. The hairless tail is much longer than that of the house mouse and can break off if it is caught by a predator, without causing the owner undue harm. Wood mice are nocturnal, living underground in tunnels. Some tunnels may be nearly three metres in length and extending to depths of 1.5 metres. They occupy a wide variety of habitats, but prefer good cover, relatively dry ground, and generally avoid urban areas. Dr Chris Smal studied the small mammals of the Reenadinna yew wood on the Muckross peninsula. Here he recorded a density of 92 woodmice per hectare, the highest density recorded for this species anywhere. This was principally due to the numerous grykes and fissures in the limestone terrain. This added a third dimension to the habitat and allowed the mice to reduce their territory size.

The third small rodent found in Kerry is the bank vole, which was first discovered in Ireland in 1964 near Listowel. The original introduction of voles probably arrived off a ship-load of timber or other material at Foynes harbour. Judging by their rate of spread, it is estimated that their initial arrival was around 1950. Bank voles are smaller than wood mice, with much shorter tails, rich chestnut-coloured fur and a more herbivorous diet. They are more diurnal than field mice and can sometimes be seen scurrying about by roadside banks and ditches, wherever there is good cover. Bank voles prefer tall

Bank vole

vegetation which provides some protection from aerial predators such as kestrels and harriers. The dense growth found in young forestry plantations is ideal for their needs. This provides good cover and an ample food supply of seeds and other vegetable matter, including tree bark. They can cause considerable damage to young trees by bark-stripping, but it has been found that grazing such plantations at appropriate times with sheep and cattle reduces the ground cover and thus the impact of bank voles.

Since their initial discovery their range has increased remarkably. Their rate of advance has been calculated at an average of 4.5 kilometres per year. They have now spread as far as Galway and Kildare, although they appear not to have penetrated far onto the Dingle peninsula.

Our smallest mammal is the pygmy shrew, the only member of the shrew family in Ireland. They are readily distinguished from the small rodent species by their tiny size, long, pointed snout, small ears and tiny eyes. Despite their size, they are ferocious hunters and very pugnacious towards their own species. Because of their small size and insectivorous nature, pygmy shrews must eat virtually continuously to stay alive. They will die if deprived of food for more than a few hours. Their diet consists of beetles, woodlice, insect larvae, spiders and other small animals;

they will tackle virtually anything they can subdue but generally avoid earthworms, slugs and snails. Pygmy shrews remain active day and night, with frequent short periods of rest.

A pygmy shrew

Pygmy shrews are highly territorial, thus allowing individuals to become familiar with their patch and the food resources within it. This territoriality breaks down somewhat during the mating season in early summer. Litter size varies from two to eight young. Densities vary from 20 to 40 animals per hectare, the highest densities being found in grassland. Life is short for these little creatures, with an average life span of less than six months. Shrews show the remarkable adaptation of actually shrinking in size between autumn and winter. Their weight decreases by about ¹/₃, their body shortens as their weight drops and the skull becomes smaller. This extraordinary change is due to resorption of some of the bone, that is its breakdown and assimilation into the bloodstream.

Hedgehogs are widely if thinly distributed throughout Kerry. However, even where apparently suitable habitat is found, their densities are often low. This may be linked to the presence of badgers, which are known to prey on hedgehogs. Recent work from Poland suggests that where badger densities are high, hedgehog densities are low, and vice-versa. Unfortunately for the majority of us, our only encounter with hedgehogs are when they have been killed by road traffic.

A hedgehog after its rescue from a cattle grid

Hedgehogs are largely nocturnal and eat earthworms, caterpillars, beetles, slugs, as well as small mammals, birds and their eggs. Some people attract hedgehogs by putting out milk and other foodstuffs and are lucky enough to have hedgehogs as visitors to their gardens. Hedgehogs hibernate overwinter, remaining curled up among dense mounds of fallen leaves and dead vegetation.

All seven species of bat which occur in Ireland have been recorded in Kerry, although some species are very rare. By day they roost in attics, old buildings, caves and hollow trees, emerging at dusk to forage. If you are fortunate enough to have bats in your attic, they can be readily counted as they depart for their night's hunting. Most bats depart their summer roosts of trees and buildings in late autumn. They prefer to winter underground in caves and old tunnels, where a constant temperature is maintained. Bats hunt over a wide variety of habitats. Individual species avoid undue competition by hunting over varying habitats, at different heights, or going for different sized prey, ranging from mosquitoes up to moths.

The most abundant species, the pipistrelle, prefers to roost in houses and old buildings, generally just between the slates and the felt lining. There are hundreds of roosts known in Kerry, and many more unknown. Some roosts can be quite large – I've counted over 500 individuals departing from one house on their evening flight.

The lesser horseshoe is one of the most distinctive species. If examined in the hand, the peculiar nose-leaf readily identifies this species. When roosting, they are the only species which hang vertically from the ceiling of the cave, tunnel or attic, rather than against the walls. Lesser horseshoes only occur in the western counties of Ireland, which is a major European stronghold for this species. Kerry has at least 50 colonies. These range in size from one to 300 animals, including colonies in old houses, ice houses, caves and tunnels.ranging in size from one to 300 animals, including colonies in old houses, ice houses, caves and tunnels.

THE COMMON PIPISTRELLE

The common pipistrelle, Pipistrellus pipistrellus, *has recently been shown on genetic evidence to consist of two species. One species vocalises at a different wavelength than the other and is believed to congregate in much smaller breeding colonies. At this point in time, no decision has been taken regarding a new name, so the two species are provisionally referred to as P. pipistrellus 45kHz and P. pipistrellus 55 kHz.*

Another distinctive species is the brown long-eared bat. They roost in old houses, castles, churches, etc., sometimes singly but often in the company of other species such as pipistrelles. This bat is well named, with ears averaging 35 millimetres in length, not much shorter than the entire length of the head and body. When sleeping, the ears are folded back along the body and can be very difficult to see, so causing some initial confusion with identification. They are highly manoeuvrable in flight, hunting close to large shrubs and trees, where they take insects offthe leaves. Long-eareds probably hunt more by sight and the sounds made by their prey than by echolocation. There are only about a dozen known roosts in Kerry, with colonies numbering from one to 54.

These three species are probably our most common bats. Our knowledge of the distribution of the other four species is sketchy. Ireland is an important stronghold for Leisler's bats, which have become rare in Europe. Only six sites have been recorded in Kerry, mainly in old houses, with colony size varying from one to 30. They are our largest species, with thick fur which covers the forearm and part of

TABLE 15
KERRY MAMMALS LISTED IN THE *IRISH RED DATA BOOK* – VERTEBRATES

INTERNATIONALLY IMPORTANT SPECIES	SPECIES THREATENED OR EXTINCT
Hedgehog	Whiskered bat
Lesser-horseshoe bat	Natterer's bat
Daubenton's bat	Grey wolf
Leisler's bat	
Pipistrelle bat	
Brown long-eared bat	
Irish hare	
Pine marten	
Badger	
Otter	

the wing membrane. In winter they are thought to migrate from quite long distances to form a few large roosts in caves and cellars.

Daubenton's bat prefers to roost and hunt over water. They are a medium-sized species, generally roosting in crevices under bridges and other buildings near water. Daubenton's specialise in catching insects over lakes, rivers and ponds, using their large feet to trawl the water surface for insects, particularly those just hatching. At least eleven colonies have been recorded in the county, with from one to twenty animals.

Natterer's bat is a medium sized species with a diagnostic fringe of hair along the edge of the tail membrane, that patch of skin which joins the legs and tail. They are one of our most elusive species, and only two colonies are known to occur in Kerry, with one and fifteen animals respectively. A colony of 150 which occurred in an old church deserted the site when it was restored, a common problem which many species face. Natterer's frequently feed on the ground, catching earwigs, centipedes and other invertebrates. They prefer to roost in large open roost spaces such as churches and old barns. Most bats swarm outside a roost in the morning before retiring for the day, but Natterer's swarm inside, where no one sees them, so they can be easily missed. Natterer's require direct uninterrupted flight to a permanently open aperture in the joists, so blocking up their entrance way during restoration will effectively exclude them.

Long-eared bat

Whiskered bats are our rarest species, with

only 34 roosts in Ireland, all quite small. In Kerry, they are only known from three sites near Killarney but are probably more widespread. One of the most recent discoveries was in 1994, when one animal, which somehow managed to end up on the floor of a hallway, was saved from being swept out by a sharp-eyed naturalist!

Despite being fully protected under the Wildlife Act, bats face many threats. The chemicals used to treat roof timbers are often extremely toxic to bats. Non-toxic varieties are obtainable and should be requested by anybody considering such treatment. Many old bridges have recently had their cracks and crevices filled with liquid cement by local authorities, entombing bats within their roosts. The felling of old trees, bulldozing of hedgerows and knocking of old houses all reduce bat habitat. Dr Kate McAney, working for the National Parks and Wildlife Service and the Vincent Wildlife Trust has done sterling work on improving our knowledge of bat distribution and habits in Ireland. She has produced an excellent educational Bat Pack, obtainable free from the N.P.W.S. This should be read by anybody interested in bats and by those involved in building restoration or bridge maintenance.

Any keen naturalist can contribute valuable information on the distribution of bats. One can search old buildings and other likely sites for signs of bats and identify remains of bats found dead. By using a bat-detector, (an easily made electronic device which converts their ultrasonic squeaks and sounds into audible clicks), our knowledge of the distribution and habits of these animals can be greatly extended.

AMPHIBIANS

NATTERJACK TOADS

The night was quite still and the croaking could be heard from Kieran's house over a kilometre away. After walking down a series of boreens, we quietly stalked to the water's edge The croaking stopped, only to restart further away after a few moments. We decided to sit on a large boulder and await events. In the gathering darkness, an otter swam past less than 15 metres away, its head just breaking the surface. The croaking started up again, seemingly right beside us, but the source remained invisible among the low vegetation. Then we noticed a tiny ripple among the waterplants. In the narrow beam of a small torch, we saw a small frog-like animal, but darker, with a yellow stripe along its spine – our first natterjack toad of the evening.

Natterjacks are Kerry's highest profile amphibian and Ireland's only toad species. They have a distinctive running gait, rather than the hopping motion of frogs, and the yellow dorsal stripe is diagnostic. Because of poisonous substances in their skin, natterjacks are rarely preyed upon by otters or other predators. Their voice is among the loudest and most strident animal noises to be heard anywhere in Europe. Except for a couple of other locations on the south coast where they have been introduced, they occur nowhere else in Ireland, and Kerry's population is very important in European terms. Even in Kerry their distribution is restricted due to their quite specific habitat requirements. They are confined to a few coastal sites around Dingle and Tralee bays, with a small population at Derrynane. Natterjacks are a *Red Data Book* species and protected under the Wildlife Act.

Natterjacks need open, sandy areas with short vegetation, and access to shallow spawning ponds nearby. The sandy soil allows them to dig burrows which they shelter in. This habitat provides a warmer micro-environment than normally found elsewhere. Adults range in size from four to eight centimetres, weighing up to 21 grams. Females are larger than males. Adults are most active between dusk and midnight, and have a home range of 200-400 square metres. They are active hunters; their running gait allows them to chase their invertebrate prey at speed

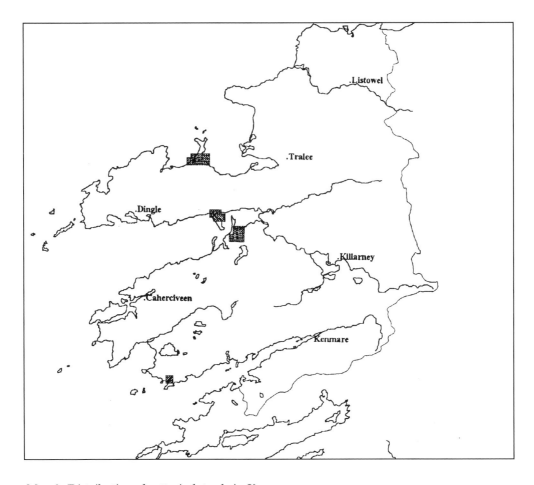

Map 9: Distribution of natterjack toads in Kerry

over short distances. Their burrows average 15-20 centimetres in length, but they can also be found under stones, logs and other objects.

Natterjacks have a long mating season from April to June, but a significant proportion of matings occur during the first two weeks of the season. Males have two different mating strategies. Some visit one pond, and call from it during the season, others move irregularly between ponds. The same animals use the same strategy each year. Females are more attracted to ponds with the highest density of calling males. Movements attract the male's attention up to two metres away, and the first animal of whatever sex will be quickly approached and seized – a frustrating and time-consuming behaviour. When a female is finally caught, the male clutches the female about her abdomen in a position called amplexus. This is a male's way of denying other males access to the female. Once a male couples with a female, he remains in amplexus with her until she is ready to spawn, which is usually on the same night she arrives at the pond. Their spawn is quite distinctive, being laid in long chains, with each female laying up to 4,000 eggs.

Their tadpoles are smaller than those of frogs, and suffer from a peculiar form of competition with them. If both species are present in the same pond, the presence of the frog tadpoles inhibits the growth, development rate and survival of the natterjacks' tadpoles. This is caused by the presence of a unicellular organism in tadpole faeces which is known to cause this inhibition.

THE COMMON FROG

In the middle of January, when winter winds and rains are still making life seem very raw, it always comes as a pleasant surprise to find the first frog-spawn appearing in ponds and puddles all over the region. Although the texts state that spawning normally begins in February, it probably begins earlier in Kerry because of our mild winters. I have found spawn on 22 December! Common frogs will travel quite long distances to reach traditional ponds, and it is not unusual to come across such mass movements. During mating male and females remain in amplexus for some days. When the female is ready she lays 1,000-3,000 eggs which the male simultaneously fertilises. The gelatinous covering of the eggs swells immediately on absorbing water, giving the familiar appearance of frogspawn. Any semi-permanent small water body will suffice, though in a particularly dry summer some of the smaller ponds may almost dry out. This leaves the hapless tadpoles thrashing about in any muddy areas remaining and exposed to a wide variety of predators. If they survive predators and drought, the tadpoles develop into froglets after about three months.

The common frog is widely distributed about the county, but may have suffered local declines due to land drainage. They feed on a wide variety of invertebrates including spiders, beetles, earthworms and slugs. They are themselves important prey of herons, otters, and other animals.

SMOOTH NEWTS

Our third amphibian is the smooth newt. Little is known about its distribution, but they occur in habitats such as bog pools, overgrown lowland ponds and flooded quarries. They measure up to 10 centimetres in length, are greenish-brown above, spotted with dark flecks of green or black. The sexes differ somewhat, particularly during the breeding season, when the male develops a bright, orange-coloured belly with dark spots and a dorsal crest. Outside the spawning season they live on land, hiding by day and emerging at night to feed on worms, slugs, snails and various insect species. During the breeding season they prefer ponds with hard water and a relatively high concentration of metallic ions. Courtship is an elaborate affair. When the female is receptive, the male places a small bag of sperm on the bed of the pond. She moves over it, taking the bag up into her cloaca. Fertilisation then occurs internally.

The female lays her eggs singly among the leaves of aquatic vegetation, secreting a fluid which seals it firmly to the leaf. The tadpoles have three pairs of feathery external gills, and unlike frog tadpoles, develop their front legs earlier than their hindlegs. Most young newts leave the water in August or September, but some overwinter still in tadpole form.

KERRY'S REPTILES

If you are out walking the hills or bogs on a warm summer's day, your eye may be attracted by the scurrying of a long, slender creature among the grass or heather. If you are especially lucky, you may be fortunate enough to spot one of these elusive creatures, a viviparous lizard, basking on a rock. Measuring up to 18 centimetres in length, they are our only native reptile and are usually yellowish or brownish in colour. They occur at altitudes of up to 800 metres. Being cold-blooded, they require the sun to warm their bodies to about 30^{0} C before they can hunt their prey of spiders, small worms and insects. Thus lizards normally start their day by basking, flattening their bodies against the ground to maximise their exposure to the sun's warming rays.

Lizards overwinter in hibernation, living on reserves of stored fat. Emergence occurs about mid-March, males appearing before females. Individuals often have their own den or burrow, where they shelter at night or in bad weather. They spend several hours per

A viviparous lizard

day hunting, patrolling their territories along regular pathways, which invariably take advantage of sunny areas. A few weeks after emergence, females will enter males' territories to mate. Unlike most reptiles, the young are born live, in litters of 3 to 15. They grow rapidly, and by hibernation time in the autumn have moulted two or three times.

SNAKES IN KERRY

A couple from Northern Ireland holidaying in Kerry during 1994 received quite a shock when they found a long, thin snake in their rented bungalow near Tralee. It was caught by Gardai, who transported it to Killarney, where it was identified by local naturalist Toby Hodd as a garter snake. These attractive yellow and black reptiles are natives of North America, but being docile and non-poisonous are commonly kept as pets. They normally feed on earthworms and fish. This specimen was nearly 60 centimetres long and about as thick as an index finger. It probably escaped from its previous owners while they were on holidays, and may have been present in the house for some time.

INSECTS AND OTHER TERRESTRIAL INVERTEBRATES

THE IMPORTANCE OF INVERTEBRATES

The invertebrates comprise the microscopic protozoa, worms, molluscs, and arthropods, which includes spiders, crustaceans, myriapoda and insects. Approximately 200,000 species have been described for Europe alone compared to about 900 vertebrates. Worldwide, 15-20,000 species new to science are described each year. The sheer biomass of invertebrates is staggering. In Europe each hectare of soil produces up to one tonne of invertebrates annually. To this one could add 100 kilos of flying invertebrates produced in a temperate European forest. This huge volume of invertebrates has a major function in degrading and mineralising plant and animal organic material, returning it to the soil for re-use. By their physical action on soil or their elimination of processes which restrict soil productivity, invertebrates are crucial in assisting plant productivity. We tend to take all this for granted, and do not begin to appreciate the consequences if this system were to break down.

Apart from their important biological function, we depend upon many invertebrates for our food supply. In both temperate and tropical regions invertebrates constitute an important food source. Marine and freshwater crustaceans (crabs, lobsters), and marine and terrestrial molluscs (mussels, oysters, snails) are all utilised as foodstuffs and sustain employment in farming, harvesting and commercial activities. Invertebrates are vital to soil fertility, and more than 80% of our fruits, vegetables, and natural textile fibres, as well as some medicinal preparations depend upon invertebrates for fertilisation and production. The potential of invertebrates as a source of further medicinal preparations is unknown. In agriculture, the use of biological pest control methods has been found to be more practical, economical and environmentally friendly than artificial ones. Many invertebrate groups are increasingly being used as highly sensitive indicators of environmental quality.

Kerry has attracted the attention of invertebrate specialists, particularly entomologists, for nearly 150 years. This interest probably began with an English collector called Mr Weaver, who published an article in 1848. Since then Kerry has possibly been visited by more entomologists than any other part of the country and some have chosen to live here. These include Edwin Bullock, a renowned specialist on beetles, Raymond Haynes, who lived in Killarney and specialised in Lepidoptera and Tim Lavery of Castlemaine, whose particular interest is empids, or dance flies. This is a group of predacious flies which are frequently used as environmental indicators.

BUTTERFLIES

Of the 750 species of butterfly which occur in Europe, only 28 species are native to Ireland. A further eight species are migrants to our shores. Butterflies are under serious threat wherever they occur due to clearance and degradation of habitats. Even in Kerry butterfly numbers are declining seriously, and much needs to be done to stop this decline.

While butterfly caterpillars feed on plant leaves, the adults mainly feed on nectar from flowers. This is sipped through their long proboscis, which is rolled up when not in use. Life for butterflies is fraught with dangers. They are subject to predation from a wide range of insects, birds and mammals, including spiders, wasps, and dragonflies, mice and frogs, and many more. The caterpillars are important food sources for many predators. Both the caterpillars and adults use many ingenious adaptations to avoid being eaten. These include camouflage, being distasteful to eat, or using eye-spots on their wings to startle would-be attackers.

To improve your chances of attracting butterflies to your garden, you should create a special wild area, allowing native plants such as nettles, clovers, native grasses and devil's-bit scabious to thrive. Planting flowering bushes such as buddleia, hebe, and honeysuckle will also enhance the attractiveness of your garden.

The butterflies of mountainous regions tend to be active, fast flying species. One such species is the large heath, found locally in areas of wet moorland and bogs. The bright green caterpillar feeds on white-beak sedge or cotton grass, overwintering among the roots before completing its growth in spring. Smaller but more distinctive than the large heath is the green hairstreak, which also occurs in various lowland habitats. At rest, the adults can be very difficult to spot, but in flight, their small size and bright green colouration are distinctive. They are very fast flyers – the greyhounds of the butterfly world. The caterpillars feed on gorse, heathers and brambles, pupating under a loose web at the base of the plant. The pupa produces a strange squeaking sound if disturbed, a remarkable defensive behaviour.

THE MIGRANT BUTTERFLY RECORDING SCHEME

Three Milltown-based students entered the 1995 Aer Lingus Young Scientists competition with a study of migrant butterflies and moths. Karen Cronin, Kerina Foley and Cathriona O'Dowd, were all students at Milltown Presentation Secondary school. Their project was encouraged by their teacher, Tim Lavery, himself an experienced entomologist. The girls computerised the data from the Irish Migrant Lepidoptera Survey, which is the second-longest running scheme in Europe. By using this information in combination with weather data, they were able to compute the possibility of tracking where migrants had originated from. At least 52 migrant species have been recorded in Ireland, so the girls concentrated their efforts on the painted lady, a butterfly which frequently turns up in Kerry. In 1993 Karen took on the responsibility of migrant lepidoptera recorder for Ireland, and in 1995 became the co-ordinator for the new European Migrant Lepidoptera Survey, covering 10 countries.

One of our largest woodland butterflies, with orange-coloured wings speckled and streaked with black spots, is the silver-washed fritillary. This butterfly is so called because the greenish underside of its wings are streaked with silver scales. When males locate a potential partner, the two butterflies circle upwards in a series of loops, and it is believed that the male releases an 'arrestant' pheromone to induce the female to settle and mate. The female lays her eggs in crevices in tree bark. Although the larvae hatch during August, they stay active only long enough to eat their egg cases before finding a spot to hibernate. In spring, the caterpillars descend to the ground to begin feeding on their foodplants, the violets. Much rarer is the purple hairstreak, which is very scarce throughout Ireland, but occurs in the Killarney valley. The males have a purple patch across the forewings. The species occurs in oak woodland, the caterpillars feeding mainly on the young foliage of oak. It is not often seen, as the adults usually fly high among the canopy. The adults sometimes feed on the honeydew deposited by aphids. A very scarce but distinctive species, confined mainly to limestone areas, is the brimstone. Males are a beautiful sulphur-yellow colour, females are lemon-yellow. The caterpillars feed on both common and alder buckthorn, both rare species in Co. Kerry. This may well be the species which gave rise to the term 'butterfly', because of its striking colouration.

One of our best known and easily identified butterflies is the peacock, with its large 'eyes' on each wing. Peacock caterpillars feed on nettles, while the adults sip at the flowers of bramble and hogweed. Adults overwinter in hollow trees and outhouses before reappearing in early spring. If disturbed during hibernation, they can produce a hissing sound by rubbing their wings together, so frightening off or confusing would-be predators. Male peacocks are highly territorial and will defend their territories against other males. They are so aggressive that they will investigate any large dark object passing overhead and can be confused by low-flying birds and falling leaves. If the 'intruder' is a female, courtship and hopeful-ly, mating will follow. Though male and female peacocks look similar, you can deduce the sex of a butterfly by flicking a stone over it: a male peacock will fly upwards to investigate, a female will show no reaction.

The orange tip is a species of open, damp areas, where its caterpillars feed on lady's smock and related plants. Only the male has the orange-tipped forewings, which are hidden when the wings are folded at rest. These are one of the earliest species to be seen in spring, as the adults are on the wing during April and May. Orange tips are one of the species most affected by drainage and 'improvement' of wet meadows. Another butterfly of open situations is the small copper, found in fields, hedgerows and woodland edges. These have a wingspan of less than three centimetres and metallic orange forewings with black spots. Their flight is quick and darting. The caterpillars feed on dock and sorrel. The marsh fritillary is a species associated with certain types of old pasture in Ireland. It is regarded as an internationally threatened species due to its recent decline in certain parts of Europe. The larvae feed under the protection of a silken web which is spun around the food plant, devil's-bit scabious. They hibernate over winter under the cover of these 'tents', before continuing to grow and feed from February onwards, finally emerging as adults in late May. Males emerge a few days earlier than females. Some large colonies of marsh fritillaries exist in Kerry, mainly at coastal sites on the Iveragh and Dingle peninsulas.

The small blue is a scarce species confined to sand dune areas, and all of Kerry's dune systems have important colonies of them. The adults are a powdery blue colour with white fringes to their wings. The caterpillars feed on the devel-oping seeds of kidney vetch.

The wood white, a frail looking white butterfly with a slim body, has an inter-esting distribution in Kerry. They are a species of limestone areas, their larvae feeding on meadow vetchling, clovers and bird's-foot trefoil. Apart from the Killarney area, their Kerry distribution is mainly along trainlines. This is partly due to the fact that the ballast used in the building of train lines is normally lime-stone, which provides good conditions for the growth of their food plants. The profile of many of the cuts through which the lines run reflects the sun's heat inwards, providing a degree of local warmth and shelter from strong winds, an important point for this weak flyer. These same factors, along with the overgrown and relatively undisturbed nature of many such sites ensure that train lines are good places for many insects and other creatures.

MOTHS

Moths are closely related to butterflies, but most people are far less aware of them. Most fly by night and many are difficult to identify, but as a group they are well worth our attention. Some species tend to be extremely abundant, and many are important food sources for other insects and particularly birds. Some birds such as tits have adapted their breeding season to take advantage of the superabundance of caterpillars during early summer. Many moth species are of commercial interest to us, as they can damage or defoliate trees, flowers and vegetable crops. Night-flying species are actively preyed upon by bats, and many have developed interesting anti-predator defences.

The fox moth is a common moorland species. The adults are chunky, rust-coloured insects, with two narrow pale stripes on each forewing. The caterpillars are frequently seen on moorland and bogs, where they feed on heather, bilberry and bog myrtle. They are a large caterpillar, black with dense brown hairs, with shorter, redder hairs down the back. These hairs are part of the caterpillar's defences, being irritating to the eyes of any predator which might try eating it.

A large, dramatically coloured moth is the garden tiger, a common species of woodlands, parks and gardens, where the caterpillars feed on a wide variety of wild and garden plants. The adults have mottled brown and cream coloured forewings, with black-dotted orange hindwings. Though brightly coloured, this moth flies mainly at night, when it is often attracted to lights. Another common and closely related species is the white ermine. The adults are brilliant white with small black specks, and have what looks like a white, hairy cloak thrown about their head and thorax. The caterpillars feed on the foliage of many herbaceous plants and are often found in gardens.

Female emperor moth

The green oak tortrix is a small species of oak woodlands, whose numbers can increase so enormously in certain years that whole forests of oaks can be stripped of their leaves by the caterpillars. In the early 1990s there were so many tortrix caterpillars feeding on the oaks in some Killarney woods that you could hear the rain of caterpillar frass (droppings) on a still day. The trees were so bare by June that one would have been forgiven for thinking it was mid-winter. However, the oaks put out a second flush of leaves, and no long term damage was done.

Two species of daytime-flying moths are the cinnabar and the six-spot burnet.

Both are basically black with red spots, a good indication that both are poisonous to eat. The cinnabar obtains its poison from its principal food plants, ragwort and groundsel, both of which are rich in poisonous alkaloids. These are stored in the caterpillars' bodies in a form which does not kill them, but proves a highly effective deterrent against predators. The poisons are passed on through the chrysalis to the adult, making it one of our most poisonous moths. The six-spot burnet feeds on clover, vetches and trefoils and are most common in coastal areas. Their bodies contain cyanide derivatives, which the caterpillars obtain from their food plants.

ANTI-PREDATOR RESPONSES OF MOTHS

The principal enemies of night-flying moths are bats, and the moths have developed a variety of methods to avoid becoming 'takeaway' snacks. Many moths have bodies which are covered with soft hairs; a sound-absorbing integument which acts like 'acoustic camouflage' and hardly reflects the ultrasound of their enemies. Others have achieved virtually noiseless flight by having a narrow fringe of hairs along the rear edge of their wings. This avoids the formation of air eddies which produce noise.

The Noctuidae, Geometridae and the Arctiidae have special ears for listening into the enemy's transmitter and may take early evasive action on hearing the bat's high-pitched squeaks, including performing intricate loop-the-loops, zig-zagging, or dropping to the ground and walking. Many produce a distinctive, high-pitched sound which is audible to bats. Some of these species are distasteful to bats and it is thought that the bats learn to associate this sound with a distasteful insect and do not attack. Recent work on an American species of bat has shown that the moth species under study only emitted their sound when the bat was at the final stage of its attack. The moth's sound seemed to mimic the echo of the bat's call, not the calls themselves. Thus the moths were effectively jamming the bat's echo-location signals.

A very rare species for which Kerry is probably the Irish headquarters is the satin lutestring. It is a nondescript brown coloured species, found in mature woodland, where its larvae feed on birch. The species is single-brooded, and is on the wing during August and September. The welsh clearwing is a small, narrow-bodied moth with transparent wings trimmed with brown. It is found only in Kerry and Cork and is very rare in Britain. It is a day-flying moth which uses traditional sites, different generations using the same trees each year. It is only found in old birchwoods and may be an indicator of really ancient woodlands. The welsh clearwing is one of the few insect species whose larvae feed within living birch trees, leaving distinctive 5 millimetre wide holes in

Six-spot burnet moths

the trunks. The warm, south-facing cliffs overlooking the north shore of Dingle bay are the only Irish location of the sandhill rustic, first discovered in 1962. The larvae feed on the roots of sand couch grass and hard-grass and the adults are on the wing during August and September.

THE MYSTERY OF THE WHITE-PROMINENT

One of the most sought-after moths, known from only two, possibly three, sites in Britain and Ireland, is the white prominent. It is a small white species measuring up to 42 millimetres in length, with distinctive orange markings on the forewings. The white prominent is widely distributed on the Continent, but was only positively recorded once in Britain about 130 years ago. This gem was first recorded in Kerry on the Herbert Estate at Muckross, in 1858 and again in 1859, by Peter Bouchard, a lepidopterist from Surrey. It was then collected sporadically during the late 1800s and into the early part of this century from districts as far apart as Glencar and Ardtully, near Kenmare. The last known specimen collected was taken by Mrs Lucas, near Killarney, in 1938. Although it hasn't been seen since then, despite extensive searching, its preferred habitat of wet birch-rich areas still remain, and it has been predicted to turn up again.

GRASSHOPPERS, CRICKETS, AND THEIR RELATIVES

If you spend any time outdoors on a summer's day, particularly in open, sunny areas, you will probably hear the distinctive reeling 'song' of grasshoppers and with difficulty may catch a glimpse of one before it leaps away. This group of insects is readily identified by their enlarged hind legs, used for jumping, and by the males habit of 'singing'. Some species produce the song by rubbing the hind legs against the forewings. This is known as stridulation, and serves to bring the two sexes together. Each species has its own characteristic song, some of which are identifiable to the human ear, although some species do not stridulate. Grasshoppers are vegetarian and diurnal in habit, being most active on warm, sunny days. They lay their eggs below ground in clusters of up to 14, in a tough case called an egg pod. A frothy liquid is then poured over it, which solidifies rapidly, forming a spongy protective layer for the eggs over winter.

Our largest grasshopper is the large marsh with females measuring up to 35 millimetres. Their distribution is restricted to boggy areas in the west and south west, where they are associated with bog asphodel and cotton-grass. The first adults rarely appear before July. It stridulates quite loudly, producing a pronounced 'ticking' sound at the rate of one to three per second. The mottled grasshopper is a much smaller species, grey and brown in colour, and with distinctly clubbed antennae. The females measure up to 18 millimetres. It is typical of drier moorlands and sand dunes, where it feeds on grasses.

Crickets are mostly omnivorous, devouring other insects as well as plant material. They are distinguished from grasshoppers by their long thread-like antennae, which usually sweep back past their abdomen. Females of some species have large blade-like ovipositors. The speckled bush cricket measures up to 14 millimetres in females, males being somewhat smaller. They are a bright green colour with numerous small dark brown spots. This species normally occurs in sunlit patches of scrub, usually within a metre of the ground. Bramble patches are good sites. The eggs are laid on plant stems and hatch in May and June. Speckled bush crickets are unable to fly, moving in a series of short hops. Their song is faint and barely audible to our hearing beyond a distance of a metre or so.

The house cricket was introduced to Ireland some centuries ago. It measures up to two centimetres in length, is a yellowish or greyish-brown colour and are more flattened in appearance than bush crickets. The females lay several hundred eggs in concealed places, which hatch after two or three months, depending on temperature. They are omnivorous, feeding on most kinds of organic material, but due primarily to increasing standards of hygiene, have become scarce in recent years. Their song is described as a bird-like warble, normally produced at dusk and overnight.

BUGS

The order of Hemiptera (bugs) contains over 75,000 species worldwide. They naturally show tremendous variation in form, but all species possess a piercing beak called the rostrum, which is like a miniature hypodermic needle. The presence of this rostrum distinguishes bugs from beetles, which have biting mouthparts. The rostrum is normally folded back beneath the bug's body and is brought into play to suck juices from plants and other animals. Some, such as the aphids, are serious crop and garden pests, reducing yields and transmitting diseases. Most are harmless to our economic interests. Many species occur in Kerry – one entomologist caught 92 species in one week during 1981. Some of the families which occur are examined below.

LEAFHOPPERS AND FROGHOPPERS

As their name suggests, these are all small jumping bugs found in a wide variety of habitats. The nymphs of most species of froghoppers live in masses of froth, which is generally attached to various plants upon which they feed. This gives rise to their other common names of cuckoo-spit insects and spittle bugs. Some species which have been recently recorded in Kerry include *Tachycixius pilosus*, found in Derreen wood near Kenmare, *Javesella dubia* and *Javesella obscurella*, found on Rossdohan island in Kenmare bay, and *Oncopsis albi* found near Muckross House, Killarney.

SHIELD BUGS

Shield bugs are so-called because of their characteristic shape. Their other name is stink bugs, because some species emit pungent fluids when alarmed. Many species hibernate over winter as adults, reappearing again in spring. The hawthorn shield bug feeds on the leaves and fruit of hawthorns and other trees such as whitebeam or oak. The adults are a green colour with red markings on their wing cases. *Elasmucha grisea* is a species which is known to exhibit parental care for its eggs and larvae. The female lays 30-40 eggs on a birch leaf, in a compact diamond-shaped mass. She maintains guard over the eggs for the two to three weeks which they take to hatch. After hatching, when the female moves around, the larvae follow, using their antennae to stay in contact. She is not merely a passive protector, but will interpose herself between the brood and an introduced twig or finger.

SOME OTHER BUGS

The marine bug is a small, predatory greenish creature which lives among rocks and seaweeds on the lower shore, generally in family groups. It has a mainly Atlantic distribution – the south coast of Ireland, parts of the Channel coast, and the Atlantic coasts of France and Spain. *Dichrooscytus rufipennis* is a bright green and red capsid bug, found only in Kerry and Dublin. Its principal food plant is Scots pine, although it occasionally turns to other conifers. The larva is also bright green with crimson wingpads. Adults are on the wing from June to August.

BEETLES

This is the largest order of insects, with over 300,000 species described worldwide. Beetles have tough, horny front wings, known as elytra, which usually cover the whole abdomen, meeting neatly in the mid-line of the body. Most species can fly, but they spend the majority of their time on or close to the ground, where their tough elytra provides valuable protection. They exploit many different habitats and foods, including other insects, spiders etc., dung, living plant material and the dry wood of dead trees. The ability of beetles to exploit such a wide range of foods is made possible by their possession of powerful, biting jaws. Some species are major pests of grain, wood and other valuable commodities, and are thus of economic interest.

The green tiger beetle is one of our more dramatic looking species. They are common on sandy or rocky coastal areas, where they can be seen basking. Though somewhat variable in colour, they are typically a bronzed emerald green above with yellowish spots and have coppery-coloured legs and undersides. They are one of the fastest-running insect species, moving at speeds of up to 60 centimetres per second when chasing other insect prey. The larva lives in a vertical shaft up to

30 centimetres deep, waiting at the entrance for passing insects, especially ants, which they grab with their powerful jaws.

Soldier beetles have relatively soft elytra. *Cantharis livida* is an orange-brown colour with a dark abdomen, common in coastal areas. They are often seen on flowers such as sea holly, searching and probing among the flowerheads for soft-bodied prey. Mating takes a long time compared to some other insects, which is why one often finds mating pairs. The larvae hunt on the ground.

The black and orange sexton beetle is one of nature's undertakers. These beetles bury the carcasses of small birds, mammals, etc., as food for their offspring. They are reputed to be able to smell a carcass over three kilometres away. While her eggs are hatching, the female protects the carcass from other predators, parasites and 'undertakers', eating any other maggots which may hatch before hers. The large, rounded, black dor beetle is an important 'recycler'. It is one of the dung beetles, which specialise in burying the droppings of various mammals. Different

---

BIRCH AND ITS INVERTEBRATE FAUNA

Ask the average Irish naturalist which native tree is the most important for invertebrate fauna and you would probably be told it was oak, or perhaps elm. Few would appreciate the importance of birch. Faunistically, birch has probably the most complete invertebrate fauna of any tree species in Ireland, including poorly represented components such as old-tree species, which need dead and decaying wood.

One such group are the attractively marked longhorn beetles, so-called because of their exceptionally long antennae. Sixteen species occur in Kerry, including the only Irish record of Anoplodera sexguttata, *which is rarely seen anywhere in Europe. They are recognised as being more efficient at dispersal than most other insect groups. Many species are among the first wave of invaders to colonise dead and decaying wood, particularly oak and elm. However, Ireland has only 20 indigenous species of longhorns compared to 57 species found in Britain. Dr Martin Speight, an entomologist with the National Parks and Wildlife Service, has written a very enlightening paper on the reasons for the paucity of these beetles in Ireland. He argues that the principal reason is the lack of mature and over-mature trees. He estimates that more than 50% of the cerambycid (longhorn beetle family) fauna has been eradicated in historical times due to man's clearance of forest. This phenomenon is not restricted to this one family. The oak forest fauna in Ireland shows this same feature for many insect families, due, he believes, to faunal eradication by man's activities.*

Birch has been present in the country since just after the close of the Ice Age, so has had time to build up a diverse invertebrate fauna. It is a fast-growing tree with a relatively short life-span, so there is a good turnover of ageing and decaying trees. This is an important attraction for many insect species. Birch, however, is generally regarded as a poor timber and firewood tree and has been neglected by man compared to more valuable species like oak and elm, which are usually cut in their prime. So the saproxylic community of birch has survived while that of oak and other species has been depleted.

species utilise different types of droppings – cattle, rabbit, etc. The female rolls pieces of the droppings into small balls and then buries them in specially-dug shafts up to 60 centimetres deep. After laying an egg on top of the dung ball, she defends it from predators until the larva hatches. The devil's coach horse is one of the rove beetles. In Irish folklore it was a symbol of corruption, reputed to be able to kill on sight. It is a long, black beetle which, when disturbed, cocks its abdomen upwards and opens its jaws in a threatening manner.

Click beetles are so-called because of their ability to leap into the air and right themselves when turned over on their backs. This action is accompanied by a loud click. One of the rarest species in Kerry is *Ampedus pomonae*, a bright red beetle, whose only known British or Irish location is Lickeen wood in Glencar. Its larvae live in decaying birch trees. Another county speciality is *Pyropterus nigroruber*, a one centimetre long, red-brown flattened beetle. It also forms part of Ireland's old-forest fauna. Its larvae live colonially in rotten deciduous trees, in wood which has been subject to attack by brown rot fungi. First recorded in south-west Kerry in 1866, and very rare in Britain, it is one of the species prone to having its habitat destroyed by the removal of rotten wood.

A montane rarity is *Stenus glacialis*, a small beetle thought to be a glacial relict. In 1993 Dr Ken Bond, a Cork-based entomologist specialising in micro-lepidoptera or micro-moths, and Sean Ryan, mountaineer and expert on red deer, came across a specimen of *Stenus glacialis* under a stone near the summit of Carrauntouhil. This species has only been recorded twice before in Ireland, both from montane sites in Mayo and Donegal.

DIPTERA – TRUE FLIES

Leatherjackets are well known to most gardeners and farmers. These grey, tough-skinned grubs are the larvae of the crane flies or daddy-long-legs. The most common species is *Tipula oleracea*, whose larvae feed just under the soil surface on the roots of grasses and other plants. If you watch carefully in short grass areas from June onwards you may spot the female laying her eggs. Her body will be arched up into the air, with her long ovipositer inserted almost vertically into the ground. Each female will lay several hundred black, seed-like eggs, which hatch after a fortnight. The grubs are much sought after by rooks, hooded crows, starlings and other birds, which will use their strong beaks to probe among the grass tufts for the juicy morsels.

Closely related to *T. oleracea* is *Ctenophora pectinicornis*, a species of cranefly first discovered in Ireland in May 1992 by Martin Speight. *C. pectinicornis* is a large black and yellow fly up to three centimetres in length, which makes the fact that it has escaped our attention up until recently all the more remarkable. Dr Speight points out that this is probably because it is very localised in occurrence, being only found in a few hectares of old woodland on the Muckross peninsula. Its larvae feed within the rotten trunks of old birch, alder and other trees. The adults are unusual among craneflies in being on the wing during daylight hours, especially on calm, sunny afternoons.

The empididae or danceflies are all small to medium-sized, mainly bristly flies. They are so-called because of the habits of some species of congregating in swarms over ponds, ditches and even small puddles. Here they perform rapid aerial manouverings, seemingly 'dancing' up and down in intricate flight patterns. Both sexes have a stiff, downward-projecting proboscis adapted for piercing. They are predatory on other insects, chiefly diptera, chasing and catching their prey in flight. Dance flies are found in a wide variety of habitats, from mountains to saltmarshes.

The largest species is *Empis tessellata*, a dull, grey fly, sometimes found in large numbers on hawthorn or umbellifer blossoms. One common species, *Hilara maura*, performs intricate swarming dances. They mate in flight, the male catching a small fly such as a midge, wrapping it in a ball of silken thread and offering it to the female. After accepting this gift, she sucks the juices during copulation and discards the remains after the mating ceremony is complete. *Tachypeza nubila* is a small, elongated, glossy black fly, usually found from May to September running in a swift, jerky fashion on trees or fence posts. Rather than taking to the wing when threatened, it runs around the tree trunk out of sight.

At least 25 of the scarcer species have been recorded in Kerry. Some of these are confined to restricted habitats such as the spray zone of waterfalls. Two such specialists are *Clinocera bipunctata* and *Wiedmannia insularis*, which are mainly found among algae and moss close to waterfalls and streams.

Xylophagus ater is a rare species of Irish diptera, first recorded in Ireland in 1928. It has been found in only five Irish counties, including Kerry, where it has been recorded in the Derrycunnihy and Muckross areas of the Killarney valley. The adult gives the appearance of being a rather delicate-looking fly and is a weak flier, with a long, narrow body and an overall blackish colour. It is confined to relict patches of ancient woodland and pasture woodland in the wetter, mountainous parts of the county. It breeds in recently dead broad-leaved trees, the larvae developing beneath the bark. They feed on other insect larvae, but their mode of attack is uncertain; it is thought they may first inflict an injury on a healthy larva and then wait for it to weaken before feeding.

Odinia bolentina is a small fly associated with old woodlands. It is attractively marked with a grey, dusted appearance and banded legs. Its larvae are predatory on the larvae or pupae of wood and fungus-boring beetles. Adults are usually found on bracket fungi. Females are thought to lay their eggs on the underside of these fungi, and when they hatch their larvae prey on the grubs within the brackets.

TICKS AND LYME DISEASE

Ticks have been found to transmit a debilitating bacterial infection to humans called Lyme disease, called after the town of Old Lyme, Connecticut, USA, where serious epidemics of arthritis were first noted among school-children in 1975. It is not a new disease as such, as it had been first noted as long ago as 1908 in Sweden, and the link with ticks was made in 1921. However, it wasn't until recently that the causal organism, a spirochaete bacterium called Borrelia burgdorferi was identified. The commonest symptom in infected people is a spreading rash, which occurs in about 60% of cases, sometimes accompanied by flu-like symptoms. If not caught and treated at this early stage when it is easily treated with antibiotics, other problems such as meningitis, arthritis and neuritis may occur.

Not every tick, however, can transmit the infection, and not every individual who becomes infected will develop further symptoms. One Irish survey has revealed a background infection in people without symptoms of up to 15%, yet the number of diagnosed cases of Lyme disease remains very low. But anyone who walks in tick habitat, i.e,. long grass, bracken, etc., should take care to expose as little skin as possible to ticks, and should check themselves as a matter of routine afterwards and remove any ticks which they might have picked up.

HOVERFLIES

A walk about the countryside or in your garden on a summer's day will almost certainly bring you into contact with a member of the Syrphidae or hoverfly family. This is a large, fascinating family of nectar-feeding insects, with a particular fondness for umbellifers. They have a distinctive hovering and darting flight, with the ability to fly forwards, backwards and sideways in an effortless manner. They are often very colourful, and many are mimics of wasps and bees. The larvae occupy a wide variety of habitats and include vegetarians, predators and scavengers.

Early flowers such as the winter heliotrope are particularly attractive to honeybees and other insects in late winter. Among the bees you may see a bee-mimic, the drone fly, a species of hoverfly named for its close resemblance to a honey-bee drone. Unlike bees and like all flies, it has just a single pair of large wings. The larvae of the drone fly live in stagnant ditches, farmyard drains and even in the liquid putrefaction of carcasses. Each one has a long breathing tube protruding from its rear end, earning it the unsavoury name of 'rat-tailed maggot'. Another bee-mimic is the narcissus fly. The body is black with grey, tawny or black hair, with red or buff-coloured abdomens, so mimicking a variety of bumblebee species. Its larvae feed on the roots of bluebells, as well as garden daffodils, and can be a serious horticultural pest.

Microdon mutabilis is also a bee mimic. Its larvae, which are always found in wood ants nests, was first described as a mollusc, because it looked like a slug. Another species associated with ants is *Brachypalpoides lenta*, which is wasp-like with a red body. It is a rare species, found on Ross island near Killarney. Its larva

---

NASTY BITING THINGS

We in Ireland are fortunate in having very few nasty or unpleasant creatures to make life miserable for us. However, at times there are a number of invertebrate species which are a considerable pest to outdoor enthusiasts. From May onwards, a number of species of biting midges can make standing around impossible, particularly in warm humid weather. One such is Culicoides pulicaris, *a common midge with dark stripes on their tiny wings. The attacks of these creatures can often be so bad that a ramble can become an ordeal, particularly if one's pace is slow. Only the females have piercing mouthparts; she needs to obtain a meal of blood before eggs can be laid.*

Horseflies are members of the large family called Tabanidae. The females are equipped with dagger-like organs, and are ferocious blood-suckers. The bite is quite painful and the irritation lasts for some days afterwards. The males subsist mainly on nectar. Each species tends to go for particular areas of the body. The brightly-patterned Chrysops caecutiens, *with red and green iridescent eyes, buzzes around the head and neck. The grey, mottled 'cleg',* Haematopota pluvialis, *flies slow and silently, landing on wrists, elbows and upper legs, while the much larger* Tabanus *species, thankfully relatively scarce, go for the legs.*

Members of the Hippoboscidae, or flat-flies, can be an unpleasant nuisance to those handling birds or mammals. These flies are all flattened laterally to enable them to crawl between the fur or feathers of their hosts. Stenepterx hirundinis *occurs on martins and swallows. Bird ringers in particular are well aware of these flies, as they have a disconcerting habit when disturbed of abandoning their hosts and flying directly towards one's face. I know of at least one Irish bird ringer who, unaware that he had collected one such unwanted guest in his beard, felt it run across his face while chatting later to a friend in a pub!*

Ticks are close relatives of spiders, but far less pleasant, as they are blood suckers and transmitters of disease. Our most common tick is the sheep tick, which lives in well vegetated areas. They have three life phases, larva (one millimetre), nymph (three millimetre) and adult (six millimetre). Each stage spends some days attached to the skin of a bird or mammal, feeding on blood, before dropping off into the vegetation where it will spend some months maturing into the next stage. Ticks mainly feed on small mammals, especially mice, but the adult must feed on large mammals such as livestock, dogs or deer. Adults rarely bite people, but the larvae and nymphs have no such qualms.

---

which looks like a hunched-up slug, is adapted to eating pellets of food discarded by ants.

ANTS

Ants are widespread and important members of the invertebrate community, found in a variety of habitats. The garden black ant is one of our more common species. They tend their own herds of aphids, feeding on the sugary 'honeydew' produced by these sap-suckers. In return for these offerings, the ants benefit the aphids by removing the eggs and larvae of ladybirds and hoverflies, their major predators. During August, millions of winged male and female ants take to the air for their annual courtship and mating period. These huge swarms provide rich feeding for swallows, martins and other aerial feeders. When the ants return to earth and discard their wings, more predators await them. Despite these depredations, some of the young mated queens survive to set up new nests in crevices.

The wood ant is one of our larger species, but is scarce throughout Ireland. They build large nests consisting of mounds of leaves and other vegetable debris. The nests are built in sunlit areas at woodland edges or within clearings. To maximise the warmth from the sun, they assiduously keep the nest area clear of overhanging ferns and vegetation which might shade the mound. There are a number of colonies in the Killarney valley area, but our knowledge of their distribution elsewhere is very sketchy. Wood ants are omnivorous, with a bias towards animal food. They do not possess a sting, but can shoot formic acid from their rear end if disturbed or threatened.

Wood ants are regarded as a keystone species; that is a species upon which the whole insect community structure depends. These ants have a positive effect on those insect herbivores such as aphids which they tend and a negative effect on others upon which they prey. As some species are more prone to their predation than others, the nett effect of their presence is to change the insect community structure.

OTHER INSECTS

Because of its importance entomologically, quite a few other insect groups in Kerry have received some attention. Ken Bond from UCC, already mentioned, has carried out a lot of work on micro-lepidoptera, or mini-moth species. The larvae of these make the distinctive leaf-mines to be seen on holly and other tree species.

Others have carried out work on fungus gnats, of which Kerry has 118 species, lacewings, chironomids, bees, beetles and other groups – one could fill a book on the insects of Kerry alone!

SPIDERS AND THEIR ALLIES

Spiders and harvestmen are an important part of the food web, being both active predators as well as prey items for other creatures up to the size of birds and voles. Spiders' bodies are divided into the relatively hard cephalothorax at the front, and the softer abdomen behind. They have six or eight simple eyes and four pairs of legs. The males have clubbed appendages at the front of the cephalothorax called palps. These are used during courtship and mating.

Many but not all spiders produce silk to spin elaborate webs to trap insects. Others are active hunters, while some lie in wait and ambush passing prey. Apart

---

A MOST UNUSUAL INSECT

One insect species which has certainly been introduced is the smooth stick insect, which probably came in accidentally on plants from New Zealand. They are now naturalised on Rossdohan island in Kenmare bay. Stick insects are a light greenish/beige in colour, measure up to 10 centimetres, and have long spindly legs. When disturbed they stiffen immediately, stretching their two front legs forward, and look just like a piece of twig.

All stick insects are vegetarian, feeding mainly on bramble leaves. They are nocturnal, remaining motionless by day, blending in well with their surroundings. They exhibit a curious swaying motion, the cause for which is unknown. The eggs are usually just dropped singly to the ground by the female. They have thick shells and a small 'lid' to enable the young to emerge easily.

---

from making webs, spiders use silk to wrap prey, make life-lines and shelters, and to encase their eggs. Most spiders overcome their prey by injecting venom into them, followed by digestive juices to liquefy the tissues, as spiders can only ingest liquid food.

Those spiders which spin webs normally have waxy hairs on their feet to prevent themselves sticking to their webs. The spider normally retreats to a nearby shelter, but stays in touch via a signal thread. Male spiders are generally much smaller than females, and during courtship have to approach the females cautiously to avoid being eaten themselves. Males often have an elaborate courtship procedure. In some species this involves presenting gifts of silk-wrapped food items to distract the female's attention.

Little recent work has been carried out on Irish spiders and we owe much of our present knowledge to the efforts of people like G.H. Carpenter (1865-1938), who was a professor at the Royal College of Science in Dublin until 1922 and D.R. Pack-Beresford (1864-1942), who lived in Carlow.

A common species is the garden spider, a large brown species with a white abdominal cross. The young take up to two years to mature. *Araneus quadratus* is a common moorland species with a very rounded abdomen. It ranges in colour from deep green to a brick red, but always has four prominent pale spots. *Pisaura mirabilis* is common everywhere from woodlands to open moorland, hunting in dense vegetation. It has a light brown abdomen with longitudinal yellowish stripes. They sunbathe on leaves with their front two legs stretched out forward and very close together. The female carries the egg cocoon in her fangs. Just before the young hatch, she spins a tent-like covering in which they remain until they disperse. The small black and white zebra spider is common on sunny walls from May to August. It is one of the jumping spiders, which catch their prey by stalking and leaping on them from a distance away.

A number of spiders have distributions which are confined solely or mainly to Kerry, based on our present knowledge. *Scotina celans* is a small, rare southern species found in woods or heathery areas. It is a yellowish colour overlaid with a pattern of paler stripes and chevrons. *Hyctia nivoyi* is a thin, narrow-bodied yellowish spider with a relatively massive front pair of legs. It is almost incapable of leaping, but when disturbed will run quickly backwards with its forelegs raised in front of its head. It has a distinctly coastal distribution in Kerry. *Arctosa cinerea* is one of our largest spiders, measuring up to 17 millimetres, with a dark brown or grey body. It is found among stones in riverbeds and by lakes, where it builds a silken tube. *Dipoena tristis* is a scarce, localised species, found on low bushes and trees. It is very small, measuring less than 3 millimetres, and is a glossy black colour covered with short bristles.

Harvestmen resemble spiders, but have an undivided body with very long legs. They are mainly nocturnal and are carnivorous. Their diet includes other harvestmen, snails, worms, millipedes, spiders and a wide variety of other creatures. A harvestman imprisons its prey between its legs and drops upon it from above. They need to be in moist conditions at all times to avoid desiccation. Harvestmen defend themselves by secreting a nauseous fluid which deters certain attackers. If caught by a leg, they can cast it but do not regenerate it like spiders. Some species sham death, becoming rigid with their legs in unnatural positions.

Mitopus morio is a common species, especially against the base of walls and buildings where vegetation is present. *Oligolophus tridens* is commonest in woodlands, occupying low foliage or occasionally ascending trees. It has a dark central saddle. *Nemastoma bimaculatum* is a blackish-coloured species with relatively short legs for a harvestman. It is generally distributed, found under logs, stones and amongst low herbage.

MANY-LEGGED ANIMALS

Lift any rotten wood, large stone or pile of leaves and you will probably disturb some of the multi-legged centipedes and millipedes. Centipedes are distinguished by having one pair of legs on each body segment, whereas millipedes have two pairs on most segments. Centipedes are predators, eating a wide variety of small creatures including woodlice and insects. Millipedes feed on soft plant tissue, either dead or alive. None of our centipedes have eyes, relying on vibration and touch to catch their prey. These are killed by injecting a poison delivered by their front legs, which have been modified into sharp fangs.

The common centipede is orange-coloured, measuring about 30 millimetres in length. It is found in woods, gardens and indoors in sheds and greenhouses. It shelters by day under logs and stones, emerging to hunt after dark. When running, it holds its body rigid, whereas most other centipedes move with a side-to-side motion. One such species is *Necrophlaeophagus longicornis*, which is yellowish, measuring up to 35 millimetres in length. It can be identified by its dark head and first few segments. One of the most easily recognised millipedes is the pill millipede, being shorter than the usual millipedes and with black and yellow banding. When threatened it rolls up into a ball.

WOODLICE

Woodlice are one of the few terrestrial relatives of crabs and lobsters, which all belong to a large class of animals called crustaceans. Their ancestors evolved from ocean-dwelling creatures and made their homes in dark, damp places. Not having evolved a waterproof covering like beetles, they are only active by night when darkness protects them from desiccation. Woodlice eat soft vegetable material and decaying plant matter including fungi and wood, and perform a valuable function by recycling the material back into the soil. Like rabbits, they eat their own droppings to extract the maximum amount of nutrients from their food. This is a process which is aided by bacteria in the droppings which break down any undigested particles.

Of the 28 species recorded in Ireland, only 11 have been found in Kerry, which is probably a reflection of a lack of interest in this group. The most common is *Oniscus asellus*, which is distinguished from other woodlice by the pale edges to its 'shell'. *Oniscus* can tolerate quite dry areas, and is about the only species to be found in lime-deficient sites such as peatbogs. The pill bug is black with yellow markings, and can also tolerate dry conditions. When disturbed it rolls up into a complete ball. It is found in the Banna dune system near Ardfert. *Philoscia muscorum* is very common in damp places and is subject to a wide variation in colours; even bright red and yellow specimens have been known to occur. *Porcellio pictus* prefers much drier habitats than other species, being found commonly in warm, dry, south-facing walls. Finally, *Metoponorthus cingendus* is a species whose main centre of distribution is Kerry and Cork, being especially common in mountainous districts.

EARTHWORMS

Earthworms play a vital part in maintaining the fertility of our soils. Every hectare of grassland contains up to 5 million earthworms, each one of which is a natural garbage disposal unit and rotovator combined. One of the most abundant and widespread species is *Lumbricus terrestris*. These can grow to a length of 30 centimetres and lives in tunnels up to 1.5 metres deep. Their manner of feeding is simple; they ingest large quantities of soil, digesting the bacteria and other organic debris, then excrete the remainder behind them in their tunnels. Fallen leaves on the soil surface are also pulled down into their tunnels, where the worm can eat them out of reach of birds and other predators. By these actions, minerals which have been leached by rain from the soil surface out of reach of plant roots are returned to the surface and the soil is aerated.

Charles Darwin, author of *The Origin of Species*, was an expert on earthworms whose works are still referred to. He estimated that earthworms bring 20 to 25 tonnes of soil annually to the surface of a hectare of land. *Allolobophora longa* is another common species which makes the casts frequently found on lawns. The small pink worm with the orange-tinted saddle often found under rocks or in your compost heap is *Eisenia rosea*, which measures up to 30 millimetres in length. Despite their obvious importance, some people dislike worms in their lawns because they find their casts to be unsightly. I know of at least one Kerry golf club where organochlorine chemicals are spread on the greens to kill off the worms because their casts interfere with golf balls and mowers. These pesticides can accumulate in the bodies of birds and other animals which pick up the dead worms, ultimately leading to their death. The same club then spends time and money on aerating the greens because of soil compaction, principally due to the lack of worms. Surely there must be a better way!

LAND SNAILS AND SLUGS

Snails and slugs are ubiquitous throughout Kerry, from our seashores to mountain tops. Snails are identified by the presence of a large shell, into which the animal withdraws when threatened or during dry weather. Most slugs, however, have shells too, but in the majority it is reduced to a rudimentary one within the animal's body. Both snails and slugs have soft, wet skin, and generally become inactive on warm days or during dry periods to avoid desiccation. They move on a muscular foot, producing copious quantities of mucus to aid movement. They breathe through a respiratory opening situated on the mantle. In slugs is the distinct raised area on the front half of the body and in snails it is just beneath the shell.

One of the most widespread species of slug is *Arion ater*, a large black slug up to 15 centimetres in length. There are various colour forms, ranging from all black (the most common form) to a greyish/white. This species is widespread at all altitudes, and may be especially obvious on the hills after wet weather. *Arion lusitanicus* is a very local species confined mainly to south-west Ireland and Co. Donegal. It measures up to 10 centimetres and varies in colour from grey/green to brownish, often with a dark lateral stripe on each side of its body. The shield slug is one of the few species with an external shell. The cream or pale yellow body is wider towards the tail, where the small, whitish shell is attached. They prey on earthworms and other species of slug.

Our best known slug is the Kerry spotted slug. This is a large handsome slug,

---

TERROR FROM THE SOUTHERN HEMISPHERE

One of the latest introductions to Ireland which has recently reached Kerry is the New Zealand flatworm. It is dark purple-brown above and pale yellow underneath and as their name indicates, look like flattened worms. Their size and weight vary according to season and feeding habits, but they can measure up to 30 centimetres long. Their mouthparts are on their underside, approximately halfway along the body.

The New Zealand flatworm is a serious predator of earthworms and was first noticed in Northern Ireland in 1963. It was believed to have been introduced as eggs on the rootstock of imported plants and this is how it has probably spread into Kerry, where it occurs around the Muckross area and probably elsewhere. They can elongate themselves and crawl into burrows after worms, where they wrap themselves around their hapless prey and secrete a strong digestive substance over the worm before eating it. Unlike other predators, however, whose numbers are often controlled by the abundance of their prey, flatworms can eat out virtually all the earthworms in a field and then survive without food for up to a year. This they manage by resorbing their own tissues and producing fewer offspring. Large numbers therefore remain to knock out any attempted resurgence in earthworm numbers. Studies in Northern Ireland have found that in trial plots the entire earthworm population had been eaten out within five years. This results in increased soil compaction and reduced soil aeration and fertility. Productivity in fields affected is estimated to have declined by up to one-third.

The flatworms have no known predator in this country, as their toxic secretions make them inedible to birds and mammals and are harmful to human skin, causing severe irritation. In their own countries they are animals of cool, temperate beech woodlands and cannot survive in temperatures greater than 20^0C. In Ireland, however, with its cool, moist climate, they are able to spread freely into fields and prey on the worms there. A survey of horticultural and garden centres around the county would be of interest to establish just how widespread they are. As they can often be found under potted plants, particularly in greenhouses, they are easy to locate if present. Apart from causing concern to agriculturalists, the long-term effect on animals and birds which depend to a large extent on worms is unknown.

---

endemic to Europe where it is found only on the Iberian peninsula and in southwest Ireland – a classic 'Lusitanian' distribution. Within Kerry and west Cork it only occurs in the sandstone regions. Two colour forms are found depending on habitat. The open country form is a charcoal colour with numerous white spots. Its mucus is whitish. The woodland form is bronze/ginger in colour with yellow/gold spots and yellowish mucus. Each form thus blends in well with their surroundings. It is believed that Kerry slugs were originally animals of old forest, and survive in open country only where the climate is mild and humid. Apart from its colour, the other main distinguishing feature is that it curls into a ball when disturbed, rather than contracting like other slugs. Its body is very pliable and sinuous and their powers of elongation are renowned; animals which measured four to five centimetres at rest can reach 12 centimetres when stretched. This ability allows the animal to withdraw deep into narrow crevices during dry weather to avoid desiccation.

Kerry spotted slugs eat a wide range of lichens, fungi, liverworts, mosses and algae, often concentrating on the fruiting bodies of these organisms. Their eggs are laid in batches of 18-30 between July and October, with hatching taking place after about two months. The young reach sexual maturity after approximately two years. They are long-lived; animals have been kept in captivity for over six years.

Because they need calcium to build their shells, the best places for snails are in limestone regions and sand dune areas. Few species are found in areas of acidic soils. There are a variety of different shell shapes from flattish disks to tall columnar shapes, which can be found in an attractive range of colours, from plain to multi-banded. Most species are herbivorous, but some are carnivorous on other snails or soil-dwelling organisms.

The common garden snail is *Helix aspersa*, with a wheel-shaped shell measuring 2.5 – 4 centimetres across. The shell is usually a pale brown with up to five dark spiral bands. The dark-lipped banded snail is another large species. Its normal shell colour is yellow with five dark bands. Two scarce species of wet grasslands, river and lake margins are *Vertigo lilljeborgi* and *Vertigo angustior*. Both are small cylindrical-shaped snails, yellow to yellowish-brown in colour. *V. lilljeborgi* is only found in a few areas along the western seaboard, while *A. angustior* is known from less than 10 locations throughout the country.

GLOSSARY OF ECOLOGICAL TERMS NOT EXPLAINED IN THE TEXT

OLIGOTROPHIC   Lakes which are poor in plant nutrients and therefore plant life, but rich in oxygen, are said to be oligotrophic

SAPROXYLIC   An organism which is dependent upon over-mature trees and dead or dying timber. It may hibernate in or eat rotten wood, or eat other animals in rotten wood.

LAKES AND RIVER LIFE

Aquatic habitats show almost as much variation as terrestrial ones, ranging from the smallest trickling stream, large slow-flowing rivers to puddles, ponds and deep lakes. Kerry is rich in such aquatic habitats, although the distribution of still-water bodies is markedly southern, with few lakes on the shales of north Kerry. Many of the streams and rivers of the peninsulas are relatively short and swift flowing whereas most of our largest rivers occur in a narrow band across central Kerry.

Freshwater bodies can be broadly classified on their chemistry. Oligotrophic waters are nutrient-poor, but generally oxygen rich. Their lack of calcium in particular makes the water 'soft', and they usually have comparatively poor flora and fauna. Such waters are normally found in upland areas. Waters rich in nutrients are called eutrophic, and in limestone districts the presence of calcium makes the water 'hard'. The process of eutrophication is a naturally occurring one taking thousands of years, but is often speeded up enormously by the influence of man.

All lakes contain an abundance of small floating or planktonic plants and animals. Among the tiniest are a variety of microscopic, single-celled organisms. They include plants such as the algae and diatoms which contain green chlorophyll and can manufacture their own food by photosynthesis. These phytoplankton are of great importance as they form the basis of food for all other aquatic life. The abundance of the phytoplankton varies during the year, with a peak in late spring followed by a lesser peak in autumn. The timing of these peaks is largely dictated by weather.

Euglena is a single-celled species which looks like a miniature slug, with a single, whip-like flagella. It is one of the organisms responsible for 'green water' in ponds and aquaria. *Chlamydomonas* is also a single-celled, pear-shaped organism, with two whip-like flagellae. It is very common in standing water amongst vegetation. Scientists are not sure which category to place these groups in, as they can photosynthesise in the light but are able to feed on organic material in conditions of low light.

The algae include desmids such as *Staurastrum*, a single-celled organism made up of two distinct halves, or colonial green algae such as *Volvox*, which may consist of up to 500 tiny, green cells equally spaced over the surface of a hollow sphere of mucilage. The numerous protruding flagellae give the appearance of a prickly green ball.

Rotifers are among the most abundant of freshwater animals and are characterised by a ring of thread-like hairs or cilia on the head. This structure is called the wheel organ. Although very tiny, the largest species measuring only two millimetres, rotifers are complex, multi-cellular animals. The wheel organ is used for propelling the animal through the water and for feeding on bacteria and small, organic particles. Many species are solitary, but some such as *Conochilus unicornis* are colonial. The majority are free-swimming, but many are capable of attaching themselves temporarily to the substratum with their adhesive-tipped foot.

The genus *Cyclops* are general-purpose copepods (from the Latin 'oar-footed ones'), which occupy a diversity of watery habitats from tree holes to open lakes, and may be free-swimmers or bottom-dwellers. These crustaceans range in size from 0.5-3 millimetres in length. The majority of species are greenish or brownish, but some species are brilliantly coloured. They eat small animal or plant organisms as well as organic detritus. The fish louse is a parasitic copepod, capable of

---

CHERNOBYL AND ITS EFFECT ON KERRY

On 26 April 1986 a serious accident at the Chernobyl nuclear power reactor resulted in widespread contamination of terrestrial and aquatic environments in Europe. Large quantities of radioactive caesium-134 and caesium-137, which have half-lifes of two and 30 years respectively, were released into the atmosphere. When the Chernobyl 'cloud' was passing over Ireland in early May, 1986, the heavy rainfall of that period encouraged radiocaesium deposition over various parts of the country, particularly in the west and north west. Another source of contamination has been the atmospheric testing of nuclear weapons carried out in the late 1950s and early 1960s. Radiocaesium deposition from this testing is found to correlate closely with mean annual rainfall. Thus the highest weapons fallout occurred along the western seaboard of Ireland.

After preliminary post-Chernobyl studies, the Nuclear Energy Board began a monitoring programme of upland Irish lakes, including Looscaunagh Lough and Lough Leane in Kerry. Sediment samples from lake shores and bottoms were examined, as well as samples of fish from each lake. Radiation doses absorbed by persons with an average daily intake of 50 grams of freshwater fish per day were calculated.

The highest radiation doses were received by lakes in the north and west of the country. For the Kerry lakes, radiocaesium concentrations in trout were less than 50 Bq/kg (becquerels per kilogram), with Looscaunagh Lough reporting the highest sediment concentration of 771 Bq/kg. For a person consuming fish daily, the radiation dose would be less than 5 per cent of the internationally recommended annual dose limit, and approximately 1 per cent of the dose received annually by members of the public from all sources of radiation, about 90 per cent of which is due to naturally occurring radiation.

---

swimming freely in search of a host such as salmon or sea trout. Measuring up to 12 millimetres, it has a flattened, translucent body with two large suckers. It uses these to attach itself to a fish's body before proceeding to suck its blood. A heavy burden of these lice on a fish can have a serious debilitating effect on the host.

Water fleas are a very numerous and diverse group of small crustaceans which feed by filtering small organisms out of the water. They vary in size from 0.2-10 millimetres long, have a single eye and two antennae, the larger one of which is used for swimming. One of the more familiar is *Daphnia*, measuring about three millimetres in length and mostly reddish or greenish in colour. They can be quite easily seen with the naked eye. *Leptodora kindtii* is one of our largest water fleas, measuring up to 10 millimetres, with very long antennae and no outer shell. They are predators on other small crustaceans.

The green hydra is an unusual, plant-like animal, measuring about six millimetres long. They look like umbrellas without the fabric covering. Hydras attach themselves to plants, and use stinging cells on their tentacles to paralyse small prey items such as water fleas. If necessary they can move to another area by employing a somersaulting action. The body of a hydra is like a long hollow tube formed from an inner and outer layer of cells separated by a jelly-like substance. The central cavity is lined with digestive cells and terminates in a single aperture surrounded by the tentacles. The green colour of this species is due to the presence of zoochlorellae, symbiotic green algae found within the cells. These small plants photosynthesise to produce sugars, some of which are used by the hydra. In return the alga benefits from the protection of the hydra.

SOME INVERTEBRATES OF UPLAND STREAMS AND LAKES

Upland streams are typically characterised by steep, swift water courses, interspersed with long, deep sections where the river flows through valley bottoms. Along their routes will be found numerous waterfalls, rapids and riffles.

In our wet upland climate, water flows rapidly along, carrying with it numerous stones and particles of sand and debris, all acting like a giant scouring agent. Few water plants can survive in these conditions and insect life is generally restricted to those species which are adapted to the fast flowing water. Many species such as mayflies and stoneflies have flattened nymphs, which cling beneath the stones. Others such as caddisfly larvae anchor themselves to the stream bottom in silken nets, or weigh themselves down with tubes of tiny stones and vegetable matter glued together. As the water in these areas is normally poor in calcium, very few species of snails are found in this habitat. The streams can quickly be swelled to a raging torrent after a few hours of heavy rain. In this state, the stream bed is further scoured out and the banks undercut.

Stoneflies are one of the more common insects of these fast-flowing streams. The nymphs are medium-sized inconspicuous insects, which can be distinguished by their sluggish habits and the presence of only two jointed tails or cerci. The smaller species feed on diatoms, algae and organic debris, but the larger species are active predators of worms, other fly larvae and nymphs. They use their long, jointed antennae to locate their prey, which is then quickly attacked and eaten. During their long period underwater, up to three years in some species, the nymphs may moult up to 30 times before climbing out onto the bank or a stem for the final moult. The adults are weak flyers and short-lived; their main concern being to mate and lay eggs. After the female lays her eggs on the surface of the water, they sink to the bottom and hatch in about three weeks. Stoneflies are intolerant of water pollution and their presence is a good indicator of clean, well-oxygenated water.

Nineteen species have been recorded in Ireland, of which 17 have occurred in Kerry since 1940. There is a pre-1940 record for one other species, *Protonemura meyeri*, but its current status is uncertain. Stoneflies have undergone dramatic declines in Europe generally. Of 24 species recorded in Holland, 10 were extinct by 1940, and at least four more since. Half of the species once found in the larger rivers of Italy have become extinct, and the five remaining species are seriously threatened.

In Kerry, common species of upland streams include *Siphonoperla torrentium*, a yellowish-brown species distinguished by the almost circular outline of its wing-buds and its hairy cerci. *Amphinemura sulcicollis* is distinguished by the two tufts of white gills under its chin. Other species include *Nemoura cinerea*, which is wide-spread in waters ranging from oligotrophic to eutrophic, and *Leuctra fusca;* the only species to emerge in autumn. Stoneflies are much less common in lakes, pre-ferring well oxygenated rivers. *Leuctra hipposus* is a common species of wave-beat-en, stony lakeshores and streams. The nymph has a slender, yellowish coloured body up to eight millimetres long. It carries out most of its growth in the autumn, and is one of the earliest species to emerge, hatching from February to May. The adults are called needleflies.

Of the scarcer species, *Capnia atra* is an Arctic and subalpine species, confined to a few lakes in Kerry, including the Devil's Punchbowl on Mangerton mountain, as well as in Connemara and Mayo. The adults have short wings; an adaptation to life at high altitudes where strong winds are frequent. *Diura bicaudata* is another scarce species which is to be found infrequently in lakes and rivers. *Dinocras cephalotes* is only known from a few Donegal localities, the Galway's river near Killarney and the Cottoners river near Killorglin.

The water bugs include the waterboatmen, water crickets, pond skaters and related species. Water bugs evolved during the Jurassic period and have become a highly successful group. They show a bewildering variety of adaptations for catching prey, respiration and locomotion. Waterboatmen are widespread in most still-water habitats. Most species are predatory, floating upside down on the water surface, lying motionless with the first two pairs of legs and the tip of the abdomen just touching the surface film, sensitive to any underwater disturbance. Insects, tadpoles and small fish are quickly attacked and overpowered by their short but powerful beaklike rostrum and toxic saliva, which partially digests the soft parts. The resultant soupy mix is then sucked up through the rostrum. The larger species should be handled with care as their bite is very painful to humans. When diving, they carry their air supply with them; a bubble of air is carried pressed to the abdomen by a longitudinal series of bristles.

The most common waterboatman of infertile pools and lakes is *Sigara scotti*, which is often one of the more visible species, as it can live in exposed sites with little vegetation cover. It occurs at altitudes up to 750 metres, overwintering as an adult, but in mountainous regions eggs are not laid until mid-May. *Notonecta mamorea* is more localised in occurrence, being found in northern Kerry chiefly in brackish pools and ditches in coastal areas. Another waterboatman of brackish pools is *Sigora selecta*, recorded from coastal ponds just above the high water mark on the beach at Ventry.

A very rare species which occurs only in Galway and Killarney is *Glaenocorisa propingua*, found in deep, upland pools. It is believed to be a glacial relict. *Glaenocorisa* is a large-eyed nocturnal feeder and is thought to be predatory. Swimming rapidly near the surface, it strains planktonic organisms such as copepods and water fleas out with the long hairs on its front limbs. Another Irish rarity found close to one of the same pools as *Glaenocorisa* is *Corixa dentipes*.

The water scorpion is common and widespread, found in shallow muddy ponds and lake margins. Its body is flattened and leaf-like, with a long breathing tube protruding from its abdomen. Due to its cryptic appearance and slow movements it is easily overlooked. The female lays her eggs shortly after dusk, usually in the stems and leaves of water plants just beneath the water's surface. The larvae and adults breath through the respiratory tail, poking it through the water film. They prey on small fish, larvae and other water bugs, using their powerful front legs to catch these. The water scorpion shows many features of interest: it becomes rigid when handled – called 'death-feigning' – and there are accessory hearts in the wings to enable body fluids to circulate more freely.

Pond skaters are specialised for hunting on the water's surface. They exploit the surface tension of the water, which, stretched like thin elastic, can support light weights. Their front legs are adapted to grasp prey, the middle pair move simultaneously to row the insect along and the hind legs function as twin rudders when steering. The most widely distributed species is the common pondskater, which has been found at up to 600 metres in bog pools in Kerry. Overwintered bugs first appear in late April or early May, and egg-laying occurs in May. Hatching takes 12 to 14 days. *Gerris lateralis* is a much rarer species, with one record for Kerry. It prefers still or stagnant water in ditches and bog pools. Oviposition is on damp moss, sometimes above surface level, each female laying over 100 eggs.

The freshwater beetles have, like their terrestrial counterparts, biting rather than sucking mouthparts and wing cases which meet along the centre line of their body instead of overlapping. Their larvae are mostly active and ferocious predators with powerful, pincer-like jaws. The adults of most species can fly well, and may move around from one pond or waterbody to another. Freshwater beetles are often one of the first species to invade new aquatic habitats. One of the best known groups are the whirlygig beetles, (*Gyrinus*) which can be seen gyrating on the surface of even the smallest pools. At the opposite end of the scale is the great diving beetles (*Dytiscus*) which may measure up to 50 millimetres in length. In September 1986 L.E. Laurie collected freshwater beetles from small rivers and ponds in upland peaty habitats. In three days of sampling, 31 species were recorded, included in which were five species which had not been recorded since 1936 and one species new to Ireland, *Anacaena butescans*. At the time of collecting, the

TABLE 16
THE WATER BUGS OF THE KILLARNEY AND IVERAGH DISTRICTS
AFTER O'CONNOR, O'GRADY AND BRACKEN 1985

Arctocorisa germari	Lough Leane, gravel pits
Callicorixa praeusta	Lough Leane, Lough Guitane, gravel pits
Callicorixa wollastoni	Bog pools and loughs to 800 metres
Corixa dentipes	Looscaunagh Lough
Corixa panzeri	Gravel pits
Corixa punctata	Gravel pits, bog pools near L. Guitane
Cymatia bonsdorffi	Gravel pits, bog pools
Glaenocorisa propinqua	Escabehey Lough, Lough Keal
Hesperocorixa castanea	Killarney, Kenmare
Hesperocorixa linnei	Ardagh Lough, gravel pit
Hesperocorixa sahlbergi	Aghadoe, Ardagh Lough, Lough Guitane
Micronecta poweri	Cahernane, Derrycunnihy, Flesk river
Sigara concinna	Ardagh Lough, gravel pits
Sigara distincta	Widespread
Sigara dorsalis	Widespread
Sigara falleni	Lough Leane, Upper lake, gravel pits
Sigara fossarum	Gravel pits
Sigara lateralis	Ardagh Lough, Minish, gravel pits
Sigara nigrolineata	Bog pools and loughs to 750 metres
Sigara scotti	Widespread, to 800 metres
Sigara semistriata	Kenmare, gravel pits

weather was unusually dry and most beetles found were confined to patches of *Sphagnum* and small trickles.

The predatory water spider is our only truly aquatic spider and is physically similar to its terrestrial cousins. It collects air from the surface and stores it within special bell-shaped webs attached to underwater plants. Water spiders feed on insect larvae, small crustaceans and small fish. Water mites are much smaller than water spiders. They are carnivorous, but unlike water spiders can absorb oxygen directly from the water. Many species lay their eggs in jelly masses on plants and stones. Their larvae are parasitic on aquatic insects.

DRAGONFLIES AND DAMSELFLIES
Walk the banks of any lake or stream during summer and you will notice large, sleek-looking insects patrolling stretches of water, their shimmering wings making an audible sound. Sometimes you might see two such creatures joined together in a most peculiar manner, resting on the surface of the water or the leaves of a river-

side plant. Others may be chasing each other in spectacular aerial 'dogfights'. These will be dragonflies or damselflies, large, colourful and very distinctive insects. Most damselflies hold their wings above their backs when resting, while dragonflies hold them out horizontally. All are predatory, both as larvae and adults. The larvae spend up to two years underwater, where they feed on tadpoles and other animals up to the size of small fish. Adults catch insects in flight, snatching them with their bristle-covered forelegs, which act like a trapping 'basket'. They are very agile in flight; each pair of wings operate independently, allowing them to hover and even fly backwards. Their vision is very keen with up to 30,000 facets in each eye.

Males patrol a distinct territory. These may be along streams, drains, roadways or woodland clearings, where they seek food and females and chase off rival males. Two adults grasped together in flight will be a mating pair. In some species the male 'mate guards' the female in this way until she is ready to lay her eggs. Apart from the Killarney area, little is known about the distribution of these in Kerry, where there is plenty of suitable habitat. As there are relatively few species, this would be an excellent area of research for a keen amateur.

Eight species of dragonfly occur in Kerry. The common hawker is a large brown species with blue spots in the male, green in the female. In flight from late June to mid-October, they circle high over ponds or streams, generally following a definite beat. The brown hawker has few spots, and has pale amber-tinted wings. They usually fly directly forwards and backwards along a special beat, often down the centre of a stream. The hairy dragonfly is a scarce species, preferring lowland streams and drains; it has the hairiest thorax of all the dragonflies. It has been recorded around the Killarney area and is in flight from mid-May to early July. The female only approaches water when ready to mate and lay her eggs. The downy emerald is another scarce species, with a brown abdomen and downy, green thorax. They are fast flyers, making short but regular patrols at the edge of ponds. The downy emerald has only been recorded from Glengariff and parts of Kerry. The northern emerald has a dull black-bronze abdomen and a hairy thorax. It hunts quite high along woodland fringes, flying in erratic spurts and figure-of-eight manoeuvres. The northern emerald has only been recorded from Kerry and Scotland.

The keeled skimmer is only common in the mountainous areas of Kerry and is in flight from June to September. The adult males are a bright blue colour, females and juvenile males are yellowish. They have a pronounced affinity for sphagnum-filled bog pools, as long as some open water is available too. Their wings, which appear very long in flight, are held downwards and forwards when at rest. The four-spotted chaser is a common species which inhabits boggy pools and ponds. Many males may be found sharing the same pond, but keeping to their own small territory unless challenged by a rival. Both sexes have conspicuous dark spots on the leading edge of each wing. The body is flattened and broader than other Irish dragonflies.

The black darter is primarily an upland species, but does occur in boggy low-land areas, and has been recorded in the Glencar region. Their colour varies with age; males are yellow and black as juveniles, maturing to an all black colour. Females are yellowy-brown marked with black and large groups of both sexes may sometimes be found over favoured bog pools and flushes. The black darter is one of the more approachable species, often landing quite soon after taking flight. The common darter is often the last species to be seen in the year, although the species is on the wing from mid-June. Males have red abdomens, females orange-brown, with dark marks on the tip of their abdomen. They are fond of skirting the edges of ponds, but are equally at home in woods, frequently returning to the same warm spot to settle.

Damselflies are more slender bodied than dragonflies and are generally much weaker fliers. Their eyes are well separated on either side of their heads, resembling miniature hammer-heads. Ten species have been recorded from Kerry. The two species of demoiselles are very striking creatures. Male banded demoiselles have metallic blue bodies and distinctive patches of colour on their wings, vary-ing from light purple-brown to deep prussian blue, depending on age. The females have a greenish body and greenish-brown wings. Males display their wing colours to females during courtship flight, vibrating their wings rapidly in front of the female, before flying with her in tandem. They prefer slow-flowing streams with muddy bottoms. The banded demoiselle was not recorded in Kerry from 1938 until 1986, which shows how much work remains to be done even in relatively well-worked areas. Both sexes of the beautiful demoiselle are similar in body colour to the previous species, but in the male, almost the whole wing is coloured purple-brown to blue-violet, depending on age. The female's wings are a dull pur-ple brown. They prefer fast flowing streams with pebbly / sandy bottoms.

The scarce emerald is a rare species in Ireland and may be extinct in Britain, but has been recorded in Kerry. The overall colour is an emerald green, the male having blue eyes and blue patches on the abdomen. They prefer ponds and marsh-es with dense stands of vegetation. The emerald damselfly is very similar to, but slightly smaller than the scarce emerald and has a wider distribution. Both species rest with their wings half open. The large red damselfly is one of the earliest species to occur in spring. It is a widespread and common species, found in a broad variety of habitats. Both sexes are a striking red colour, with black marks on the tips of the abdomen.

The blue-tailed damselfly has a black body with blue tips to the abdomen, and prefers slow flowing, weedy waterways. It can even tolerate moderately polluted waters. The scarce blue-tailed damselfly has been recorded from one site in the Derrynane area. It is very rare throughout the country, but again may be overlooked; it prefers very shallow pools, and has even been seen ovipositing in roadside puddles.

Species of the genus *Coenagrion* are all somewhat similar in appearance, and require care in identification. All have bright blue bodies with a variety of black markings, depending on the species. The common blue damselfly is widespread throughout, preferring large bodies of water with plentiful marginal vegetation. The azure damselfly prefers wet meadows or well vegetated ditches and streams and is a relatively common species throughout. The variable damselfly is very similar in appearance, and inhabits similar marshy areas.

LOUGH LEANE; A VERY SPECIAL LAKE

Lough Leane is probably the most studied lake in Kerry, due to its large size, variety of habitats and the threats posed to it by its proximity to Killarney. The western and southern shores shelve steeply and are mainly composed of Old Red Sandstone, the shallower eastern and northern shores overlie limestone. Some farmland abuts onto part of its northern and eastern shores, while the rest is surrounded by forests of sessile oak, yew and other species.

Under normal conditions the environment of the deep water zone (profundal) of Lough Leane is relatively simple when compared with the complex and ever changing conditions in the shallow water or littoral zone. The dominant variables are dissolved oxygen levels and the supply of decaying animal and plant detritus descending from the surface high above. The dominant algae present in Lough Leane exhibit a characteristic seasonal pattern. During the winter-spring period the dominant species are diatoms such as *Melosira*, a columnar shaped group, *Fragilaria*, elongated in shape with narrowed ends and *Asterionella* which generally form star-shaped colonies. In early summer these are replaced by green algae such as *Oedogonium,* which often forms floating masses and *Spirogyra*, a filamentous alga which forms floating rafts or tangled masses amongst larger vegetation. In late summer the dominant species are *Oscillatoria* and *Anabaena*. Each group in turn dies and drifts down to the lake bottom, becoming food for detritus feeders.

There are a number of bays of various sizes around the lake. The largest is Castlelough bay, at the eastern end of the lake. This is surrounded by a mixture of low limestone cliffs, gently-sloping rocky shores and stretches of sandy shoreline, formed principally from the deposition of large quantities of material from the river Flesk which enters here. The shoreline in front of the fifteenth-century Muckross abbey is a shallow, limestone area and here one of a number of sampling stations has been monitored intermittently since 1974. Let us now look at some of the animals of these shallows.

The oligochaetes include a wide variety of worms of varying shape and size,

---

EUTROPHICATION

Eutrophication is a natural process whereby lakes age, a process which normally takes thousands of years. Certain lakes are naturally eutrophic, receiving excessive amounts of nutrients from their catchments and thereby increasing the productivity of the lake. Most lakes gradually accumulate nutrients over a long period of time, become more fertile and eventually fill with sediments and choke with vegetation. This process often leads to the formation of fens and eventually bogs.

In recent times, concern has been expressed at the number of lakes which are undergoing rapidly accelerating cultural eutrophication, a process primarily influenced by man. Cultural eutrophication is the process whereby waters become over-enriched by the addition of nutrients, especially nitrogen and phosphorus compounds. This leads to an increase in the productivity of the lake, the production of massive algal blooms and severe deoxygenation leading to fish kills. Apart from the impact on the lake's natural flora and fauna, it severely impacts on the value of the lake for human uses such as angling, tourism, bathing and as drinking water. Where a lake system is suffering from an excessive loading of nutrients, severe algal 'blooms' can occur, particularly in warm, dry, calm weather. This has occurred in a number of Kerry lakes such as Lough Leane, Lough Gill and Caragh lake. Decomposition of these algae can lead to deoxygenation, possibly resulting in fish kills. In many instances all that prevents algal blooms from occurring more often is heavy rainfall, periodic flash flooding and the effects of wind.

In Kerry, the principal sources of nitrogen and phosphorus entering lake and river waters are animal slurry, artificial fertilisers, run-off from poorly managed silage pits and farmyards and domestic sewage. These are the most widespread sources. Locally, other potential sources include discharges from effluent treatment plants, agri-industries, chemical plants and other industries.

---

from small colourless forms to large, pigmented earthworm types. The red-bodied species have large amounts of haemoglobin in their blood, which allows them to live in poorly oxygenated waters. The majority of species feed by ingesting large volumes of mud and detritus, digesting the organic particles and excreting the remainder. *Lumbriculus variegatus* is a common reddish species of lakes, ponds and even woodland pools, where they live in vertical mud tubes. They resemble small, thin earthworms, measuring up to 10 centimetres. *Stylaria lacustris* has a yellowish, transparent body with bristles, eyespots and a long proboscis. It measures up to 18 millimetres long, and swims with a stiff, wriggling action.

Flatworms are small, common animals up to four centimetres long, found in most freshwater habitats, some of which look like miniature spear heads. Most are carnivorous, feeding on insect larvae and small crustaceans. They are common amongst debris, beneath rocks and clinging to the underside of leaves. Some of the more common flatworms are *Polycelis*, measuring up to 15 millimetres and *Dugesia*, 20 to 30 millimetres in length. Roundworms are thin, unsegmented cylindrical animals, rarely longer than two or three millimetres. They move with a distinctive thrashing or writhing motion. The numerous species are very similar in shape and actions, making identification to species level a very difficult task. They feed on most organic matter, with various species specialising in a particular food type, e.g., diatoms. On the abbey shore they have reached densities in excess of 1,000 animals per square metre, but can reach much higher densities in sites affected by organic enrichment.

Leeches are readily recognised by their muscular, contractable bodies and the presence of suckers at each end, which they use to adhere to any firm surfaces. The head is located at the narrow end of the body and has up to 10 dark eyespots, depending on species. Their mouthparts, which are located within the front sucker, may consist of an extendible proboscis, inserted into the prey when feeding, or biting and piercing jaws. They are formidable predators, which gorge themselves when feeding, so that well fed specimens are considerably larger than hungry ones. Some leech species suck the blood of fish and various invertebrates, others prey on snails, worms and insect larvae, which they may swallow whole.

Helobdella stagnalis has a creamy-white or transparent, leaf-shaped body, speckled with green, brown or grey. It prefers still ponds and lake edges, feeding on small snails. *Glossiphonia complanata* has a green or brown, rubbery body, measuring up to three centimetres in length, with two or more dark bands running longitudinally down the body. They usually have three pairs of eyes. *Glossophonia* species are unusual among leeches in brooding their eggs and the newly-hatched young beneath their bodies. They are found commonly in running or still water, where they feed on snails. *Erpobdella octulata* has a cylindrical or slightly flattened, brown body up to four centimetres long with a variable amount of black flecking. It is very common in a wide range of habitats, where it hunts any small invertebrates it can swallow. The horse leech is our largest species, measuring up to 30 centimetres in length when extended. They are found in wet areas at the margins of streams and peat bogs. Horse leeches are dark grey or greenish in colour, flecked with black, with greenish-yellow lateral stripes. They prey on most invertebrates, but despite their name do not suck the blood of horses or any mammal. The duck leech has one of the most unusual lifestyles. It is a yellow-green colour and somewhat translucent. It enters the nostrils of ducks as they are dabbling, particularly the young, where it attaches itself to the lining of the nasal cavity and sucks the blood.

Freshwater shrimps are amphipods, members of a group that also includes the marine sandhoppers. Most species are a light brown colour and are narrowly compressed from side to side. They frequent well-oxygenated waters which have good

Main photograph: Where crag and moorland and farmland meet, near Glenbeigh.
Top inset: Snow on the MacGillycuddy's Reeks; *middle inset:* 118,000 year-old pre-glacial Peat near Spa, Tralee bay; *bottom left inset:* Conglomerate rock; *bottom right inset:* Ancient, pre-bog pine stumps near Cromane.

Top main photograph: Killarney's upper lake.
Top inset: Killarney fern; *bottom inset:* Royal fern.

Bottom main photograph: Moss-rich woods at Derrycunnihy.
Top inset: Arbutus fruits; *bottom inset:* A wealth of lichens cover a branch.

Main photograph: Winter oakwoods.
1: A mixed clump of gorse and broom provides a dramatic splash of colour on Ross island, Killarney; *2:* Yew fruits;
3: The Irish spurge flowers early in spring; *4:* Ramsons carpet a woodland floor in Killarney.

Main photograph: *Rhodendron ponticum* in flower on the Beara peninsula.
Top inset: Kidney saxifrage; *middle inset:* Montbretia; *bottom inset:* Fuschia abounds in west Kerry.

Main photograph: Cloonaghlin Lough.
Top inset: Sphagnum pulchrum; *middle inset:* Meadowsweet and purple loostrife abound in wet ditches near Camp *bottom inset:* Gorse fire.

Main photograph: Rossbeigh strand and Dingle bay.
1: Sea radish; *2:* Sea kale; *3:* Wild pansy; *4:* Sea aster; *5:* Sea holly.

Main photograph: Kerry lily.
Bottom left inset: Thrift; *bottom right inset:* Bladder campion and common bird's-foot trefoil at Cromane;

Main photograph: The Magharee peninsula and Lough Gill; *inset:* Irish hare.
Top left: Caterpillars of the cinnabar moth on common ragwort; *top centre:* Kerry spotted slug; *top right:* Fox cub at play; *bottom left:* Natterjack toad; *bottom right:* Stonechat male at nest.

Main photograph: Muckross yew wood.
1: Woodcock; *2:* A female bullfinch feeds on fallen yew berries; *3:* Sika stag in velvet; *4:* Badger cub yawning;
5: Irish stoat; *6:* Silver-washed fritillary.

Main photograph: Muckross lake,
Killarney.
Top inset: Brook lampreys moving pebbles;
middle inset: A 10cm long freshwater
mussel; *bottom inset:* Four-spotted libellula.
Bottom: Common frog.

Main photograph: Seashore being exposed on ebb tide, Dingle bay.
Top inset: Brent geese near Cromane; *second inset:* A boulder encrusted with sponges and red algae;
third inset: Blue-rayed limpet on kelp stalk; *bottom inset:* Topshells – painted top shell, purple top shell and thick top shell.

Main photograph: Sunset over Kenmare bay.
1: A flounder lies partially covered by sand at low tide; *2:* Velvet crab on the seashore; *3:* Beadlet anemones; *4:* Common prawn.

stands of vegetation. They have two pairs of long antennae which are used to locate decomposing plant and animal material on which they feed. *Gammarus duebeni* is the most common Irish species of freshwater, preferring well-oxygenated lakes and rivers. Originally a species of brackish waters, it has adapted in many areas completely to a freshwater existence. It reaches densities in the Killarney lakes in excess of 6,000 animals per square metre. Its Latin name, *duebeni*, means 'twice blessed', referring to its ability to tolerate brackish and freshwater. It is 25-30 millimetres in length, with a curved body flattened from side-to-side. They have two long pairs of antennae which assist in finding the decomposing organic matter on which they feed. During mating, the male and female swim in tandem for about a week. After fertilisation, the female keeps the eggs in a special brood pouch beneath her. Here the eggs develop into miniature versions of the adults. In Britain, however, it is still mainly confined to brackish water, while its place in freshwater is occupied by *Gammarus pulex*, a species which has only recently been discovered in Ireland.

The water louse, *Asellus meridianus*, is a freshwater crustacean and very similar to the terrestrial wood louse. They are found principally on muddy bottoms, spending their lives crawling among plant debris and feeding on detritus. At first sight they look similar to the freshwater shrimp but are generally found in more sluggish water conditions, even tolerating moderate levels of pollution. High numbers of these in a watercourse is an indication that all may not be well.

Approximately 140 species of chironomid are known to occur in the Killarney lakes, as well as other riverine species. They often form dense clouds hanging over the water on still evenings. Although not all species bite, it only needs a few specimens of the biting species to make for an unpleasant experience. The most numerous species are *Cricotopus*, *Pentaneurini*, *Tanytarsus* and *Synorthocladius semivirens*. One species with an interesting history, first discovered in the river Flesk, is *Eukiefferiella ancyla*. When initially discovered in the river in 1976, it could not be identified from the known literature and it was not until 1986 that it was described from Sweden. *E. ancyla* is associated with the freshwater limpet, its bluish larvae living in silken tubes which are attached to the inner rim of the limpet's shell. Apart from the Flesk, it is only known from a few sites in Britain and Sweden.

Adult mayflies are delicately built insects, not brightly coloured, with three cerci. Mayflies spend most of their lives underwater as nymphs which graze on algae and other vegetable matter. After two to three years underwater, the adults emerge after undergoing an intermediate stage unique to mayflies called the sub-imago, which is similar in appearance to the adult, but with downy wings giving a duller appearance. After a period ranging from a few minutes to 30 hours depending on species, these moult into the full adult or imago. The imagos are unable to feed because of degeneration of their mouth-parts, and concentrate on mating. *Ephemerella ignita* and *Caenis moesta* are the commonest mayflies of the lakeshore, but in fast flowing streams their place is taken by *Baetis rhodani.*

Caddis flies are dull-coloured, moth-like insects with hairy wings, normally most active at night. Their larvae are fascinating creatures, due to the habit of many species of building tube-shaped cases to protect their soft bodies. These are made from a variety of materials, depending on species and include sand grains, small stones, twigs, leaves or pieces of vegetation cut to size, bound together with a silk-like secretion. Other species are caseless, but construct a net or tube of silk, attached to stones or vegetation, in which they live and snare their food. Caddis fly larvae are found in most clean, aquatic habitats, living on the bottom or under stones. The most common species of caddis fly near the Abbey shore is *Tinodes waeneri.* Other common species of Kerry's lakes and rivers are *Agapetus fuscipes,* which makes its case of small stones. These are flat below and rounded above, measuring about 10 millimetres long. *Polycentropus flavomaculatus* is a widely dis-tributed species whose larva spins a net stretched between stones to trap prey. *Ithytrichia clavata* is a scarce species which was first discovered in Ireland in 1973, on the Curraheen river near Camp. *Apatania auricula* is a large species with an interesting history. Though first discovered in Ireland in 1887, it was mis-identi-fied as *Apatania fimbriata.* This error was rectified in 1951 when the original speci-mens were re-examined. It is widespread and often abundant in south-west Ireland, but not recorded from Britain, though known from the Baltic regions and Scandanavia. Adults may be found throughout the year, including winter. On the Killarney lakes, *Apatania auricula* is reputed to be the 'plain rail' of the angler. This problem of mis-identification of species is not uncommon; aided by more modern equipment and better identification keys, articles regularly occur in various jour-nals correcting the mistakes of earlier workers.

FRESHWATER MOLLUSCS

The most common shelled creature of freshwater in Lough Leane is the Jenkin's spire shell. Less than five millimetres tall, it varies in colour from light to dark brown. Until the end of the last century, these tiny snails were confined to brack-ish coastal waters. In 1893 it was first noticed in freshwater, and has since spread throughout much of Britain and Ireland. The vast majority are females, reproduc-ing by parthenogenesis, or virgin birth. They are extremely abundant, in some years reaching densities in excess of 16,000 per square metre and are an important food for other species up to the size of tufted ducks. The wandering snail is one of the commonest European species, brown in colour, measuring two to three cen-timetres in length. It occurs in a variety of habitats from lowland ponds to moun-tain streams, in both hard and soft water areas. Its principal foods are organic debris, algae and fish eggs. Snails of this genus are the hosts in one stage of the life cycle of the liver fluke, a serious parasite of livestock and deer.

Another common species is the river limpet, which is closely related to the better known marine limpet. It has evolved a very similar mode of life, attaching itself to rocks and water plants with its muscular foot. Measuring about six millimetres in length, their shell colour ranges from dark brown to black. The shell is cone-shaped with a curved top, perfectly adapted to the fast flow of the water. River limpets are intolerant of silt and are usually found in fast-flowing stony rivers, or the rocky margins of lakes where there is sufficient water movement to prevent silting.

The pea mussels rarely exceed 10 millimetres in diameter and are whitish yellow or brown in colour. They move about on a tongue-shaped foot which projects between the valves of the shell. These mussels are hermaphrodites, but cross-fertilisation takes place by releasing sperm into the water. Once fertilised, the eggs are retained within the adult in brood pouches until they are fully developed. After many months the transparent young emerge as miniature adults.

One of our largest freshwater bivalves is the swan mussel, which is noted for its long life-span, often living in excess of 10 years under normal conditions. They feed and breathe by taking water in through a tube-like structure called a siphon. This action draws oxygen through the gills and traps small organisms and algae for food. The water is then expelled through a second siphon. The shell is yellowish-green in colour, up to 20 centimetres long, with distinct growth lines marking the surface. The front end of the shell always lies buried in the substrate, but the siphons at the posterior end are always exposed.

The pearl mussel is another large, slow-growing species, once harvested for the small pearls they sometimes contain. They are the longest-lived European animal, with some individuals reaching 120 years of age. The elongated, kidney-shaped shell is yellowish-brown when young, turning to dark brown or black when mature. They prefer large, fast-flowing rivers in soft-water districts and are locally distributed in a number of south Kerry rivers. One such river has recently been assessed as having one of the largest mussel populations of any European waterway. In most rivers, however, juveniles appear to be very scarce, indicating that something may be amiss in these populations. Many of the riverbeds are overgrown with algae, indicating organic enrichment of the waters, probably due to local farm intensification. This algae is probably detrimental to the juveniles and adults by impacting on their feeding, breathing or spawning processes. Other factors may also be involved.

The life cycle of the last two species differs from that of the smaller pea mussels. The females produce up to a million eggs, which are retained within a special brood pouch called a marsupium for some months. These develop into a distinctive larvae called *glochidia*, a Latin name meaning 'arrowhead'. These are brooded internally over winter and released into the water in spring, where they drift with the current. The glochidia possess a two millimetres long, sticky thread, by which it adheres to the skin of a passing fish. Salmonids – salmon and trout – are the commonest hosts. It then clamps itself onto the fish's gills by shutting its valves, and becomes encapsulated into the gills. Here it lives for a period until it develops into a tiny mussel, when it drops off into the substrate.

TABLE 17

FISH SPECIES FOUND IN KERRY WHICH ARE LISTED IN THE *IRISH RED DATA BOOK*

Arctic charr	River lamprey
Brook lamprey	Sea lamprey
Killarney shad	Twaite shad

LOUGH LEANE'S FISH

Minnows are a small, shoaling fish measuring up to 10 centimetres in length, and well known by most children. They are usually dark above, mottled with golden-brown and green, with a dark lateral line running the length of their bodies, ending in a black spot near the tail. At spawning time this dark lateral line becomes greenish, and males develop a reddish colour along the throat and belly. Minnows prefer rivers with clear water and sandy or gravelly bottoms of the sort preferred by trout. They are normally found along the slower flowing margins and among waterweed. They form an important part of the diet of kingfishers, fish, water beetles and dragonfly larvae.

The stone loach is a small, bottom-dwelling species, in colour a mosaic of yellows, green, brown and grey. They have an elongated body up to 12 centimetres in length, three pairs of barbels around its mouth, a square-cut tail and small eyes. They inhabit fast flowing streams with a sandy or gravelly bottom, as well as the shallow areas of lakeshores. They spend the day hidden beneath stones, emerging at night to hunt bottom-dwelling invertebrates such as crustaceans and shrimps, feeling for their prey with their barbels.

Two species of stickleback occur in Kerry waters. The commonest is the three-spined stickleback, which are found in most water bodies from ditches to the lower reaches of rivers. They are dark brownish-green above and silvery below, measuring up to 10 centimetres in length. In spring the males develop breeding colours of a red throat and belly and bright blue eyes. During courtship he performs a zig-zag courtship dance, enticing the female to the nest that he has carefully built of thread-like algae and mosses. More than one female may be enticed to lay in each male's nest. The female enters the nest and lays her eggs. After fertilising them the male guards them and later the young fish until they leave. The nine-spined stickleback has in the past been called the ten-spined stickleback, although the number of spines varies from seven to 12 Their distribution is more localised than the three-spined stickleback's, being found mainly in sheltered bays with dense weedcover. The male's spring colours are less dramatic, the greenish throat turning black. Both species feed on insect larvae, molluscs and crustaceans.

An Arctic charr from Lough Leane

Arctic charr are a trout-like, cold water fish of Arctic regions of which a number of land-locked populations exist in Ireland. Their colour is variable according to habitat, sex and breeding condition, but they are normally olive or blue-grey above, lighter on the flanks, and with pale spots. They are probably best told by the pure white edges of the pelvic, pectoral and anal fins. In the spawning season these fins, along with the belly, turn bright red. Exceptional fish can measure up to 60 centimetres in length, weighing up to three kilograms, but the average size is less than half of this. Several different races are recognised, including the Coomasaharn charr and the blunt-nosed charr of the Killarney lakes and Lough Acoose. Charr are now regarded as rare in Lough Leane, possibly due to pollution during the 1970s and more recently.

For most people, Atlantic salmon are the king of freshwater fish. Large salmon migrate from the open ocean to the coast in May, smaller individuals follow slightly later. Both have built up large reserves of fat and from this time until spawning they scarcely feed at all. Once in freshwater they survive on their fat reserves, and towards spawning time in October/November change colour to brown or greenish with orange or red mottling. The adult male's lower jaw develops a hook or kype and active fighting between rival individuals takes place. The female chooses a suitable stretch of river with a sandy or gravelly bottom where she digs a spawning nest or redd with her body and tail. Into this she lays a large number of eggs, which are fertilised by the male. She then prepares another redd. Up to 26,000 eggs are laid in a number of redds over a period of two weeks.

The heavy, slightly sticky eggs lie embedded among the gravel throughout the winter, hatching into larvae in April or May. When their yolk sac is depleted, the young fry start to hunt for insects and other invertebrates. After remaining in freshwater for a year or more, the young salmon, now called smolts, return to the estuaries and thence to the sea.

The life history of the brown trout is similar in many ways to salmon, but they spend all their life in freshwater. Niall O' Maoileidigh carried out a major study of the Lough Leane fishery from 1985 to 1989. Spawning takes place in local streams,

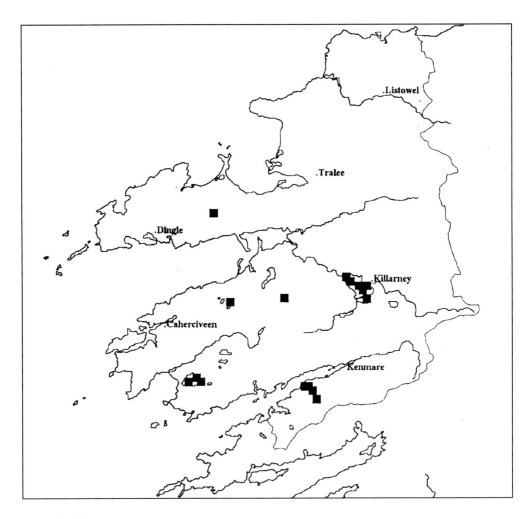

Map 10: Distribution of Arctic charr in Kerry

with the vast majority of trout migrating to the lake as one year-old fish. Most mature in their second year, but only a small proportion of trout spawn in any one year. Their life expectancy is relatively short, with few brown trout living to more than three years of age. In a 1991 study of the fish stock of Lough Leane, Martin O'Grady of the Central Fisheries Board found that the lake had the highest density of brown trout ever recorded in an Irish fishery. He estimated the total trout population for fish over 19.8cm to be in excess of 670,000. A combination of factors are responsible for the high density. These include the moderately productive status of the lake, a large catchment area with many suitable spawning streams, and the absence of pike, a major trout predator, in the lake.

TABLE 18
FISH STOCK SURVEY OF LOUGH LEANE (FROM O'GRADY, 1993)

Brown trout	819		Sea trout	1
Shad	252		Perch	166
Eel	25		Salmon	16
Charr	8		Flounder	57
Roach	1			

The ferox trout or 'great lake trout' is considered to be a distinct form of the brown trout, possibly the descendants of an 'ancestral' trout lineage which entered Ireland after the Ice Age. They mainly occur in deep, oligotrophic lakes over 100 hectares in area where shoaling fish such as charr are present. Ferox trout show a marked increase in growth rate between the fourth and eighth year of life, but no fish older than 11 years were caught in either study. This spurt in growth rate is attributed to the trout changing to a predominately fish diet. All ferox trout stomachs examined contained fish, including charr, shad, perch and eel. The largest fish caught weighed 7.7 kilograms, but heavier ferox trout have been captured on the lake. While they are considered by local anglers to be rare, in O'Maoileidigh's study they constituted a minimum of 3.6 % of the total number of trout caught.

Sea trout are regarded as a migratory form of the brown trout. They are most common in the short, spate rivers of the Kerry peninsulas. Although their numbers declined during the late 1990s, there are recent indications of an increase in the number of returning adults. Many reasons have been put forward for the collapse in numbers, including disease, overfishing, predation, pesticides, acidification and the proliferation of sea lice associated with intensive salmon rearing at sea. Studies at the Salmon Research Agency in Co. Mayo suggests that most of these factors cannot explain the collapse in stocks and that the principal cause of the decline is due to the proliferation of sea lice, operating in conjunction with natural factors which usually regulate sea trout numbers.

Twaite shad are a herring-like, shoaling fish which live at sea but enter rivers and lakes during spawning. They are silvery in colour, measuring up to 40 centimetres in length. They feed principally on small fish. While they have occurred as far upstream as the Killarney lakes, their full status in Kerry is unknown. A substantial stock of Killarney shad also occur in the lake. This is regarded as a non-migratory sub-species of the twaite shad and one of the most unique fish in Britain and Ireland. Their Irish distribution is confined to the Killarney lakes, where they are believed to have been present since the early post-glacial period. They are smaller in size than the twaite shad, a maximum of 23 centimetres and have a larger number of gill rakers, which look like the teeth of a comb, on the first branchial arch. The higher number of gill rakers in the Killarney shad enhance the ability of the fish to capture and feed on planktonic food items.

They feed mainly on *Daphnia*, particularly *Daphnia longispina*, which comprises over 9% of all food items taken. Their life span is short, averaging four to five years. Males mature in their third year, females in their fourth. Spawning takes place when they reach a size of 17-20 centimetres, between mid-July and mid-August, probably in shallow bays or in the river Laune. Females produce an average of 19,600 eggs.

Tench are a large, slow-moving fish which were introduced to Ireland, probably at the beginning of the nineteenth century. They are a dark blackish or greenish colour, with a deep body, square tail, rounded fins and a small barbel at each corner of its mouth. They inhabit the bottom of weedy ponds and the sheltered bays of lakes and slow-flowing lowland rivers. In Kerry, tench occur in Lough Leane in sheltered bays and large ponds. In O'Maoileidigh's study the majority of fish taken were less than four years old, but some females reached their tenth year. After their fourth year, females grow considerably faster than males. Tench in Lough Leane had a better growth rate than in other Irish fisheries, probably due to the milder temperature regime in Kerry. However, their growth rate is still poor by European standards, due to the shorter growing seasons and lower water temperatures here. Tench hibernate during winter and early spring, which further curtails their growing season to the period from mid-July to November. Small tench have a predominately planktonic diet, but larger fish eat more molluscs, chironomid larvae and other insects. Female fecundity is related to size; the smallest female examined had 1,730 eggs, the largest held approximately a quarter of a million eggs.

One of the most surprising finds of Martin O'Grady's survey was of a single roach. Roach are a silvery grey colour, with orange fins and reddish eyes. They were first introduced into Ireland in 1889, when numbers were released into the Munster Blackwater. They have a tremendous capacity for increasing in numbers, when they actively compete with trout, shad and other fish for food, so the introduction of roach to the lakes is a cause for serious concern.

A large stock of European eels also exists in the Killarney lakes, and probably in other Kerry fisheries. The peculiar life history of the eel begins in the Sargasso Sea off the West Indies. Here they spawn at some depths, hatching into small, colourless larvae known as leptocephalus. These have been found in March and April at depths of 100-300 metres. The larvae are drifted by the Gulf Stream to Europe, a journey which lasts about a year. Shortly before they arrive they metamorphose into elvers, measuring about 65 millimetres long. The elvers move into brackish waters and start moving upstream in mid-winter, generally staying close to the banks of the river. This phenomena can be observed in the river Laune in late winter, where a dark, wriggling mass of elvers may be seen for a period of some weeks. They gradually develop into adults, eating worms, molluscs, insect larvae, shrimps, crayfish and small fish. At an age of six to seven years they undergo a change from their yellow and brown colour to become dark grey and silver, and cease feeding. By this time, males may be up to 50 centimetres long, with females measuring up to a metre and weighing over three kilograms. In September and October these 'silver eels' migrate to sea and disappear into the ocean depths.

Lampreys are eel-like in appearance, but lack pectoral fins and have rows of circular, gill-like openings behind the eyes. River lampreys measure up to 35 centimetres in length, and possess a circular mouth disc with a row of horny teeth. They are parasitic, principally on herring and sprat, feeding by rasping the skin off fish and sucking their blood. To prevent the blood coagulating they secrete a substance into the wound which also acts to dissolve the host's tissues. They spend most of their time feeding in estuarine and inshore waters, migrating into rivers and lakes to breed. The female may lay up to 40,000 eggs, with both adults dying after spawning. The larvae return to the sea after metamorphosing into the adult form when they reach a length of 9-15 centimetres. Brook lampreys are non-migratory and measure less than eight centimetres. They are brownish in colour, and are distinguished from the river lamprey by their tail and dorsal fin being continuous. From late spring onwards, careful examination of spring fed streams and the upper reaches of rivers may reveal small spawning groups of brook lampreys, sometimes in a writhing, intertwined mass. At first glance they look like young eels but their unusual behaviour will quickly distinguish them. Using their sucker mouths, they remove small stones from patches of sandy or gravelly bed, where the female excavates a shallow nest and lays up to 1,200 eggs. After spawning the adults die. The worm-like larvae feed on organic particles in the mud, taking up to five years to reach maturity.

One of the most unexpected fish to occur frequently in Lough Leane is the flounder. They are a dull brown or greyish green flatfish sometimes marked with pale, orange blotches. They are the only flatfish which are tolerant of freshwater, and are known to migrate into many Irish lakes where they may spend up to six months feeding, returning to the ocean with the onset of cold weather. They spawn at sea between February and May. Most of those caught in Lough Leane are between two and six years of age, and their diet consists mainly of molluscs, particularly freshwater cockles and the Jenkin's spire shell.

Chapter 4

MARINE LIFE

LIFE ON THE SEASHORE

THE OPEN SEA and its shoreline hold a special fascination for most people. With its daily cycle of tides and surf and the interplay of water, light and movement, there exists a powerful aesthetic appeal. Added to this is the presence of a varied and somewhat mysterious flora and fauna which most of us only glimpse as pieces of cast-up seaweed and shells.

With its long and varied coastline, Kerry has much to offer the explorer of this unique environment. Although the total area of the narrow coastal strip is negligible in comparison to the land area of Kerry and only an insignificant part of the vast expanse of the seas around us, the interest to be discovered in this narrow strip is out of all proportion to its extent.

In this section we shall deal with that narrow belt of land left exposed at low tide – the inter-tidal zone. In this region an enormous variety of habitats exist, as different as mountains, moorlands and meadows on dry land. But whereas zonation exists on dry land over a vertical range of hundreds of metres, in this inter-tidal zone it is telescoped into a range of a few metres. It is a difficult region for animals and plants to live in, neither entirely marine nor fully terrestrial, and a wide variety of adaptations have evolved to cope with this environment. Only the hardiest and most adaptable plants and animals can survive in this hostile region, yet this zone displays an incredible richness of life, occupying almost every conceivable niche.

The most important factor facing inter-tidal animals and plants is the twice-daily ebb and flow of the tides, caused by the gravitational pull of the sun and moon. When these large bodies are at right angles to each other, at the first and last quarter of the moon, the effect on the oceans is reduced, and the tide neither comes in too high nor retreats too far out – a neap tide. A neap tide floods in at a relatively leisurely pace, reaching its highest point about three-quarters of the way up the shore. After a short period of slack water it gradually turns and recedes equally sedately to a low point about three-quarters of the way down the shore.

When the sun, moon and earth are aligned, their gravitational pull is magnified and very high and low spring tides are the result. Spring tides flood in more quickly to the high-water spring tide level, turn quickly and recede down the shore to the low-water spring tide level. For complex astronomical reasons, the strongest tidal effect is observed in the days after the full and the new moon, rather than at the peak of these lunar phases. Strong onshore winds can have a surprisingly marked effect on tides, pushing the water higher up the shore than usual and delaying its turning. Certain spring tides are particularly dramatic and the equi-noctial spring tides of February and March are among the best of the year and should not be missed by the naturalist wishing to reach sections of shore exposed only once a year.

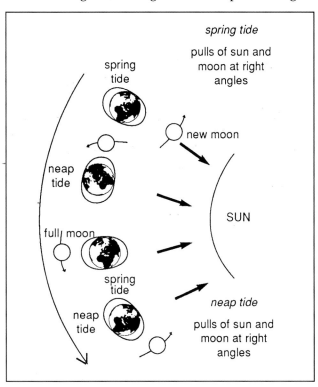

Figure 3: The Lunar Cycle

During neap tides, the timing of full tide is about an hour later than the previous day, whilst during spring tides it arrives about 40 minutes later. Thus if high tide is at 0900 hours one day during a neap tide, it will be at about 1000 hours the day after. The average tidal range on the Kerry coast is about three metres during neap tides, but as much as 4.5 metres during spring tides. The tide times for Dingle are published in the national daily newspapers. The tide is full in at the same time in Kilmakilloge harbour in Kenmare bay, but for Cromane and Tralee add about 35 and 13 minutes respectively, and subtract 25 minutes for Valentia harbour.

This repeated ebb and flow of the tides poses a number of problems for those animals and plants living in this environment. As the vast majority of these organisms are of marine origin, the first problem which they face is desiccation – most marine animals use gills to breathe and must keep them continually wet. One feature which many intertidal animals have evolved is a shell. These originally evolved as an anti-predator device, but being waterproof are a pre-adaptation for inter-tidal life. The shells of animals such as common winkles are closed by an operculum, a hinged flap which creates a water-tight fit. Limpets can pull their shells tight against the rock, which serves the same function. Behavioural adaptations to prevent drying out include seeking out crevices, retreating deeper into the substrate or to rock pools and clumping together.

Other organisms have evolved physiological tolerances to the problem of desiccation. Intertidal organisms display varying degrees of tolerance so species progressively replace each other along a gradient from deep water to the high shore. Plant species such as the channelled wrack, the seaweed most often found at the highest point on the shore, can withstand a loss of 80% or more of its weight. Many high shore animals are white or pale coloured to reflect light and heat, while darker coloured ones such as winkles may seek out the protection of crevices on hot days. Another problem is temperature stress. As the intertidal zone warms up beneath a spring sun, it is not unusual for the surface temperature to reach 20°C or more, to be suddenly cooled to 10°C or less as the tide floods in.

Varying salinity is another important ecological factor. Oceanic water has a salinity of 35 parts per 1,000 or 3.5%, declining to about 3.3% in coastal zones. Where large volumes of freshwater enter an estuary, the salinity varies quite dramatically twice daily. In the upper and middle reaches, the salinity of the water will range from almost fully freshwater at low tide to almost completely saltwater at high tide. The salt water, being denser and heavier than the fresh, flows in along the bottom of the channel, while the lighter fresh water fans out as a layer above it. Even a small stream flowing onto a rocky shore will cause a variation in salinity while the tide is out and often has interesting localised effects on the flora and fauna.

Transplantation experiments have shown that many of the common animals and plants of the intertidal zone often thrive and fare better when moved to the lower shore, but their present restriction to the upper shore is principally determined by their interaction with other organisms. Thus the lower limits of species such as mussels and barnacles is largely restricted by predation from whelks. Grazing and predation by mobile shore animals such as limpets and dogwhelks is important on the lower shore when the tide is in. Conversely, predation by birds such as oystercatchers, turnstones and even hooded crows is greater on the upper shore or at low tide.

ESTUARIES

Our own journey of discovery begins in the estuaries of Kerry, where the rivers of the county meet the waters of the Atlantic ocean. The combination of varying salinity, continual deposition of mud and reduced light levels makes estuaries a particularly difficult environment for organisms, especially plants, which need light to photosynthesise. However, vast quantities of nutrients are deposited by the river and tides. Relatively few animal species have managed to make the necessary adaptations required, but those that have often have enormous populations. One of the smallest creatures is *Hydrobia*, a tiny snail measuring only 5-6 millimetres long. It spends much of its life on the mud surface, feeding on the film of algae present. The population of *Hydrobia* may exceed 30,000 per square metre, and it forms an important part of the diet of many birds and fish. Another numerous and important organism is *Corophium volutator*, a crustacean which dwells within u-shaped burrows. When the tide is in, *Corophium* crawls over the mud surface picking up small fragments of organic debris with its legs.

Burrowing is a particularly common *modus operandi* of estuarine organisms. One of the commonest animals is the baltic tellin, a bivalved mollusc which remains hidden below the mud surface, but which uses feeding tubes called siphons to filter organic material from the water. The common cockle has very short siphons and hardly burrows at all, remaining just below the mud surface, with the upper edges of its two valves protruding above the mud. Though more common on clean, sandy beaches, they are also a frequent component of the mud flat community and an important food source for many animals including man. The mounds of discarded cockle shells found on kitchen middens, some quite ancient, are a testimony to the long-standing importance of cockles as food for humans. Such middens are to be found at Inch, Ballybunion and other coastal sites.

The common ragworm lives in semi-permanent mucus-lined burrows. It is recognised by the distinctive red line of its dorsal blood vessel which runs the length of its back and the numerous leg-like outgrowths or parapodia, each of which is equipped with bristles. Each parapodium also acts as a gill, absorbing oxygen from the water. Ragworms are active predators of small shrimp and other creatures, locating them with their eyes and antennae before seizing them with their strong jaws.

At low tide we may find clumps of mud-coloured tubes protruding from the substrate, which appear relatively uninteresting. When the tide floods in, however, their occupants, the peacock worm, enliven the muddy bottom with a display of multi-coloured fans. The fans are composed of feathery tentacles which are sensitive to changes in light levels and vibrations and are immediately withdrawn if danger threatens. These tentacles are highly modified gills which absorb oxygen and filter food from the water.

The shore crab is equally abundant on rocky shores, mud flats and salt marsh pools. It grows to about nine centimetres in length, with a shell colour ranging from blackish-green to dark red, with sharp serrations along its front edge. It is a scavenger, eating almost anything dead or alive and is quite pugnacious, as its French name *le crab enrage* indicates. Crabs grow by periodically moulting their old shell to expose the new, soft shell beneath. Most species mate only when the female is soft and the male may carry her with him for some days until she moults.

Goose barnacles on driftwood

Kerry is well endowed with extensive sandy beaches, particularly from Rossbeigh to Ballybunion as well as in south Kerry. Such sandy beaches are particularly difficult habitats for organisms. Sand forms a movable, shifting substrate of unstable nature, so that few living things can establish themselves in its uppermost layers. Most occupants of this habitat are burrowers. One such animal is the lugworm, which leave the familiar worm casts on sandy beaches from the middle shore downwards to the sea. They live in u-shaped burrows, the walls of which are lined with mucus to keep them intact. Near the cast will be a shallow depression marking the head end of the worm. They feed by swallowing large quantities of sand, absorbing the organic content and ejecting the remainder onto the surface. Beaches with a high content of organic matter may have lugworm densities in excess of 25,000 animals per hectare. Spawning takes place towards the end of October. Males shed their sperm in synchrony, while fertilisation takes place in the female's burrows. The fertilised eggs hatch into larvae, and for safety's sake, the entire population ceases feeding until the minute juveniles have been carried by tides to silty areas further upshore, where they are an important food source for wintering waders.

Sheltered sandy beaches are home to a wide variety of crabs. The masked crab is elongated, with its legs situated well to the rear of the carapace, a long rostrum and extremely long antennae in front. Its name derives from the resemblance of furrows on its upper shell to a human face. By day these crabs lie buried beneath the sand, breathing through a special arrangement of their antennae. The inner edges of these are lined with hairs, which interlock to form a breathing tube.

Common shrimps are locally abundant on sandy beaches and in sheltered bays and estuaries. They are well camouflaged, cautious and nocturnal, so are quite difficult to observe. They grow to about five centimetres in length, ranging in colour from grey to brown, generally matching that of the sand. They emerge at night to feed, walking steadily over the surface to search for food with their antennae. Shrimps eat small fish, worms, small crustaceans and vegetable and animal debris.

A walk along any sandy beach will give a hint of the wide variety of shelled animals which live offshore. Discarded shells of many species may be found, including various species of cockles, tellins, carpet shells, edible oysters and pod razor shells, to name but a few. A good seashore guide such as the *Marine Field Course Guide. 1. Rocky Shores,* published by Immel or the *Collins Pocket Guide to the Seashore* will greatly enhance the enjoyment of a beach or shoreline walk.

EXPOSED ROCKY SHORES

While estuarine and sandy shores may appear somewhat devoid of life, a quick glance at a rocky shore will show this to be a tremendously rich and varied habitat, abounding with creatures and plants. Such rocky, seaweed covered shores are good places to search for and study intertidal animals. Look for areas with a good mixture of pools and crevices, but take care not to slip into these. It is essential to remember that, especially in summers, daytime low tides are potentially lethal for intertidal animals. If you move overhanging curtains of wracks you will find rich communities of worms,

A seashore naturalist

sponges, sea squirts and cnidarians, but just a few minutes of strong sunlight can destroy the entire community. Be sure to replace the seaweed cover! Turning over large rocks will expose communities of encrusting animals such as sponges and bryozoans, as well as brittlestars, small crabs and molluscs. However, most will swiftly perish unless you carefully return the rock to its original position. If you wish to get endless enjoyment from your seashore visits, be sure to replace the rocks and seaweeds.

One of the major problems faced by organisms of exposed shores is the force of breaking waves. Inhabitants of the open ocean can sink into deep water to avoid rough seas, but shore-dwellers have no such refuge. The exposed coasts of Kerry receive some of the most violent surf in the world, driven by winds that have had a huge expanse of ocean to sweep across. Waves release tremendous energy as they break upon the shore, sometimes delivering blows of awesome force. Yet very few coasts have completely defeated the attempts of life forms to colonise them. The most inhospitable habitats are boulder and pebble beaches which shift in the surf, grinding one stone against the other, and easily eroded cliffs composed of soft materials. Even in these seemingly impossible circumstances some life almost certainly exists, living deep within the interstices between the rocks or cliff face.

Organisms living on rocky shores are more exposed to the rigours of the environment than those living in softer sediments such as sand and mud. One of their principal problems is maintaining a hold and remaining in position. To this end a variety of adaptations have evolved. These range from the holdfasts of seaweeds to the adhesive foot of snails, the byssus threads of mussels and the modified, sucker-like fins of pool-dwelling fish. Other creatures bore into the rock, use crevices or form dense aggregations to expose a smaller surface area.

A fine example of an exposed, rocky shore is found at Parkmore Point on the western tip of the Dingle peninsula. The flora and fauna of this site was first described by J.R. Lewis in his classic book, *The Ecology of Rocky Shores*. On the steeply sloping rocks four different zones can be easily recognised.

Working from clifftop to bottom we first enter the splash zone, the transition area between land and sea. On a calm, summers day it is dry and awash with colour. During winter storms, however, this region is drenched by breaking waves and salt spray, conditions intolerable to most terrestrial organisms. We first notice patches of the greenish-grey lichen *Ramilina siliquosa* or sea ivory, mixed with odd splashes of the yellow lichen *Xanthoria parietina* and the reddish-orange *Caloplaca thallincola*. Below these lichens extends a dark band of two black lichen species; *Lichina confinis* uppermost, resembling a scattering of soot, and *Verrucaria maura*, adhering so closely to the rock that, in spite of its finely cracked thalus, it looks like a thin layer of tar or black paint. *Verrucaria* is the dominant species, in places up to 20′ to 30′ in width. It lies entirely above the high tide level and extends as far as the eye can see along the adjacent coast. Small insects and spiders exist among the foliose lichens or in the deeper cracks, along with the five millimetre high, small periwinkle, which occurs above the high-water line. Lower down the *Verrucaria* belt numbers of rough periwinkles occur in the deeper clefts. These measure up to 20 millimetres high and have a distinct rough, ridged shell which varies in colour from yellow, white, grey or green to reddish-brown. They feed by scraping off micro-particles of detritus or algae with their rasping, file-like radula. This is a special organ consisting of chitin which lies like a continuous belt on the floor of the pharynx. Rough periwinkles are viviparous, the female retaining her eggs within special cocoons in her body until they hatch into fully developed young.

Below the black lichen zone lies the whitish-looking barnacle zone. It averages about a metre in depth on steeper rock faces. The dominant barnacle species is *Chthamalus stellatus*. The dividing line between the two zones is quite abrupt, often less than 15 centimetres in width, leaving one with the impression of someone having drawn a sharp line along the rock face. Above this line a few *Chthamalus* occur in crevices. A comparison of adjacent situations suggests that the upper limit of *Chthamalus* is most ragged where splashing and wave surge can be expected at high tide. Barnacles have evolved two major adaptations to assist their survival.

The base of their cone-shaped shell is fixed to the rock with a natural cement of extraordinary strength, and their low conical shape deflects the force of the wave. In the upper section the barnacles are conical and well formed. Lower down, however, where competition for space is greater and densities are much higher, many are elongated and columnar in shape. Here the barnacles may reach densities of 400,000-600,000 per square metre, each barnacle having only a tiny area of attachment to the rock substrate, depending largely upon lateral support from its neighbours. Barnacles are not snails but belong to the crustacea, that group which includes lobsters, crabs, shrimps and sand-hoppers. When the tide is in they feed by opening their opercular plates and projecting their cirri (modified legs). The waving action of the cirri draws food and oxygen-rich water to the barnacles. It has been said that barnacles feed by kicking food into their mouth with their feet while standing on their heads!

The common limpet is another creature well-suited to life on exposed shores, becoming progressively more abundant lower down. They are a simple and primitive snail that have developed a cone-shaped shell, and which anchor themselves to the rock with a suction cup of fleshy tissue. The force of pounding water serves to press their shell against the surface more firmly, strengthening their grip on the rock. When the tide is out, limpets remain firmly attached to the rock face. But when the tide returns, limpets move about over the rocks grazing algae as they move. They feed mainly on the algal sporelings and effectively prevent seaweeds from establishing themselves. There is a complex balance on rocky shores between limpets and their algal food, tilted in favour of limpets by increasing exposure to wave action. If limpets are experimentally removed from exposed shores, algal growth develops unimpeded, indicating their importance as grazers.

When feeding, limpets leave a chemical trail behind them and return unerringly to their home scars when the tide starts to recede. On soft rocks such as limestone the limpet grinds down a depression or, on hard rock, has its shell worn down to fit the rock perfectly. Due to this perfect fit, water for breathing can be retained within the shell during low tide. Limpets have a complex reproductive strategy. As they become sexually mature, most are males. As they age, a proportion of the population becomes female, whereas others remain as males. They start breeding in November, induced to spawn by falling temperatures and wave shock. After a few days their free-swimming larvae settle in crevices and pools on the middle and upper shore.

Below the barnacle belt there is a very sudden transition to the blue-black mussel zone, which stretches in a continuous belt along the rocky shore. Common mussels are one of the most numerous animals of rocky shores, reaching densities of many thousands per square metre. Measuring up to eight centimetres in length, they are commercially and ecologically important. Mussels attach themselves using byssus threads which are secreted as a thick fluid which hardens on contact with water. Young mussels can reabsorb their threads and move about until they find a suitable place to attach themselves, but older mussels rarely move. When the tide is in, they feed by drawing water in through their frilly siphon and emitting it through another, plain one. A female produces 5-12 million eggs which hatch after a couple of weeks into tiny larvae. These are free-swimming for two to three weeks, when they settle on rocks. Mussels themselves act as a substrate for

the attachment of barnacles and other creatures, as well as algae. In the steeper situations, scattered plants of two red algae *Lithothamnion arbuscula* and *Porphyra umbilicalis* occur. Here and there on patches of bare rock tufts of bladder wrack appear, a species of exposed shores throughout Ireland. Its fronds have a distinct mid-rib with pairs of air bladders on either side, which ensure that the wrack floats upwards towards the light.

Common starfish, an important predator of mussels

Below this mussel zone seaweeds predominate. Where wave action is most severe *Alaria esculenta* is dominant. This grows to two metres in length, with long undivided fronds and a distinctive midrib. In more sheltered sites oarweed becomes common. This has thin, root-like holdfasts, a cylindrical stalk and oar-shaped fronds divided into many ribbons. Beneath the large seaweeds there is an almost complete cover of the calcareous alga *Corallina officinalis*, while the presence of pink, encrusting seaweeds such as *Lithothamnion* gives a pinkish colour to the rock. The fronds of *Corallina* are impregnated with calcium and magnesium salts, which gives the plant a distinctive hard, brittle feeling and reduces its palatability to grazing molluscs and other animals.

SHELTERED ROCKY SHORES

On gently shelving rocky shores, it is easier for us to explore the differing micro-habitats. In sheltered areas a wider variety of organisms may be found, although the general zonation will be similar to that found at Parkmore point. If we travel across Dingle bay and around the Iveragh peninsula we will find that another world awaits us in the naturally protected inlet of Kenmare bay.

The most obvious features of these shores are the masses of brown seaweeds, or algae, which are found draped over the rocks. In spite of the limitations imposed by excessive wave action and voracious grazers, most temperate, rocky shores support algal vegetation. They provide a surface for the attachment of epiphytic organisms, food for herbivores, a sheltering breakwater when the tide is in and a moist protective blanket from the sun, rain and air when the tide is out.

Seaweeds thrive best on sheltered or semi-sheltered shores. They do not resist the waves, but yield readily to them. They do not require the supporting stem or trunk of terrestrial plants, as the water supports them. Thus pliability and elasticity are more important assets than simple strength. They also lack the roots of terrestrial plants, as they do not need to absorb minerals from the soil. Being almost continuously bathed in seawater, they live within a solution of all the necessary minerals needed. They do, however, have root-like structures called holdfasts, which are flattened, disc-like expansions at the base of the plant. These look as if a bit of the plant had melted, spread out and congealed, thus creating a very powerful attachment to the rocks. The most striking distribution pattern exhibited by littoral seaweeds is their vertical zonation. The extent of exposure to air inhibits the shore-ward distribution of some species, while competition, grazing and lack of light limit their seaward extent.

On moderately exposed shores one finds a mosaic of seaweeds, bare rock, barnacles and limpets, whereas on sheltered shores a continuous cover of algae can be seen. The upper shores are dominated by swathes of channelled wrack, which has inward-curling edges to its bladder-less fronds, forming distinctive channels. This seaweed is physiologically adapted to withstand prolonged exposure and may spend up to 80% of its time out of water. When exposed to sun and air for prolonged periods it blackens and turns crisp, so one would be excused for thinking it had died. On being immersed in seawater again, however, its normal colour and texture is restored. In summer and autumn the plants will produce swollen, orange-coloured reproductive bodies at the tips of its fronds. Further down the shore we find bladder wrack and knotted wrack; the largest species of wrack which may grow up to three metres long. It has oval bladders down the middle of each frond, and yellowish, raisin-shaped, fruiting bodies borne on slender side branches. Growing on it and almost exclusive to this species, will be found a tufted dark red alga called *Polysiphonia lanosa*. The cells of brown seaweeds contain both chlorophyll, which gives the green algae and most terrestrial plants their green colour, and brown pigments such as fucoxanthin which masks the green of the chlorophyll. In rock pools and on the lower shore we find toothed wrack, with serrated edges to its fronds and no air bladders. Here too we find species such as dulse and pepper dulse. The former has flat fronds which are sometimes divided palmately, arising directly from a small disc holdfast. It is dark red with purple reflections. Pepper dulse is rusty-red in colour, with tough, flattened fronds which branch alternately from the main stem.

When the equinoctal spring tides expose the lowest sections of shore, it is possible for us to search for seaweeds and other organisms rarely seen at other times. Here the dominant algae are the kelps. Three species are widespread and common. *Laminaria digitata* is one of the largest species. Its fronds are divided into 'fingers', and it has a flexible, oval stalk. *Laminaria hyperborea* is somewhat similar, but has a stiff, round stalk which causes it to stand upright when the tide recedes. The sugar kelp has a small holdfast, a short stipe and long, undivided fronds which have crinkly edges. One of the most beautiful species which may be found in the narrow zone above the kelps or in deep rock pools is the rainbow bladder weed, a prickly-looking shrubby perennial which has a striking blue iridescence. This is a warm water species which is at the northern end of its range in Ireland.

The kelps extend well below the low water mark, often forming dense forests. They have a considerable influence on the communities of plants and animals which can survive there. Their dense canopies reduce light penetration to lower levels, while the sweeping action of their fronds keeps nearby rocks free of other organisms. Their survival in heavy waves is mainly a matter of chemistry. Large amounts of alginic acid and its salts are contained within their tissues. This creates a tensile strength and elasticity which enables it to withstand the tearing and pounding action of waves.

The reproductive strategies of the common seaweeds are complex and varied. Some species such as bladder wrack and toothed wrack have plants of separate sex, whereas the spiral wrack has both male and female parts on the same plant. Some have alternate phases in their life history which look so dissimilar that it was once believed they were different plants. The egg wrack reproduces primarily by vegetative means from existing clumps, some of which are believed to be tens to hundreds of years old. Most species have a dispersive phase in their life cycle, which drift in the water before settling on the rock and growing into a tiny plant or sporeling. These form the preferred food of many of the grazing animals.

Turning over a handful of seaweeds we will frequently find the edible common winkles. Growing to a length of 30 millimetres, they are dark grey or black in colour, with a horny plate – the operculum – which is used to seal the entrance to the shell when the tide is out or when danger threatens. Mating occurs in spring, after which the female releases lens-shaped egg capsules into the sea. Each capsule measures about one millimetre across and contains up to nine eggs. After about six days these hatch into minute larvae which drift in the plankton for a few weeks before settling on the lower shore during mid-summer.

Common winkles and limpets

Top shells have a conical shape and a broad base to the shell. They prefer long, broken reefs or undisturbed boulder beaches. The purple top is greenish in colour with purple bands. It is more common on the west coast than on the east, except in areas of freshwater influence, strong currents or silting, factors

180

known to affect its distribution. The thick top shell is a southern, warm water species found along the west and south coasts of Ireland. Measuring up to 25 millimetres high, it is greyish or greenish in colour with indistinct, purple zigzag markings. In some specimens the cone of the shell may be worn, exposing the silvery mother-of-pearl. If we search the lower shore carefully, we may find the painted top shell, the most striking species of the group. They have a pointed, conical shape and dramatic pink stripes. Top shells and limpets are all grazers, feeding mainly on the newly-germinated seaweed sporelings which settle on the rocks. Species such as the green seaweed *Enteromorpha intestinalis* and the sea lettuce *Ulva lactuca* are particularly prone to grazing and are often only found where a freshwater stream flows across a rocky shore. Most of the grazing molluscs are only active in fully saline conditions and cannot tolerate freshwater, so the algal sporelings have a chance to germinate and grow in herbivore-free conditions. One of the few grazers which feeds directly on the stipes and fronds of the large kelps is the blue-rayed limpet. Measuring less than 25 millimetres in length, they have four to six rows of vivid blue spots running the length of their shell. The deep cavities they excavate can badly weaken the plants.

Scattered over the middle and lower shore one sees numerous dog whelks, an important predator of barnacles and mussels. Their thick, spiralled shells are usually whitish, up to 30 millimetres long, with a distinct groove running from the shell opening into the interior. This is the siphonal canal, through which the dog whelk extends its tube-like siphon, which it uses to breathe and sense food. When feeding, they settle on their prey and secrete a chemical which softens and dissolves the shell. With the aid of its file-like radula, the dogwhelk rasps a hole through the softened shell, injects digestive enzymes into the animal and ingests the liquified contents.

Another grazer of young algae is the purple sea urchin, one of the specialities of the Irish west coast, particularly on more exposed stretches. You will definitely need a low spring tide to find these, sheltering in cavities or beneath rocks on the lower shore. In deeper pools there may be hundreds per square metre, giving a purplish hue to the pool bottom. The strong suction of their tube feet enable sea urchins to graze on vertical rock faces and kelp stems. Their five strong teeth are used to scrape the sporelings of algae and small animals such as sea mats and sea firs off the substrate. In suitable conditions, sea urchins may reach very high densities, preventing regeneration of algae over large areas.

Sponges brighten our rocky shores, existing in an astonishing variety of sizes, colour and shapes. They are simple animals which feed by pumping water in through their porous surfaces and extracting suspended plankton and bacteria. The filtered water is discharged through larger openings called oscula visible on their surface. Their skeletons consist of gelatinous material strengthened with minute needles or spicules composed of silica, calcium carbonate (chalk) or a fibrous material called spongin. The bath sponge of the Mediterranean and warm water areas has spicules composed of spongin. Sponges occur on both exposed and sheltered shores, from the middle shore seawards, usually on shaded rocks and under overhangs. Those exposed to fast currents or strong wave action tend to conform in shape to the substrate, thus enabling them to withstand the turbulence. Most species are hermaphrodites, with both male and female sex cells. After fertilisation occurs the eggs develop into tiny larvae which are released through the osculum. These spend some time in the plankton before settling on the seabed.

One of the most common species is the breadcrumb sponge, so-named because of the manner in which it crumbles when handled. Its vivid green colour make it easy to recognise, forming patches up to 20 centimetres across and two centimetres in thickness. Numerous volcano-like oscula cover its surface. The bright colour is due to the presence of algae which live in the sponge. In shaded sites the algae are absent and the sponge is yellow in colour. *Hymeniacidon perleve* is orange or yellowy-red in colour, up to 50 centimetres across and a centimetre in thickness. Its surface is covered by indistinct oscula and is broken by irregular ridges and furrows.

Sponges have been described as living hotels. The larger species in particular act as hosts to a wide range of animals such as worms, crabs and small fish. Others have a more complicated relationship with animals. The boring sponge burrows into the shells of scallops and oysters, probably by secreting an acid which dissolves the shell.

If you examine bare areas of rock, shells and the large fronds of kelp, you will often find a variety of hard, white encrustations. These are the homes of the serpulid worms. These animals secrete and live inside a calcareous tube, which is

A large colony of honeycomb worms, near Rossbeigh

normally cemented to a rock or kelp frond. The tubes may be irregularly bent and triangular in cross-section, as in the keel worm, measuring up to two centimetres long. When visible, the feeding tentacles have a banded appearance. Others have spiral-shaped tubes such as the coiled tube worm, whose tiny tubes are twisted in a clockwise direction. The tube opens at its wider end, from where the animal extends feathery tentacles to catch suspended particles of food. At low tide the opening is plugged by an operculum. Dense clusters of these organisms may be seen on rocks and seaweeds from the middle shore downwards. One of the most fascinating of the tube building worms is the honeycomb worm. This worm forms its tube from sand grains, living in colonies which build into large honeycomb structures. They are found on the lower shore, in areas of rocks and boulders where sand is also present. Their distribution around Kerry's coast is patchy, but extensive colonies up to a metre across can be seen on the rocky shore between Kells and Rossbeigh.

The large pools often found on rocky shores hold brightly coloured anemones. They are simple animals related to jellyfish and hydroids. Their bodies consist of a columnar structure, with a base at one end and a mouth at the other. The mouth is surrounded by a ring of tentacles armed with stinging cells. When touched by a passing animal, these stinging cells explode and discharge microscopic threads which impale the victim.

The beadlet anemone is the most common species on shores and in rock pools. They are quite variable in colour, ranging from red to brown or green. This species can be identified when open by the ring of blue warts lying at the base of each tentacle. If two beadlets come into contact with each other, one will often attack the other, the aggressor stinging its opponent's column with its warts, until the weaker of the two retreats. Studies suggest that the red types are the most aggressive. This behaviour is thought to space the animals out, thus reducing competition for food. The jewel anemone is widespread on shaded rocks on the lower shore and occurs in a range of colours from scarlet to white. One of the largest species is the dahlia anemone, measuring up to 20 centimetres across and occurring in almost any colour. Their columns are covered in sticky warts, to which pieces of gravel and shells adhere. These help camouflage the animal when the tide is out.

Hidden at the bottom of pools you may disturb a velvet crab. They are an aggressive species, with bold leg markings, bright red eyes and strong claws. If threatened, it will sit back on its rear legs and spread its claws wide apart in an intimidating manner. The flattened hind legs enable them to swim rapidly away from predators.

Rocky shores are the haunt of blennies – chunky large-headed fish with long dorsal fins. They live in rock pools or in damp crevices beneath seaweed. The shanny is the most common fish of such areas, measuring up to 16 centimetres long and a dull brown in colour, blotched with darker markings. After spawning, which occurs in early summer, the male guards and cares for the eggs constantly until they hatch. The young feed on small invertebrates but also nip the feet off feeding barnacles. The goby is another small fish, but with two separate dorsal fins and a single, fused pelvic fin. They are mainly sandy coloured with a variable amount of blotching and can be difficult to identify to species level. They are found in sandy or muddy areas of the seashore.

Most shore fish move seawards with the onset of winter and cooler temperatures. Sand gobies, which are abundant in shallow pools during summer, disappear abruptly once the water temperature drops below 5^0C. The butterfish, however, is a winter breeder, and from October onwards females can be discovered brooding eggs beneath stones or in empty bivalve shells in the low intertidal zone. Butterfish are dark greyish/brown in colour with a line of 9-13 dark spots along the base of the dorsal fin. They grow to 25 centimetres in length and occur at depths of up to 30 metres, feeding on small crustaceans and other invertebrates.

In this brief survey of Kerry's intertidal zone we have noted some of the more common species of animals and plants. It is one of the most fascinating and least explored wildlife habitats in the county, rewarding the curious naturalist with new experiences on nearly every visit.

BEYOND THE INTERTIDAL

The enormous variety of sea-life beyond the intertidal fringe is well beyond the scope of this book to cover. However, a number of interesting aspects about Kerry's marine life are worth mentioning. Kerry has a number of advantages over other coastal regions for the shore-based naturalist who wishes to glimpse this fauna. Its location on the south-west corner of Ireland and the geography of the county mean that many migratory species pass close enough inshore to be seen. Also, the presence of a major fishing port at Dingle gives us a greater insight into the variety of fish and other marine life to be encountered offshore.

Of the commoner species of fish, the thick-lipped grey mullet is a typical estuarine species which may grow up to 75 centimetres long. Their feeding method is unusual – they suck up the mud and extract small animals, or graze the surface algae. The thick, muscular wall of their stomach grinds the mud and food to a smooth consistency and improves their digestive efficiency. The flounder is the most estuarine of the flatfish and can even tolerate freshwater. They measure up to 50 centimetres long and are brownish or greyish-green in colour, sometimes with pale orange spots. As we saw in the previous chapter, large numbers frequently penetrate quite far upriver during summer. In estuaries they feed on worms, crustaceans and molluscs.

In rocky areas a number of species of wrasse occur. The ballan wrasse is the largest species, growing to 60 centimetres long and weighing up to 3.5 kilograms. They are slow-growing, long-lived and highly territorial, found from the intertidal zone down to 30 metres depth. Their food consists of molluscs and crustaceans, which they macerate with their powerful throat teeth. Their life cycle is rather unusual. No juvenile males have ever been found and the population consists of more females than males. All ballan wrasse are born as females, becoming sexually mature at about six years of age. As they mature, some individuals change sex to males, although there is no external difference between the sexes. In another species, the cuckoo wrasse females are red in colour, with black marks near the tail. When the sex change occurs, she becomes predominantly blue above and orange below. It is thought that these changes are controlled by social pressures. When an older, dominant male dies, his territory may be taken by a large female, which then undergoes a sex change to become the dominant male.

Many rare and unusual fish, mammals and other animals are caught or reported every year by trawlers operating out of Dingle. As the average temperature of the waters around Ireland appears to be increasing, probably due to climate warming, it is to be expected that more southern species will appear in our waters. In 1995 the seawater temperature reached 22⁰C, the highest ever recorded. In the same year, Spanish and Irish trawlers were fishing for tuna, normally regarded as a warm-water species, in waters north of the Shannon estuary.

A sample of rare fish which have occurred off Kerry is listed in table 19.

TABLE 19
SOME UNUSUAL FISH CAUGHT OFF THE KERRY COAST

Black-mouthed dogfish	Sunfish
Barrel-fish	Swordfish
Bluefin tuna	Scaldfish
Boarfish	Triggerfish
Bogue	Wreckfish
Six-gilled shark	

Triggerfish are brown or greyish deep-bodied fish which lack pelvic fins. They are primarily found in tropical Atlantic waters and grow to 40 centimetres in length. In late summer, they sometimes appear in numbers in north European waters. The wreckfish is a deep-water species, usually living at depths down to 1000 metres. It has powerful, sharp teeth, capable of cracking the shells of lobster. Measuring up to 66 centimetres in length, its normal distribution is 20⁰ north and south of the Equator, but it has occurred as far north as Norway and appears to be expanding its range into north European waters. There have been less than 30 Irish records, mostly from the south and south-west coasts. Although a deep-water species, it has a habit of following floating objects near the surface. Specimens recorded off our coast tend to be tame and approachable. In 1975, a wreckfish was photographed by divers off Great Skellig as it sheltered under a large, floating container unit.

One of the most unusual looking species is the sunfish. Measuring up to three metres long, sunfish have a short, laterally-compressed body, a much-reduced tail, and long dorsal and anal fins. These are modified to form paddles which the fish can only move from side-to-side. Although they are a tropical fish, spawning in the Sargasso sea, they are frequently seen in Irish waters during summer, drifting at the surface while lying on their sides. It is believed that this basking behaviour is used by the fish to allow the sun to kill off lice attached to their bodies. Sunfish feed on animal plankton, eel larvae and small, deep-sea fishes.

TURTLES

The marine turtles are among the more dramatic animals which frequent our off-shore waters. Four species have been recorded in Irish waters; leathery turtle, loggerhead, hawksbill and Kemp's ridley. All are long-lived, spending most of their time at sea and only leaving the water to lay their eggs on tropical and sub-tropical beaches, where some species face their most serious problems; tourist developments, egg-collection and the adults being killed for food and shells.

THE ANIMAL WITH THE SAILS

The basking shark is the largest fish in European waters and the second largest in the world. It occurs in most of the earth's temperate oceans, usually appearing off the Irish coast from April to November, when water temperatures reach a minimum of 11.5⁰C.

Because of its habit of cruising the surface of the waters, or basking, its other common name is the sunfish, but its Gaelic name of ainmhidhe na seolta *(animal with the sails) is more evocative. These giant fish, measuring up to nine metres long and weighing up to seven tonnes, cruise through the seas with their mouths agape, filtering vast quantities of planktonic animals from the water. Their gill arches carry a large number of long, slender horny gill rakers which act as filters. At a swimming speed of two knots, the basking shark can filter the plankton from 1,500 tonnes of water per hour. Their skin exudes a black, slimy substance, which probably has a function in discouraging skin parasites.*

1993 saw the launch of a basking shark sighting scheme to determine the abundance and distribution of these animals off the Irish coast. In its first year, 142 sighting records were made of 425 individuals, with observations from all around the Irish coast. The greatest number of observations, totalling in excess of 160 animals, were off south-west Ireland, particularly off north Kerry. Sightings peaked in June, with a lesser peak in September. Anybody out sailing, fishing or sea watching who sees some of these magnificent animals should send details to the Irish Whale and Dolphin Group.

The leathery turtle, the largest living reptile, is the most common species in our waters and is the most widely distributed reptile in the world. They average up to two metres in length and 750 kilograms in weight. The largest known specimen, a male which was found dead on a Welsh beach in 1988, measured nearly three metres in length and weighed 916 kilograms. Instead of the usual rigid, horny shell, these turtles have a thick leathery skin which gives them their name. They are very strong swimmers, ranging far into high latitudes in pursuit of jellyfish, their preferred prey. Due to a number of physiological adaptations – their large size, the presence of blubber and a heat exchange mechanism at the base of the flippers – they can tolerate the very cold temperatures which they encounter while in northern waters. They often dive deeply in pursuit of prey and have been recorded down to 1,200 metres.

A young common seal

All turtles are protected in Irish waters, and are frequently encountered by fishermen and other seafarers. Thanks to the goodwill and interest shown by such mariners, Gabriel King, a turtle enthusiast, was able to carry out a comprehensive survey of turtle sightings around our coast. By doing so our knowledge of turtle numbers and distribution has increased dramatically – leathery turtles are frequently seen off the Kerry coast during the summer months, while occasionally large numbers have been seen passing the headlands of Cape Clear, Co. Cork. Other large turtles, possibly loggerheads, have been encountered in deep waters, while smaller ones occur closer inshore. They are sometimes washed up onshore, particularly after prolonged westerly gales. Turtles face a number of other hazards. Some are drowned in nets before they can be released, while others are killed or injured in collisions with the propellers of boats. A more serious threat is marine pollution, particularly the presence of plastics and other debris floating in the water. Turtles are known to mistake such material for prey, sometimes resulting in obstruction to the gut or asphyxiation.

MARINE MAMMALS

A day's outing to any of Kerry's offshore islands is often rewarded by views of seals. Both species of seal inhabit the coasts of Kerry. The smaller and scarcer species is the common seal, measuring up to 1.7 metres in length. The smaller dog-like head distinguishes the common seal from the bigger grey seal, which has a large flat forehead. Common seals prefer sheltered waters within bays such as Kenmare bay, where an average of 30 animals occur, out of a total Irish population of about 700. Common seals give birth to their pups in July.

Grey seals prefer our more exposed coastal headlands and islands. Both species haul out frequently on rocks and large congregations of up to 50 grey seals can be seen on some islands, particularly during the breeding season. They breed on the Magharee, Blaskets, Skelligs,

The long sloping head of the grey seal distinguishes it from the common seal

187

Valentia and Scariff islands as well as on Brandon Head. During October, the males come ashore to establish territories, to be joined shortly afterwards by the females, some already pregnant from the previous year. After the birth of the pups, the young are suckled for about three weeks, then left to fend for themselves, while the adults mate again. Grey seals are prodigious travellers. One animal which was radio-collared on the Farne islands on the east coast of England was tracked to the Orkneys and the Faroe islands, before finally losing its collar somewhere off the coast of Galway.

A MOST UNUSUAL VISITOR

In early 1994 a large seal-like animal was washed up dead on the shore near Sybil head on the Dingle peninsula. Its most obvious distinguishing feature was a pair of 30 centimetre long tusks protruding from its mouth, identifying it as an adult male walrus. These are animals of Canadian Arctic waters and a very rare visitor to our side of the world. From its relatively fresh state it had probably died only a short time before it washed up. Walruses measure up to three metres long and have grey, wrinkled skin overlaying a thick layer of blubber. Adult males may weigh up to 300 kilos. Their tusks are actually elongated canine teeth.

WHALES AND DOLPHINS

Our visit to the Great Blasket island had gone very well, with a calm sea journey across to the island and excellent weather. As we ate our lunch in the middle of the Iron Age hilltop fort near the summit, a keen-eyed member of the group spotted something in the water 300 metres below – a herd of 12 dolphins. Their blunt, rounded heads, slow-swimming behaviour, lack of beak and an extensive whitish area between the head and the tall, sickle-shaped dorsal fin indicated that these were Risso's dolphin. At least three calves were present, with one particularly large animal, probably the dominant male. They cruised the shoreline slowly, sometimes diving out of view as if feeding, before finally disappearing around the point of the island. For all present, it was the highlight of the day. Risso's travel in groups of up to 30 animals, measure up to 4.3 metres in length and weigh up to 680 kilograms. The whitish area on the upper body of the older animals is caused by numerous scratches and scars, some of which may be caused by encounters with squid on which they feed almost exclusively.

Thanks to the work of Dr Simon Berrow and members of the Irish Whale and Dolphin Group, Kerry has been highlighted as one of the best locations in Ireland or Britain, if not Europe, for seeing cetaceans – dolphins, porpoises and whales. By watching from suitable vantage points, particularly during summer, many species can be seen on passage around our headlands. In September and October 1992, the

IWDG organised a survey of cetaceans around the Irish coast. Twenty-six sites were chosen as vantage points, including four in County Kerry and a watch was kept for periods of 100 minutes. One of the best sites was Slea Head, on the Dingle peninsula, with four sightings per 100 minutes.

Many other species occur off our coast apart from Risso's. Partly because of its inshore distribution, the harbour porpoise is the most commonly recorded cetacean around the Irish coast and is especially numerous off the south-west coast. Approximately 20,000 may be present during summer. It is the smallest cetacean, measuring up to 1.8 metres in length, with a black upper body, whitish underparts, a short blunt head, no beak, and a small, triangular dorsal fin at the mid-point of their back. Their diet includes sand-eels, flatfish, crabs, herring and mackerel. In 1988 a very rare, white harbour porpoise was enmeshed in nets off the Blasket islands.

Common dolphins are also frequently recorded. They grow to 2.4 metres in length and have a dark grey to brownish back with a distinctive hour-glass pattern of yellow patches on their sides. They travel in parties of up to 20 animals and are frequently reported bow-riding yachts and fishing vessels or leaping clear of the water, revealing their flank pattern.

Striped dolphins are very similar to common dolphins, but lack the yellow flank markings. They tend to occur in very deep water (greater than 1000 metres), with an average surface temperature of 19°C. There has been an increase in the number stranded on the Irish coast during the last decade, which taken in conjunction with an increase in the numbers of warm water fish occurring, may reflect an increase in sea temperature.

Kerry's most famous dolphin is Fungi, a bottle-nosed dolphin which has been to residence at the mouth of Dingle harbour since the winter of 1983. Bottle-nosed dolphins are slaty-blue or grey above, whitish below, with a short snout about 75 millimetres long and a slender, sickle-shaped fin. They can grow to four metres in length, weighing over 400 kilograms. Fungi quickly became a centre of attraction and soon became accustomed to the divers, swimmers and canoeists who arrived to see him. Local boatmen also appreciated that other visitors were interested in going out to see Fungi close-up and a lively business in dolphin-watching developed. An estimated 150,000 people travel to Dingle each year to see Fungi, which generates over £750,000 in cetacean-watching revenue.

White-sided dolphins grow up to three metres in length and have a distinctive light patch on the side. Their numbers are believed to have increased in recent decades. Large 'bachelor' herds, composed entirely of male animals, are frequent in the north-west Atlantic. As a greater proportion of males than females are reported stranded on the Irish coast, a similar pattern may occur off Irish coasts.

Pilot whales, which measure up to six metres long, are blackish in colour with white underparts. They have large bulbous foreheads and a prominent, rounded dorsal fin set quite far forward. They are highly gregarious, travelling in quite large herds, often of many hundreds. Squid and shoaling fish are their chief prey.

DOLPHINS IN THE SHANNON ESTUARY

Two separate populations of bottle-nosed dolphins are believed to occur in the North Atlantic, an offshore population and a coastal population scattered around various bays and estuaries. The Shannon estuary has had a well-established population for many years which ranges between Tarbert/Killimer to the east and Kerry head and the Magharee islands to the west. Since 1993, this population of dolphins has been studied by Dr Simon Berrow of University College Cork and his colleagues, partly to establish whether it would be feasible to run regular dolphin-watching trips from local harbours. A minimum population of 60-70 animals in several distinct groups occur in the estuary, of which they have been able to individually identify over 30 animals by the presence of notches and scars on fins and body. The presence of young calves each season since the study began indicates that the area is an important breeding ground.

For land-based observers, Beal point and Leck point have been found to be good locations to watch these dolphins from the Kerry side of the estuary, particularly about one to two hours after high water. In examining the commercial viability of dolphin watching, Dr Berrow pointed out that bottle-nosed dolphins are protected by Irish and European law and that studies elsewhere had found that they react negatively to disturbance from boats. As a commercial proposition, Dr Berrow suggested that cetacean-watching was potentially viable in the estuary, but should be carefully monitored and properly licensed if necessary to ensure the safety and welfare of the dolphins.

Killer whales are regular in small numbers along the coast. Their black bodies have large, white areas on the throat and belly with a distinctive lens-shaped patch behind the eye. Adult males may reach nine metres in length and are recognisable by the dorsal fin which may grow to 1.8 metres tall. Some groups of killer whales are predominantly fish hunters, others feed on birds, seals, porpoises and other large prey. The average lifespan is 50 years for females and 30 years for males. Females have their first calf at 14 years and bear one every six years or so thereafter.

Sperm whales are the largest toothed whale, growing up to 20 metres in length and weighing up to 36 tonnes. These giants are the deepest diving mammal of all, capable of diving to three kilometres and staying submerged for up to 90 minutes. They feed on giant squid and other deep-sea creatures. A number have stranded on Irish coasts. A 20 metre long sperm whale was found at Trabeg strand, Lispole in January 1987, with flukes four metres across. The head was two metres deep and 80 centimetres wide. Severe south-west gales the week before probably accounted for the whale being washed ashore. Another at Feoghanach in 1975 measured 15.5 metres in length. The most recent stranding was at Minard beach on the Dingle peninsula in October 1990.

Minke whales are the most likely large cetacean to be observed from land. They measure up to 8.5 metres long and are dark grey or black in colour with a distinctive white bar across each flipper. The small dorsal fin is set well back on the body. Minke whales are filter feeders, having a series of horny plates or baleen in the mouth each with a bristly fringe, through which they strain plankton and small fish from the water.

Fin whales are probably the most common large whale in the north-east Atlantic, although their stocks have been much depleted this century due to over-exploitation. They are dark grey in colour, with a small dorsal fin set well back. Fin whales grow to 24 metres, second in size to the blue whale, the largest animal on earth. They are normally solitary or found in small groups. Their blow rises six metres into the air and can be spotted up to eight kilometres away in calm conditions.

Other species occur off our coast, though in smaller numbers, but every year a number of whales and dolphins are washed up on our shores. Although some are already dead when they arrive onshore, others are very much alive but rarely last long.

Whales were once hunted in Irish waters, details of which can be read in Professor James Fairley's book *Irish Whales and Whaling*. Since 1991, however, all Irish territorial waters out to our 200 mile limit have been designated as a whale and dolphin sanctuary, the first such sanctuary in European. Interest in cetaceans has increased enormously in recent years, thanks largely due to the efforts of bodies such as the Irish Whale and Dolphin Group, who would welcome further support and reports of observations of cetaceans at sea and stranded on land. They can be contacted through the address in Appendix 3.

In 1993, whale-watching was estimated to be worth £1.2 million to the Irish economy, with excellent potential for growth. Much of this revenue was earned in Dingle, through the interest in Fungi-watching and the organised whale-watching trips which operate from there. Other coastal communities in Kerry such as Ballybunion, Valentia and Derrynane could well profit from similar ventures, but the organisers of such ventures should bear in mind their responsibilities to the welfare of these special creatures.

TABLE 20
RECORDS OF STRANDED CETACEANS ON THE KERRY COAST: **1980-1994**

SPECIES	NUMBER	DATE	LOCATION
Harbour porpoise	2	April 1982	Inch
	1	April 1982	Castlegregory
	2	April 1982	Banna
	1	Sept. 1992	Derrynane
	1	Dec. 1994	Inch
White-sided dolphin	1	April 1981	Dingle
	2	April 1989	Ballyferriter
Common dolphin	1	Jan. 1981	Tralee
	6	Jan. 1984	Fermoyle
	1	Aug. 1992	Smerwick
	1	Sept. 1992	Ventry
Euphrosyne dolphin	2	Sept. 1992	Dingle
Bottle-nosed dolphin	1	April 1989	Rossbehy
Risso's dolphin	1	Sept. 1992	Feohanagh
Pilot whale	1	March 1983	Waterville
	1	March 1988	Caherdaniel
Cuvier's beaked whale	1	May 1983	Brandon
Sperm whale	1	July 1982	Dunquin
	1	Jan. 1987	Near Dingle
	1	Oct. 1990	Minard
Fin whale	1	Nov. 1994	Ballyheigue
Minke whale	1	Sept. 1990	Fermoyle

Chapter 5

CONSERVATION

Each of us are brief tenants; we do not really own anything, but are just here for a short time. Whoever owns property, whatever he or she does to that property should not diminish the biological diversity of that piece of land, and should somehow provide for public access, not for everybody at once, but for some people at some time.

David Brower, founder of 'Friends of the Earth'

BIOLOGICAL DIVERSITY OR biodiversity is a term describing the multitude of different life forms which exist in a particular place. Over the past few centuries, but particularly over the latter decades of this century, we have seen a reduction in biodiversity in Kerry, with many species becoming extinct. Of the more obvious species, the golden eagle was exterminated by the end of the twentieth century, and the corncrake ceased to breed within the last 10 years. The rapidly increased rate of development, afforestation and farm intensification has seen the virtual extinction of many wildflower species and their associated invertebrate fauna. Natural ecosystems have been described as being like a series of inter-linked building blocks. If you continue to take out blocks, in due course the whole structure will collapse. If we continue to allow species to become extinct, the natural ecosystem will also collapse, with catastrophic results for all who share this planet.

By trying to stop and if possible reverse this trend towards a reduction in biodiversity, nature conservation strives to promote a state of harmony between people and the land. The conservation and wise use of our land, seas and natural resources is of immense importance for the future welfare of the people of Kerry, where so many people depend on these for their livelihoods. Despite the ravages of the last few decades, there are indications that we are beginning to appreciate the value of conservation. Let us look at some of the areas which show promise, before we examine some of the problems which remain.

EDUCATION

It is encouraging to see the increased emphasis being placed on environmental education by schools throughout Kerry. More and more classes participate in environmental courses, join in outdoor activities and undertake natural history projects. Some classes enter national environmental competitions. Kerry students have won a number of prestigious awards in the biological categories of the Aer Lingus Young Scientist of the Year competition. Every school should promote the principals of nature conservation from a child's earliest years, to value our land and water and all that depend on it. Larger schools should develop their own wildlife club and carry out projects on their grounds and elsewhere. These could include creating wildlife gardens and flowerbeds, digging ponds, building nestboxes and tree planting. As the voters of the future, school groups also have the power to influence political decisions affecting our environment, particularly at the local level.

The principal centre for conservation-orientated education in the county is the Killarney National Park. The park offers an audio-visual introduction to its landscape and wildlife, a modest interpretative centre and an excellent range of publications on its landscape, birds, butterflies, oakwoods and the Muckross gardens. A number of informal educational activities are run by the park management and rangers. These include a series of autumn talks and guided walks for school and university groups. Staff also liaise with visiting biologists and visit schools and other organisations to give talks on the National Park and local natural history. The park also offers practical work experience on conservation projects for students from Ireland and abroad.

The park also fulfils an important research role. This is carried out by the rangers, visiting students and amateur and professional researchers. Such work is important in guiding the park management in their efforts to conserve, enhance and interpret this unique area and its wildlife.

Part of the park's educational role is fulfilled by the Killarney National Park Field Studies Centre, based in Knockreer House. The centre organises and runs courses on ecological subjects for schools, scouts, guides and other groups.

The Cappanlea Outdoor Education Centre is involved in a range of activities from hillwalking to canoeing, as well as offering a variety of conservation-orientated courses. The high level of environmental awareness shown by its staff reduces the potential for conflict with conservation interests in Kerry.

RED DATA BOOKS

The concept of a Red Data Book *has been around for some 30 years since Sir Peter Scott first proposed and later defined it as 'a register of threatened wildlife that includes definitions of derees of threat' (Scott et al 1987). Many countries have published* Red Data Books *covering threatened plants and animals within their borders. Ireland now has* Red Data Books *on vascular plants, vertebrates and stoneworts, while another on byrophytes is due for publication.*

Red Data Books summarise the available information on species believed to be rare or endangered, covering aspects such as its history, current distribution, status, threats and conservation measures needed. As such they are invaluable working guides for those involved at the 'coal-face' of conservation.

THE LOCAL CONSERVATION MOVEMENT

As conservationists, we should not leave the development and implementation of policies that effect our environment entirely to central government. As voters, tax-payers and consumers we have the power to influence governmental, industrial and agricultural practices. Much can be done by ordinary members of the public, whether at a local, national or international level. The principal qualification needed is perseverance and a desire not to be fobbed off.

The past decade has seen a tremendous growth in involvement by individuals and communities in local and national conservation issues. In Kerry, a number of conservation groups now exist as a result of this growing interest. Apart from their field activities, such groups have an important role to play in monitoring potential environmental problems and influencing important decisions. One way of raising the level of awareness about particular local or national issues is through your own local politician, be they county councillor, TD or MEP. At local level you should identify the brighter individuals and feed them with information and ideas. Make sure the information is factually correct and can be readily verified if possible – hear-say or second-hand information is not good enough. You should find out who currently leads the thinking on particular topics. At national level you should lobby your own local politician, especially if they are members of relevant committees. These days, European Laws are setting the pace for environmental controls and standards in Ireland and our MEPs are often anxious to be seen to be staying in touch with local issues. They should also be made aware of your concerns.

Conservation groups also have a function in the generation, collating and dissemination of factual information on important sites in their areas. Apart from its possible political value, much of this information would be of everyday practical use in the development of educational packs for local schools, youth clubs, farm organisations and other groups.

One such organisation is the Killarney Nature Conservation Group, which is very active in many practical ways. It has campaigned on a number of environmental issues. It carries out frequent local clean-ups and clearance of invasive rhododendron and runs field trips to other areas such as the Burren. The group also run a series of popular 'Nature for all' courses over the winter months, with guest speakers and weekend outings.

Birdwatch Ireland, formerly called the Irish Wildbird Conservancy, has had a strong Kerry branch since the earliest days of its inception. Blennerville-based ornithologist Frank King has been the main driving force behind the branch for many years, leading most of the frequent branch outings. An Taisce (the National Trust) has played a leading role in environmental protection for many years, and has been particularly strong on planning issues. As one of the oldest environmental organisations in the country, An Taisce was active in the protection of our environment long before the term 'green issues' came into vogue. The Irish Wildlife Trust, through its subsidiary, Groundwork, undertakes important voluntary conservation work annually in the Killarney National Park. By removing invasive rhododendron, Groundwork volunteers have helped save some of the oldest woods in Kerry from the threat posed by this plant.

Another way in which we can all be involved is by changing the way in which we use the environment, so that the earth's resources are actually renewed. This kind of preventative medicine may not yield immediate results but in the long term will pay handsome dividends. One way of putting this philosophy into practice is by living more locally. In the case of food supply, much of what we in Kerry eat is obtained from overseas or far afield. Apart from some beef and dairy products, relatively little of the food we consume is locally produced. The American Briarpatch and the Dutch Kleine Aarde (Small Earth) movements are examples of groups which encourage local, organically-based food production and consumption. Supporting such locally-based initiatives would reduce the need for huge amounts of packaging, preservatives and fuel, as well as having beneficial effects for local job creation.

SOME CONSERVATION ISSUES

There is still much conservation work to be done and issues which need to be addressed. Agricultural activities have the single biggest impact on the environment in Kerry. Farming practices are changing rapidly and many of the more recent developments are not particularly environmentally friendly. The demise of tillage and hay-making in the county has led to a reduction in floral diversity and its associated invertebrate fauna – when was the last time you sat in a flower-rich meadow and listened to grasshoppers and the hum of other insects? The introduction of silage-making has caused increased levels of water pollution, causing problems for fish, freshwater invertebrates, plants and our own drinking wells. New practices, sometimes originally hailed as being environmentally friendly, often lead to different problems. A case in point is the introduction of round bale silage-making. This practice was believed to be less polluting than silage pits, but we now have other problems. These include trampling and pollution of numerous, widely-scattered feeding sites, even worse littering, and the blockage of natural soakways by carelessly disposed plastic leading to increased flooding.

Conservation work

Apart from the National Parks and Nature Reserves, there exist throughout the county many locally important patches of wildlife habitat which survive as much through neglect as through design. Others are vanishing every year to farm improvement, overgrazing, dumping and other factors. Most landowners, however, are sympathetic to conservation if made aware of the importance of a particular site on their property. There is quite a scope for local voluntary conservation groups to involve themselves in management agreements with landowners to conserve and maintain such wildlife habitats. These may be sand dune systems, areas of woodland and scrub, old hay meadows or marshes. All that may be needed is the maintenance or slight modification of existing land use practices, but in some cases more active management may be required. This may include rubbish clearing, fencing or the control of invasive species, particularly where a rare plant or invertebrate species is threatened. The priorities for each site would need to be identified in consultation with experienced local naturalists. Such projects would provide a valuable educational facility in their areas and some would also have potential as tourism attractions.

Peatbogs are a case in point. These are often regarded as being a very unique Irish ecosystem. The wide range of uses to which bogs have been put has created a special bond between people and bogland. This applies especially in Kerry, where so much of our land area is bog. I have already discussed the importance of our few remaining intact bogs of high conservation interest, but we also have vast areas of cutaway bog around the county, often being used for no more than dumping sites. A selection of such areas would make exciting restoration projects for community and school groups. Wetter areas could be encouraged to redevelop their natural bog vegetation, ponds could be created and any suitable dry sites planted with alder, willow and other native tree species.

In the uplands, the intensification of sheep farming has led to overgrazing, hill erosion, the spread of bracken and pollution of water supplies. This problem is further exacerbated by the burning of heather, much of it in a uncontrolled fashion and often at the wrong time of the year. The shift towards sheep farming has led to increased fencing of commonage and mountainous areas. This has reduced the ease of access which people traditionally had to these areas and the inappropriate siting of many fences has impinged upon the scenic value of many parts of Kerry. Here, a small change in farming practices would greatly enhance the aesthetic appearance and ecological value of a farm. In recent years, Kerry has seen many farm boundaries, originally enclosed by stone walls, fenced with sheep wire. Much of this new fencing has been erected on top of the original stone wall. This not only offends aesthetically, but because of overstocking with sheep has led to the virtual elimination of many flower species which thrive in this habitat. If such fences are needed, their placement just inside the wall rather than on top would encourage the growth of flowers, shrubs and their associated fauna, and reduce their visual impact.

RURAL ENVIRONMENTAL PROTECTION SCHEME

The launch in 1994 of the Rural Environment Protection Scheme (REPS) has raised hopes that we may see some reversal of the worst problems caused by agriculture. The objective of REPS is to introduce environmentally friendly farming practices which produce quality food while protecting wildlife habitats, threatened species of flora and fauna and the wider landscape. Farmers who agree to participate in the scheme do so for a five year period and are paid a basic annual payment per hectare up to a maximum of 40 hectares. In consultation with environmental and agricultural advisors, a management plan is drawn up for each farm. This covers subjects such as soil analysis, stocking rates, nutrient management and waste disposal, the protection of watercourses, retention of wildlife habitats and hedgerow management. The plan also deals with improving the visual appearance of the farm buildings, old walls, and the protection of archaeological features. Additional payments are made to farmers who participate in certain supplementary measures, or have a Natural Heritage Area on their land. The supplementary measures include the rejuvenation of degraded areas, farming organically, rearing rare local breeds and the provision of public access.

While the Rural Environment Protection Scheme has generally been broadly welcomed, it remains to be seen how effective it is in solving the problems it addresses. This will largely depend on its uptake by farmers, the quality of the management plans put in place and the effectiveness of monitoring procedures. The scheme is most attractive to farmers in marginal areas and does little to solve conservation problems in areas of intensive farming.

FORESTRY

With the attractive grants and premiums now being paid on forestry, tree planting has become a big business. Despite the substantially greater grants for planting hardwoods, the majority of planting in Kerry is still of introduced conifers, principally sitka spruce. The use of such species has been widely criticised on ecological, economic and aesthetic grounds. They offer habitats for relatively few, common species of birds and invertebrates and shade out most other plant species.

NATURAL HERITAGE AREAS

Natural Heritage Areas are the the best representatives of natural or semi-natural habitats in the county, or contain a rare species or natural phenomenon. They stem from an original list of 70 sites of Areas of Scientific Interest in Kerry, drawn up during the early 1970s by An Foras Forbatha. Additional areas have been subsequently added to this original list. Natural Heritage Areas will have to be taken into account by the County Council, Department of Agriculture, Food and Forestry and other agencies when considering development applications. Unlike the original ASIs, there is extensive consultation with farmers and landowners who have NHAs on their property and an appeal system will be set up to arbitrate on areas of disagreement.

They may also cause acidification of lakes and rivers. This could have long term negative effects on all water life.

With the shift from planting bog-covered hillsides to marginal farmland, many of our most scenic valley areas are now being targeted for afforestation. Some of these are on major tourist routes such as the Ring of Kerry. Few voices, however, have been raised to question their suitability or desirability for planting. Before long many well known views will have been lost behind a wall of dark green conifers. If tree planting along scenic routes is considered desirable, we should insist that a good mix of tree species is used, with a high proportion of native hardwoods.

In all forestry operations, unplantable areas should be left to develop a natural vegetation, ponds created for invertebrates and wildfowl and specimens of native tree species already present allowed space to flourish. Much of the earlier tree planting is now approaching time for the final cut. Rather than large scale clear-felling, such work should be carried out in more discrete blocks and the second generation of trees should be of a broader species mix. This would reduce both the ecological and visual impact of these clearfells and greatly improve their wildlife value.

The planting of trees throughout the county is having a major ecological and visual impact. The public have a right to demand that this is done in the most sensitive manner possible. Here again conservation and tourism interests should get together to ensure this is done before it is too late.

SPECIAL PROTECTION AREAS (SPAs) AND SPECIAL AREAS OF CONSERVATION (SACs)

The EC Directive on the Conservation of Wild Birds (79/409/EEC), known as the 'Birds Directive' was adopted by the Council in 1979 and obliges member states to adopt measures to protect wild birds and their habitats, so as to maintain their populations at ecologically sound levels. This directive places special emphasis on the conservation of important bird habitats and requires member countries to designate networks of Special Protection Areas (SPAs). In Kerry the more important SPAs to be designated are Castlemaine harbour, Tralee bay and Killarney National Park.

The EC Directive on the Conservation of Natural Habitats and of Wild Fauna and Flora (Directive 92/43/EEC), known as the 'Habitats Directive' aims to conserve natural habitats and wild flora and fauna and, where necessary, to restore these to a favourable state. Under this directive member states are to establish a core of Special Areas of Conservation (SACs); areas of particular wildlife importance, containing rare plants, animals or special habitats. In Ireland, SACs have been selected from the list of proposed Natural Heritage Areas. These SACs and SPAs will be included in a European-wide network of conservation sites called 'Natura 2000'. In March 1997, an initial selection of 207 candidate SACs were advertised in the national press. A large tract of Kerry uplands, as well as lowland sites, were included in this first list.

The principal object of SAC designation is to protect those lands from future harmful development and to restore traditional, low impact farming and land management regimes to areas already damaged. A number of public meetings have been held throughout the county to explain the implications of SPAs and SACs to landowners and land-users.

PUBLIC ACCESS TO LAND

Access to the countryside, free of the danger, fumes and noise of passing traffic, is in danger of becoming a luxury in this country. Many of the traditional boreens, droving trails and mass paths have become overgrown or blocked by fences, gates

Walkers on the Kerry Way

and buildings. Elsewhere, landowners and farming organisations are discouraging access to property which people generally enjoyed. In the present climate of insurance and litigation problems, it is understandable that landowners are wary of encouraging freer access. The introduction in 1995 of the Occupiers Liability Act governing the rights and responsibilities of landowners and land-users went a long way to address the fears of landowners about being sued by people walking their land. The REPS initiative and some local tourism organisations are attempting to encourage landowners to develop walking trails and old footpaths across their land, but much more work could be done. Here again, local community groups could play a greater part by helping to maintain rights-of-way, boreens and other trackways.

IMPORTING NON-NATIVE SPECIES

As the rules governing the importation of non-native species are gradually relaxed under EU regulations, our wild populations face new threats. With the growth in deer farming, red deer have been brought in from eastern European countries to supply this new market. A number of these have already escaped, posing a threat to the genetic integrity of our native red deer. Similarly, there is growing concern that farmed salmon escaping from sea cages pose a threat to wild stocks. The New Zealand flatworm, a serious earthworm predator, is now an established part of our fauna. It was probably brought in as eggs in pot plant containers. Other examples exist in the areas of agriculture, horticulture and mariculture. Such non-native species may pose other threats through predation, competition, hybridisation or the spread of parasites and diseases. Is anybody monitoring the effects of such introduced organisms on our wild populations? In our rush to be good Europeans, must we agree so readily to the relaxation of regulations governing such importations?

LITTERING AND DUMPING

One of the worst scourges which Kerry suffers from is that of littering. Every hedgerow, boreen, and roadside is lined with tin cans, bottles, disposable nappies, household and agricultural plastic. The high tide mark on every beach is lined with a variety of plastics. Most peatbog tracks lead to local rubbish dumps. Abandoned cars, fridges and other objects ruin the scenery in many areas. Our beaches are frequently used for the dumping of rubble, which, combined with large-scale, illegal removal of sand, rapidly degrades their amenity, protective and conservation value. Nowhere is safe from the scourge, and few, if any, prosecutions are taken under the littering or dumping laws.

Surveys have shown that the Irish public view litter as one of our major environmental problems, yet we are being increasingly swamped by a rising tide of rubbish. In 1995, the government launched a major initiative to counter the litter problem. The main objectives of the programme are to direct the public's attention on litter as an urgent environmental problem, to improve anti-litter legislation and step up its enforcement, and to develop new and on-going anti-litter measures over the following years. Such initiatives deserve our fullest support.

TOURISM

As the county's second largest source of revenue, tourism plays a vital part in the region's development. Tourism interests are particularly fond of spreading the message that we have a pristine, unpolluted environment. As long as we believe this we fool ourselves into thinking that we need do little to protect or enhance our environment. While our problems may not be on the same scale as many parts of

Europe, our environment is a long way from being pristine. It is high time we were honest with ourselves and set about correcting our deficiencies.

These same tourism interests could play a more powerful role in protecting our environment. By lobbying strongly for more sensitive management of farmlands, peatlands, sand dunes and forestry, tourism groups could greatly enhance our countryside for the benefit of our wildlife and human populations. By supporting or organising local clean-ups, monitoring illegal burning and dumping, and sponsoring environmentally orientated activities, such groups would be doing a great service to their own industry and local communities. The latter point of sponsorship is particularly relevant, as tourism gains so much from having a clean environment that the industry should be seen to be doing something in return. By directly sponsoring a particular group's activities or running environmental competitions, the tourism industry would greatly benefit in a number of ways, not least from the probability of extra business generated by the ensuing goodwill.

Eco-tourists on the Great Blasket

A number of tourism developments pose serious conflicts of interests with nature conservation. The huge growth in golfing has led to the creation of new courses, some of which have been in or are proposed for areas of prime environmental importance. While golf courses may superficially seem to be environmentally friendly, their siting is of crucial importance. Environmentally sensitive areas such as sand dunes and wet woodland systems have been or are threatened with damage by such developments, often because they can be acquired cheaply. The application of herbicides and pesticides on greens and fairways is another cause for concern.

The promotion of Kerry as an attractive venue for walkers and cyclists has led to increased erosion in frequently used areas. This highlights the need for a conservation corps to tackle footpath work, stile erection and erosion control. Here again the tourism industry, as the main beneficiary of this promotional work, could contribute more to allieviate these problems.

Rather than being on opposing sides of the fence, there is a need for tourism and conservation interests to work in close co-operation. Such a relationship would greatly benefit nature conservation for the good of resident and visitor alike.

THE FUTURE

With rapid agricultural changes and afforestation, we are witnessing the most dramatic changes in our landscape in over 100 years. Many of these changes will impact directly on our flora and fauna, as well as on the everyday lives of the people of Kerry. We have a right and a moral obligation to ensure that the mistakes and misdeeds of the past are not allowed to happen again.

The conservation of our threatened flora, fauna and special habitats cannot be approached in a piece-meal fashion. These species and areas do not exist in a vacuum, but are part of the wider countryside. What we need for Kerry is a comprehensive land-use strategy. This would involve local authorities, state conservation agencies, farm organisations, foresters, tourism and fishery interests. Most importantly, input should be also be sought from local people and conservation groups.

Much of what we have already lost and stand to lose in the future has no obvious economic value. Biological diversity, however, is a key quality of the environment which attracts people to a locality: the contrast between water and land, trees and grass or cultivation and wilderness. Fortunately, diversity is also an essential element of rich, healthy biological communities. It is in all our interests to protect that diversity and, if possible, to restore some of what has been lost already. If we fail to do so, we impoverish and even threaten our own future and that of our children.

Appendix I

Species List

Plants

English	Latin
Adder's-tongue fern	*Ophoiglossum vulgatum*
Alder	*Alnus glutinosa*
Alder buckthorn	*Frangula alnus*
Allseed	*Radiola linoides*
Alpine bistort	*Polygonum viviparum*
Alpine hair-grass	*Deschampsia caespitosa*
Alpine lady's-mantle	*Alchemilla alpina*
Alpine meadow-grass	*Poa alpina*
Alpine saw-wort	*Saussurea alpina*
Alpine scurvygrass	*Cochlearia pyrenaica*
American skunk cabbage	*Lysichiton americanus*
Annual sea-blite	*Sueda maritima*
Ash	*Fraxinus excelsior*
Aspen	*Populus tremula*
Autumn gorse	*Ulex gallii*
Autumn hawkbit	*Leontodon autumnalis*
Awlwort	*Subularia aquatica*
Barren strawberry	*Potentilla sterilis*
Beaked tasselweed	*Ruppia maritima*
Beech	*Fagus sylvatica*
Beech fern	*Phegopteris connectilis*
Betony	*Stachys officinalis*
Bilberry	*Vaccinium myrtillus*
Bird's-nest orchid	*Neottia nidus-avis*
Biting stonecrop	*Sedum acre*
Black spleenwort	*Asplenium adiantum-nigrum*
Blackthorn	*Prunus spinosus*
Bladder wrack	*Fuscus vesiculosus*
Blue-eyed grass	*Sisyrinchium bermudiana*
Bluebell	*Hyacinthoides non-scripta*
Blunt-flowered rush	*Juncus subnodulosus*
Bog asphodel	*Narthecium ossifragum*

Bogbean	*Menyanthes trifoliata*
Bog cotton	*Eriophorum spp.*
Bog myrtle	*Myrica gale*
Bog orchid	*Hammarbya paludosa*
Bog pimpernel	*Anagallis tenella*
Bracken	*Pteridium aquilinum*
Brittle bladder-fern	*Cystopteris fragilis*
Broad-leaved cottongrass	*Eriophorum latifolium*
Broad-leaved dock	*Rumex obtusifolius*
Broom	*Cytisus scoparius*
Buddleia	*Buddleja spp.*
Chaffweed	*Anagallis minima*
Channelled wrack	*Pelvetia canaliculata*
Chanterelle	*Cantharellus cibarius*
Chilean pine	*Araucaria araucana*
Common bent	*Agrostis capillaris*
Common bird's-foot trefoil	*Lotus corniculatus*
Common butterwort	*Pinguicula vulgaris*
Common centaury	*Centaurium erythraea*
Common cottongrass	*Eriophorum angustifolium*
Common knapweed	*Centaurea nigra*
Common reed	*Phragmites australis*
Common saltmarsh-grass	*Puccinellia maritima*
Common scurvy-grass	*Cochlearia officinalis*
Common twayblade	*Listera ovata*
Common water-crowfoot	*Ranunculus aquatilis*
Corky-fruited water-dropwort	*Oenanthe pimpinelloides*
Corncockle	*Agrostemma githago*
Cornflower	*Centaurea cyanus*
Cornish moneywort	*Sibthorpia europea*
Cow parsley	*Anthriscus sylvestris*
Creeping bent	*Agrostis stolonifera*
Creeping buttercup	*Ranunculus repens*
Crested dog's-tail	*Cynosurus cristatus*
Crested hair-grass	*Koeleria macrantha*
Cross-leaved heath	*Erica tetralix*
Crowberry	*Empetrum nigrum*
Curled dock	*Rumex crispus*
Cyperus sedge	*Carex pseudocyperus*
Dandelion	*Taraxacum sp.*
Deergrass	*Tricophorum cespitosum*

Devil's-bit scabious	*Succisa pratensis*
Dodder	*Cuscuta epithymum*
Douglas fir	*Pseudotsuga menziesii*
Dove's-foot cranes-bill	*Geranium molle*
Dulse	*Rhodymenia palmata*
Dwarf spike rush	*Eleocharis parvula*
Dwarf willow	*Salix herbacea*
Elder	*Sambucus nigra*
Elm	*Ulmus sp.*
Foxglove	*Digitalis purpurea*
Fragrant orchid	*Gymnadaenia conopsea*
Fringed rock-cress	*Arabis brownii*
Fuchsia	*Fuchsia magellanica*
Giant rhubarb	*Gunnera tinctoria*
Greater tussock-sedge	*Cladium mariscus*
Greater woodrush	*Luzula sylvatica*
Green spleenwort	*Asplenium viride*
Groundsel	*Senecio vulgaris*
Grey willow	*Salix caprea*
Gypseywort	*Lycopus europaeus*
Hard fern	*Blechnum spicant*
Hart's tongue fern	*Asplenium scolopendrium*
Hawthorn	*Crataegus monogyna*
Hazel	*Corylus avellana*
Hebe	*Hebe spp.*
Hemlock water dropwort	*Oenanthe crocata*
Henbane	*Hyoscyamus niger*
Hoary whitlowgrass	*Draba incana*
Holly	*Ilex aquifolium*
Holly fern	*Polystichum lonchitis*
Honeysuckle	*Lonicera spp.*
Horse chestnut	*Aesculus hippocastanum*
Intermediate bladderwort	*Utricularia intermedia*
Irish Lady's tresses	*Spiranthes romanzoffiana*
Irish spleenwort	*Asplenium onopteris*
Ivy	*Hedera helix*
Ivy-leaved bellflower	*Wahlenbergia hederacea*
Juniper	*Juniperus communis*
Kelp	*Laminaria spp.*
Kidney saxifrage	*Saxifraga hirsuta*
Kidney vetch	*Anthyllis vulneraria*

Knotted wrack	*Ascophyllum nodosum*
Lesser bladderwort	*Utricularia minor*
Lesser twayblade	*Listera cordata*
Lodgepole pine	*Pinus contorta latifolia*
Male fern	*Dryopteris filix-mas*
Marram grass	*Ammophilia arenaria*
Marsh clubmoss	*Lycopodium inundatum*
Marsh fern	*Thelypteris palustris*
Marsh hawk's-beard	*Crepis paludosa*
Marsh marigold	*Caltha palustris*
Marsh ragweed	*Senecio aquaticus*
Meadowsweet	*Filipendula ulmaria*
Monterey cypress	*Cupressus macrocarpa*
Monterey pine	*Pinus radiata*
Moonwort	*Botrychium lunaria*
Mountain male-fern	*Dryopteris oreades*
Mountain sorrel	*Oxyria digyna*
Narrow-leaved helleborine	*Cephalanthera longifolia*
Oak	*Quercus spp.*
Oblong-leaved sundew	*Drosera intermedia*
Pale butterwort	*Pinguicula lusitanica*
Peat mosses	*Sphagnum spp.*
Pedunculate oak	*Quercus robur*
Pepper dulse	*Laurencia pinnatifida*
Pillwort	*Pilularia globulifera*
Pipewort	*Eriocaulon aquaticum*
Plantain	*Plantago spp.*
Purple loostrife	*Lythrum salicaria*
Purple moor-grass	*Molinia caerulea*
Rainbow bladder weed	*Cystoseira tamariscifolia*
Ragged-robin	*Lychnis flos-cuculi*
Rhododendron	*Rhododendron ponticum*
Roseroot	*Sedum rosea*
Round-leaved sundew	*Drosera rotundifolia*
Rowan	*Sorbus aucuparia*
Royal fern	*Osmunda regalis*
Rusty-back fern	*Ceterach officinarum*
Sand cat's-tail	*Phleum arenarium*
Sanicle	*Sanicula europaea*
Scots pine	*Pinus sylvestris*
Sea campion	*Silene maritima*

Sea-holly	*Eryngium maritimum*
Sea lettuce	*Ulva lactuca*
Sedge	*Carex spp.*
Serrated wrack	*Fucus serratus*
Sessile oak	*Quercus petraea*
Sitka spruce	*Picea sitchensis*
Slender cicendia	*Cicendia filiformis*
Slender cottongrass	*Eriophorum gracile*
Slender naiad	*Najas flexilis*
Smooth brome	*Bromus racemosus*
Sorrel	*Rumex spp.*
Sphagnum	*Sphagnum spp.*
Spiral wrack	*Fucus spiralis*
Stinging nettle	*Urtica dioica*
Sycamore	*Acer pseudoplatanus*
Thistle	*Cirsium spp.*
Three-nerved sandwort	*Moehringia trinervia*
Thrift	*Armeria maritima*
Tunbridge filmy-fern	*Hymenophyllum tunbrigense*
Toothed wrack	*Fucus serratus*
Toothwort	*Lathraea squamaria*
Townsend's cord-grass	*Spartina townsendii*
Tormentil	*Potentilla erecta*
Tree lungwort	*Pulmonaria lobaria*
Tree mallow	*Lavatera arborea*
Tufted hair-grass	*Deschampsia cespitosa*
Velvet bent	*Agrostis canina*
Viviparous fescue	*Festuca vivipara*
Water chickweed	*Myosoton aquaticum*
Water crowfoot	*Ranunculus aquatilis*
Water mint	*Mentha aquatica*
Wavy hair-grass	*Deschampsia flexuosa*
White beak-sedge	*Rhynchospora alba*
White water-lily	*Nymphaea alba*
Whorled caraway	*Carum verticillatum*
Wild angelica	*Angelica sylvestris*
Wild carrot	*Dancus carota*
Wild garlic	*Allium ursinum*
Wild pansy	*Viola tricolor*
Wild strawberry	*Fragaria vesca*
Wild thyme	*Thymus praecox*

Willow	*Salix spp.*
Wilson's filmy fern	*Hymenophyllum wilsonii*
Wood blewit	*Tricholoma nudum*
Wood horsetail	*Equisetum sylvaticum*
Wood sorrel	*Oxalis acetosella*
Wood vetch	*Vicia sylvatica*
Woodruff	*Galium odoratum*
Wych elm	*Ulmus glabra*
Yellow bartsia	*Parentucellia viscosa*
Yellow centaury	*Cicendia filiformis*
Yellow iris	*Iris pseudacorus*
Yellow water-lily	*Nuphar lutea*
Yew	*Taxus baccata*

Appendix II

Animals

English	Latin
American mink	*Mustela vision*
Arctic charr	*Salvelinus alpinus*
Arctic tern	*Sterna paradisaea*
Azure damselfly	*Coenagrion puella*
Badger	*Meles meles*
Ballan wrasse	*Labrus bergylta*
Banded demoiselle	*Calopteryx splendens*
Bank vole	*Clethrionomys glareolus*
Bar-tailed godwit	*Limosa lapponica*
Barn owl	*Tyto alba*
Barnacle goose	*Branta leucopsis*
Barrel-fish	*Hyperoglypha perciforma*
Basking shark	*Cetorhinus maximus*
Bath sponge	*Spongia officinalis*
Beadlet anemone	*Actinia equina*
Beautiful demoiselle	*Calopteryx virgo*
Bewick swan	*Cygnus columbianus*
Black darter	*Sympetrum danae*
Black-mouthed dogfish	*Galeus melastomus*
Blackbird	*Turdus merula*
Blue tit	*Parus caeruleus*
Blackcap	*Sylvia atricapilla*
Blue-tailed damselfly	*Ischnura elegans*
Bluefin tuna	*Thunnus thynnus*
Blue-rayed limpet	*Patina pellucida*
Boarfish	*Capros aper*
Bogue	*Boops boops*
Boring sponge	*Cliona celata*
Bottle-nosed dolphin	*Tursiops truncatus*
Breadcrumb sponge	*Hymeniacidon perleve*
Brent goose (light-bellied)	*Branta bernicla hrota*
Brimstone	*Gonepteryx rhamni*
Brook lamprey	*Lampetra planeri*
Brown hawker	*Aeshna grandis*

Brown hawker	*Aeshna grandis*
Brown long-eared bat	*Plecotus auritus*
Brown trout	*Salmo trutta*
Butterfish	*Pholis gunnellus*
Carpet shell	*Tapes decussatus*
Chough	*Pyrrhocorax pyrrhocorax*
Chaffinch	*Fringilla coelebs*
Cleg	*Haematopota pluvialis*
Cinnabar moth	*Tyria jacobaeae*
Coal tit	*Parus ater*
Coiled tube worm	*Spirorbis borealis*
Collared dove	*Streptopelia decaocto*
Common blue damselfly	*Enallagma cyathigerum*
Common darter	*Sympetrum striolatum*
Common dolphins	*Delphinus delphis*
Common frog	*Rana temporaria*
Common goby	*Pomatoschistus microps*
Common gull	*Larus canus*
Common hawker	*Aeshna juncea*
Common limpet	*Patella vulgata*
Common lobster	*Homarus gammarus*
Common mussel	*Mytilus edulis*
Common ragworm	*Nereis diversicolor*
Common rat	*Rattus norvegicus*
Common sandpiper	*Actitis hypoleucos*
Common scoter	*Melanitta nigra*
Common seal	*Phoca vitulina*
Common seal	*Phoca vitulina*
Common shore crab	*Carcinus maenas*
Common shrimp	*Crangon crangon*
Common tern	*Sterna hirundo*
Cormorant	*Phalacrocorax carbo*
Corncrake	*Crex crex*
Cuckoo	*Cuculus canorus*
Cuckoo wrasse	*Labrus mixtus*
Curlew	*Numenius arquata*
Cuvier's beaked whale	*Ziphius cavirostris*
Dahlia anemone	*Urticina felina*
Daubenton's bat	*Myotis daubentonii*
Devil's coach horse	*Staphylinus olens*
Dog whelk	*Nucella lapillus*

Dor beetle	*Geotrupes stercorarius*
Dotterel	*Charadrius morinellus*
Downy emerald	*Cordulia aenea*
Drone fly	*Eristalis tenax*
Duck leech	*Theromyzon tessulatum*
Dunlin	*Calidris alpina*
Edible cockle	*Cerastoderma edule*
Edible periwinkle	*Littorina littorea*
Emerald damselfly	*Lestes sponsa*
Euphrosyne dolphin	*Stenella coeruleoalba*
Fallow deer	*Dama dama*
Feral goat	*Capra hircus*
Fin whale	*Balaenoptera physalus*
Flounder	*Platichthys flesus*
Four-spotted chaser	*Libelulla quadrimaculata*
Fox	*Vulpes vulpes*
Fox moth	*Macrothylacia rubi*
Freshwater shrimp	*Gammarus duebeni*
Froghopper	*Philaenus spumarius*
Fulmar	*Fulmarus glacialis*
Gannet	*Sula bassana*
Garden black ant	*Lasius niger*
Garden spider	*Araneus diadematus*
Garden tiger moth	*Arctica caja*
Garden warbler	*Sylvia borin*
Garter snake	*Thamnophis sirtalis*
Goldcrest	*Regulus regulus*
Golden plover	*Pluvialis apricaria*
Goldeneye	*Bucephala clangula*
Goldfinch	*Carduelis carduelis*
Goosander	*Mergus merganser*
Great black-back gull	*Larus marinus*
Great northern diver	*Gavia immer*
Great scallop	*Pecten maximus*
Great tit	*Parus major*
Great-crested grebe	*Podiceps cristatus*
Green hairstreak	*Callophrys rubi*
Green oak tortrix	*Tortrix viridana*
Green tiger beetle	*Cicindela campestris*
Greenfinch	*Carduelis chloris*
Greenland white-fronted goose	*Anser albifrons flavirostris*

Grey heron	*Ardea cinerea*
Grey plover	*Pluvialis squatarola*
Grey seal	*Halichoerus grypus*
Grey wolf	*Canus lupus*
Guillemot	*Uria aalgae*
Hairy dragonfly	*Brachytron pratense*
Harbour porpoise	*Phocoena phocoena*
Hawksbill turtle	*Eretmochelys imbricata*
Hawthorn shield bug	*Acanthosoma haemorrhoidale*
Hen harrier	*Circus cyaneus*
Herring	*Clupea harengus*
Herring gull	*Larus argentatus*
Honeycomb worm	*Sabellaria alveolata*
Hooded crow	*Corvus corone cornix*
Horse leech	*Haemopus sanguisuga*
House cricket	*Acheta domesticus*
House mouse	*Mus musculus*
Irish hare	*Lepus timidus hibernicus*
Irish stoat	*Mustela erminea hibernica*
Jack snipe	*Lymnocryptes minimus*
Jackdaw	*Corvus monedula*
Japanese sika deer	*Cervus nippon*
Jay	*Garrulus glandarius*
Jenkin's spire shell	*Potamopyrgus jenkinsi*
Jewel anemone	*Corynactis viridis*
Keel worm	*Pomatoceros triqueter*
Keeled skimmer	*Orthetrum coerulescens*
Kemp's ridley	*Lepidochelys kempii*
Kerry spotted slug	*Geomalacus maculosus*
Kestrel	*Falco tinnunculus*
Killarney shad	*Alosa fallax killarnensis*
Killer whale	*Orcinus orca*
Kittiwake	*Rissa tridactyla*
Knot	*Calidris canuta*
Lapwing	*Vanellus vanellus*
Large heath butterfly	*Coenonympha tullia*
Large marsh grasshopper	*Stethophyma grossum*
Large red damselfly	*Pyrrhosoma nymphula*
Leach's petrel	*Oceanodroma leucorhoa*
Leathery turtle	*Dermochelys coriacea*
Leisler's bat	*Nyctalus leisleri*

Lesser black-backed gull	*Larus fuscus*
Lesser horseshoe bat	*Rhinolophus hipposideros*
Lesser yellowlegs	*Tringa flavipes*
Linnet	*Acanthis cannabina*
Little egret	*Egretta garzetta*
Little tern	*Sterna albifrons*
Loggerhead turtle	*Caretta caretta*
Long-eared owl	*Asio otus*
Lugworm	*Arenicola marina*
Mackerel	*Scomber scombrus*
Mallard	*Anas platyrhynchos*
Manx shearwater	*Puffinus puffinus*
Marine bug	*Aepophilus bonnairei*
Marsh fritillary	*Eurodryas aurinia*
Masked crab	*Corystes cassivelaunus*
Meadow pipit	*Anthus pratensis*
Merlin	*Falco columbarius*
Minke whale	*Balaenoptera acutorostrata*
Minnow	*Phoxinus phoxinus*
Mottled grasshopper	*Myrmeleotettix maculatus*
Mute swan	*Cygnus olor*
Natterer's bat	*Myotis nattereri*
Natterjack toad	*Bufo calamita*
Needlefly	*Leuctra fusca*
New Zealand flatworm	*Artiposthia triangulata*
Nine-spined stickleback	*Pungitius pungitius*
Nightjar	*Caprimulgus europaeus*
Northern emerald	*Somatochlora arctica*
Orange tip	*Anthocaris cardamines*
Otter	*Lutra lutra*
Oyster	*Ostrea edulis*
Oystercatcher	*Haematopus ostralegus*
Painted top shell	*Calliostoma zizyphinum*
Pea mussel	*Pisidium spp.*
Peacock butterfly	*Inachis io*
Peacock worm	*Sabella pavonina*
Pearl mussel	*Margaritifera margaritifera*
Pectoral sandpiper	*Calidris melanotos*
Perch	*Perca fluviatilis*
Peregrine	*Falco peregrinus*
Pheasant	*Phasianus colchicus*

Pied wagtail	*Motacilla alba yarrellii*
Long-finned pilot whale	*Globicephala melas*
Pine marten	*Martes martes*
Pintail	*Anas acuta*
Pipistrelle bat	*Pipistrellus pipistrellus*
Pochard	*Aythya ferina*
Pod razor shell	*Ensis siliqua*
Puffin	*Fratercula arctica*
Purple hairstreak	*Quercusia quercus*
Purple sandpiper	*Calidris maritima*
Purple top	*Gibbula umbilicalis*
Purple sea urchin	*Paracentrotus lividus*
Pygmy shrew	*Sorex minutus*
Rabbit	*Oryctolagus cuniculus*
Raven	*Corvus corax*
Razorbill	*Alca torda*
Red deer	*Cervus elaphus*
Red grouse	*Lagopus lagopus scoticus*
Red squirrel	*Sciurus vulgaris*
Red-breasted merganser	*Mergus serrator*
Red-throated diver	*Gavia stellata*
Redshank	*Tringa totanus*
Ring ouzel	*Turdus torquatus*
Ringed plover	*Charadrius hiaticula*
Risso's dolphin	*Grampus griseus*
River lamprey	*Lampetra fluviatilis*
River limpet	*Ancylus fluviatilis*
Roach	*Rutilus rutilis*
Robin	*Erithacus rubecula*
Rook	*Corvus frugilegus*
Rough periwinkle	*Littorina saxatilis*
Salmon	*Salmo salar*
Sand goby	*Pomatoschistus minutus*
Sandhill rustic	*Luperina nickerlii knilli*
Sandwich tern	*Sterna sandvicensis*
Satin lutestring	*Tetheella fluctuosa*
Scarce blue-tailed damselfly	*Ischnura pumilio*
Scaup	*Aythya marila*
Sea lamprey	*Petromyzon marinus*
Sea trout	*Salmo trutta*
Scaldfish	*Arnoglossus laterna*

Shag	*Phalacrocorax aristotelis*
Shanny	*Lipophrys pholis*
Short-eared owl	*Asio flammeus*
Silver-washed fritillary	*Argynnis paphia*
Siskin	*Carduelis spinus*
Six-gilled shark	*Hexanchus griseus*
Six-spot burnet	*Zygaena filipendulae stephensi*
Skylark	*Alauda arvensis*
Small blue	*Cupido minimus*
Small copper	*Lycaena phlaeas*
Small periwinkle	*Littorina neritoides*
Smooth newt	*Triturus vulgaris*
Smooth stick insect	*Clitarchus hookeri*
Snipe	*Gallinago gallinago*
Snow bunting	*Plectrophenax nivalis*
Song thrush	*Turdus philomelos*
Speckled bush cricket	*Leptophyes punctatissima*
Sperm whale	*Physeter catodon*
Starling	*Sturnus vulgaris*
Stone loach	*Meomachilus barbatulus*
Stonechat	*Saxicola torquata*
Storm petrel	*Hydrobates pelagicus*
Striped dolphin	*Stenella coeruleoalba*
Sunfish	*Mola mola*
Surf scoter	*Melanitta perspicillata*
Swan mussel	*Anodonta cygnea*
Swift	*Apus apus*
Swordfish	*Xiphias gladius*
Teal	*Anas crecca*
Tench	*Tinca tinca*
Thick top shell	*Monodonta lineata*
Thick-lipped grey mullet	*Mugil chelo*
Three-spined stickleback	*Gasterosteus aculeatus*
Tree sparrow	*Passer montanus*
Treecreeper	*Certhia familiaris*
Triggerfish	*Ballistes capriscus*
Tufted duck	*Aythya fuligula*
Turnstone	*Arenaria interpres*
Twaite shad	*Alosa fallax*
Twite	*Carduelis flavirostris*
Variable damselfly	*Coenagrion pulchellum*

Velvet crab	*Liocarcinus puber*
Viviparous lizard	*Lacerta viviparus*
Walrus	*Odobenus rosmarus*
Wandering snail	*Lymnaea peregra*
Water louse	*Asellus meridianus*
Weasel	*Mustela nivalis*
Welsh clearwing	*Synanthedon scoliaeformis*
Whiskered bat	*Myotis mystacinus*
White ermine	*Spilosoma lubricipeda*
White prominent	*Leucodonta bicoloria*
White-rumped sandpiper	*Calidris fuscicollis*
White-sided dolphin	*Lagenorhynchus acutus*
Whooper swan	*Cygnus cygnus*
Wigeon	*Anas penelope*
Willow warbler	*Phylloscopus trochillus*
Wilson's phalarope	*Phalaropus tricolor*
Wood ant	*Formica rufa*
Wood mouse	*Apodemus sylvaticus*
Wood warbler	*Phylloscopus sibilatrix*
Wood white	*Leptidea sinapsis*
Woodpigeon	*Columba palumbus*
Wreckfish	*Polyprion americanus*
Wren	*Troglodytes troglodytes*

Appendix III

List of Relevant Organisations

An Bord Pleanála (Planning Appeals Board), Floor 3, Blocks 6 & 7, Irish Life Centre,
    Lower Abbey St, Dublin 1 (01) 8728011 Fax (01) 8722684
An Taisce (The National Trust), Tailors Hall, Back lane, Dublin 8.
    (01) 4541786 Fax (01) 4533255
Birdwatch Ireland, Ruttledge House, 8 Longford Place, Monkstown,
    Co. Dublin   (01) 2804322 Fax (01) 2844407
Bord Failte Eireann (Irish Tourist Board), Baggot St Bridge, Dublin 2.
    (01) 6765871 Fax (01) 6764764
Bord Iascaigh Mhara (Irish Sea Fisheries Board), Crofton Rd., Dun Laoghaire,
    Co. Dublin   (01) 2841544 Fax (01) 2841123
Bord Na Mona (Irish Peat Board), Lower Baggot St., Dublin 2.
    (01) 6688555 Fax (01) 6601800
Central Fisheries Board, Head Office, Mobhi Boreen, Dublin 9.
    (01) 8379206 Fax (01) 8360060
Coillte Teoranta (Irish Forestry Board), Spruce House, Leeson Lane, Dublin 2.
    (01) 6615666 Fax (01) 6789527
District Office, 17 Castle St., Tralee, Co. Kerry.   (066) 21529 Fax (066) 23868
Crann Woodland Trust, Aughavas, via Cavan, Co. Leitrim.
    (078) 36020 Fax (078) 36020
Department of Agriculture, Food and Forestry, Kildare St., Dublin 2.
    (01) 6789011 Fax (01) 6616263
Regional Office, Government Offices, Spa Rd., Tralee. (066) 25811 Fax (066) 22227
Department of Arts, Culture and the Gaeltacht, 43 Mespil Rd, Ballsbridge, Dublin 4.
    (01) 6670788
Department of Education, Marlborough St., Dublin 1. (01) 8734700 Fax (01) 8729553
Department of the Environment, Custom House, Dublin 1.
    (01) 6793377 Fax (01) 6789527
Department of the Marine, Leeson Lane, Dublin 2.   (01) 6785444 Fax (01) 6618214
Department of Tourism and Transport, Kildare St., Dublin 2.
    (01) 6789522 Fax (01) 6763350
Earthwatch Kerry, c/o Matthew Hodd, Coolies, Muckross, Killarney, Co. Kerry.
    (064) 33970
ENFO – The Environmental Information Service, 17 St Andrew St, Dublin 2.
    (01) 6793144 Fax (01) 6795204

Environmental Research Unit, St Martin's House, Waterloo Rd., Dublin 4.
(01) 6602511 Fax (01) 6504929

Farming and Conservation Liaison Group, c/o David Hickie, An Taisce, Tailor's Hall,
Back Lane, Dublin 8. (01) 4541786 FAx (01) 4533255

Foroige (National Youth Development Organisation), Irish Farm Centre, Bluebell,
Dublin 12. (01) 4501022 Fax (01) 4501166

Geographical Survey of Ireland, Beggars Bush, Haddington Rd., Dublin 4.
(01) 6609511 Fax (01) 6681782

Irish Biogeographical Society, c/o National Museum of Ireland, Natural History
Division, Kildare St, Dublin 2.   (01) 6618811 Fax (01) 6766116

Irish Countrywomens Association, 58 Merrion Rd, Dublin 4.
(01) 6680453 Fax (01) 6609423

Irish Farmers Association, Irish Farm Centre, Bluebell, Dublin 12.
(01) 4501166 Fax (01) 4551043

Regional Office, F.B.D. Building, Ashe St., Tralee.   (066) 23279 Fax (066) 23279

Irish Organic Farmers and Growers Association, 59 Blessington St., Dublin 7
(01) 8307996

Irish Peatland Conservation Council, Capel Chambers, 119 Capel St, Dublin 1.
(01) 8722384

Irish Wildlife Trust, 132A East Wall Rd., Dublin 3.   (01) 8366821 Fax (01) 8366821

Kerry County Council, County Buildings, Tralee, Co. Kerry (066) 21111 Fax(066) 22466

Killarney Nature Conservation Group, c/o Jim O'Malley, Cullina, Lower Beaufort,
Killarney, Co. Kerry. (064) 44592

Macra na Feirme, Irish Farm Centre, Bluebell, Dublin 12.
(01) 4501166 Fax (01) 4514908

National Botanic Gardens, Glasnevin, Dublin 9. (01) 8374388 Fax (01) 8360080

National Heritage Council, Department of An Taoiseach, Government Buildings,
Upper Merrion St, Dublin 2.   (01) 6763546 Fax (01) 6789037

National Museum of Ireland, Kildare St, Dublin 2.   (01) 6618811 Fax (01) 6766116

National Parks and Wildlife Service, Dúchas, The Heritage Service, Dublin 2.
(01) 6613111 Fax (01) 6610747

Regional Office, Killarney National Park, Co. Kerry.   (064) 31440 Fax (064) 33926

Organic Trust, Charlotte Colchester Islands, Urlingford, Co. Kilkenny.
(056) 31411

Royal Dublin Society, Merrion Rd, Ballsbridge, Dublin 4.
(01) 6680645 Fax (01) 6604014

Royal Irish Academy, 19 Dawson St, Dublin 2.   (01) 6764222 Fax (01) 6762346

Salmon Research Agency of Ireland Inc., Farran Laboratory, Newport, Co. Mayo.
(098) 41107 Fax (098) 41107

Shannon Regional Fishery Board, Thomond Wier, Limerick.
(061) 455171 Fax (061) 326533

South West Regional Fishery Board, 1 Nevis Tce., Masseytown, Macroom, Co. Cork.
 (026) 41222 Fax (026) 41223

Teagasc (Agriculture and Food Development Authority), 19 Sandymount Ave.,
 Ballsbridge, Dublin 4.   (01) 6688188 Fax (01) 6688023

Regional Office, The Pavillion, Austin Stack Park, Tralee.
 (066) 25077 Fax (066) 25558

Tralee Regional Technical College, Clash, Tralee, Co. Kerry.
 (066) 24666 Fax (066) 24711

Tree Council Of Ireland, 33 Botanic Rd, Glasnevin, Co. Dublin.
 (01) 8306996 Fax (01) 8306948

BIBLIOGRAPHY

The Bibliography contains 1206 references to natural history in County Kerry, including scientific articles, books, magazines, university theses, published and unpublished reports. Although comprehensive, it is not exhaustive and I apologise to any authors whose publication I have missed.

GENERAL

Anon., 1972 *County Kerry Agricultural Resource Survey*, Kerry County Committee of Agriculture Tralee.

Anon., 1972, *Killarney National Park Management Plan*, Office of Public Works, Dublin.

Barrington, T.J., 1976, *Discovering Kerry. Its history, heritage and topography*, Dublin

Barry, E., 1989, *Phosphorus loads in Lough Leane and Muckross*, Kerry County Council report (Unpublished).

Beaumont, W.I., 1900, 'The fauna and flora of Valencia harbour on the west coast of Ireland, 7, Report on the results of dredging and shore collecting', *Proc. R. Ir. Acad.* 5 (5): 754-798.

Beeftink, W.G., 1978, 'Salt marshes', *In* Barnes, R.S.K., *The coastline, a contribution to our understanding of its ecology and physiography in relation to land-use and management and the pressures to which it is subject,* Wiley and Sons, Chichester., 1978

Boaden, P.J.S. and Seed, R., 1985, *An introduction to coastal ecology,* Blackie and Sons, Glasgow.

Boyd, R.J., O'Ceidigh, P. and Wilkinson, A., 1973, 'Investigations of the plankton of the west coast of Ireland VI.', *Proc. R. Ir. Acad.* 73B: 383.

Bracken, J.J. and Casey, T.J., 1976 *Final Report of the Killarney Valley Lake Survey (1971 - 1975)'*, Limnological Research Unit, University College Dublin.

Bracken, J.B. and Murray, D.A. 1987, *A limnological survey of the Killarney valley area,* Unpublished Report to Office of Public Works.

Brennan, E., 1978 *An investigation of the spatial distribution of the littoral zoobenthos of Lough Leane, Co. Kerry*, B.Sc. thesis (Unpublished) University College, Dublin.

Browne, E.T., 1900 'The fauna and flora of Valencia harbour on the west coast of Ireland', *Proc. R. Ir. Acad.* 5: 667-854

Buitléar, E. de, 1993 *Ireland's wild countryside*, Boxtree, London.

Cabot, D., Whilde, A., Taylor, N., Lloyd, C., and Goodwillie, R., 1981, *Areas of scientific interest in Ireland,* An Foras Forbartha, Dublin.

Collins, J.F., and Neefjes, J., 1990 'Soils of Cores-Ferta area of Killarney National Park Co. Kerry', *Soil Bull.* 9, University College, Dublin.

Conry, M.J., De Coninck, F., Bouma, J., Cammaerts, C., and Diamond, J.J., 1972 'Some brown podzolic soils in the west and south-west of Ireland', *Proc. R. Ir. Acad.* 72B: 359-402.

Cooke, J., 1902 *Murray's handbook for travellers in Ireland,* London.

Corbet, G.B., 1961 'Origin of the British insular races of small mammals and of the 'Lusitanian' fauna', *Nature, Lond.* 191: 1037-1040.

Craig, A.J., 1984 'National parks and other conservation areas'. *In* Jeffrey, D.W.,(ed.) *Nature conservation in Ireland: progress and problems,* R. Ir. Acad. Dublin, 122-134.

Craig, A.J., 1989 'Die nationalparke Irlands', In Bibelriether, H., and Schrieber, R.L., (Eds.) Die nationalparke Europas, *Suddeutsher Verlag,* Munchen, 126-131.

Douglas, D. J., and Murray, D.A., 1987 'The palaeolimnology of Lough Leane, Killarney, Co. Kerry', *Ir. J. Env. Sci.* 4 (2): 33-41

Erwin, D., and Picton, B., 1987 *The Marine Conservation Society guide to inshore marine life,* Immel Publications, London.

Fehily, J., and Shipman, P., 1967 *The Killarney valley survey,* An Foras Forbartha, Dublin.

Field, E.M., and Goode, D.A., 1981 *Peatland ecology in the British Isles: a bibliography,* Institute of Terrestrial Ecology and Nature Conservancy Council, Banbury.

Finch, T.F., 1957 *Reconnaissance soil survey of Kerry,* Unpublished report to An Foras Taluntais, Republic of Ireland.

Fitter, R., and Manuel, R.,1986 *Field guide to the freshwater life of Britain and North-West Europe,* Collins, London.

Flanagan, P.J., and Toner, P.F., 1975 *A preliminary survey of Irish lakes,* An Foras Forbatha, Dublin.

Godwin, H., Suggate, R.P., and Willis, E.H., 1958 'Radio-carbon dating of the eustatic rise in ocean level', *Nature* 181: 1518-1519.

Griffin, L., and Duggan, F., 1993 *Irish environmental statistics,* Environmental Research Unit, Dublin.

Hawkins, S.J., and Jones, H.D., 1992 *Marine field course guide,* 1, Rocky shores, Immel Publishing, London.

Hayward, R., 1970 *In the Kingdom of Kerry,* Dundalgan Press, Dundalk.

Hazlett, A., and Seed, R., 1976 'A study of *Fucus spiralis* and its associated fauna in Strangford Lough, County Down', *Proc. R. Ir. Acad.* 76B: 607-618.

Hiscock, K., and Hiscock, S., 1980 'Sublittoral plant and animal communities in the area of Roaring Water Bay, south-west Ireland', *J. Sherkin Is.* 1: 7-48.

Hoare, R.C., 1807 *A journal of a tour in Ireland,* London.

Inglis, H.D., 1834 *A journey throughout Ireland during 1834,* London.

Johnson, J., 1844 *A tour in Ireland,* London.

Keane, T., (Ed.) 1986 *Climate, weather and Irish agriculture,* Agriculture Trust, Dublin.

Lennox, L.J., and Toner, P.F., 1980 *The national survey of Irish rivers, a third report on water quality,* An Foras Forbatha, Dublin.

Lewis, S., *1837 A Topographical Dictionary of Ireland,* Kennikat Press, London.

Lewis, J. R., 1964 *The ecology of rocky shores*, E.U.P. London.

Lewis, J.R., 1978 'Rocky foreshores', *In* Barnes, R.S.K., *The coastline, a contribution to our understanding of its ecology and physiography in relation to land-use and management and the pressures to which it is subject*, Wiley and Sons, Chichester.

Limnology Research Unit, 1971, *A preliminary report on the University College Dublin Killarney valley lake survey*, Unpublished report to Office of Public Works.

Limnology Research Unit, 1973 *An interim report on the University College Dublin Killarney valley lake survey*, Unpublished report to Office of Public Works.

Limnology Research Unit, 1976, *Final report on the Killarney valley lake survey. (1971-1975)*, Unpublished report to Office of Public Works.

Lloyd, E., 1712 'Some further observations relating to the antiquities and natural history of Ireland', *Phil. Trans.* 27: 524-526.

Lovegrove, R.R., Byrne, E.J. and Rear, D., 1965 'Notes on a visit to the Great Skellig rock, Co. Kerry', *Ir. Nat. J.* 15 (2): 47-49.

Lynam, J., (Ed.) 1982 *Irish peaks*, Constable, London.

Lynch, A., 1981 *Man and environment in south-west Ireland*, British Archaeological Reports, British Series 85, Oxford.

MacGinnet, M., 1979 *Dúlra agus dúchas – Our heritage*, Government Stationary Office, Dublin.

McCracken, E., 1957 'Charcoal-burning ironworks in seventeenth and eighteenth century Ireland', *Ulster Journal of Archaeology*, 20: 123-138.

McCracken, E., 1971 *The Irish Woods since Tudor Times*, David and Charles, Newton Abbot.

McGee, E., 1988 *A report to the Office of Public Works on the preliminary investigation of the extent and causes of peat erosion in the National Parks*, Unpublished report to Office of Public Works.

McLysaght, E., 1991 *The Kenmare papers*, Ir. Manuscripts Commission, Dublin, 1942

McWilliams, B.E., (Ed.), *Climate change – studies on the implications for Ireland*, Stationary Office, Dublin.

McWilliams, B., 1994 *Weather eye*, Lilliput Press, Dublin.

Meldon, J., 1992 *Structural funds and the environment – problems and prospects*, An Taisce, Dublin.

Mitchell, G.F., 1976 *The Irish landscape*, Collins, London.

Mitchell, G.F., 1986 *The Shell guide to reading the Irish landscape*, Country House, Dublin.

Mitchell, G.F., et al, 1987 *The book of the Irish countryside*, Town House, Dublin.

Mitchell, F., 1989 *Man and environment in Valencia island*, Royal Irish Academy, Dublin.

Mitchell, F., 1990 *The way that I followed – a naturalist's journey around Ireland*, Country House, Dublin.

Mitchell, P.I., Sanchez-Cabeza, J.A., Ryan, T.P., McGarry, A.T., and Vidal-Quadras, A.,1990 'Preliminary estimates of cumulative caesium and plutonium deposition in the Irish terrestrial environment' *Journal of Radioanalytical and Nuclear Chemistry*, 138: 241-256.

Monk, M.A., 1993 'People and the environment: In search of the farmers', *In* Shee Twohig, E. and Ronayne, M., (Eds.) *Past perceptions: The prehistoric archaeology of south-west Ireland*, Cork University Press.

Mould, D.D.C.P., 1955 *The mountains of Ireland*, Batsford, London.

Murray, D.A., 1979 'The evolution of pollution as evidenced by lake sediment pseudofossils', In *Biological aspects of freshwater pollution*, 77-91, Pergamon Press. London.

Murray, D.A., and Douglas, D.J., 1977 'Eutrophication, past, present and future'. in *Lake pollution eutrophication control*, Government Publications Office, Dublin.

Murray, D.A., and O'Byrne-Ring, N.,1981 'Lake sediments as indices of productivity, studies on Irish and Italian lakes', *Ir. J. Env. Sci.* 1: 235-40.

O'Donoghue, J., 1960 *In Kerry long ago*, London.

O'Ruadhain, M., 1956 'The position of nature protection in Ireland in 1956', *Ir. Nat. J.* 12: 50-55.

O'Siocfradha, P., 1939 *An Seabhac, Triocha-Cead Chorca Dhuibhne*, Baile Atha Cliath.

O'Sullivan, T.F., *1931 Romantic hidden Kerry*, The Kerryman Ltd., Tralee.

O'Sullivan, M., and McGarry, A.T., *1995 Radioactivity monitoring in Irish upland lakes, 1988-1992*, Radiological Protection Institute of Ireland, Dublin.

Pochin Mould, D., 1978 *Valentia, portrait of an island*, Blackwater Press, Dublin.

Praeger, R.Ll., and Sollas, W.J., 1897 'Report of the committee appointed by the Royal Dublin Society to investigate the recent bog-flow in Kerry', *Scient. Proc. R. Dubl. Soc.* 8: 475-508.

Praeger, R.Ll., 1937 *The way that I went*, Allen Figgis, Dublin.

Praeger, R.Ll., 1950 *Natural history of Ireland*, Collins, London.

Quirke, W., 1987 *Limnological investigations of the Killarney lakes, (1986-1987)*, unpublished report to the Office of Public Works.

Radcliff, T., 1814 *Report of the Agriculture and Livestock of the County of Kerry*, W. Porter, Dublin.

Rohan, P.K., 1968 *The climate of Munster*, Meteorological Service, Dublin.

Rohan, P.K., 1986 *The climate of Ireland*, Meteorological Service, Dublin.

Rubel, E.A., 1912 'International phytogeographical excursion to the British Isles V. the Killarney oakwoods', *New Phytologist* 11: 54-57.

Scott, P., Burton, J.A., and Fitter, R., 1987 'Red Data Books: the historical background', In Fitter, R., and Fitter, M., (Eds.) *The road to extinction*, IUCN, Gland: 1-5.

Shee Twohig, E., and Ronayne, M., 1993 *Past perceptions: The prehistoric archaeology of south-west Ireland*, Cork University Press.

Smith, C., 1756 *The antient and present state of the county of Kerry,* Erving, Faulkner, Wilson and Exshaw, Dublin.

Smith, A. G., 1970 'Late – and post-glacial vegetational and climatic history of Ireland: A review', in Nicholas Stephens and Robin Edgar Glasscock (eds). *Irish Geographical Studies in honour of E. Estyn Evans:* 65-88, Belfast.

Southward, A.J., 1965 *Life on the seashore,* London.

Stack, M., 1968 *A bibliography of County Kerry,* Thesis for the Fellowship of the Library Association of Ireland.

Stephens, N., 1970 'The coastline of Ireland', In Nicholas Stephens and Robin Edgar Glasscock (Eds.), *Irish geographical studies in honour of E. Estyn Evans*: 125-145, Belfast.

Twomey, H., 1989 *Limnological investigations of the Killarney Lakes, 1989,* Unpublished report to Office of Public Works.

Twomey, H., 1990 *Limnological investigations of the Killarney Lakes, 1990,* Unpublished report to Office of Public Works.

Twomey, H., 1991 *Limnological investigations of the Killarney Lakes, 1991,* Unpublished report to Office of Public Works.

Twomey, H., 1992 *Limnological investigations of the Killarney Lakes, 1992,* Unpublished report to Office of Public Works.

Twomey, H., 1992 *Compilation report integrating the results of biological and physical/ chemical monitoring of the Killarney lakes,* Unpublished Report to the Office of Public Works.

Whilde, A., *Irish red data book 2,* vertebrates, HMSO, Belfast.

GEOLOGY

Bailey, W.H., 1860 'List of fossils from west flank of Caherconree, Co. Kerry', *J. Geol. Soc. Dubl.* 8.

Bassett, M.G., Cocks, L.R.M., and Holland, C.H., 1976 'The affinities of two endemic Silurian brachiopods from the Dingle peninsula, Ireland', *Palaeontology* 19: 615-625.

Brennand, T. P., 1965 'The upper carboniferous (Namurian) stratigraphy north east of Castleisland, Co. Kerry, Ireland', *Proc. R. Ir. Acad.* 64 B (4): 41-63.

Bridge, J.S., Van Veen, P.M., and Matten, L.C., 1980 'Aspects of the sedimentology, palynology and palaeobotany of the upper Devonian of southern Kerry Head, Co. Kerry, Ireland', *Geological Journal* 15: 143-170.

Bryant, R.H., 1966 'The 'pre-glacial' raised beach in south-west Ireland', *Ir. Geogr.* 5 (3): 188-203.

Bryant, R.H, 1968 *A study of the glaciation of South Iveragh,* Co. Kerry, Ph.D. dissertation, (Unpublished) University of Reading.

Bryant, R.H., 1974, 'A late-Midlandian section at Finglas river near Waterville Kerry', *Proc. R. Ir. Acad.* 74 B (12): 161-178.

Capewell, J.G., 1951 'The Old Red Sandstone of the Inch and Annascaul district, Co. Kerry', *Proc. R. Ir. Acad.* 54B:141-168.

Capewell, J.G., 1957 'The stratigraphy and structure of the country around Sneem, Co. Kerry', *Proc. R. Ir. Acad.* 58B: 167-183.

Capewell, J.G., 1965, 'The Old Red Sandstone of Slieve Mish, Co. Kerry', *Proc. R. Ir. Acad.* 64B:165-174.

Capewell, J.G., 1975 'The Old Red Sandstone group of Iveragh Co. Kerry', *Proc. R. Ir. Acad.* 75B: 155-171.

Charlesworth, J. K., 1928 'The glacial retreat from central and southern Ireland', *Q. J. Geol. Soc. Lond.* 84: 293-344.

Charlesworth, J.K., 1963 *The historical geology of Ireland,* Oliver and Boyd, London.

Charlesworth, J.K., 1966 *The geology of Ireland,* Oliver and Boyd, London.

Clayton, G., Graham, J.R., Higgs, K., Holland, C.H. and Naylor, D., 1980 'Devonian rocks in Ireland: a review', *J. Earth Sci.* R. Dubl. Soc. 2: 161-183.

Close, M., 1870 'On some corries and their rock-basins in Kerry', *J. R. Geol. Soc. Ir.* 12: 236-248.

Coe, K. and Selwood, E.B., 1968 'The Upper Palaeozoic stratigraphy of west Cork and parts of south Kerry', *Proc. R. Ir. Acad.* 66 B (9): 113-131.

Cole, G.A., 1899 'Geology of Kenmare district', *Ir. Nat.* 8 (3): 62.

Cole, G.A.J., 1908 'Probable Cretaceous and Cainozoic outliers off the coast of Co. Kerry', *Geol. Mag. N.S.* Dec. 5 (5): 463-464.

Cole, G.A.J., 1922 *Memoir and map of localities of minerals of economic importance and metalliferous mines in Ireland,* Mem. Geol. Surv. of Ireland, Dublin.

Cole, G.A.J. and Crook, T., 1910 *On rock specimens dredged from the floor of the Atlantic off the coast of Ireland, and their bearing on submarine geology,* Memoirs of the Geological Survey of Ireland, Dublin.

Coleman, J.C., 1965 *The caves of Ireland,* Tralee.

Coxon, P., 1993 'Irish Pleistocene biostratigraphy', *Ir. J. Earth Sci.* 1312: 83-105.

Diemer, J.A., Bridge, J.S. and Sanderson, D.J., 1987 'Revised geology of Kerry Head, Co. Kerry', *Ir. J. Earth Sci.* 8 (2): 113-138.

Dolan, J.M., 1984 'A structural cross-section through the Carboniferous of northwest Kerry, *Ir. J. Earth Sci.* 6: 95-108.

Doran, R.J.P., Holland, C.H. and Jackson, A.A., 1973 'The sub-old red sandstone surface in southern Ireland', *Proc. R. Ir. Acad.* 73B: 109-128.

Edwards, K.J., and Warren, W.P., (Eds.), 1985 *The Quarternary history of Ireland,* Academic Press, London.

Ehlers, J., Gibbard, P.L. and Rose, J., 1991 *Glacial deposits in Great Britain and Ireland,* Balkema, Rotterdam.

Fahy, G., 1972 *Geomorphology,* Educational Company of Ireland, Dublin.

Farrington, A., 1931 'The Loo valley, Co. Kerry', *Proc. R. Ir. Acad.* 40 B (10): 109-120.

Farrington, A., 1947 'Unglaciated areas in southern Ireland', *Irish Geog.* 1: 89-97.

Farrington, A., 1954, 'A note on the correlation of the Kerry-Cork glaciations with those of the rest of Ireland', *Ir. Geogr.* 3(1): 47-53.

Farrington, A., 1959 'The Lee Basin, Part one: glaciation', *Proc. R. Ir. Acad.*60 B (3): 135-166.

Foot, F., 1856 'On the trappean rocks of the neighbourhood of Killarney, *J.Geol.Soc. Dublin* 7: 167.

Gardiner, C.I. and Reynolds, S.H., 1902 'The fossiliferous Silurian beds and associated igneous rocks of the Clogher Head district, Co. Kerry', *Q. Jl. Geol. Soc. Lond.* 58: 226-266.

Griffith, R.J., 1839 'On the principle of colouring adopted for the geological map of Ireland and on the geological structure of the south of Ireland', *Jl. Geol. Soc. Dubl.* 2: 78-90.

Griffith, R.J., and McCoy, F., 1846 *A synopsis of the Silurian fossils of Ireland,* Dublin.

Guilcher, A., 1965 'Drumlin and spit structures in the Kenmare river, south-west Ireland', *Ir. Geogr.* 5 (2): 7-19.

Guilcher, A., 1966 'Les grandes falaises et megafalaises des Cotes sud-ouest et ouest de l'Irlande', *Annals. Geogr.* 75: 26-38.

Guilcher, A., King, A.M., and Berthois, R., 1961 'Spits, tombolos and tidal marshes in Connemara and west Kerry, Ireland', *Proc. R. Ir. Acad.* 61B (17): 283-338.

Hamilton, C.W., 1838 'An outline of the geology of part of the county of Kerry', *Jl. Geol. Soc. Dubl.* 1: 276-285.

Hancock, J.M., 1963 'The hardness of Irish chalk', *Ir. Nat. J.* 14: 157-164.

Harper, J.C., and Brenchley, P.J., 1972 'Some points of interest concerning the Silurian inliers of south west central Ireland in their geosynclinal context: A statement', *Jl. Geol. Soc. Lond.* 128: 257-262.

Herries Davies, G.L. and Stephens, N., 1978 *The Geomorphology of the British Isles; Ireland,* Methuen, London.

Holland, C.H., 1969 'The Irish counterpart of the Silurian of Newfoundland, Gander Symposium 1967', *Mem. Am. Ass. Petrol. Geol.* 12: 298-308.

Holland, C.H., 1977 'Ireland', *In* House, M.R. et al. A correlation of Devonian rocks in the British Isles, *Geol. Soc. special Report,* No. 8: 54-66.

Holland, C.H., 1979 'Augmentation and decay of the Old Red Sandstone Continent, Evidence from Ireland', *Palaeogeog. Palaeoclimat. Palaeoecol.* 27: 59-66.

Holland, C.H., 1981a *A geology of Ireland,* Scottish Academic Press.

Holland, C.H., 1981b 'Devonian', in Holland, C.H., (ed.) *A geology of Ireland,* Scottish Academic Press. pp. 121-146.

Horne, R.R., 1970 'A preliminary re-interpretation of the Devonian palaeogeography of western County Kerry', *Geol. Surv. Ireland Bull.* 1: 53-60.

Horne, R.R., 1974 'The lithostratigraphy of the late Silurian to early Carboniferous of the Dingle peninsula, Co. Kerry', *Bull. geol. Surv. Ireland*. 1: 395-428.

Horne, R.R., 1975 'The association of alluvial fan, aeolian and fluviatile facies in the Caherbla Group (Devonian) Dingle peninsula, Ireland', *J. of Sedimentary Petrology* 45: 535-540.

Horne, R.R., and MacIntyre, R., 1975 'Apparent age and significance of Tertiary dykes in the Dingle peninsula, s.w. Ireland', *Scient. Proc. R. Dubl. Soc. Series* A 5 (18): 293-299.

Howard, D.W., 1975 'Deep-seated igneous intrusions in Co. Kerry', *Proc. R. Ir. Acad.* 75 B (7): 173-183.

Hudson, R.G.S., Clarke, M.J., and Brennand, T.P., 1966 'The Lower Carboniferous (Dinantian) stratigraphy of the Castleisland area, Co. Kerry', *Scient. Proc. R. Dubl. Soc.* 2(A): 297-317.

Hull, E., 1879a 'On the geological age of the rocks forming the southern highlands of Ireland generally known as the "Dingle Beds" and the "Glengariff grits and slates",' *Q. Jl. Geol. Soc. Lond.* 35: 699-723.

Hull, E., 1879b 'On the relations of the Carboniferous, Devonian and Upper Silurian rocks of the south of Ireland to those of north Devon', *Sci. Proc. R. Dubl. Soc.* 1: 135-150.

Inamdar, D.D. and Horne, R.R., 1971 'A magnetic survey of North Kerry, Part 1, The Dingle Bay – Castlemaine Valley area', *Bull. Geol. Surv. Ireland* 1: 113-118.

Jackson, J.S.,1968 'Bronze Age copper mining on Mount Gabriel, County Cork, Ireland', *Archaeologica Austriaca* 43: 92-114.

Jessen, K., 1949 'Studies in late Quarternary deposits and flora history of Ireland', *Proc. R. Ir. Acad.* 52B: 85-290.

Jones, P.C., 1974 'Marine transgression and facies distribution in the west Cork Beds (Devonian: Carboniferous) of west Cork and Kerry', *Proc. Geol. Assoc.* 85: 159-188.

Jukes, J.B.,1862 'On the mode of formation of some river valleys in the south of Ireland', *Qrt. J. Geol. Soc. London* 18: 378-403.

Jukes, J.B. and Du Noyer, G.V., 1857 'On the geological structure of the Dingle promontory, Co. Kerry', *Br. Ass. Advmt. Sci.* 27: 70-73.

Jukes, J.B. and Du Noyer, G.V., 1858 'On the geological structure of the Caherconree mountain, ten miles west of Tralee', *Jl. geol. Soc. Dubl.* 8: 106-109.

Khan, M.F.H., 1955 'The Old Red Sandstone of the Kerry Head anticline, Co. Kerry,' *Proc. R. Ir. Acad.* 57B (6): 71-78.

Khan, M.F.H., 1970 'Old Red Sandstone of the Kerry Head anticline',. *Proc. R. Ir. Acad.* 57 B (6): 71-78.

Kinahan, G.H., 1857 *On the Valentia trap-district*, Report of the 27th. Meeting of the British Ass. For the Advancement of Science, p.75.

Kinahan, G.H., 1878a 'Cambro-Silurian and Silurian rocks of the south and the western part of Ireland', *Jl. R. geol. Soc. Ireland* 5: 118-121.

Kinahan, G.H., 1878b *Manual of the geology of Ireland,* C.K. Paul and Co., London.

Kinahan, G.H., 1878c 'Slates and clays (bricks, etc.) with introduction and building notes by R. Clark', *Sci. Proc. R. Dubl. Soc,* New Series, 6: 84-156.

Kinahan, G.H., 1879 *Manual of the geology of Ireland with ill. and maps,* 8 vols., London.

Kinahan, G.H., 1879 'Dingle beds and Glengariff grits', *Geol. Mag.* 6: 349.

Kinahan, G.H., 1887a 'Irish marbles and limestones', *Sci. Proc. R. Dubl. Soc.* 5:383-492.

Kinahan, G.H., 1887b 'Irish arenaceous rocks, sands, sandstones, grits, conglomerates, quartz-rocks, and quartzites', *Sci. Proc. R. Dubl. Soc.* 5: 567-571.

Kinahan, G.H., 1888 'Granite, elvan, porphyry, felstone, whinstone and metamorphic rocks of Ireland', *Sci. Proc. R. Dubl. Soc.* 6: 213-215..

Kinahan, G.H., 1894 'The recent Irish glaciers', *Ir. Nat. 3* (11): 236-240.

Kinahan, G.H., 1899 'The geological structure of the Kenmare district', *Ir. Nat.* 8:28..

King, C.A.M. and Gage, M., 1961 'The extent of glaciation in part of west Kerry', *Ir. Geog.* 4 (3): 202-208..

Lewis, C.A., 1967 'The glaciation of the Behy valley, County Kerry', *Ir. Geogr.* 5 (4): 293-301.

Lewis, C.A., 1974, 'The glaciations of the Dingle peninsula, County Kerry', *Scient. Proc. R. Dubl. Soc.* Series A 5 (13): 207-235.

Matten, L.C., Lacey, W.S., and Edwards, D., 1976 'An Upper Devonian/Lower Carboniferous transition flora from southwest Eire', *Courier Forschungen Senckenberg* 17: 87.

Matten, L.C., May, B.I., and Lucas R.C., 1980 'A megafossil flora from the Upper Devonian/Lower Carboniferous transition zone near Ballyheigue, Co. Kerry', *Reviews of Palaeobotany and Palynology* 29: 241.

McHenry, A., and Watts, W.W.,1898 *Guide to the collection of rocks and fossils belonging to the Geological survey of Ireland,* H.M.S.O., Dublin.

McHenry, A.,1912 'Report on the Dingle beds', *Proc. R. Ir. Acad.* 24B: 229-234.

Mitchell, G. F.,1970 'The Quaternary deposits between Fenit and Spa on the north shore of Tralee Bay, Co. Kerry', *Proc. R. Ir. Acad.* 70 B (6): 141-162.

Mitchell, G.F., 1981, 'The Quaternary – until 10,000 B.P', In Holland, C.H., (ed.) *A geology of Ireland,* Scottish Academic Press. pp. 235-258.

Mitchell, G. F., Coxon, P., and Price, A., 1983 *Guide book to north-west Iveragh,* Kerry, Irish Association for Quarternary Studies, Dublin.

Mitchell, G. F., Penny, L. F., Shotton, F. W. and West, R. G., 1973 'A correlation of Quaternary deposits in the British Isles', *Geol. Soc. Lond.,* Special Report No. 4: 1-99.

Morris, P., 1973 'Density, magnetic and resistivity measurements on Irish rocks', *Dubl. Inst. Adv. Stud. Geophys. Bull.* 31: 1-48.

Morris, P., 1974 'A Tertiary dyke system in south-west Ireland', *Proc. R. Ir. Acad.* 74 B (13): 179-184.

Morris, P., 1980 'An analysis of some small scale gravity variations over the Iveragh peninsula', *Ir. J. Earth Sci.* 3 (2): 147-153.

Murphy, T., 1986 'Comments on: An interpretation of the Killarney and Leinster gravity anomalies in the Republic of Ireland', *In*: Emenike , E.A., 'An interpretation of the Killarney and Leinster gravity anomalies in the Republic of Ireland', *Ir. J. Earth Sci.* 7: 125-132.

Naylor, D., 1978 'A structural section across the Variscan fold belt, south-west Ireland', *Ir. J. Earth Sci.* 1 (1): 63-70.

Parkin, J.R., 1974 'Silurian rocks of Inishvickillane, Blasket Islands, Co. Kerry', *Scient. Proc. R. Dubl. Soc.* 5A: 277-291.

Parkin, J., 1976a 'Silurian rocks of the Bull's Head, Annascaul, and Derrymore Glen inliers, Co. Kerry', *Proc. R. Ir. Acad.* 76 B (35): 577-606.

Parkin, J., 1976b 'The geology of the Foze Rocks, Co. Kerry: A review', *Ir. Nat. J.* 18: 308.

Phillips, J. St. J., 1898 'Geology; Part 4 of the report of the second triennial conference and excursion of the Irish Field Club Union, held at Kenmare, July 7-13th, 1898', *Ir. Nat.* 7: 228.

Piper, D.J.W., 1969 *Silurian sediments in western Ireland*, Ph.D. thesis, (Unpublished) University of Cambridge.

Proudfoot, V.B., 1954 'The glaciation of the Dingle peninsula', *Ir. Geog.* 3: 36-38.

Redmond, T., 1974 The post-glacial developmental history of Doo Lough, Muckross peninsula Killarney. Co. Kerry, B.Sc.thesis (Unpublished) University College, Dublin.

Rowan, A.B., 1852 'Limestone boulders of Corkaguiney, County of Kerry', *J. Geol. Soc. Dubl.* 5: 201-203.

Russell, K.J., 1978 'Vertebrate fossils from the Iveragh peninsula and the age of the Old Red Sandstone', *Ir. J. Earth Sci.* 1 (1): 151-162.

Sevastopulo, G.D., 1981a 'Lower Carboniferous', *In* Holland, C.H., 1981, (ed.) *A geology of Ireland*, Scottish Academic Press. pp. 147-171.

Sevastopulo, G.D., 1981b 'Upper Carboniferous', *In* Holland, C.H., 1981, (ed.) *A geology of Ireland*, Scottish Academic Press. pp. 173-187.

Sevastopulo, G.D., 1981c 'Hercynian structures', *In* Holland, C.H., 1981, (ed.) *A geology of Ireland*, Scottish Academic Press. pp. 189-199.

Sevastopulo, G.D., 1981d 'Economic geology', *In* Holland, C.H., 1981, (ed.) *A geology of Ireland*, Scottish Academic Press. pp. 273-301.

Shackleton, R.M., 1940 'The succession of rocks in the Dingle Peninsula', *Proc. R. Ir. Acad.* 46B: 1-12.

Squire, R. and Squire, J.E.,1964 'Caves in the Tralee area, Co. Kerry', *Proc. Univ. Bristol Spelaeo. Soc.* 10: 139-148.

Thomson, S.M.,1899 'Glacial geology of Kerry,' *Ir. Nat.* 8 (3): 61.

Twomey, H., 1994, *Biological investigations of Lough Leane,* Killarney National Park, Unpublished report to the Office of Public Works.

Walsh, P.T., 1959-60 'Specimens from an occurrence of Cretaceous chalk in the Killarney district, Eire', *Proc. Geol. Soc.* 1581: 112-113.

Walsh, P.T., 1960 'Cretaceous rocks near Killarney', *Proc. Geol. Soc.* 1581: 112-113.

Walsh, P.T., 1965 'Possible Tertiary outliers from the Gweestin valley, Co. Kerry', *Ir. Nat. J.* 15 (4): 100-104.

Walsh, P.T.,1966 'Cretaceous outliers in south-west Ireland and their implications for Cretaceous palaeogeography', *Q. J. Geog. Soc. Lond.* 122: 63-84.

Walsh, P.T., 1968 'The Old Red Sandstone of Killarney Co. Kerry', *Proc. R. Ir. Acad.* 66B: 9-26.

Warren, W.P., 1978 *The glacial history of the McGillycuddy's Reeks and the adjoining area,* Ph.D. thesis (Unpublished) University College, Dublin.

Warren, W.P., 'Fenetian (Midlandian) glacial deposits in Ireland', 1991a *In* Ehlers, J., Gibbard, P.L. and Rose, J., (Eds.), *Glacial deposits in Great Britain and Ireland,* Balkema, Rotterdam. pp. 69-88.

Warren, W.P., 1991b 'Glacial deposits of southwest Ireland', *In* Ehlers, J., Gibbard, P.L. and Rose, J., (Eds.) *Glacial deposits in Great Britain and Ireland,* Balkema, Rotterdam. pp. 345-353.

Warren, W.P., 1991c 'Till lithology in Ireland', *In* Ehlers, J., Gibbard, P.L. and Rose, J., (Eds.) *Glacial deposits in Great Britain and Ireland*, Balkema, Rotterdam. pp. 415-420.

Watts, W. A., 1963 'Late-glacial pollen zones in western Ireland', *Ir. Geogr.* 4 (5): 367-376.

Weaver, T., 1838 'On the geological relations of the south of Ireland', *Trans. Geol. Soc. London* Series 2, Vol. 5(1).

White, C., 1894 'Geological notes of the scenery of the Killarney district', *Brit. Naturalist:* 184-190.

Whittow, J. B., 1975 *Geology and scenery in Ireland*, Penguin, Middlesex.

Williams, M., 1964 'Glacial breaches and sub-glacial channels in south-western Ireland', *Ir. Geogr.* 4 (6): 432-441.

Williams, M., 1964 'Glacial breeches and sub-glacial channels in south-western Ireland', *Ir. Geogr.* 5: 83-95.

Wilson, H.E., 1981 'Permian and Mesozoic', *In* Holland, C.H., 1981, (ed.) *A geology of Ireland*, Scottish Academic Press.

Wingfield, R., 1968, *The geology of Kenmare and Killarney,* Ph.D. thesis (Unpublished) Trinity College Dublin.

Wright, W.B., 1927 ' The geology of Killarney and Kenmare', *Mem. Geo. Surv. Ireland,* 1-111.

Wyse Jackson, P., 1994 *The geology of Kerry,* Trinity College Dublin.

FLORA
FLOWERS AND VEGETATION

Allen, D. E., 1993 'Further Irish bramble records', *Ir. Nat. J.* 25: 249-253.

Andrews, W., 1941a 'Account of a botanical excursion through a portion of Clare and Kerry', *In*: Anon., 'Proceedings of Learned Societies', *Dublin Nat. Hist. Soc. Ann. Mag. nat. Hist.* 6: 382-385.

Andrews, W., 1841b 'Lecture note. A naturalist ramble in Kerry. Lecture to Dublin Natural History Society, presented 5 November 1841'. *In: Intellectual Observer* May 1864, 229.

Andrews, W., 1844 'Saxifrages exhibited from Brandon', *Phytologist* 1: 1032.

Andrews, W., 1871, 'On some Irish saxifrages' *Proc. Dub. Nat. Hist Soc.* 6: 84-6.

Andrews, W., 1856 '*Saxifraga geum* in the Great Blasket island', *Proc. Dubl. Nat. Hist. Soc.* 1: 66.

Anon., 1988 *An overview of the rhododendron control situation in Killarney National Park,* Unpublished report, Groundwork.

Anon., 1989 *Assessment of oakwood rhododendron infestation in Killarney National Park.* Unpublished report., Groundwork.

Babington, C.C., 1841 'Notes on *Saxifraga umbrosa*', *Dublin Nat. Hist. Soc. Ann. Mag. nat. Hist.* 7: 47-48.

Babington, C.C., 1842 'On the saxifrages of the Robertsonia, or London pride group, which are found in Ireland', *Dublin Nat. Hist.Soc. Ann. Mag. nat. Hist.* 8: 321-323.

Babington, C.C., 1844 'On the difference between the Robertsonian saxifrages of Ireland and those of the Pyrenees', *Dublin Nat. Hist.Soc. Ann. Mag. nat. Hist.* 10: 465-466.

Babington, C.C., 1865 'On *Hedera canariensis* as an Irish plant', *J. Bot.* 8: 381.

Balfour, J. H., 1853 'Botanical trip to Ireland', *Phytologist* 1005-1007.

Ballantyne, R.M., 1859 'The lakes of Killarney', *The Arbutus* 109-111.

Barbour, J.H., 1898 'Plants of Killarney', *Sci. Gossip, New Series* 4: 108-109.

Barnosky, C.W., 1988 'A late-glacial and post-glacial pollen record from the Dingle peninsula', *Proc. R. Ir. Acad.* 88 B (2): 23-27.

Barrington, M., 1947 'Wild flowers of west Cork and Kerry' In Moore, C. (Ed.) *Introducing Ireland*, Countrygoer.

Barrington, R. M., 1881 'Report on the flora of the Great Blasket island', *Proc. R. Ir. Acad.* 13: 368-391.

Beesley, S., 1979 'The sea-pea, *Lathyrus japonicus* Willd. in Co. Kerry', *Ir. Nat. J.* 19: 328.

Bellamy, D., 1986 *The wild boglands,* Country House, Dublin.

Bennett, A., 1887 'Notes on British plants', *J. Bot.* 35: 244-64.

Bennett, A., 1892 '*Carex aquatilis* Wahlb and its British forms', *Ir. Nat.* 1: 48-50.

Bennett, A., 1895 '*Juncus tenuis* Willd in Great Britain', *J. Bot.* 33: 39-40.

Boatman, D.J., 1961, 'Vegetation and peat characteristics of blanket bogs in Co. Kerry. *J. Ecol.* 49: 507-517.

Boggitt, G., 1932, 'Ten days in Co. Kerry', *Bot. Exchange Club of the Brit. Isles* 9: 786.

Bond, M.K., 1927 'A second station for *Spiranthes gemmipara* (as *romanzoffiana*) in Co. Kerry', *Ir. Nat. J.* 1: 277.

Bradshaw, R.H.W., and Browne, P., 1987 'Changing pattern in the post-glacial distribution of *Pinus sylvestris* in Ireland', *Journal of Biogeography,* 14: 237-248.

Bree, W.T., 1841 '*On Saxifraga umbrosa* and the Kerry saxifrages', *Dublin Nat. Hist. Soc. Ann. Mag. nat. Hist.* 6: 401-402.

Brenan, S.A., 1896 'Irish hawkweeds, etc.', *Ir. Nat.* 5 (1): 27.

Britten, J., 1915 '*Juncus tenuis* in Kerry', *J. Bot.* 54: 307.

Carrington, J.T., 1899 'Natural science in Ireland', *Sci. Gossip, New Series* 5: 129.

Carroll, I., 1854 'Notes on new or scarce Irish plants', *Phytologist* 5: 76-78.

Carroll, I., 1857, 'Notes of scarce Irish plants', *Phytologist New Series* 2: 76-77.

Chapman, V.J., 1960 *Salt marshes and salt deserts of the world,* Hill, London.

Charlesworth, J.K., 1932, 'The distribution of the Irish peats', *Ir. Nat. J.* 4 (2): 37-39.

Clabby, G., and Osborne, B.A., 1994 'History, distribution and ecology of *Mycelis muralis* (L.) Dumort (Asteraceae) in Ireland', *Biology and Environment* 94 B: 57-73.

Clapham, A.R., Tutin, T.G., and Warburg, E.F., 1962 *Flora of the British Isles,* Cambridge University Press, Cambridge

Clapham, A.R., Tutin, T.G., and Moore, D.M., 1987 ' *Flora of the British Isles,* 3rd. edition', Cambridge University Press, Cambridge.

Colgan, N., 1886 'Scrambles in the Kerry highlands', *Dubl. Univ. Rev:* 2: 484-493.

Colgan, N., 1918 'A botanical parallel: Lusitania and Kerry', *Ir. Nat.* 27: 20-26.

Collingwood, C., 1853 'Jottings of a naturalist at Killarney', *The Naturalist* 3: 9.

Craig, A.J., 1992 Woodland conservation in Killarney National Park and elsewhere in Ireland, *Int. Seminar on Conservation of Atlantic Woodlands,* Galicia, Spain, (Unpublished) 21pp.

Cross, J.R., 1973 *The ecology and control of Rhododendron ponticum L. with special reference to the Killarney National Park,* Ph.D. thesis (Unpublished) Trinity College Dublin.

Cross, J.R., 1975 'Biological flora of the British Isles: *Rhododendron ponticum* L.', *J. Ecol.* 63: 345-364.

Cross, J.R., 1981 'The establishment of *Rhododendron ponticum* in the Killarney oak-woods, s.w. Ireland', *J. Ecol.* 69: 807-824.

Cross, J.R., 1982 'The invasion and impact of *Rhododendron ponticum* in native Irish vegetation', *J. Life Sci.* 209-220.

Curtis, T.G. F., 1993 '*Polygonum viviparum* in Ireland, with particular reference to the flora and vegetation of the Mount Brandon range, Co. Kerry', *Ir. Nat. J.* 24: 274-280.

Curtis, T.G.F., and Harrington, T.J., 1987 'A second station for *Ranunculus tripartitus* D.C. in Kerry (H1)', *Ir. Nat. J.* 22 (5): 204.

Curtis, T.G.F., and McGough, H.N., 1988 *The Irish red data book, 1; Vascular plants,* Government Stationary Office, Dublin.

Delap, A., 1893 *'Lavatera arborea,* the tree mallow in Ireland', *Ir. Nat.* 2: 112.

Dodson, J.R., 1990 'Holocene vegetation of a prehistorically inhabited valley, Dingle peninsula', *Proc. R. Ir. Acad.* 90 B (9): 151-174.

Donaldson, F., Donaldson, F. and McMillan, N. F., 1976 'The present status of tear-thumb *(Polygonum sagittatum L.)* in Ireland, and notes on some other Kerry plants', *Ir. Nat. J.* 18: 331-332.

Donaldson, F., Donaldson, F. and McMillan, N. F., 1978 *'Polygonum sagittatum L.* Its status in Co. Kerry', *Ir. Nat. J.* 19 (5): 168.

Donaldson, F. and McMillan, N. F., 1981 'The habitat of the sea-pea *Lathyrus japonicus* Willd.', *Ir. Nat. J.* 20: 206-207.

Doogue, D., Kelly, D.L., and Wyse Jackson, P.S., 1985 'The progress of *Epilobium ciliatum Rafin. (E. aderiocaulon* Hausskn.) in Ireland, with some notes on its hybrids', *Ir. Nat. J.* 21 (10): 444-446.

Douglas, C., Garvey, L., Kelly, L., and O'Sullivan, A., 1989 'A survey to locate blanket *bogs of scientific interest in County Kerry and County Sligo',* Unpublished report to the Office of Public Works.

Doyle, J., 1937 *'Geranium pusillum* in Co. Kerry', *Ir. Nat. J.* 6: 195.

Doyle, G.J., 1987 'The Killarney fern *(Trichomanes speciosum* Willd.) can still be found in Killarney oakwoodlands (Blechno-Quercetum)', *Ir. Nat. J.* 22: 353-356.

Druce, G.C., 1908 'Notes on the flora of Cork, Kerry and Dublin', *J. Bot.* 29: 304- 307.

Druce, G.C., 1907 'Notes on a botanical expedition in Ireland', *Ir. Nat.* 16: 146-153.

Druce, G.C., 1909 'On *Thymus* forms', *J. Bot.* 47: 384.

Druce, G.C., 1910 'Three new species to "Cybele Hibernica" and "Irish Topographical Botany"', *Ir. Nat.* 19: 237.

Druce, G.C., 1911 'Two plants new to Ireland', *Ir. Nat.* 20: 198.

Druce, G.C., 1912 'Notes on Irish plants', *Ir. Nat.* 21: 235-240.

Edees, E. J., and Newton, A., 1988 *Brambles of the British Isles,* Ray Society, London.

Faris, R.C., 1974 *'Spiranthes romanzoffiana* Cham. at Caragh Lake, South Kerry', *Ir. Nat. J.* 18: 93.

Fitzpatrick, H.M., 1933 'The trees of Ireland, native and introduced', *Sci. Proc. R.D.S.* 20 (41): 597-656.

Forbes, A.C., 1933 'Tree planting in Ireland during four centuries', *Proc. R. I. Acad.* 41C: 168-199.

Fryer, A., 1889 'Irish potamogetons', *J. Bot.* 27: 183-184.

Gimingham, C.H., Chapman, S.B., and Webb, N.R., 1979 'European heathlands', *In* Specht, R.L., (ed.) *Ecosystems of the World,* Elsevier Scient. Publishing, Oxford. pp. 365-413.

Gray, A.J., 1985 'Adaptation in perennial coastal plants - with particular reference to heritable variation in *Puccinellia maritima* and *Ammophila arenaria*',*Vegetatio* 61: 179-188.

Gray, A.J., 1992 'Saltmarsh plant ecology: zonation and succession revisited', *In* Allen, J.R.L., and Pye, K., (eds) *Saltmarshes – morphodynamics, conservation and engineering significance*, Cambridge Univ. Press, Cambridge.

Gordon, V., 1970 '*Ranunculus tripartitus* DC in south Kerry', *Ir. Nat. J.* 16: 396.

Groves, H., and Groves C., 1898 '*Ranunculus tripartitus* DC., In Ireland', *J. Bot.* (Lond.) 36: 277.

Harrison, J.H., 1950 '*Orchis fuchsii* ssp. *hebridensis* Wilmott, in Co. Kerry', *Ir. Nat. J.* 10: 57.

Harron, J., 1974 'Plant records for some Irish counties', *Ir. Nat. J.* 18: 88.

Hart, H.C., 1882a 'Notes on mountain plants in Kerry', *J. Bot.* 20: 174-175.

Hart, H.C., 1882b 'Report upon the botany of the Macgillicuddy Reeks, Co. Kerry', *Proc. R. Ir. Acad.* 8: 573-593.

Hart, H.C., 1884 'Notes on the plants of some of the mountain ranges of Ireland', *Proc. R. Ir. Acad.* 14: 211-251.

Hart, H.C., 1891 'On the range of flowering plants and ferns on the mountains of Ireland', *Proc. R. Ir. Acad.* 17: 512-570.

Harvey, W.H., 1855 'On two recently discovered plants new to Ireland – *Saxifraga andrewii* and *Simethis bicolor*', *R. Dubl. Soc. Reports* 6-7.

Hayes, C., Dower, P., Kelly, D.L., and Frazer, F.J.G., 1991 *The establishment of permanent quadrats for the monitoring of grazing and its effects on tree regeneration in the Killarney oakwoods.* Unpublished report to the Office of Public works.

Healy, M., 1986 *The history of woodland on Muckross peninsula, Killarney, in late glacial and postglacial times.* M.A. thesis (Unpublished) U.C.C.

Heijnis, H., Ruddock, J., and Coxon, P., 1993, 'A uranium-thorium dated Late Eemian or Early Midlandian organic deposit from near Kilfenora between Spa and Fenit, Co. Kerry, Ireland', *J. Quart. Sci.* 8 (1): 31-43.

Henderson, A., 1982 'Strawberry trees', *The Garden* 107: 191-194.

Hennessy, H., 1867, 'On the origin of the south European plants found in the west and south of Ireland', *Proc. R. Ir. Acad.* 10: 66-7.

Hind, W.M., 1857a 'Three days at Killarney', *Phytologist, New Series* 2: 25-28.

Hind, W.M., 1857b 'Dingle and its flora', *Phytologist, New Series* 2: 97-100.

Hodd, M., 1995, *Tree surveys in the Killarney National Park*, Unpublished Report to the Office of Public Works.

Hogg, J., 1858 'On four varieties of British plants', *J. Linnean Soc.* 2: 133-137.

Ingram, R., 1967 'On the identity of the Irish populations of *Sisyrinchium*', *Watsonia* 6 (5): 283-289.

Ingram, R., 1964 The taxonomy and cytology of the genus *Sisyrinchium*, Ph. D. Thesis, University of Durham.

Iremonger, S.F., 1986 *An ecological account of Irish wetland woods; with particular reference to the principal tree species*, Ph.D. thesis (Unpublished) Trinity College Dublin.

Iremonger, S.F., 1990 'A structural analysis of three Irish wooded wetlands'. *J. Veg. Sc.* 1: 359-366.

Iremonger, S.F., and Kelly, D.L., 1988   'The response of four wetland tree species to raised soil water levels', *New Phytologist* 109: 491-497.

Jacob, D.J., 1990 *Ancient woodland in the Killarney National Park.* B.A. (Mod.) thesis (Unpublished) Trinity College Dublin.

Jenner, B.C., 1918 'Note, *Lathyrus japonicus* Willd.' *Wild Flower Mag.* December 1918: 7-8.

Jessen, K., 1949 'Studies in late Quaternary deposits and flora history of Ireland', *Proc. R. Ir. Acad.* 52B: 85-209.

Kelly, D.L., 1970 *Studies on the vegetation of the National Park at Muckross, Killarney.* B.A. (Mod.) thesis (Unpublished) Trinity College Dublin.

Kelly, D.L., 1975 *Native woodlands in western Ireland with especial reference to the region of Killarney*, Ph.D. thesis (Unpublished) Trinity College Dublin.

Kelly, D.L., 1981 'The native forest vegetation of Killarney, s.w. Ireland: An ecological account', *J.Ecol.* 69: 437-462.

Kelly, D.L., 1984 'A note on the vice-county boundary between south and north Kerry: Is Derrycunnihy in H1 or H2?', *Ir. Nat. J.* 21(8): 36.

Kelly, D.L., and Kirby, E.N., 1982 'Irish native woodlands over limestone', *J. Life Sc.* 3: 181-198.

Kelly, D.L., and Moore, J.J., 1974 'A preliminary sketch of the Irish acidophilous oak-woods', *Colloques Phytosociologiques* 3: 375-387.

Kelly, F., 1976, 'The old Irish tree-list', Celtica 11: 107-124.

Kent, D. H., and Allen, D. E., 1984, *British and Irish herbaria*, Botanical Society of the British Isles, London.

Lernihan, A.A., 1991, *The vegetation on a disused copper mine on Muckross peninsula, Killarney National Park, Co.Kerry.* B.Sc. (ed.) thesis (Unpublished) Thomond College of Education.

Lev, A., 1887, '*Thalictrum alpinum* in Kerry', *J. Bot.* 25: 374.

Linton, E.F., 1910, '*Saxifraga geum x serratifolia*', *J. Bot.* 48: 202.

Linton, E.F., 1866, '*Naias flexilis* Rostk. at Killarney', *J. Bot.* 24: 83-84.

Linton, E.F., 1894, '*Hieracium cerinthiforme* in Co. Kerry', Ir. Nat. 3: 136.

Linton, E.F., 1896, '*Alchemilla vulgaris* L. and its segregates'. *Ir. Nat.* 5: 296.

Linton, E.F., and Linton, W.R., 1886, 'Notes of a botanical tour in west Ireland', *J. Bot.* 24: 18-21.

Lovegrove, R.R. et al, 1965, 'Notes on a visit to the Great Skellig rock, Co. Kerry, *Ir. Nat. J.* 15: 47-49.

Lowe, J., 1897, *Yew trees of Great Britain and Ireland*, McMillan, New York. .

Bibliography

Lucas, A.T., 1960, *Furze - a survey of its uses and history in Ireland,* National Museum of Ireland.

Lüdi, W., 1952, 'Fragmente zu waldstudien in Irland *In* "Die Pflanzenwelt Irlands". Veröff. Geobot. Inst. Rübels, Zürich, 25H: 214-230.

Lyne, G.J., and Mitchell, M.E., 1985, 'A scientific tour through Munster: The travels of Joseph Woods, architect and botanist, in 1809', *North Munster Antiquarian J.* 37: 415-436.

MacKay, J.T., 1806, 'A systematic catalogue of rare plants found in Ireland' *Trans. R. Dubl. Soc.* 5: 121-184.

MacKay, J.T., 1836, *Flora Hibernica, comprising the flowering plants, ferns, characeae, musci, lepaticae, lichen and algae of Ireland, according to the natural system with a synopsis of the genera according to the Linnaean system.* Part 1-2, 8 vols., Dublin.

Marchant, C.J., 1967, 'Evolution in *Spartina* (Gramineae), 1, The history and morphology of the genus in Britain. *Bot. J. Linn.* Soc. 60 (381): 1-24.

Marshall, E.S., 1910, '*Epipactis atropurpurea* (as *Helleborine atroviridis)* in Ireland', *J. Bot.* 48: 109.

Marshall, E.S., 1912, 'South Kerry plants', *J. Bot.* 1: 197.

Marshall, E.S., 1917, 'South Kerry plants', *J. Bot.* 4: 56.

McCracken, E., 1971, *The Irish woods since Tudor times,* David and Charles, Newton Abbot.

McHenry, M.J., 1906, 'Notes on the *Arbutus* at Killarney', *J. R.S.A.I.* 36: 433-435.

McNally, A., and Doyle, G.J., 1981, 'Tree ring series – A valuable source of ecological and environmental information', *Ir. For.* 38 (1): 7-18.

McNally, A., and Doyle, G.J., 1985, 'Tree productivity models based on annual ring widths for contemporary and subfossil Scots pine in Ireland', *Ir. For.* 42: 33-43.

Matten, L.C., Lacey, W.S., and Edwards, D., 1975, 'Discovery of one of the oldest gymnosperm floras containing culpate seeds', *Phytologia* 32: 299-303.

Meinertzhagen, R., 1947, 'October in Co. Kerry - plants and birds', *Ir. Nat. J.* 4: 63.

MhicDaeid, C., 1976, *A phytosociological and ecological study of the vegetation of peatlands and heaths in the Killarney valley.* Ph.D. thesis (Unpublished) Trinity College Dublin.

Minchin, D., and Minchin C., 1996, 'The Sea-pea *Lathyrus japonicus* Willd. in Ireland, and an addition to the flora of west Cork (H3) and Wexford (H12)' *Ir.Nat. J.* 25 (5): 165-169.

Mitchell, F.J.G., 1987, *Recent woodland history in the Killarney valley, south west Ireland.* Ph.D. thesis (Unpublished) Trinity College Dublin.

Mitchell, F.J.G., 1988, 'The vegetational history of the Killarney oakwoods, sw Ireland: evidence from fine spatial resolution pollen analysis', *J. Ecol.* 76: 415-436.

Mitchell, F.J.G., 1990, 'The impact of grazing and human disturbance on the dynamics of woodland in s.w. Ireland', *J. Vegetation Sc.* 1: 245-254.

Mitchell, F.J.G., 1990, 'The history and vegetation dynamics of a yew wood *(Taxus baccata L.)* in s.w. Ireland', *New Phytol.* 115: 573-577.

Mitchell, F.J.G., and Bradshaw, R.H.W., 1984, 'The recent history of native woodland in s.w. Ireland', *Brit. Ecol. Soc. Bull.* 15 (1): 18-19.

Moore, D., 1864, 'On *Potamogeton nitens* Weber, as an Irish plant', *J. Bot.* 11: 325- 326.

Moore, D., and More, A.G., 1866, *Contributions towards a Cybele Hibernica, being outlines of the geographical distribution of plants in Ireland,* 8 Vol., Hodges, Smith and Co., Dublin.

Murphy, E., 1829, 'Contributions towards a Cybele Hibernica', *Mag. Nat. Hist.* 1: 436-438.

More, A.G., 1877, '*Naias flexilis* in Kerry', *J. Bot.* 15: 350.

More, A.G., 1882, '*Sisyrinchium bermudiana* in Kerry', *J. Bot.* 20: 8.

More, A.G., 1892a, '*Silene maritima* growing inland', *J. Bot.* 30: 87.

More A.G., 1892b, '*Cuscuta epithymum* in Ireland', *J. Bot.* 30: 14.

Nelson, E.C., and Brady, A., 1979, 'Ireland's flora: its origin and composition', In Nelson, E.C., *Irish gardening and horticulture*, RHSI, Dublin, pp. 17-35.

Nelson, E.C., 1979, 'Historical records of the *Irish Ericaceae,* with particular reference to the discovery and naming of *Erica mackiana*', *J. of Nat. Hist.* 9: 289-299.

Nelson, E.C., 1982, 'Historical records of the *Irish Ericaceae* - additional notes', *Ir.Nat. J.* 30: 364-369.

Nelson, E.C., 1986, 'Sea peas among tropical drift seeds', *B.S.B.I. News* No. 44: 16-17.

Neff, M.J., 1974, 'Woodland conservation in the Republic of Ireland', *Colloques Phytosociologiques,* 3: 273-285.

Newman, E., 1854, 'Contributions towards the history of an Irish *Asplenium* (A. *acutum,* Bory)', *Phytologist* 5: 36.

Oliver, D., 1853a, '*Carex punctata* in Ireland', *Phytologist* 4: 1095.

Oliver, D., 1853b, '*Agrimonia odorata* in Kerry', *Phytologist* 4: 1096.

O'Malley, J., 1996, 'New plant records for south Kerry (H1) and north Kerry (H2)', *Ir. Nat. J.* 26 (8): 298-299.

O'Sullivan, A., 1986, '*A fire history study in the Killarney National Park. B.A.* (Mod.) thesis', (Unpublished) Trinity College Dublin

O'Sullivan, A., 1991, '*Historical and contemporary effects of fire on the native woodland vegetation of Killarney, s.w. Ireland*'. Ph.D. thesis (Unpublished) Trinity College Dublin

O'Sullivan, A.M., 1967 '*Reconnaissance botanical survey of the Bourn Vincent Memorial Park, Killarney, Co. Kerry*', Irish Vegetation Studies, No. 1, An Foras Taluntais, Dublin.

Paul, D., 1902, 'Excursion of the Scottish Alpine Botanical Club to Co. Kerry', *Bot. Soc. Edinburgh* 22: 156.

Perring, F. H., and Walters, S. M., 1962, *Atlas of the British Flora,* London and Edinburgh.

Peterken, G.F., and Lloyd, P.S., 1967, 'Biological flora of the British Isles: *Ilex aquifolium* L.', *Journal of Ecology,* 55: 841-859.

Phillips, R.A., 1908, 'Some Irish brambles', *Ir. Nat.* 17: 54-56.

Pilcher, J.R., and Baille, M.G.L., 1980, 'Six modern oak chronologies from Ireland. *Tree-Ring Bull.* 40: 23-24.

Praeger, R. Ll., 1898, 'Botany; Part 3 of the report of the second triennial conference and excursion of the Irish Field Club Union, held at Kenmare, July 7-13th. 1898', *Ir. Nat.* 7: 227.

Praeger, R. Ll., 1901, *Irish topographical botany,* 8 Vols., Hodges Figgis and Co., Dublin.

Praeger, R. Ll., 1902a, 'Additions to Irish topographical botany', *Ir. Nat.* 11: 1-8.

Praeger, R. Ll., 1902b, 'Gleanings in Irish topographical botany', *Proc. R. Ir. Acad.* 24B: 61-94.

Praeger, R. Ll., 1902c, 'On the types of distribution in the Irish flora', *Proc. R. Ir. Acad.* 8B: 1-60.

Praeger, R. Ll., 1903, 'Additions to Irish topographical botany', *Ir. Nat.* 12: 23-40.

Praeger, R. Ll., 1904, 'Additions to Irish topographical botany', *Ir. Nat.* 13: 1-5.

Praeger, R. Ll., 1905, 'Additions to Irish topographical botany', *Ir. Nat.* 14: 21-29.

Praeger, R. Ll., 1906a, 'Additions to Irish topographical botany', *Ir. Nat.* 15: 47-61.

Praeger, R. Ll., 1906b, 'A colour variety of *Pinguicula grandiflora*', *Ir. Nat.* 15: 154.

Praeger, R. Ll., 1908, 'Additions to Irish topographical botany', *Ir. Nat.* 17: 28-37.

Praeger, R.Ll., 1912a, 'Notes on the flora of the Blaskets', *Ir. Nat.* 21: 157-163.

Praeger, R.Ll., 1912b, 'A note on the Robertsonian saxifrages', *Ir. Nat.* 21: 205-206.

Praeger, R. Ll., 1913, 'Additions to Irish topographical botany', *Ir. Nat.* 22: 103-110.

Praeger, R. Ll., 1929, 'Report on recent additions to the Irish fauna and flora (terrestrial and freshwater', *Ir. Nat.* 22: 103-110.

Praeger, R. Ll., 1930, 'Notes on Kerry plants', *J. Bot.* 68: 249-250.

Praeger, R. Ll., 1934, *The botanist in Ireland,* Hodges Figgis, Dublin (Reprinted by E P Publishing, Yorkshire, 1974).

Praeger, R. Ll., 1938, *'Spiranthes gemmipara* in Co. Kerry', *Ir. Nat. J.* 7: 11.

Quirke, W., 1991, *The rhododendron clearance programme in the western woods of Killarney National Park, 1981-1991,* A ten year progress report. unpublished report to the Office of Public Works.

Randall, R.C., 1977, 'The past and present status and distribution of sea-pea *Lathyrus japonicus* Willd. in the British Isles' *Watsonia* 11: 247-251.

Rasor, J., 1882, *'Arbutus unedo',* *Sci. Gossip* 18: 18.

Redfern. N., and Askue, O.R., 1992, *Plant galls,* Naturalists handbooks No. 17. Rich Publishing, Slough.

Reynolds, S.C.P., 1993, 'Records of alien and adventive plants in Ireland', *Ir. Nat. J.* 24: 339-342.

Reynolds, S.C.P., 1996, 'Records of casual and alien plants in Ireland', *Ir. Nat. J.* 25: (5): 186-189.

Rich, T.C.G., Kay, G.M., and Kirschner, J., 1995, 'Floating water plantain *Luronium natans* (L.) Raf. (Alismataceae) present in Ireland', *Ir. Nat. J.* 25 (4): 140-145.

Ridley, H.N., 1884, 'Kerry plants', *J. Bot.* 22: 91-92.

Rowan, A.B., 1855, 'A natural history query', *Kerry Mag.* 2: 129-130.

Räbel, E.A., 1912, 'The Killarney oakwoods', *New Phytologist* 11: 54-57.

Russell, P.J., Flowers, T.J., and Hutchings, M.J., 1985, 'Comparison of niche breadths and overlaps of halophytes on salt marshes of differing diversity', *Vegetatio* 61: 171-178.

Ryall, Thomas, 1989, 'The Pitcher-Plant *Sarracenia purpurea* L. in Co. Kerry (H2)', *Ir. Nat. J.* 23 (4): 160.

Scannell, M.J.P., and Synott, D.M., 1987, '*Census catalogue of the flora of Ireland*. 2nd. ed., Government Stationary Office, Dublin

Scannell, M.J.P., 1995, '*Equisetum x dycei* C.N. Page in Ireland', *Ir. Nat. J.* 25 (4): 154.

Scholten, M., and Rozema, J., 1990, 'The competitive ability of Spartina anglica on Dutch salt marshes' In A.J. Gray and P.E.M. Benham (eds) Spartina anglica - a *research review,* Institute of Terr. Ecology Research Publication No. 2, HMSO, London. 39-47.

Scully, R.W., 1888, 'Notes on some Kerry plants', *J. Bot.* 26: 71-78.

Scully, R.W., 1889a, 'Further notes on Kerry flora', *J. Bot.* 27: 85-92.

Scully, R.W., 1889b, '*Juncus tenuis* in Kerry', *J. Bot.* 27: 335-336.

Scully, R.W., 1890, 'Plants found in Kerry, *J. Bot.* 28: 110-116.

Scully, R.W., 1891a, 'Plants found in Kerry, *J. Bot.* 29: 143-148.

Scully, R.W., 1891b, 'Ancient and unverified Kerry records', *J. Bot.* 24: 324-329.

Scully, R.W., 1902, 'Notes on the Kerry flora', *Ir. Nat.* 11: 156-159.

Scully, R.W., 1903, 'Notes on the Kerry flora', *Ir. Nat.* 12: 113-116.

Scully, R.W., 1904, 'Notes on the Kerry flora', *Ir. Nat.* 13: 77-80.

Scully, R.W., 1908, 'Notes on the Kerry flora', *Ir. Nat.* 17: 50-54.

Scully, R.W., 1912a, '*Arbutus unedo*', *Ir. Nat.* 21: 64.

Scully, R.W., 1912b, 'Some introduced plants in Kerry', *Ir. Nat.* 21: 214-217.

Scully, R.W., 1914, '*Rumex maritimus* in north Kerry', *Ir. Nat.* 23: 125.

Scully, R.W., 1915, '*Ranunculus auricomus* in north Kerry', *Ir. Nat.* 24: 106.

Scully, R. W., 1916, *Flora of County Kerry,* Dublin.

Scully, R.W., 1918, 'Reappearance of *Lathyrus maritimus* in Kerry', *Ir. Nat.* 27: 113- 115.

Scully, R.W., 1921, '*Spiranthes gemmipara* (as *romanzoffiana*) in Co. Kerry', *Ir. Nat.* 30:79.

Scully, R.W., 1933, 'Does *Juncus trifidus* occur in Ireland?', *J. Bot.*71: 104.

Scully, R.W., 1934, '*Utricularia ochroleuca* Hartm. In Kerry', *J. Bot.* 72: 209-210.

Sealy, J.R., 1949, '*Arbutus unedo*', *J.Ecol.* 37: 369-388.

Sealy, J.R., 1949, 'The swollen stem base in *Arbutus unedo*', Kew Bull. 241-251.

Sealy, J.R., and Webb, D.A., 1950, 'Biological flora of the British. Isles, *Arbutus unedo* L.', *J. Ecol.* 38: 223-236.

Simpson, D.A., 1986, 'Taxonomy of *Elodea Michx* in the British Isles', *Watsonia* 16: 1-40.

Slatter, T.J., 1890, '*Sisyrinchium bermudiana*', *Sci. Gossip* 26: 235.

Stace, C., 1991, *New flora of the British Isles,* Cambridge University Press.

Stelfox, A.W., 1935, '*Alnus incana* Willd. in south Kerry', *Ir. Nat. J.* 5: 308.

Stelfox, A.W., 1936a, 'A further note on *Alnus incana* ', *Ir. Nat. J.* 6: 150.

Stelfox, A.W., 1936b, '*Rosa stylosa* in south Kerry ', *Ir. Nat. J.* 6: 72-73.

Stelfox, A.W., 1947, 'Extension of known range of *Sibthorpia europaea* in Kerry ', *Ir. Nat. J.* 9: 101.

Stelfox, A.W., 1947, 'The willowherb *Epilobium* on Brandon mountain in south Kerry', *Ir. Nat. J.* 9: 101.

Stelfox, A.W., 1948, 'Hart's station for *Polygonum viviparum* in Kerry and its flora ', *Ir. Nat. J.* 9: 121-123.

Stelfox, A.W., 1950a, 'Goldilocks (*Ranunculus auricomus*) in Co. Kerry ', *Ir. Nat. J.* 10: 80-81.

Stelfox, A.W., 1950b, '*Carex acutiformis:* an addition to the flora of Kerry ', *Ir. Nat. J.* 10: 84.

Stewart, S.A. 1879, 'A trip from Galway to Dingle', *Belfast Naturalists' Field Club* 2: 352-353.

Stewart, S.A. 1890, 'Report on the botany of south Clare and the Shannon', *Proc. R. Ir. Acad.* 31: 343-369.

Synnott, D., 1972, 'The Oxford ragwort (*Senecio squalidus* L.) in County Kerry', *Ir. Nat. J.* 17: 281.

Tansley, A.G. , 1911, Types of British vegetation, Cambridge.

Tansley, A.G., 1949, The British islands and their vegetation, Cambridge.

Taylor, J.A., 1983, 'Peatlands of the British Isles', In Gore, A.J.P., *Ecosystems of the World*, 4B, Elsevier Scient. Publishing. pp. 1-46.

Thompson, H.S. and Elliot, A., 1910, 'Notes on south Kerry plants', *J. Bot.* 48: 227-228.

Threlkfeld, C., 1726, *Synopsis stirpium Hibernicarum, etc.* Dublin.

Turner, J.S., and Watts, A.S., 1939, 'The oakwoods (Quercetum sessiliflora) of Killarney, Ireland', *J. Ecol.* 27: 202-233.

Ui Chonchubhair, M., and O'Conchuir, A., 1994, *Flora Chorca Dhuibhne*. Oidhreacht Chorca Dhuibhne.

Van Doorslaer, L., 1986, *The effects of the 1984 fire on the vegetation of Killarney* National Park, B.A. (Mod.) thesis (Unpublished) Trinity College Dublin

Vokes, E., 1966, *Late-glacial and post-glacial vegetation of Killarney*, Co. Kerry. M.Sc. thesis (Unpublished) Trinity College Dublin

Vokes, E., 1967, 'The late and post-glacial vegetation development on sandstone and limestone at Killarney, County Kerry', *J. Ecol.* 55: 57-58.

Walsh, W.F., Ross, R.I., and Nelson, E.C., 1983, *An Irish floregium*, London.

Watt, A.S., 1955, 'Bracken versus heather, a study in plant sociology', *J. Ecol.* 43:490-506.

Watts, W. A., 1970, 'Tertiary and interglacial flora in Ireland', *In* Nicholas Stephens and Robin Edgar Glasscock (eds), *Irish Geographical Studies in honour of E. Estyn Evans*: 17-33, Belfast.

Watts, W.A., 1984, 'Contemporary accounts of the Killarney woods 1580-1870', *Ir. Geography*, 17: 1-13.

Webb, D.A. 1948, 'Miscellaneous plant notes', *Ir. Nat. J.* 9: 213.

Webb, D.A., 1952, 'Narrative of the ninth I.P.E.' In *Die Pflanzenwelt Irlands'*, Veröff. Geobot. Inst. Rübels, Zürich, 25H: 9-31.

Webb, D.A., 1952, 'The flora and vegetation of Ireland', In *Die Pflanzenwelt Irlands'*. Veröff. Geobot. Inst. Rübels, Zürich, 25H: 46-84.

Webb, D.A., 1959, '*Hydrocotyle moschata* Forst. f. In south Kerry', Proc. *Bot. Soc.* Brit. Isles 3: 288.

Webb, D.A., 1961, 'Some observations on *Arbutus* in Ireland', *Ir. Nat. J.* 9: 198-203.

Webb, D. A., 1993, 'The Irish and British plants in the herbarium of Trinity College Dublin, II. The non-vascular plants', *Ir. Nat. J.* 24: 69-72.

Webb, D. A., and Ackeroyd, J.R., 1991, 'Inconstancy of sea-shore plants' *Ir. Nat. J.* 23: 384-385.

Webster, M.M., 1952, 'Meeting of the Botanical Society of the British Isles in Co. Kerry, June 1952', *Ir. Nat. J.* 11: 18-21

West, W., 1911, 'Mural ecology', *J. Bot.* 49: 59-61.

Westrup, A.W., 1959, 'Reprint of a meeting at Killarney', *Proc. Bot. Soc. Brit. Isles* 3: 247.

Woods, J. 1855, 'Some botanical notes made during a tour through a part of Ireland in June and July 1855, with occasional remarks on scenery etc., in a letter to the editor', *Phytologist, New Series* 1: 121-127, 156-159, 207-210.

Woodward, S.P., 1844, 'Notes of a botanical excursion in Warwickshire, Worcestershire, Wales and Ireland: a paper read before the Botanical Society of London, Nov. 1843', *Phytologist* 1: 875-879.

Wright, E.P., 1905, '*Euphrasia occidentalis* in Ireland', *Notes Bot. Sch. Trinity College Dublin* 1: 237.

Wyse Jackson, M.B., 1995, Annotated records for rare, critical or under-recorded vascular plant taxa from Ireland', *Ir. Nat. J. 25(2): 44-57.*

FERNS AND THEIR ALLIES

Andrews, W., 1856a, 'On Madeiran forms of ferns at Killarney', *Nat. Hist. Rev.* 3: 53.

Andrews, W., 1856b, '*Trichomanes speciosum* from Kerry; Iveragh and Killarney', *Proc. Dubl. Nat. Hist. Soc.* 1: 43.

Derrick, J., N., Jermey, A.C. and Paul A.C., 1987, 'Checklist of European Pteridophytes', *Summerfeldtia* 6: 1-94

Douery, C.T., 1901, '*Osmunda regalis'*, Gardeners Chronicle Series 3, 30: 156.

Harvey, W.H., 1853, '*Trichomanes speciosum* at Valentia', Phytologist 4: 1007.

Jermey, A.C., Arnold, H.R., Farrell, C., and Perring, F.H., 1978, *Atlas of ferns of the British Isles, Botanical Society of the British Isles and British Pteridological* Society, London.

Kinahan, G.H., 1863, '*Trichomanes* from Iveragh', *Proc. Dubl. Nat. Hist. Soc.* 4: 78.

Kinahan, G.H., 1865, '*Trichomanes radicans* near Waterville', Proc. Dubl. *Nat. Hist. Soc.* 77-78.

Newman, E., 1856, 'Notes on *Equisetum limosum* of Linnaeus', *Phytologist* 2 25.

Moore, D., 1845, 'Memorandum on *Equisetum variegatum, E. wilsoni* and other plants observed in Ireland', *Phytologist* 2: 129-130.

Moore, D., 1846, 'Remarks on *Equisetum variegatum, E. wilsoni* and other plants observed in Ireland', *Phytologist* 3: 576-578.

More, H.K., 1914, 'My native ferns', *Brit. Fern Gazett.* 2: 179.

Rasor, J., 1882, 'Notes on the ferns of Killarney', *Sci. Gossip* 18: 162.

Scannell, M.J.P., 1982, 'Southern elements in the cryptogamic flora of Ireland', *J. Life Sci. R. Dubl. Soc.* 3: 267-276.

Scully, R.W., 1893, '*Asplenium obovatum lanceolatum* in Kerry', *J. Bot.* 31: 20-21.

Stelfox, A.W., 1951, 'The beech fern and the wall rue at about 2,000' on Brandon mountain in south Kerry; and the old record for *Thalictrum alpinum*', *Ir. Nat. J.* 10: 138-139.

Synnott, D.M., 1980, *Irish Ferns,* Folens, Dublin.

Willmot, A., 1983, 'An ecological survey of the ferns of the Killarney district Co. Kerry', *Fern Gaz.* 12: 249-265.

MOSSES AND LIVERWORTS

Conrad, M.S., 1937, 'British Bryologists at Killarney', *Bryologist* 40.

Crundwell, A.C., 1951, 'Some bryophytes from the Dingle peninsula', *Ir. Nat. J.* 10: 309-311.

Jones, D.A. 1913, 'Mosses and hepatics of Killarney', *J. Bot.* 51: 188-182.

Long, D.G., 1984, 'The moss *Fissidens rivularis* (Spruce) B.S.G. in Kerry, new to Ireland', *Ir. Nat. J.* 21(8): 347-348.

McArdle, D., 1900, 'The Hepaticae of Ross island, Killarney', *Ir. Nat.* 9: 23-26.

McArdle, D., and Lett, H.W., 1899, 'Hepaticae collected at Torc waterfall', *Proc. R. Ir. Acad.* 3: 52.

Mitchell, F.J.G., and Averis, A.B.G., 1988, *Atlantic bryophytes in three Killarney* woods. Unpublished report of Praeger fund bursary.

More, A.G. 1876, '*Lycopodium inundatum* in Kerry', *J. Bot.* 14: 373.

Paton, J.A. 1976, 'Distribution maps of bryophytes in Britain and Ireland', *J. Bryol.* 9: 109.

Paton, J.A. 1987, 'Bulbils in *Telaranea nematodes* (Gott. ex Aust.) Howe in Ireland', *J. Bryol.* 14: 792-793.

Ratcliffe, E.A., 1968, 'An ecological account of Atlantic bryophytes in the British Isles', *New Phytologist,* 67: 365-439.

Richards, P.W., 1938, 'The bryophyte communities of a Killarney oakwood' *Annls. Bryol.* 11: 108-130.

Synnott, D., 1976, *'Plagiochila atlantica* F. Rose (*P. Ambagiosa* Auct.)', *Ir. Nat. J.* 18: 347.

Wallace, E.C., 1952, 'The British Bryological Society's field meeting in Co. Kerry 1951', *Ir. Nat. J.* 10: 259-263.

Watson, W., 1937, 'British Bryological Society at Killarney, 1935; list of records', *Ir. Nat. J.* 6: 161-165.

LICHENS

Bailey, R.H., 1973, 'Some Irish lichen records', *Ir. Nat. J.* 17: 392.

Bailey, R.H., 1975, 'Lichens from the Skellig rocks', *Ir. Nat. J.* 18: 163.

Leighton, W., 1879, *'Lichen flora of Great Britain, Ireland and the Channel Islands'*, 3rd. Ed., Privately Published, Shrewsbury.

Mitchell, M.E., 1964, 'Lichens occurring on *Arbutus* at Killarney', *Ir. Nat. J.* 14 (11): 277-278.

Mitchell, M.E., 1993, 'First records of Irish lichens', *Officiana Typographica.*

Mitchell, M.E., and Henssen, A., 1966, 'New and noteworthy lichens from Ireland', *Ir. Nat. J.* 15 (5): 143-145.

FUNGI

Adams, J., and Pethybridge, G.H., 1910, 'A census catalogue of Irish fungi', *Proc. R. Ir. Acad.* 28B: (4): 120-166.

Bullock, D.J., 1975, 'Fungi collected on the Blaskets, Co. Kerry', *Ir. Nat. J.* 18: 150.

Doppelbaur, H., 1975, 'Some rust fungi from Ireland', *Ir. Nat. J.* 18: 198.

Frazer, W., 1856, 'Remarks on specimens of fungi obtained adhering to old trees under a bog near Tralee', *Proc. Dubl. Nat. Hist. Soc.* 1: 34-35.

Ing, B., and McHugh, R., 1988, 'A review of the Irish Myxomycetes', *Proc. R. Ir. Acad.* 88B: 7-117.

Ing, B., and Mitchell, D., 1980, 'Irish Myxomycetes', *Proc. R. Ir. Acad.* 80B: 277-304.

Mangan, A., 1974, 'Botanical note: Truffles', *Ir. Nat. J.* 18: 126.

Muskett, A.E., and Malone, J.P., 1980, 'Catalogue of Irish fungi - II - Hymenomycetes', *Proc. R. Ir. Acad.* 80B: 197-276.

Muskett, A.E., and Malone, J.P., 1980, 'Catalogue of Irish fungi – III – Teliomycetes', *Proc. R. Ir. Acad.* 80B: 343.

Pearson, A.A., *et al* 1948, 'Fungal flora of Kerry', *Ir. Nat.* 9: 181-185.

Pim, G., 1885, 'Preliminary report of the fungi of Glengariff and Killarney', *Proc. R. Ir. Acad.* 14: 475-485.

ALGAE

Batters, E. A. L., 1902, 'A catalogue of the British marine algae', *J. Bot. Lond.* 40 (suppl) (2): 1-107.

Brennan, A. T., 1945, 'Notes on the distribution of certain marine algae on the west coast of Ireland', *Ir. Nat. J.* 8 (7): 252-254.

Brennan, A. T.,1950, 'Notes on some common Irish seaweeds', Dublin

Burrows, E. M., and Dixon, P. S., 1959, 'List of marine algae from the west of Ireland collected by members of the Third International Seaweed Symposium', *Br. Phycol. Bull.* 1 (7): 47-60.

Cooke, P.J., 1975, *'Halopitys incurvus* Batt. An addition to the algae of the west coast of Ireland', *Ir. Nat. J.* 18: 200.

Cullinane, J. P., 1973, *'Phycology of the south coast of Ireland'*, Cork Univ. Press. UCC.

Cullinane, J. P., 1971a, *'Seaweeds collected from the Dun Chaoin district. September 1970'*, Unpublished.

Cullinane, J. P., 1971b, *'List of seaweed specimens from the Kerry coast in the DBN'*, Unpublished.

Cullinane, J. P. 1971c, *'Seaweeds collected from Kenmare – Parknasilla district in December 1970'*, Unpublished.

De Valéra, M., 1958, *'A topographical guide to the seaweeds of Galway Bay with some brief notes on other districts on the west coast of Ireland'*, Institute for Industrial Research and Standards, Dublin.

Groves, H., and Groves, J., 1880, 'A review of the British Characeae', *J. Bot.* 18: 97-103.

Groves, H., and Groves, J., 1893, 'Notes on Irish Characeae', *Ir. Nat.* 1: 163-164.

Groves, H., and Groves, J., 1895a, 'The distribution of the Characeae in Ireland', *Ir. Nat.* 4: 7-11.

Groves, H., and Groves, J., 1895b, 'Notes on the British Characeae', *J. Bot.* 33: 289-292.

Irvine, L.M., Irvine, D.E.G., and Guiry, M.D., 1978, 'Notes on Irish marine algae 2, *Platoma marginifera* (J. Agardh) Batters (Rhodophyta)', *Ir. Nat. J.* 19 (6): 188.

Lund, S., 1949, 'Remarks on some Norwegian marine algae', *Saertrykk au Blyttia.* Bind. 7. Oslo.

Moore, K.A., 1979, 'Current status of Characeae (stoneworts) in the British Isles', *Watsonia* 12: 297-309.

Moore, K.A., 1986, *Charophytes of Great Britain and Ireland,* Botanical Society of the British Isles.

Murphy, J.P., 1981, 'Marine algae on peat' *Ir. Nat. J.* 20 (6): 254.

Parks H.M., 1946, *Marine algae collected at Waterville,* Co. Kerry. September 1946. Unpubished report.

Parks H.M., 1950, 'Records of Irish marine algae', *Ir. Nat. J.* 10: 58.

Parks, H.M., 1975, 'Records of *Codium* species in Ireland', *Proc. R. Ir. Acad.* 75 B: 125-133.

Powell, H.T,. 1954, 'The distribution, ecology and taxonomic status of forms of *Fucus inflatus* L. In Britain and Ireland', *Rapp. Commun. Vlll. Int. Bot. Congr.* 17: 135-136.

Powell, H.T., 1963, 'Speciation in the genus *Fucus L.,* and related genera', *In* Harding, J.P., and Tebble, N., *Speciation in the sea, A symposium,* Systematics Association, Publication No. 5, London.

Sanders, G., 1860, 'On the advantages to botany of local lists, and notes with reference to the algae of the east coast of Ireland', *Proc. nat. Hist. Soc. Dublin* 1: 36-39.

Scully, R.W., 1895, '*Chara canescens* Loisel. in Ireland', *Ir. Nat.* 4: 50.

Stewart, N.F., and Church, J.M., 1992, *Red data books of Britain and Ireland: Stoneworts,* Joint Nature Conservation Committee, Peterborough.

Weiss, F.E., 1900, 'Report on the algae', In: Browne, E.T. 'The fauna and flora of Valentia harbour on the west coast of Ireland', *Proc. R. Ir. Acad.* 3 (5): 667-854.

FAUNA
GENERAL

Austin, A., 1900, *Spring and autumn in Ireland,* Edinburgh and London.

Bolger, T., and Quirke, C., 1987, *Responses of surface dwelling arthropods and small mammals to infestation of the Killarney oakwoods by Rhododendron ponticum L.* Unpublished report, University College, Dublin

Bouskell, F,. 1905, 'Stray notes from south Kerry in 1903', *Trans. Leics. phil. Soc. 9* (1): 39-47.

D'Arcy, G., 1988, *Pocket guide to the animals of Ireland,* Appletree Press, Belfast.

Delap, M., and Delap, C., 1903, 'Notes on the plankton of Valentia harbour 1899-1901', *Fisheries, Ireland. Sci. Invest.* 5: 3-19.

Delap, M., and Delap, C., 1905, 'Notes on the plankton of Valentia harbour 1902-1905', *Fisheries, Ireland. Sci. Invest.* 7: 3-21.

Delap, M. J., 1924, 'Further notes on the plankton of Valentia harbour 1902-1923', *Ir. Nat.* 33: 1-6.

Forde, G., 1980, *A study of the Benthic and Periphytic fauna of Ross Bay, Lough Leane, Killarney,* B.Sc. thesis (Unpublished) University College, Dublin

Gore Cuthbert, H.K., 1898, 'An entomologist at Ballybunion, Co. Kerry', *Ir. Nat.* 7 (3): 65-68.

Huggins, H.C., 1960, 'A naturalist in the kingdom of Kerry', *Proc. S. Lond. Ent. Nat. Hist. Soc.* 1959: 176-183.

Jenkins, M., 1979, *The littoral fauna of Victoria and Ross Bays, Lough Leane, Killarney,* B.Sc. thesis (Unpublished) University College, Dublin

Muhlemann, M.F., and Wright, D.J.M., 1987, 'Emerging pattern of Lyme disease in the United Kingdom and Irish Republic', *Lancet* 260-262.

Nicholls, A.R., 1886, *In* Hadden, A.C. 'First report of the marine fauna of the south-west of Ireland', *Proc. R. Irish. Acad. Second series* 4: 599-638.

Ní Lamhna, E., 1979, *Provisional distribution atlas of amphibians, reptiles, and mammals in Ireland,* An Foras Forbatha. Dublin.

O'Riordan, C.E., 1968, 'Some interesting fauna from the Dingle area', *Ir. Nat. J.* 16: 9-12.

O'Riordan, C.E., 1971, 'Further interesting fauna from the Dingle area', *Ir. Nat. J.* 17: 12-14.

O'Riordan, C. E., 1972, 'Some noteworthy crustacea and mollusca from the Dingle bay area', *Ir. Nat. J.* 17: 252.

O'Riordan, C. E., 1973, 'Notes on marine fauna recently acquired by the National Museum of Ireland', *Ir. Nat. J.* 17: 399.

O'Riordan, C. E., 1974, 'Marine fauna notes from the National Museum of Ireland. *Ir. Nat. J.* 18: 27.

O'Riordan, C. E., 1975, 'Rare and interesting marine fauna from the Dingle bay area, Co. Kerry', *Ir. Nat. J.* 18: 129-132.

O'Riordan, C. E., 1976, 'Marine fauna notes from the National Museum of Ireland – II', *Ir. Nat. J.* 18: 337.

O'Riordan, C. E., 1977, 'Marine fauna notes from the National Museum of Ireland – IV', *Ir. Nat. J.* 19(1): 6.

O'Riordan, C.E., 1981, 'Marine fauna notes from the National Museum of Ireland – VII', *Ir. Nat. J.* 20 (8): 338-340.

O'Riordan, C.E., 1986, 'Marine fauna notes from the National Museum of Ireland – 10', *Ir. Nat. J.* 22: 34-37.

O'Riordan, C.E., and Holmes, J. M. C., 1978, 'Marine fauna notes from the National Museum of Ireland, V, – Passengers on the North Atlantic currents', *Ir. Nat. J.* 19(5): 152.

O'Rourke, F.J., 1970, *The fauna of Ireland*, Mercier Press, Cork.

Scharff, R.F., 1899, 'Some animals from the MacGillycuddy's Reeks', *Ir. Nat.* 8: 213-218.

Scharff, R.F., and Carpenter, G.H., 1899, 'Some animals from the MacGillycuddy's Reeks', *Ir. Nat.* 7: 213-218.

Southward, A.J., and Crisp, D.J., 1954, 'The distribution of certain intertidal animals around the Irish coast', *Proc. R. Ir. Acad.* 57B (1): 1-29.

Thompson, W., 1856, *The natural history of Ireland,* Reeve, Benham and Reeve.

Wallis Kew, H., 1910, 'A holiday in south-western Ireland: notes on some false-scorpions and other animals observed in the counties of Kerry and Cork', *Irish. Nat.*19: 64-73.

Wilson, J.P.F., 1983, 'The post-glacial colonisation of Ireland by fish, amphibia and reptiles', *Occ. Pub. Ir. Biogeog. Soc.* 1: 53-58.

MAMMALS

Avery, M.I., 1985, 'Winter activity of pipistrelle bats', *J. Anim. Ecol.* 54: 721-738.

Berrow, S., 1993, 'Constant effort cetacean sighting survey of Ireland', *Ir. Nat. J.* 24: 344.

Berrow, S., Evans, P.G.H., and Sheldrick, M.L., 1993, 'An analysis of sperm whale *Physeter macrocephalus* stranding and sighting records, from Britain and Ireland', *J. Zool. Lond.* 230: 333-357.

Berrow, S. D., Holmes, B., and Kiely, O., (In prep), 'Distribution and abundance of bottle-nosed dolphins *Tursiops truncatus* (Montagu) in the Shannon estuary, Ireland'.

Brindley, J.B., 1980, *Ecology and population dynamics of the lowland red deer herd in Killarney, Co. Kerry, Ireland.* M.Sc. thesis (Unpublished) University College, Dublin

Brindley, J.B., 1982, 'The dispersion of the lowland red deer herd in the Killarney valley, Co. Kerry and factors contributing to it', *Trans. Intern. Congr. Game Biol.* 14: 573-581.

Bruton, T.E., and Berrow, S., 1993, 'Records from the Irish Whale and Dolphin Group', *Ir. Nat. J.* 24: 336-337.

Burkitt, T.D., 1994, *A comparison of two census techniques and patterns of habitat use in a population of japanese sika deer over a twelve month period,* Unpublished Diploma thesis, University College Cork.

Byrne, J.M., Duke, E.J., and Fairley, J.S., 1990, 'Some mitochondrial DNA polymorphisms in Irish wood mice and bank voles', *J. Zool. Lond.* 221: 293-302.

Carruthers, T., O'Leary, P., and O'Connor, J.B., 1984, 'Sika deer hummel', *Deer 6:* 144.

Chapman, P.J., and Chapman, L.L., 1982, *Otter survey of Ireland. 1980-1981,* Vincent Wildlife Trust, London.

Cork, D., Cowlin, R.A.D. and Page, W.W. 1969, 'Notes on the distribution and abundance of small mammals in south-west Ireland', *J. Zool. Lond.* 158 (6): 216-221

Dansie, O., 1979, 'Live-catching sika deer at Killarney, south-west Ireland', *Deer 4:* 527.

Dennehy, N., 1995, *An assessment of the intestinal helminths in two wild populations of native red deer (Cervus elaphus) and introduced sika deer (Cervus nippon) by faecal analysis,* Mod. Thesis (Unpublished) Trinity College Dublin.

Dobberkau, K., and Dobberkau, K., 1987, 'Sperm whale *Physeter catadon*', *Ir. Nat. J.* 22 (8): 359.

El-Gadi and Hayden, T.J., 1988, *'Observations on the renal structure of the sika deer Cervus nippon'*, Ungulate Res. Group Conf. (Unpublished).

Evans, P.G.H., 1987, The natural history of whales and dolphins, Christopher Helm. London.

Evans, P.G.H., 1980, 'Cetaceans in British waters', *Mammal Review* 10 (1): 1-52.

Evans, P.G.H., 1990, 'European cetaceans and seabirds in an oceanographic context', *Lutra* 33 (1): 1-31.

Fairley, J.S., 1965, 'Fieldmice at high altitude in Co. Kerry, Ireland', *Proc. Zool. Soc. Lond.* 145: 144-145.

Fairley, J.S., 1970, 'Epifauna from Irish bank voles *Clethrionomys glareolus* Schreber', *Ir. Nat. J.* 16:342-346.

Fairley, J.S., 1971a, 'The present distribution of the bank vole *Clethrionomys glareolus* Schreber in Ireland', Proc. R. Ir. Acad. 71B: 183-189.

Fairley, J.S., 1971b, 'A collection of Irish bank vole skulls', *Scient. Proc. R. Dubl. Soc.* 4A: 37-44.

Fairley, J.S., 1975, *An Irish beast book,* Blackstaff, Belfast.

Fairley, J.S., 1981a, *Irish whales and whaling,* Blackstaff, Belfast.

Fairley, J.S., 1981b, 'A north-south cline in the size of the Irish stoat', *Proc. R. Ir. Acad.* 81B: 5-10.

Fairley, J.S., and McCarthy, T.K., 1985, 'Do otters prey on breeding natterjack toads?' *Ir. Nat. J.* 21 (12): 544-545.

Fairley, J.S., McCarthy, T.K., and Andrews, J.F., 1978, 'Notes on the fieldmice of Iniskea North and a large race of fieldmouse from Great Blasket island', *Ir. Nat. J.* 19: 270-271.

Fairley, J.S., and Murdoch, B., 1989, 'Summer food of otters in the lakes of Killarney', *Ir. Nat. J.* 23 (2): 36-41.

Fairley, J.S., and Smal, C.M.,, 1987, 'Feral house mice in Ireland', *Ir.Nat. J.* 22 (7): 284-290.

Forcada, J., Aguilar, A., Evans, P.G.H., and Perrin, W.F., 1990, *Distribution of common and striped dolphins in the temperate waters of the eastern north Atlantic,* European Research on Cetaceans 4. Cambridge, England.

Goggin, B., and Gresson, R.A.R., 1976, 'Carcase of sperm whale, *Physeter catodon* L. at Feohanagh, Co. Kerry', *Ir. Nat. J.* 18: 275.

Gormally, M.J., and Fairley, J.S., 1982, 'Food of otters *Lutra lutra* in a freshwater lough and an adjacent brackish lough in the west of Ireland', *J. Zool. Lond.* 186: 463-474.

Gradl-Grams, M., 1982, 'Social structure and play behaviour of sika deer', *Zool. Anz. Jena* 209 3/4: 247-268, (In German - English Abstract).

Gradl-Grams, M., 1982, 'Intraspecific aggression and rutting behaviour of sika deer', *Zool. Anz. Jena* 209 5/6: 315-332, (In German - English Abstract).

Gradl-Grams, M., 1983, 'Acoustic signals and bodily contacts of sika deer', *Zool. Anz. Jena* 210 1/2: 101-108, (In German – English Abstract).

Gresson, R.A.R., 1968, 'White-sided dolphins *Lagenorphynchus acutus* (Gray) stranded at Ventry harbour, Co. Kerry', *Ir. Nat. J.* 16: 19-20.

Harrington, R., 1973, 'Hybridisation among deer and its implications for conservation', *Ir. For.* 30: 64-78.

Harrington, R., 1982, 'The hybridisation of red deer (*Cervus elaphus* L. 1758) and Japanese sika deer (*C. nippon* Temminck 1838)', *Trans. intern. Congr. game* Biol. 14: 559-571.

Harrington, R., 1985, 'Evolution and distribution of the cervidae', *Bull. R.S.N.Z.* 22: 3-11.

Hayden, T.J., Lynch J.M., and O'Corry-Crowe, G., 1994, 'Antler growth and morphology in a feral sika deer *Cervus nippon*) population in Killarney, Ireland', *J. Zool.* 232: 21-35.

Kelly, P.A., Mahon, G.A.T., and Fairley, J.S., 1982, 'An analysis of morphological variation in the fieldmouse *Apodemus sylvaticus* (L.) on some Irish islands' *Proc. R. Ir. Acad.* 82B: 39-51.

Kelsall, J.E., 1887, 'The distribution in Great Britain of the lesser horse-shoe bat', *Zoologist* 3 (11): 89-93.

Larner, J.B., 1972, *An Irish herd of sika deer,* M.Sc. thesis (Unpublished) University College, Dublin

Larner, J.B., 1977, 'Sika deer damage to mature woodlands of southwestern Ireland', *Proc.13th. Int. Cong. Game Biol.*192-202.

Larner, J.B., 1980, *The impact of a herd of sika deer on their woodland habitat,* Ph.D. thesis (Unpublished) University College, Dublin

Larner, J.B., 1982, 'The feeding range size of Sika deer in southwest Ireland', *Trans. intern. Congr. game Biol.* 14: 545-552.

Leirs, H., Antonissen, A., Bohets, H., Vrancken, A., and Vrinssen, A. 1987, Additional data on the distribution of the bank vole *Chletrionomus glareoleous* (Schreber, 1780) on the Beara Peninsula, Counties Cork and Kerry', *Ir. Nat. J.* 22: 321-322.

Linnell, J., 1989, *The biochemical systematics of red and sika deer in Ireland,* B.Sc. thesis (Unpublished) U.C.C.

Linnell, J., and Cross, T.F., 1991, 'The biochemical systematics of red and sika deer (genus Cervus) in Ireland', *Hereditas* 115: 267-273.

Lockley, R.M., 1966, 'The distribution of grey and common seals on the coast of Ireland', *Ir. Nat. J.* 15 (10): 136-143.

Long, P., 1984, 'Killarney's native reds- the situation in '84', *Field and Countryside* 2(3).

Lowe, V.P.W., and Gardiner, A.S., 1974, 'A re-examination of the subspecies of red deer *Cervus elaphus* with particular reference to the stocks in Britain', *J. Zool. Lond.* 174: 185-201.

Lunnon, R.M., and Reynolds, J.D., 1991, 'Distribution of the otter, *Lutra lutra* in Ireland, and its value as an indicator of habitat quality', In *Bioindicators and environmental management,* Academic Press pp. 435-443.

Lynch, J.M., 1989, *Aspects of growth and morphology of Japanese sika deer from Killarney National Park,* B.Sc. thesis (Unpublished) University College, Dublin

Lynch, J.M., and Hayden, T.J., 1989, 'The use of multivariate analysis to seperate Cervid Populations in Ireland', *Proc. 3rd Ir. Zool. Meet.*

Lynch, J.M., O'Corry-Crowe, G., and Hayden, T.J., 1989, 'Morphology of the antlers of the sika deer *Cervus nippon nippon* from the Killarney Valley', *Mamm. Soc. Conf.* 14pp.

Mason, C.E., and McDonald, S.M., 1986, *Otters: ecology and conservation,* Cambridge University Press, Cambridge.

McCabe, R., 1984, 'Management recommendations for native red deer', *Proc. 15th Cong. Game Biol.*

McFadden, Y.M.T., and Fairley, J.S., 1984, 'Food of otters *Lutra lutra* (L.) in an Irish limestone river system with special reference to the crayfish *Austropotamobius pallipes* (Lereboullet)', *J. Life Sci. R. Dubl. Soc.* 5: 65-76.

Merne, O.J., 1995, 'Risso's dolphins *Grampus griseus* (Cuvier)', *Ir. Nat. J.* 25 (4): 147-148.

Merne, O.J., and Walsh, A.,1996, 'Risso's dolphins *Grampus griseus* (Cuvier)', *Ir. Nat. J.* 25 (8): 296.

Moffat, C.B., 1938, 'The mammals of Ireland', *Proc. R. Ir. Acad.* 44B: 61-128.

Molyneux, T., 1697, 'A discourse concerning the large horns frequently found underground in Ireland', *Phil. Trans.* 19: 489-512.

Murphy, P., Bolger, T., and Hayden, T. J., 1988, *The morphology of the skull of the sika deer* Cervus nippon nippon *from Wicklow and Killarney and red deer* Cervus elephas *from Donegal,* Ungulate res. group conf. (Unpublished).

Murphy, P., and Hayden, T.J., 1989, *Craniometric variation in deer populations in Ireland,* Proc. 3rd Ir. Zool. Meet. (Unpublished).

Nowlan, B., 1988, 'Fox attacking sika deer calf', *Ir. Nat. J.* 22 (11): 502.

Nowlan, B., 1989, *Niche overlap of three herbivorous species in Killarney National Park.* M.Ag.Sc. thesis (Unpublished) University College, Dublin

Nowlan, B., 1990, *The population dynamics of the Red deer herd in Killarney National Park,* Co. Kerry, Ireland, unpublished report to Office of Public Works, Dublin.

Nowlan, B., and O'Toole, P., 1991, *A preliminary survey of the lowland herd of Red deer (Cervus elephas) in Killarney National Park,* Co. Kerry, Ireland, Unpublished report to Office of Public Works, Dublin.

O'Corry Crowe, G., 1988, *Morphology of the skull and antlers of sika deer from the Killarney Valley,* B.Sc. thesis (Unpublished) University College, Dublin

O'Sullivan, W., 1991, 'The distribution of otters *Lutra lutra* within a major Irish river system, the Munster Blackwater catchment, 1988-90', *Ir. Nat. J.* 23 (11): 442-446.

O'Donoghue, Y.A., 1986, *Aspects of growth and reproduction of Japanese sika deer from Killarney National Park,* B.Sc. thesis (Unpublished) University College, Dublin

O'Donoghue,Y.A., 1991, *Growth, reproduction and survival in a feral population of Japanese sika deer,* Ph. D. thesis (Unpublished) University College, Dublin

O'Donoghue, Y.A., and Hayden, T.J., 1987, *Sika deer in the Killarney National Park,* Mamm. Soc. AGM (Unpublished).

O'Gorman, F., 1967, 'Some aspects of deer ecology in Killarney, Co. Kerry' *Abstract. Bull. Mamm. Soc.* 28: 9-10.

O'Gorman, F., and Classens, A.J.M., 1965, '*Myotis nattereri* (Kuhl), a bat new to Co. Kerry', *Ir. Nat. J.* 15 (2): 53-54.

O'Gorman, F., and Mulloy F.,1973 'The economical and recreational potential of deer in Ireland' In *The future of Irish wildlife – a blueprint for development,* An Foras Taluntais, Dublin.

O'Sullivan, B.W., Stronach, N., and Fairley, J.S., 1975, 'New records of horse-shoe bats', *Ir. Nat. J.* 18: 190-191.

O'Sullivan, H.M., Smal, C.M., and Fairley, J.S. 1984, 'A study of parasite infestations in populations of small rodents *(Apodemus sylvaticus* and *Clethrionomys glareolus)* on Ross Island, Killarney, southwest Ireland', *J. Life Sc. R. Dub. Soc.* 5: 29-42.

O'Sullivan, P.J., 1983, 'The distribution of the pine marten *(Martes martes)* in the Republic of Ireland', *Mamm. Rev.* 13 (1): 39-44.

O'Sullivan, P.J., 1994, 'Bats in Ireland', *Ir. Nat. J.* (Special Zoological Supplement).

O'Toole, P., and Long, A., 1993, *A study of the distribution of the lowland red deer population in Killarney National Park,* Internal report to the Office of Public Works, 63 pp.

Paul, J., 1989, 'Zoological note on an unusual birth date of a Grey Seal, *Halichoerus grypus* L.', *Ir. Nat. J.* 23 (1): 33.

Quirke, C., 1986, *The native red deer of County Kerry,* unpublished Report.

Quirke, C., 1991, *The diet of red deer, sika deer and Scottish blackface sheep in Killarney National Park.* M.Sc. thesis (Unpublished) University College, Dublin.

Ratcliffe, P.R., 1991, 'Sika deer, *Cervus nippon*', In Corbet, G.B., and Harris, S., (Eds.), *The handbook of British mammals,* (3rd. Edn.), pp. 504-508, Blackwell, Oxford.

Riney, J., 1974, *The red deer of County Kerry,* Unpublished Report to the Office of Public Works.

Scharff, R.F., 1918, 'The Irish red deer', *Ir. Nat.* 27: 133-139.

Sleeman, D.P., 1981, *Parasites of deer in Ireland,* M.Sc. thesis (Unpublished) University College, Dublin.

Sleeman, D.P., 1987, *The ecology of the Irish stoat,* Ph.D. thesis (Unpublished) National University of Ireland.

Sleeman, D.P., 1991, 'Home ranges of Irish stoats', *Ir. Nat. J.* 23: 212-213.

Sleeman, D.P., 1992, 'Diet of Irish stoats', *Ir. Nat. J.* 24: 151-153.

Smal, C.M., 1988, 'The American mink *Mustela vision* in Ireland', Mammal Rev. 18: 201-208.

Smal, C.M., 1991, *The national badger survey: Preliminary results for the Irish Republic'* Unpublished report, Office of Public Works. Dublin.

Smal, C.M., and Fairley, J.S., 1978, 'The spread of the bank vole since 1970', *Ir. Nat. J.* 19 (7): 237-239.

Smal, C.M., and Fairley, J.S., 1980, 'Food of woodmice *(Apodemus sylvaticus)* and bank voles *(Clethrionomys glareolus)* in oak and yew woods at Killarney, Ireland', *J. Zool. Lond.* 191: 413-418.

Smal, C.M., and Fairley, J.S., 1980, 'The fruits available as food to small rodents in two woodland ecosystems', *Holarctic Ecol.* 3: 10-18.

Smal, C.M., and Fairley, J.S., 1981a, 'Energy consumption of small rodent populations in two Irish woodland ecosystems', *Acta Theriol.* 26: 449-458.

Smal, C.M., and Fairley, J.S., 1981b, 'Primary production in two Irish woods and the fraction available to small rodents as food', *Ir. Nat. J.* 20 (5): 173-216.

Smal, C.M., and Fairley, J.S., 1982, 'The dynamics and regulation of small rodent populations in the woodland ecosystems of Killarney, Ireland', *J. Zool. Lond*. 196: 1-30.

Smal, C.M., and Fairley, J.S., 1984, 'The spread of the bank vole *Clethrionomys glareolus* in Ireland', *Mammal Rev*. 14(2): 71-78.

Stebbings, R.E., and Griffith, F., 1986, *Distribution and status of bats in Europe,* Institute of Terrestrial Ecology, Monks Wood.

Thomson, E.H., 1977, *A study of the Irish stoat (*Mustela ermina hibernica*) in the Bourn Vincent Memorial Park,* Report to Office of Public Works, Dublin, 20pp.

Thomson, E.H., and Fairley, J. S., 1978, 'Notes on the Irish stoat in the Bourn Vincent Memorial Park, Killarney', *Ir. Nat. J.* 19 (5): 158-159.

Viney, M. and Berrow, S., 1995, 'Walrus *Odobenus rosmarus* (L.) in Co. Kerry', *Ir. Nat. J.* 25 (4): 150.

Warner, P., 1983, 'An assessment of the breeding population of common seals *(Phoca vitulina vitulina L.)* in the Republic of Ireland', *Ir. Nat. J.* 21 (1): 24-26.

Whitehead, G.K., 1950, *Deer and their management in the deer parks of Great Britain and Ireland,* Country Life, London.

Whitehead, G.K., 1960, *The deer stalking grounds of Great Britain and Ireland,* Hollis and Carter, London.

Whitehead, G.K., 1964, *The deer of Great Britain and Ireland: an account of their history, status and distribution,* Routedge and Kegan-Paul, London.

Whitehead, G.K., 1972, *The wild goats of Britain and Ireland*, David and Charles, Newton Abbot.

Webb, J.B., 1976, *Otter spraint analysis,* Mammal Society, Reading.

BIRDS

Alexander, S.M.D., 1954, 'The birds of the Blasket islands', *Bird Study* 1: 148-168.

Anon. 1927, 'Snipe of Co. Kerry: big bags at Ballinagroun', *The Field*: 831.

Anon. 1898, 'Supposed great spotted cuckoo in Ireland', *Ir. Nat.* 7: 51.

Batten, L., 1976, 'Bird Communities of some Killarney woodlands', *Proc. R. Ir. Acad.* 8 (76): 285-313.

Barrington, R.M., 1900, *The migration of birds as observed at Irish lighthouses and lightships, including original reports from 1888-1897*, Porter, London.

Barrington, R.M., 1914, 'Fulmars, gannets and other seabirds on the Skelligs', *Ir. Nat.* 23: 133-135.

Brazier, H., and Merne, O.J., 1989, 'Breeding seabirds on the Blasket islands, Co. Kerry', *Ir. Birds* 4(1): 43-64.

Cabot, D., 1967, *The status and distribution of the Greenland white-fronted goose* Anser albifrons flavirostris *in Ireland*, January 1967, Publication No. 9. Irish Wildfowl Conservancy, Dublin.

Candler, C., and Candler, H., 1890, 'Notes on the birdlife of the Skellig rocks', *Norfolk Norwich Naturalists' Soc.* 5: 47.

Carpenter, G.H., et al 1898, 'Zoology: Part 2 of the report of the second triennial conference and excursion of the Irish Field Club Union, held at Kenmare July 7-13th. 1898', *Ir. Nat.* 7: 206-226.

Carruthers, T.D., 1986, 'Waterways bird survey on the river Flesk, Co.Kerry', *Ir. Birds.* 3: 229-236.

Carruthers, T.D., 1987, 'Greenland white-fronted geese associating with deer', *Ir. Birds* 3: 449-450.

Carruthers, T.D., and Larner, J., 1993, *The birds of the Killarney National Park*, Government Stationary Office, Dublin.

Carruthers, T.D., 1994, *The ecology of bogland-feeding Greenland white-fronted geese wintering in the Killarney valley*, Co. Kerry, Ireland. Diploma thesis (Unpublished), University of London.

Carruthers, T.D., 1996a, 'An unusual concentration of Chiffchaffs' *Ir. Birds* 5: 435.

Carruthers, T.D., 1996b, 'Grey heron feeding after dark' *British Birds* 89: 139.

Carruthers, T.D., 1996c, 'Great tit eating earthworm' *British Birds* 89: 143.

Carruthers, T.D., and Gosler, A.G., 1994, 'Distribution of breeding birds in relation to habitat in the Muckross yew wood, Killarney', *Ir. Birds* 5 (2): 157-164.

Carruthers, T.D., and Gosler, A.G., 1995, 'The breeding bird community of the Muckross yew wood, Killarney', *Ir. Birds* 5:308-318.

Conroy, D., and Wilson, J., 1994, *'Bird life in Ireland'*, O'Brien Press, Dublin.

Delaney, S.N., 1996a, *'I-WeBS Report 1994-95: Results from the first winter of the Irish Wetland Bird Survey'*, BirdWatch Ireland, Dublin.

Delaney, S.N., 1996b, 'Waterfowl counts in Ireland, 1994-95: A summary of the first winter of the Irish Wetland Bird Survey (I-WeBS)', *Ir. Birds* (5): 423-432.

Delaney, S.N., 1997, *'I-WeBS Report 1995-96: Results from the second winter of the Irish Wetland Bird Survey'*, BirdWatch Ireland, Dublin.

Delap, M.J., 1922, 'Swans in Valencia harbour', *Ir. Nat.* 31: 140.

Dempsey, E., and O'Clery, M., 1993, *The complete guide to Ireland's birds.* Gill and McMillan, Dublin.

Evans, P.G.H., and Lovegrove, R.R., 1974', 'The birds of the south-west Irish islands', *Irish Bird Report*, 1973: 33-64.

Fairley, J.S., and Smal, C.M.,, 1989, 'Further observations on the diet of the barn owl in Ireland', *Ir. Birds* 4: 65-68.

Fox, A.D., and Salmon, D.G., 1989, 'The winter status and distribution of gadwall in Britain and Ireland', *Bird Study* 36: 37-44.

Garcia, E.F.J., 1983, 'An experimental test of competition for space between blackcaps *Sylvia atricapilla* and garden warblers *Sylvia borin* in the breeding season. *J. Anim. Ecol.* 52: 795-805.

Gibbons, D.W., Reid, J.B., and Chapman, R.A., 1993, *The new atlas of breeding birds in Britain and Ireland,* 1988-1991, Poyser, London.

Gosler, A., 1993, *The great tit,* Hamlyn, London.

Gosler, A. G., and Carruthers, T.D., 1994, 'Bill size and niche breadth in the Irish coal tit *Parus ater hibernicus'*, *Avian Biology* 25 (3): 171-177.

Goss-Custard, J.D., and Moser, M.E., 1988, 'Rates of change in the numbers of dunlin *Calidris alpina,* wintering in British estuaries in relation to the spread of *Spartina anglica', J. Appl. Ecol.* 25: 95-110.

Green, M., Knight, A., Cartmel, S., and Thomas, D., 1988, 'The status of wintering waders on the non-estuarine west coast of Ireland', *Ir. Birds* 3 (4): 569-574.

Harrop, J.M., 1961, 'The birds on Great Skellig, Co. Kerry, June 1958', *Ir. Nat. J.* 13: 17-18.

Hillis, J.P., 1975, 'Apparent hybrid gull, *Larus argentatus* Pontopp. x L. *Fuscus* L.', *Ir. Nat. J.* 18: 229.

Hillis, P., Fairley, J.S., Smal, C.M.,, and Archer, P., 1988, 'The diet of the long-eared owl in Ireland', *Ir. Birds* 3: 581-588.

Hoodless, A.N., and Coulson, J.C., 1994, 'Survival rates and movements of British and Irish woodcock *Scolopax rusticola* in the British Isles', *Bird Study* 41: 48-60.

Hounsome, M.V., and Rear, D., 1966a, 'Turtle dove in Co. Kerry,' *Ir. Nat. J.* 15: 8

Hounsome, M.V., and Rear, D., 1966b, 'The bird population of the Great Blasket island, Illaunboy and Beginish, Co. Kerry,' *Ir. Nat. J.* 15: 169-175.

Hutchinson, C.D., 1979, *Ireland's wetlands and their birds,* Irish Wildbird Conservancy, Dublin

Hutchinson, C.D., 1989, *Birds in Ireland,* Poyser, Calton.

Hutchinson, C.D., 1994, *Where to watch birds in Ireland,* Christopher Helm, London.

Jones, E., 1979, 'Breeding of the short-eared owl in south-west Ireland' *Ir. Birds* 1: 377-380.

Kane, K.W.S., 1988, 'Eagles in Kerry in the nineteenth century - a correction', *Ir. Birds* 3 (4): 606-608.

Kennedy, A.J., 1923, 'Birds at the Tearaght lighthouse', *Ir. Nat.* 32: 7.

Kennedy, P.G., Ruttledge, R.F., and Scroope, C.F., 1954, *The birds of Ireland,* Oliver and Boyd, London and Edinburgh.

King, F., 1980, 'Red-necked phalaropes breeding at Akeragh Lough, Co. Kerry', *Ir. Birds* 1: 540-541.

Kirby, J.S., Rees, E.C., Merne, O.J., and Gardarsson, A., 1992, 'International census of whooper swans *Cygnus cygnus* in Britain, Ireland and Iceland: January 1991', *Wildfowl* 43: 20-26.

Lack, P., 1986, *The atlas of wintering birds in Britain and Ireland,* Poyser, Calton.

Mayes, E., and Stowe, T., 1989, 'The status and distribution of the corncrake in Ireland, 1988', *Ir. Birds* 4: 1-12.

McDermot, P., 1992, 'Site guide; Akeragh Lough and Tralee Bay, Co. Kerry', *Irish Birding News* 2: 121-129.

McDermot, P., 1993, 'Franklin's Gull at Black Rock, Co. Kerry', *Irish Birding News* 3: 85-90.

McDermot, P., 1994, 'Franklin's Gull in County Kerry – a species new to Ireland', *Ir. Birds* 5 (2): 203-204

Merne, O.J., and Murphy, C.W., 1986, 'Whooper swans in Ireland; January 1986', *Ir. Birds* 3: 199-206.

Merne, O.J., and Walsh, A., 1994, 'Barnacle Geese in Ireland, spring 1993 and 1994', *Irish Birds* 5: 151-156.

Mitchell, C., 1991, 'Movements and turnover of wigeon in Britain and Ireland', In Haradine, J. (ed.) *Wigeon in Ireland,* British Association for Shooting and Conservation, Rossett.

Munns, D.J., 1956, 'Further notes on the birds of the Blasket islands', *Bird Study* 3: 248-250.

Nairn, R.G.W., 1986, '*Spartina anglica* in Ireland and its potential impact on wildfowl and waders - a review', *Ir. Birds* 3: 215-228.

Norris, D.W., and Wilson, H.J., 1983, *Greenland white-fronted goose project for 1982-83,* Internal report, Forest and Wildlife service, Dublin, 9pp.

Norris, D.W., and Wilson, H.J., 1986, *Greenland white-fronted geese in Ireland, A progress report,* Forest and Wildlife service, Dublin.

Norris, D.W., and Wilson, H.J., 1987, *Greenland white-fronted geese in Ireland, 1986-87,* Office of Public Works, Dublin.

Norris, D. W., and Wilson, H.J., 1988, *Greenland white-fronted geese in Ireland, 1987-88,* Office of Public Works, Dublin.

Norris, D.W., and Wilson, H.J., 1988, 'Disturbance and flock size changes in Greenland white-fronted geese wintering in Ireland', *Wildfowl* 39: 63-70.

Norris, D.W., and Wilson, H.J., 1989, *Greenland white-fronted geese in Ireland, 1988-89,* Office of Public Works, Dublin.

Norris, D.W., and Wilson, H.J., 1991, *Greenland white-fronted geese in Ireland, 1989-90,* Office of Public Works, Dublin.

Norris, D.W., and Wilson, H.J., 1992, *Greenland white-fronted geese in Ireland, 1990-91,* Office of Public Works, Dublin.

O'Briain, M., and Healy, B., 1991, 'Winter distribution of light-bellied Brent Geese *Branta bernicla hrota* in Ireland', *Ardea* 79: 317-326.

O'Briain, M., Carruthers, T.D., and Sheridan, V., 1986, 'Transitory staging of Brent geese *Branta bernicla hrota* in Ireland', *Ir. Birds* 3: 286.

O'Clery, M., 1991, 'Site guide; Dunquin, Co. Kerry', *Irish Birding News* 2: 29-36.

O'Halloran J., Myers, A.A., and Duggan, P.F., 1987, 'Lead poisoning in swans and angling practice in Ireland', In Biological Indicators of Pollution, *Proc. R. Ir. Acad.*183-191.

O'Halloran, J., Myers, A.A., and Duggan, P.F., 1988, 'Biochemical and haematological reference values for mute swans, *Cygnus olor:* Effects of acute lead poisoning', *Avian Path.* 17: 667-678.

O'Halloran, J., Myers, A.A., and Duggan, P.F., 1988, 'Blood lead levels and free red blood cell protoporphyrin as a measure of lead exposure in mute swans', *Env. Pollution,* 51: 19-38.

O'Halloran, J., Myers, A.A., and Duggan, P.F., 1988, 'Lead poisoning in swans and sources of contamination in Ireland', *J. Zool.* London 216: 211-223

O'Halloran J., Walsh, P.M., Cross, T.F., Kelly T.C., and Hutchinson, C.D., 1985, 'Current ornithological research in Ireland', *Ir. Birds.* 3: 139-162.

O'Halloran, J., Myers, A.A., and Duggan, P.F., 1989, 'Some sub-lethal effects of lead on mute swans, *Cygnus olor'*, *J. Zool.* London 218: 627-632.

O'Meara, M., 1979, 'Distribution and numbers of corncrakes in Ireland in 1978', *Ir. Birds* 1: 381-405.

Patten, C.J., 1902, 'A list of birds observed west of Dingle, Co. Kerry', *Ir. Nat.* 11: 1 2 5 137.

Renouf, L.P.W. 1924, 'Spoonbill and great spotted cuckoo in Kerry', *Ir. Nat.* 33: 30.

Rowan, A.B., 1856, 'The barnacle', *Kerry Mag.* 3: 7-10.

Ruttledge, W., 1921, 'Iceland falcon in Co. Kerry', *Ir. Nat.* 30: 63.

Ruttledge, R.F., 1966a, 'The present breeding distribution of the tree sparrow in Ireland', *Fourteenth Annual Irish Bird Report* 1966: 50-54.

Ruttledge, R.F., 1966b, *Ireland's birds,* Witherby, London.

Ruttledge, R.F., 1970, 'Winter distribution and numbers of scaup, long-tailed duck and common scoter in Ireland', *Bird Study* 17: 241-246.

Ruttledge, R.F., and Ogilvie, M.A., 1979, 'The past and current status of the Greenland white-fronted goose in Ireland and Britain', *Irish Birds.* 1. 293-363.

Sharrock, J.T.R., 1976, *The atlas of breeding birds in Britain and Ireland,* Poyser, Berkhamsted.

Sheppard, R., 1991, 'The Irish wigeon population – distribution and changes', In Haradine, J. (ed.) *Wigeon in Ireland,* British Association for Shooting and Conservation, Rossett.

Sheppard, J.R., 1993, *Ireland's wetland wealth,* Irish Wildbird Conservancy, Dublin.

Simms, E., 1971, *Woodland birds,* Collins, London.

Smal, C.M.,, 1987, 'A study of the barn owl *Tyto alba* in southern Ireland with reference to a recently introduced species - the bank vole *Clethrionomys glareolus'*, *Bird Study* 34: 113-125.

Stroud, D.A., 1992, *Greenland white-fronted goose International Management Plan,* Proc. IWRB Conference on Goose Damage and Conservation, Lelystad, Holland.

Turle, W.H., 1891, 'A visit to the Blasket islands and the Skellig rocks', *Ibis* Series 6, 3: 1-12.

Usher, R.J., and Warren, R., 1900, *The birds of Ireland,* Gurney and Jackson, London.

Walsh, A., and Merne, O.J., 1988, 'Barnacle geese in Ireland, spring 1988', *Ir. Birds* 3: 539-550.

Walsh, P.M., and Sleeman, D.P., 1988, 'Avian prey of a wintering short-eared owl population in south-west Ireland', *Ir. Birds* 3: 589-591.

Waters, W.E., 1965, 'The birds of the Great Blasket islands, 20th. June 1964', *Ir. Nat. J.* 15 (2): 49-50.

Way, L.S., Grice, P., MacKay, A., Galbraith, C.A., Stroud, D.A., and Pienkowski, M.W., 1993, *Ireland's internationally important bird sites: a review of sites for the EC Special Protection Area network,* Joint Nature Conservation Committee, Peterborough.

Whilde, A., 1977, 'The autumn and winter food of mallard, *Anas platyrhynchos* (L.) and some other Irish wildfowl', *Ir. Nat. J.* 19 (1): 18.

Whilde, A., 1978, 'Further observations on the autumn and winter food of some Irish wildfowl', *Ir. Nat. J.* 19 (5): 149.

Whilde, A., 1986, *An ecological evaluation of potential areas in the west of Ireland for the reintroduction of white-tailed (sea) eagles* Haliaeetus albicilla L., Unpublished report for Irish Wildbird Conservancy, Corrib Conservation Centre, Oughterard.

Wilson, H.J., 1977, 'Some breeding bird communities of sessile oak woodlands in Ireland', *Pol. Ecol. Stud.* 3 (4): 245-256.

Wilson, H.J., 1982, *The breeding and wintering ecology of the woodcock* Scolopax rusticola *in Ireland,* Unpublished Report to Forest and Wildlife Service, Dublin.

Wilson, H.J. and Norriss, D.W., 1985, *Greenland white-fronted geese in Ireland 1982-83 to 1984-85: A report on its status, distribution and the impact of shooting,* Office of Public Works, Dublin.

REPTILES AND AMPHIBIANS

Beebee, T.J.C., 1983, *The natterjack toad,* Oxford University Press.

Beebee, T.J.C., 1991, *Natterjack toad* (Bufo calamita) *conservation in Ireland.* Report of an on-the-spot appraisal for the Council of Europe, 4-7 June 1991, Strasbourg.

Buckley, J., 1979, *Natterjack toad colonies in Co. Kerry 1979,* Unpublished Expedition Report.

Corbett, K., 1989, *Conservation of European reptiles and amphibians,* Christopher Helm, London.

Denton, J.S., and Beebee, T.J.C., 1993, 'Reproductive strategies in a female-biased population of natterjack toads *Bufo calamita*', *Anim. Behav.* 46: 1169-1175.

Frazer, D., 1983, *Reptiles and amphibians,* Collins, London.

Griffiths, R.A., Edgar, P.W., and Wong, A.L.C., 1991, 'Interspecific competition in tadpoles: growth inhibition and growth retrieval in natterjack toads, *Bufo calamita*', *J. Anim. Ecol.* 60: 1065-1076.

Greeson, R.A.R., and O'Dubhda, S., 1971, 'Natterjack toads *Bufo calamita* Laur. at Castlegregory and Fermoyle, Co. Kerry', *Ir. Nat. J.* 17: 9-11.

Gresson, R.A.R., and O'Dubhda, S., 1974, 'The distribution of the natterjack toad, *Bufo calamita* Laur. in County Kerry', *Ir. Nat. J.* 18: 97-103.

Mackay, J.T., 1836, 'The natterjack (*Bufo rubeta*) occurs wild in Ireland', *Mag. Nat. Hist.* 9: 316-317.

McDougald, T.J., 1942, 'Notes on the habits of the natterjack toad in Co. Kerry', *Ir. Nat. J.* 8: 21-25.

Ward, H., 1864, 'The natterjack toad in Ireland', *Intellectual Observer* 5: 227-233.

Fish

Adams, J., 1924, *The anglers guide to the Irish fisheries*, Hutchinson, London.

Andrews, W., 1860-61, 'On the cod and ling fisheries of Ireland', *J. R. Dub. Soc.* 3: 230-2

Andrews, W., 1871, 'On oyster deposits (Kenmare and Dingle)', *J. R. Geol. Soc. Ire.* 2: 13-15, 132.

Anon. 1973, *Irish sport fishes: a guide to their identification,* The Inland Fisheries Trust, Dublin.

Anon. 1975, *A preliminary survey of Irish lakes*, An Foras Forbatha, Dublin.

Aprahamian, M.W., and Aprahamian, C., 1990, 'Status of the genus *Alosa* in the British Isles; past and present', *J. Fish. Biol.* 37A: 257-258.

Berrow, S.D., and Heardman, C., 1994, 'The basking shark *Cetorhinus maximus* (Gunnerus) in Irish waters - patterns of distribution and abundance', *Biology and Environment: Proc. R. Ir. Acad.* 94B (2): 101-107.

Berrow, S.D., and Heardman, C., 1995, 'Basking sharks *Cetorhinus maximus* Gunnerus, stranded on the Irish coast', *Ir. Nat. J.* 25 (4): 152.

Bracken, J.J., and Kennedy, M., 1967, 'Notes on some Irish estuarine and inshore fishes', *Ir. Fish Invest. Ser.* B. 3: 4-8.

Farran, G.P., 1946, 'Local names of Irish fishes', *Ir. Nat. J.* 8: 420-433.

Ferguson, A., 1981, 'Systematics of Irish charr as indicated by electrophoretic analysis of tissue proteins', *Biochemical Systematics and Ecology* 9: 225-232.

Fitzmaurice, P., 1976, '*Lophius budegassa* Spinola, 1907 from Irish inshore waters', *Ir. Nat. J.* 18: 237.

Friend, G.F., 1959, 'Subspeciation in British charrs', *Publs. Systematics Ass.* 3: 121-129.

Griffith, D. de G., 1966, '*Raia undulata* (Lacépede), a species new to Irish waters', *Ir. Nat. J.* 15 (6): 166-168.

Griffith, D. de G., 1968, 'Further occurrences of *Raia undulata* (Lacépede) in Irish waters', *Ir. Nat. J.* 16: 21.

Grimble, A., 1913, *The salmon rivers of Ireland*, Kegan-Paul, Trench, Tribner, London.

Guttfield, F., 1978, *Tench Fisherman's Handbook,* 42: 1162-1169, Marshall Cavendish Partworks Ltd., Great Britain.

Healy, A.,1956, 'A specimen of Tench *(Tinca tinca L.)* from Lough Lein Killarney', *Ir. Nat. J.* 12: 109.

Hillis, J.P., 1963, 'Abnormally-coloured turbot from Co. Kerry', *Ir. Nat. J.* 14:155.

Hillis, J.P., 1966, 'Abnormal thornback ray *Raia clavata* from Kerry', *Ir. Nat. J.* 15: 6.

Hillis, J.P., 1968, 'Large whiting *Merlangus merlangus* (L.) from south-western Ireland', *Ir. Nat. J.* 16: 25.

Hillis, J.P., and Long, M., 1972, 'Abnormal flatfish from the Dingle area', *Ir. Nat. J.* 17: 204.

Kennedy, M., and Fitzmaurice, P., 1971, 'The biology of the tench *Tinca tinca* (L.) in Irish waters', *Proc. R. Ir. Acad.* 71B: 158 pp.

Lelek, A., 1980, 'Threatened freshwater fishes in Europe', *Nature and Environment Series* 18, Council of Europe, Strasbourg.

Lelek, A., 1987, *Threatened fishes of Europe,* A.U.L.A. - Verlay Wiesbaden.

Maitland, P.S., 1972, Key to British freshwater fishes. *Freshwater Biological Association Scientific Publication* 27, Freshwater Biological Association, Ambleside.

Maitland, P.S., 1979, 'The status and conservation of rare freshwater fishes in the British Isles', *Proc. Inst. Br. Freshwat. Conf.:* 237-248.

Maitland, P.S., and Campbell, R.N., 1992, *Freshwater fishes of the British Isles,* Harper Collins.

Maitland, P.S., and Lyle, A.A., 1991, 'Conservation of freshwater fishes in the British Isles; the current status and biology of threatened species', *Aquatic Conservation: Marine and Freshwater Ecosystems* 1: 25-54.

M'Intosh, W.C., 1898., 'Note on a post-larval fierasfer', *Ir. Nat.* 7 (3): 61-64.

Minchin, D., 1995, 'The red-mouthed goby *Gobius cruentatus* Gmelin (Gobiidae) from the south-west coast of Ireland', *Ir. Nat. J.* 25 (3): 98-105.

Minchin, D., and Molloy, J., 1976, 'Notes on fishes taken in Irish waters', *Ir. Nat. J.* 18: 360-363.

Minchin, D., and Molloy, J., 1978, 'Notes on fishes taken in Irish waters in 1976', *Ir. Nat. J.* 19 (5):160.

Minchin, D., and Molloy, J., 1981, 'Notes on fishes taken in Irish waters during 1979', *Ir. Nat. J.* 20 (8): 340-342.

Moriarty, C., 1972, *Eel research 1965-1971,* Dept. of Agriculture and Fisheries, Ireland.

Moriarty, C., 1978, *Eels: A natural and unnatural history,* David and Charles, Newton Abbot.

Moriarty, C., 1980, *Eel research 1978-1979,* Dept. of Fisheries and Forestry, Ireland.

Moriarty, C., 1988, *The eel in Ireland,* Went Memorial Lecture 1987, Royal Dublin Society, Dublin.

Muus, B.J., 1974, *Collins Guide to the sea fishes of Britain and north-western Europe,* Collins, London.

Muus, B.J., and Dahlstrom, D., 1985, *Collins Guide to the sea fishes of Britain and north-western Europe,* Collins, London.

O'Grady, M.F., 1993, *A fish stock survey of Lough Leane, Co. Kerry and management recommendations for this resource,* Central Fisheries Board Report to Office of Public Works, Dublin, 23pp.

O'Maoileidigh, N., 1990, *A study of fish populations in the Killarney lakes,* Ph.D. thesis (Unpublished), University College, Dublin

O'Maoileidigh, N., Cawders, S., Bracken, J.J., and Ferguson, A., 1988, 'Morphometric, meristic character and electrophoretic analyses of two Irish populations of twaite shad, *Alosa fallax* (Lacépede)', *J. Fish. Biol.* 32: 355-366.

O'Maoileidigh, N., and Bracken, J.J., 1989, 'Biology of the tench, *Tinca tinca* (L.) in an Irish lake', *Aquaculture and Fisheries Manag.* 20: 199-209.

O'Riordan, C.E., 1983, 'Third record of the dusky perch from Irish coastal waters', *Ir. Nat. J.* 21 (3): 141.

O'Riordan, C.E., 1984, 'Some interesting fishes and other marine fauna from the Porcupine bank', *Ir. Nat. J.* 21: 321-323.

Partington, J.D., and Mills, C.A., 1988, 'An electrophoretic and biometric study of Arctic charr, *Salvelinus alpinus* (L.), from ten British Lakes', *J. Fish. Biol.* 33: 791-814.

Quigley, D.T.G., and Flannery, K., 1989, 'Fish notes', *Ir. Nat. J.* 23 (3): 114-117.

Quigley, D.T.G., and Flannery, K., 1992a, 'Wreckfish *Polyprion americanus* Bloch and Schneider', *Ir. Nat. J.* 24: 80-81.

Quigley, D.T.G., and Flannery, K., 1992b, 'Black-mouth dogfish *Galeus melastomus* Rafinesque/Schmaltz', *Ir. Nat. J.* 24: 81.

Quigley, D.T.G., and Flannery, K., 1992c, 'Turbot *Schophthalmus maximus*', *Ir. Nat.* 24: 81.

Quigley, D.T.G., and Flannery, K., 1993, 'Bonito or pelamid *Sarda sarda* Bloch in Irish waters, further records and a review of the Irish records', *Ir. Nat. J.* 24: 72-75.

Quigley, D.T.G., and Flannery, K., 1995a' 'First record of red dory *Cyttopsis roseus* (Lowe 1843) in Irish waters together with a review of north-eastern Atlantic records', *Ir. Nat. J.* 25: 13-15.

Quigley, D.T.G., and Flannery, K., 1995b, 'The bogue *Boops boops* L. In Irish waters: further records and a review of Irish records', *Ir. Nat. J.* 25: 15-17.

Quigley, D.T.G., and Flannery, K., 1995c, 'Sailfin dory *Zenopsis conchifer* (Lowe 1852): further records from Irish waters and a review of north-west European records', *Ir. Nat. J.* 25: 71-76.

Quigley, D.T.G., and Flannery, K., 1995d, 'Herring *Clupea harengus* L.', *Ir. Nat. J.* 25: 81

Quigley, D.T.G., and Flannery, K., 1995e, 'Wolf-fish *Anarhichas lupus* L. In Irish waters: further records and a review of the Irish records', *Ir. Nat. J.* 25 (3): 106- 110.

Quigley, D.T.G., and Flannery, K., 1995f, 'First record of deep-sea angler fish *Cryptosarus couesi* (Gill 1983) from Irish waters', *Ir. Nat. J.* 25 (4): 145- 146.

Quigley, D.T.G., and Flannery, K., 1995g, 'Spurdog *Squalus acanthias* L.', *Ir. Nat. J.* 25 (4): 152.

Quigley, D.T.G., and Flannery, K., 1995f, 'Porbeagle shark *Lamna nasus* (Bonnaterre, 1788)', *Ir. Nat. J.* 25 (4): 153.

Quigley, D.T.G., and Flannery, K., 1996a, 'A further record of the Hair-tail *Trichiurus lepturus* L. (Pisces: Trichiuridae) from Irish inshore waters', *Ir. Nat. J.* 25 (5): 176-178.

Quigley, D.T.G., and Flannery, K., 1996b, 'Common Dolphin-fish *Coryphaena hippurus* L. in Irish and other north-eastern Atlantic waters', *Ir. Nat. J.* 25 (7): 260-263.

Quigley, D.T.G., and Flannery, K., 1997, Arctic charr *Salvelinus alpinus* L., first record from Lough Annscaul, Co. Kerry; further records from loughs Bunaveela, Kindrum and Coomasaharn; and notice of an introduction to Lough Owel, Co. Westmeath. *Ir. Nat. J.* 25 (11/12): 435-439.

Quigley, D.T.G., Flannery, K., and O'Shea, J., 1989, 'Specimens of the Greenland halibut *Reinhardtius hippoglossoides* (Walbaum 1972) from Irish waters', *Ir. Nat. J.* 23 (3): 111-112.

Quigley, D.T.G., Flannery, K., and O'Shea, J., 1991, 'Trigger fish *(Balistes carclinensis* Gremlin 1789) in Irish waters: a biogeographical review', *Biogeography of Ireland: past, present and future*, Trinity College, Dublin.

Quigley, D.T.G., Flannery, K., and O'Shea, J., 1993, 'Trigger fish *Balistes capriscus* Gmelin', *Ir. Nat. J.* 24: 223-228.

Quigley, D.T.G., Flannery, K., and O'Shea, J., 1997, 'Opah *Lampris guttatus* (Brunnich 1788) in Irish waters: further records and a review of Irish records', *Ir. Nat. J.* 25 (9): 326-331.

Quigley, D.T.G., O'Shea, J. and Flannery, K., 1997, 'Tadpole fish *raniceps raninus* L. in Irish waters: further records and a review of Irish records', *Ir. Nat. J.* 25 (9): 332-336.

Regan, C.T., 1908, 'A preliminary revision of the Irish charr', *Ann. Mag. Nat. Hist. Series 8:2.*

Regan, C.T., 1911, *The freshwater fishes of the British Isles,* Methuen, London.

Roberts, C.D., 1977, 'The wreckfish *Ployprion americanus* (Schneider, 1801) in Irish waters: an underwater sighting and review of the Irish records', *Ir. Nat. J.* 19 (4): 108.

Toner, B.D., 1957, 'Movements of salmon around Ireland', *Proc. R. Ir. Acad.* 58B: 321-8.

Trewavas, E., 1938, 'The Killarney shad or 'Goureen' (*Alosa fallax killarnensis*, Regan, 1916)', *Proc. Linn. Soc.* 150 (2): 110-112.

Twomey, E., 1957, 'A specimen of shad, *Alosa fallax killarnensis* from Lough Leane, Killarney', *Ir. Nat. J.* 12: 270.

Went, A.E.J., 1944, 'Notes on some Irish char', *Ir. Nat. J.* 8 (6): 202-205.

Went, A.E.J., 1946a, 'Irish freshwater fish', *Salmon Trout Mag.* 118: 248-256.

Went, A.E.J. 1946b, 'The greatest weaver *Trachinus draco,* L. From Dingle bay, Co. Kerry', *Ir. Nat. J.* 8: 336.

Went, A.E.J., 1948a, 'Note on a specimen of germo or longfinned tunny *Oreynus germo*, Day, from the Kerry coast, *Ir. Nat. J.* 9: 179.

Went, A.E.J., 1948b, 'Specimen of file or trigger fish captured in Dingle bay', *Ir. Nat. J.* 9: 149.

Went, A.E.J., 1949, 'File or trigger fish in Dingle bay', *Ir. Nat. J.* 9: 245.

Went, A.E.J., 1950, 'Notes on the introduction of some freshwater fish into Ireland', *Dept. of Agric. Jour.* 47 (1): 119.

Went, A.E.J., 1951, 'Sting rays *Trygon pastinaca* L. From Dingle bay', *Ir. Nat. J.* 10: 136.

Went, A.E.J., 1952, 'Specimen of *Macrurus laevis* Lowe from Dingle bay', *Ir. Nat. J.* 10: 321.

Went, A.E.J., 1953a, 'Notes on some Irish char (*Salvelinus* spp.)', IV. *Ir. Nat. J.* 11: 246-248.

Went, A.E.J., 1953b, 'The status of shads *Alosa finta* and *Alosa alosa* (Cuvier) in Irish waters', *Ir. Nat. J.* 11: 8-11.

Went, A.E.J., 1963, 'The shad', In *Irish water fishing* No. 4. E.M. Art and Publishing Ltd., Peterborough.

Went, A.E.J., 1965, 'Rare fishes taken in Irish waters in 1964', *Ir. Nat. J.* 15 (2): 38- 40.

Went, A.E.J., 1966, 'Rare fishes taken in Irish waters in 1965', *Ir. Nat. J.* 15 (6): 159-163.

Went, A.E.J., 1969, *List of Irish Fishes,* Government Stationery Office, Dublin.

Went, A.E.J., 1971a, 'The distribution of Irish char (*Salvelinus alpinus*)', Ir. Fish. Invest. 6: 5-11.

Went, A.E.J., 1971b, 'Interesting fishes from Irish waters in 1970', *Ir. Nat. J.* 17: 41.

Went, A.E.J., 1973, 'Some interesting fishes taken in Irish waters in 1972', *Ir. Nat. J.* 17: 375.

Went, A.E.J., 1974, 'Some interesting fishes taken from Irish waters', *Ir. Nat. J.* 18: 57.

Went, A.E.J., 1975, 'Interesting fishes taken in Irish waters in 1974', *Ir. Nat. J.* 18: 205.

Went, A.E.J., 1978, *The zoogeography of some fishes in Irish waters,* Fishery Leaflet 93, Department of Fisheries, Dublin.

Went, A.E.J., and Kennedy, M., 1969, List of Irish fishes, 2nd. Edition, Stationary Office, Dublin.

Wheeler, A., 1969, *The fishes of the British Isles and north-west Europe,* Macmillan,

Whelan, K., 1974, *Comparative study of the growth of brown trout (Salmo trutta L.) in Lough Leane, Killarney and other selected Irish lakes with special reference to the effects of cultural eutrophication,* B.Sc. thesis (Unpublished), University College, Dublin.

Whelan, B.J., 1976, *A comparative study of the growth and feeding of brown trout (Salmo trutta) and salmon (Salmo salar) in the Killarney valley catchment.* B.Sc. thesis (Unpublished), University College, Dublin.

INSECTS

Alexander, K.N., 1993, 'The status and distribution of *Xylophagus ater* Meigen (Diptera: Xylophagidae) in Ireland', *Ir. Nat. J.* 24: 316-318.

Alexander, K.N.A., and Clements, D.J., 1991, '*Xylophagus* - the continuing story', *Lger. Brachycera. Rec. Sch. Newsl.* Institute of Terrestrial Ecology, Grange-over-Sands. (Unpublished) 8: 1-2.

Andrews, H.W., 1914, 'Notes on some Diptera in the south of Ireland', *Ir. Nat.* 23: 136-143.

Anon., 1980, *Atlas of the bumblebees of the British Isles*, Institute of Terrestrial Ecology, Cambridge.

Ashe, P., 1977, *An investigation of the Chironomidae of the river Flesk with particular refe rence to diel periodicity of emergence.* B.Sc.thesis (Unpublished) University College, Dublin.

Ashe, P., 1982, *Ecological and taxonomic studies on the Chironomidae (Diptera: Nematocera) - A study of the Chironomidae of the river Flesk,* s.w. Ireland. Ph.D.thesis (Unpublished) University College, Dublin.

Ashe, P., 1985, 'A checklist of Irish Dixidae (Diptera)', *Bull. Irish. Biogeog. Soc.* 9: 46-50.

Ashe, P., and Murray, D.A., 1980, '*Nostococladius*, a new subgenus of *Cricotopus* (Diptera: Chironomidae)' In *Chironomidae*, Pergamon Press, Oxford 105-111.

Ashe, P., and Murray, D.A., 1984, 'Observations on and description of the egg-mass and eggs of *Buchonomyia thienemanni* Fitt. (Diptera: Chrironomidae), *Mem. Amer. Ent. Soc.* 34: 3-13.

Ashe, P., and O'Connor, J.P., 1990, 'Further records of Irish Dixidae (Diptera) including *Dixella attica* Pandazis, new to Ireland', *Bull. Ir. Biogeog. Soc.* 13: 23-28.

Ashe, P., O'Connor, J.P., and Casey, R., 1991, 'Irish mosquitoes (Diptera: Culicidae): a checklist of the species and their known distribution', *Proc. R. Ir. Acad.* 91B: 21-36.

Ashe, P., O'Connor, J.P., Stubbs, A.E., Vane-Wright, R.I., and Blackith, R., 1991, 'Crane flies new to Ireland (Diptera: Cylindrotomidae, Limoniidae, Tipulidae), *Bull.Ir. Biogeog. Soc.* 10: 72-80.

Ashe, P., O'Connor, J.P., Chandler, P.J., Stubbs, A.E., Vane-Wright, R.I., and Blackith, R.E., 1991, 'Craneflies new to Ireland (Diptera: Cylindrotomidae, Limoniidae, Tipulidae), Bull. Ir. Biogeog. Soc. 14: 54-59.

Ashe, P., and O'Connor, J.P., 1994, '*Eukiefferiella ancyla* and *Paratanytarsus grimmii* (Diptera: Chironomidae), new to Ireland, with a second record for *Orthocladius (Symposiocladius) lignicola. Ir. Nat. J.* 24: 364-366.

Atkins, L.S., 1968, '*Valella spirans* found in counties Cork and Kerry', *Ir. Nat. J.* 16: 24.

Barnard, P.C., and O'Connor, J.P., 1987, 'The populations of *Apatania muliebris* McLachan in the British Isles (Trichoptera: Limnephilidae)', *Entomol. Gaz.* 38: 263-267.

Barnard, P.C., O'Connor, J.P., and O'Connor, M A., 1987, 'Some records of Irish Neuroptera (Insecta)', *Bull. Ir. Biogeog. Soc.* 10: 72-80.

Barnard, P.C., O'Connor, J.P., and Speight, M.C.D., 1991, 'A review of published distribution data for Irish Neuroptera (Insecta), together with additional records and a check-list of the Irish species', *Bull. Ir. Biogeog. Soc.* 14: 109-123.

Baynes, E.S.A., 1964, *A revised catalogue of Irish Macrolepidoptera (butterflies and moths)*, Classey, Middlesex.

Baynes, E.S.A. 1965, 'Irish Lepidoptera: some recent discoveries', *Ir. Nat. J.* 15 (1):13-16.

Beirne, B., 1938, 'New Irish microlepidoptera', *Ir. Nat. J.* 7 (1): 12-15.

Beirne, B., 1940, 'New Irish microlepidoptera', *Ir. Nat. J.* 7 (10): 289.

Beirne, B., 1943a, 'Some Diptera from Ireland', *Ir. Nat. J.* 8 (3): 55-56.

Beirne, B., 1943b, 'Further records for Irish Diptera', *Ir. Nat. J.* 8 (4): 98-99.

Beirne, B., 1944, 'New records for Irish Lepidoptera', *Ir. Nat. J.* 8 (5): 147-148.

Beirne, B.P., and Harris, J.R., 1946, 'Light trap catches in Ireland in 1945 (Lep., Trich., Ephem., Plec.)', *Entomologist's Rec. J. Var.* 58: 46-49.

Birchall, E., 1859, 'A week at Killarney', *Zoologist* 17: 6766.

Birchall, E., 1867a, 'The Irish list of Lepidoptera', *Entomologist* 3: 192.

Birchall, E., 1867b, 'Irish insect-hunting grounds', *Entomologist* 3: 253.

Birchall, E., 1873, 'The Lepidoptera of Ireland', *Ent. mon. Mag.* 10: 155.

Birchall, E., 1874, '*Notodonta bicolora* in Ireland', *Ent. mon. Mag.* 10: 230.

Blackith, R.M., Blackith, R.E., and O'Connor, J.P., 1994, 'A check list of Irish flesh-flies (Diptera: Sarchophagidae) and their known distribution', *Ir. Nat. J.* 24: 427-434.

Bonaparte-Wyse, I.H., 1911, 'Coleoptera from south Kerry', *Ir. Nat.* 20: 55.

Bonaparte-Wyse, I.H., 1913, 'Lepidoptera and Coleoptera from Co. Kerry', *Ir. Nat.* 22: 75-76.

Bonaparte-Wyse, I.H., 1916, 'Lepidoptera from Killarney', *Ir. Nat.* 25: 73-74.

Bonaparte-Wyse, I.H., 1917, '*Notodonta bicoloria* in Co. Kerry', *Ir. Nat.* 26: 164-165.

Bonaparte-Wyse, I.H., 1920, 'Some Coleoptera and Lepidoptera from Co. Kerry', *Ir. Nat.* 29: 61-64.

Bond, K.G.M., and Van Nieukerken, E.J., 1987, 'Discovery of male *Ectodemia argyropeza* (Zeller) (Lepidoptera: Nepticulidae) in south west Ireland', *Entomol. Gaz.* 38: 191-195.

Bond, K.G.M., 1984, 'Recent records of Eriocraniidae (Lepidoptera) including three species new to the Irish list', *Ir. Nat. J.* 21(7): 323-324.

Bond, K.G.M., and Ryan, S., 1993, 'A further Irish montane record of *Stenus glacialis* Heer (Coleoptera: Staphylinidae)' *Ir. Nat. J.* 24: 338.

Breen, J., 1976, *Studies on* Formica lugubris *Zetterstedt in Ireland, (Hymenoptera: Formicidae)*. Ph.D. thesis (Unpublished) Nat. Univ. of Ireland.

Breen, J., 1977, 'The distribution of *Formica lugubris* Zetterstedt (Hymenoptera: Formicidae) in Ireland, with a discussion of its possible introduction', *Ir. Nat. J.* 19 (4):123-127.

Breen, J., 1979, 'Aphids visited by *Formica lugubris* Zetterstedt (Hymenoptera: Formicidae) including eleven species new to Ireland', *Ir. Nat. J.* 19: 349-352.

Bullock, D.J., 1974, 'Zoological note: Migrating butterflies at Ballyheigue, Co. Kerry', *Ir. Nat. J.* 18: 94.

Bullock, E., 1928, 'Coleoptera from the Killarney district of County Kerry, Ireland', *Ent. Mon. Mag.* 64: 102-4.

Bullock, E., 1928, '*Corixa dentipes* Thoms. in the Killarney district of Co. Kerry, Ireland', *Ent. Mon. Mag.* 64: 117.

Bullock, E., 1930, ' Some new records of Coleoptera from Ireland', *Ent. Mon. Mag.* 66: 140-1.

Bullock, E., 1932, 'Coleoptera from Co. Kerry, Ireland', *Ent. Mon. Mag.* 68:130.

Bullock, E., 1935, 'Coleoptera new to Ireland from Co. Kerry', *Ent. Mon. Mag.* 71: 130-1.

Butler, F.T., and O'Connor, J.P., 1994, 'A review of the Irish Ischnocera and Amblycera (Phthiraptera)', *Ir. Nat. J.* 24: 449-457.

Chalmers-Hunt, J.M., 1982, 'On some interesting Irish Lepidoptera in the National Museum of Ireland', *Ir. Nat. J.* 20 (12): 531-537.

Chandler, P.J., 1975, 'An account of the Irish species of two-winged flies (Diptera) belonging to the families of larger Brachycera (Tabanoidea and Asiloidea)', *Proc. R. Ir. Acad.* 75B: 81-110.

Chandler, P.J., 1982, 'Some Diptera of the Killarney area May 1981, including five species new to Ireland', *Ir. Nat. J.* 20(12): 555-558.

Chandler, P.J., 1987, 'New data on Irish fungus gnats (Diptera: Mycetophiloidea) including 51 species new to the Irish list', *Bull. Irish. Biogeog. Soc.* 10: 2-27.

Chandler, P.J., O'Connor, J.P., and Ashe, P., 1996, 'Notes on the Irish Sciaridae (Diptera), including five species new to Ireland', *Ir. Nat. J.* 25 (7): 258-259.

Chandler, P.J., and Speight, M.C.D., 1982, 'A preliminary list of the Irish Tephritidae (Diptera), with notes on the species', *Bull. Irish. Biogeog. Soc.* 6: 2-17.

Claessens, E.E.C.M., 1981, 'The stoneflies (Plecoptera) of the Netherlands' *Nieuwsbrief Europ. Invert. Surv. - Nederland.* 10: 73-77.

Clements, D.J., and Alexander, K.N.A., 1987, 'Distribution of the fly *Xylophagus ater* Meigen (Diptera: Xylophagidae) in the British Isles, with reference to its biology', *Proc. Trans. Br. Ent. Nat. Hist. Soc.*

Collingwood, C.A., 1958, 'A survey of Irish Formicidae', *Proc. R. Ir. Acad.* 59B (11): 213-19.

Costello, M.J., 1988, 'A review of the distribution of stoneflies (Insecta, Plecoptera) in Ireland', *Proc. R. Ir. Acad.* 88B: 1-22.

Costello, M.J., 1988, 'Preliminary observations on wing-length polymorphism in stoneflies (Plecoptera: Insecta) in Ireland', *Ir. Nat. J.* 22 (11): 474-478.

Coyler, C.N., and Hammond, C.O., 1968, *Flies of the British Isles,* Warne, London.

Cronin, K., 1995, 'A study of Lepidoptera migration with particular reference to Ireland and including an account of the implementation of a European Migrant Lepidoptera Survey', *Environment Science Report*, 2: 1-30.

Cross, J.R., 1974, '*Graphocephala coccinea* (Foster) (Hemiptera: cicadellidae), A bug new to Ireland', *Ir. Nat. J.* 18: 20.

Cuthbert, H.K. Gore, 1898, 'Hymenoptera', *Ir. Nat.* 7: 208-9

De Courcy Williams, M., 1986, '*Odinia bolentina* (Zetterstedt) (Diptera: odiniidae) new to Ireland', *Ir. Nat. J.* 22: 117-8.

Delap, A.H., 1896, '*Formica rufa*', *Ir. Nat.* 5: 167.

Donovan, C., 1932, 'Some Notodontids in Kerry' *Entomologist* 65: 238.

Donovan, C., 1936, *A catalogue of the Macrolepidoptera of Ireland and Supplement*.

Douglas, D. J., 1975, *The Chironomid fauna of the Killarney valley*, Co. Kerry. Its distribution, ecology and post-glacial history. Ph.D. thesis (Unpublished) University College, Dublin

Douglas, D. J., and Murray, D.A., 1980, 'A checklist of the Chironomidae (Diptera) of the Killarney valley catchment area, Ireland', *In* Murray, D.A. (ed.): *Chironomidae - Ecology, Systematics, Cytology and Physiology*, Pergamon Press, Oxford, 123-129.

Dowling, C., O'Connor, J.P., and O'Grady, M.F., 1981, 'A baseline survey of the Caragh, an unpolluted river in south-west Ireland: observations on the macroinvertebrates', *J. Life Sci. R. Dubl. Soc.* 2: 147-158.

Drake, C. M., 1981, *Provisional atlas of the larger Brachycera (Diptera) of Britain and Ireland*, Institute of Terrestrial Ecology, Huntington.

Dunne, R. and O'Connor, J.P., 1989, Some insects (Thysanoptera: Diptera) of economic importance, new to Ireland, *Ir. Nat. J.* 23 (2): 63-65.

Faris, R.C., 1956, Insects in a Kerry heatwave', *Ir. Nat. J.* 12: 65-68.

Fleming, S., and O'Mahony, P., 1978' 'New Munster locations for the holly blue *Celastrina argiolus* L. (Lepidoptera: Lycaenidae) and wood white *Lepidea sinapis* L. (Lepidoptera: Pieridae) butterflies', *Ir. Nat. J.* 19 (6): 193.

Foster, N.H., 1914, *Trichoniscus vividus* in Co. Kerry', *Ir. Nat.* 23: 248.

Foster, G., 1924, 'Kerry moths', *Ir. Nat.* 32: 46-47.

Foster, G., 1932, 'Stray visits to Kerry in search of moths', *Ent. Rec.* 44: 3.

Foster, G.N., 1995, 'Some records of aquatic coleoptera in Kerry, including *Helophorus griseus* Herbst (Coleoptera: Helophoridae) new for Ireland', *Ir. Nat. J.* 25: 32-34.

Foster, G.N., and Lott, D.A., 1989, 'Modern records of upland aquatic Coleoptera (Dytiscidae) in Ireland', *Ir. Nat. J.* 23 (2): 72-73.

Fowler, S.V., and Macgarvin, M., 1985, 'The impact of hairy wood ants, *Formica lugubris*, on the guild structure of herbivorous insects on birch *Betula pubescens*', *J. Anim. Ecol.* 60: 327-334.

Friday, L.E., 1987, 'New records of aquatic coleoptera from counties Cork and Kerry', *Ir. Nat. J.* 22 (8): 343-345.

Gillham, M., 1987, 'Some Auchenorrhyncha (Homoptera) collected from counties Kerry, Cork and Waterford', *Ir. Nat. J.* 22 (5): 212-213.

Graham, M.W.R. de V., 1956, 'A revision of the Walker types of Pteromalidae (Hym. Chalcidoidea). Part 1 (including descriptions of new genera and species)', *Entomologist's Mon. Mag.* 92: 76-98.

Graham, M.W.R. de V., 1969, 'The Pteromalidae of north-western Europe', *Bull. Britain. Mus. Nat. Hist. (Ent.) Suppl.* 16.

Graves, P.P., 1947, 'Odonata at Killarney', *Ir. Nat. J.* 4: 61-63.

Halbert, J.N., 1898, 'Coleoptera from Valentia Island', *Ir. Nat.* 7 (6): 149.

Halbert, J.N., 1908, 'Review of Bouskell (1905)', *Ir. Nat.* 17: 19-20.

Halbert, J.N., 1935, 'A list of Irish Hemiptera (Heteroptera and Cicadina)', *Proc. R. Ir. Acad.* 42: 211.

Hamilton, I., and Heath, J., 1976, 'Predation of *Pentatoma rufipes* L. (Hemiptera: pentatomidae) upon *Zygaena filipindulae* L. (Lepidiptera: zygaenidae)', *Ir. Nat. J.* 18: 337.

Hammond, C.O., 1983, *The dragonflies of Great Britain and Ireland*, Harley Books, Colchester.

Hancock, E.G., 1990, 'Some cranefly (Diptera:Tipulidae, Anisopodidae, Ptychopteridae) records from Kerry, Ireland, 1982', *Bull. Irish. Biogeog. Soc.* 13: 137-140.

Hardy, J.R., 1874, '*Notodonta bicolor* in Ireland', *Ent. Mon. Mag.* 10: 212.

Haynes, R.F., 1946, 'Killarney lepidoptera, spring 1946', *Ir. Nat. J.* 8: 436.

Haynes, R.F., 1961, 'Proposed Lepidoptera list for Killarney', *Ir. Nat. J.* 13: 147.

Haynes, R.F., 1977, 'Lepidoptera from Cos. Clare and Kerry', *Ir. Nat. J.* 19 (2): 51.

Haynes, R.F., 1989, 'Report on migrant insects in Ireland for 1988', *Ir. Nat. J.* 23 (3):117-119.

Haynes, R.F., and Hillis, J.P., 1981, 'Report on migrant insects in Ireland for 1980', *Ir. Nat. J.* 20 (7): 296.

Haynes, R.F., and Hillis, J.P., 1983, 'Report on migrant insects in Ireland for 1982', *Ir. Nat. J.* 21 (4): 324-325.

Haynes, R.F., and Hillis, J.P., 1984, 'Report on migrant insects in Ireland for 1983', *Ir. Nat. J.* 21 (7): 187.

Heal, H., 1965., 'The wood white *Leptidea sinapsis* L. and the railways', *Ir. Nat. J.* 15 (1): 8-13.

Heneghan, L., 1988, *The biogeography of Chironomidae (Diptera) from three Irish national parks: An analysis of pattern*, Unpublished report to the Office of Public Works.

Herbert, I. J.,1993, 'Scarce prominent *Odentosia carmelita* Esper (Lepidoptera: notodontidae) a species new to N. Ireland', *Ir. Nat. J.* 25: 263.

Hickey, S., 1976, *The influence of cultural eutrophication on the benthic macroinvertbrate communities in the littoral zone of the Killarney lakes*, B.Sc. thesis (Unpublished) University College, Dublin.

Hickin, N., 1992, *The butterflies of Ireland, a field guide*, Roberts Rinehart, Schull.

Hillis, J.P., 1976, 'Report on migrant insects in Ireland for 1975', *Ir. Nat. J.* 18: 356- 359.

Hillis, J.P., 1977, 'Report on migrant insects in Ireland for 1976', *Ir. Nat. J.* 19: 88- 90.

Hillis, J.P., 1978, 'Report on migrant insects in Ireland for 1977', *Ir. Nat. J.* 19: 243-244

Hillis, J.P., 1979, 'Report on migrant insects in Ireland for 1978', *Ir. Nat. J. 19*: 439-440.

Hillis, J.P. and Haynes, R.F., 1980, 'Report on migrant insects in Ireland for 1979', *Ir. Nat. J.* 20: 122-124.

Janson, O.E. 1914, 'Coleoptera in Co. Kerry', *Ir. Nat.* 23: 38-40.

Janson, O.E., 1920, 'Coleoptera in Co. Kerry', *Ir. Nat.* 29: 1-6.

Janson, O.B. and Bonaparte-Wyse, L.N., 1924, 'Coleoptera from south Kerry', *Ir. Nat.* 33: 125-128.

Johnston, C., 1993, *Provisional atlas of the Crytpophagidae-Atomariinae (Coleoptera) of Britain and Ireland*, Harding P.T., and Dring, J.C.M., (Eds) Biological Records Centre, Monks Wood.

Kane, W.F. de V., 1886, Report of researches at Killarney and south of Ireland; Macrolepidoptera, etc', *Proc. R. Ir. Acad. Series* 2, 14: 588-598.

Kane, W.F. de V., 1893, 'A catalogue of the Lepidoptera of Ireland', *Ent.* 26: 212.

King, J.J.F., and Halbert, J.N., 1910, 'A list of the Neuroptera of Ireland', *Proc. R. Ir. Acad.* 28 B: 29-112.

Kirby, P., 1983, 'Heteroptera recorded from the Killarney area, 28th. August-7th. September 1981', *Ir. Nat. J.* 21 (1): 45-47.

Kirby, P., 1991, 'Hemiptera (Heteroptera and Auchenorhyncha) recorded from south-west Ireland (Co.s Cork, Kerry and Clare), September 1989', *Bull. Irish. Biogeog. Soc.* 14: 90-104.

Lavery T.A., 1991, 'Report of migrant insects in Ireland for 1990', *Ir. Nat. J.* 23 (11): 458-461.

Lavery, T.A., 1991, *Killarney National Park Butterflies*, Office of Public Works.

Lavery, T.A., 1993, 'A review of the distribution, ecology and status of the marsh fritillary, *Euphydryas aurinia*, Rottemburg, 1775 (Lepidoptera: Nymphalidae) in Ireland', *Ir. Nat. J.* 24 (5): 192-199.

Lavery, T.A., 1995, 'A review of the status of the White Prominent, *Leucodonta bicoloria* ([D. & S., 1775]) in the British Isles (Lepidoptera, Notodontidae)', *Environment Science Report,* 3: 1-3.

Lavery, T.A., Speight, M.C.D., and Blackith, R. M., 1993, 'Records of some Irish dance flies, including eleven species new to Ireland and a checklist of the Irish fauna (Diptera: Empididae, Hybotidae, Microphoridae)', *Ir. Nat. J.* 24: 204-212.

Lesten, D., 1958, 'The distribution of waterbugs (Hemiptera-Heteroptera: Hydrocorisae) in Ireland, *Ent. Mon. Mag.* 94: 26-31.

Lucas, Mrs. G.E., 1938, 'Co. Kerry moths', *Ir. Nat. J.* 7: 88.

Mahdi, T., and Whittaker, J.B., 1993, 'Do birch trees (*Betula pubescens)* grow better if foraged by wood ants?', *J. Anim. Ecol.* 62: 101-116.

McCarthy, T.K., and Walton, G.A., 1980, 'Sigara selecta (Fieb.) (Hemiptera/ Heteroptera: Corixidae) new to Ireland, with notes on water bugs recorded from the Dingle peninsula', *Ir. Nat. J.* 20 (2): 64-66.

McNeill, N., 1960, 'Odonata - Irish distribution', *Ir. Nat. J.* 13 (8): 190.

McNeill, N., 1968, 'Odonata - Irish distribution', *Ir. Nat. J.* 16 (1): 25.

McNeill, N., 1973, 'A revised and tabulated list of the Irish Hemiptera-Heteroptera: part 1 Geocorisae', *Proc. R. Ir. Acad.* 73B (3): 57-60.

Mendel, H., 1988, *Provisional atlas of the click beetles (Coleoptera: Curclionoidea)*, Instituteof Terrestrial Ecology, Grange-over-Sands.

More, A.G., 1870, 'Report on the collections made in Kerry; a list of the animals observed in Kerry , July and August, 1868', *J. R. Dubl. Soc.* 5: 389-394.

Morley, C., 1931, 'A synopsis of the British Hymenopterous family Cynipidae', *Entomologist* 64: 183-186.

Morris, M.D., 1993a, Some species of weevils recorded erroneously from Ireland, and others whose status requires confirmation. (Coleoptera: Curculionoidea)', *Ir. Nat. J.* 24: 325-328.

Morris, M.D, 1993b, 'A critical review of the weevils of Ireland and their distribution', *Proc. R. Ir. Acad.* 93B: 69-84.

Murray, D.A. 1974, 'Notes on some Chironomidae (Diptera) from the Killarney area', *Ent. Tidskr.* 95: 177-181.

Murray, D.A., 1976, 'Buchonomyia thienemanni, Fittkau, a rare and unusual species (Diptera, Chironomidae) recorded from Killarney, Ireland', *Ent. Gaz.* 27: 179-180.

Murray, D.A., 1976, 'Thienemannimyia pseudocarnea N. sp. a palaearctic species of the Tanypodinae (Diptera, Chironomidae)', *Ent. Scand.* 7: 191-194.

Murray, D.A., and Ashe, P, 1981, 'A description of the larva and pupa of *Eurycnemuscrassipes Panzer*, (Diptera, Chironomidae)', *Ent. Scand.* 12: 357-361.

Murray, D.A., and Ashe, P., 1981, 'A description of the pupa of *Buchonomyia thienemanni*, Fittkau with notes on its ecology and on the phylogenetic position of the Buchonomyiinae (Diptera, Chironomidae)', *Spixiana* 4 (1): 5-68.

Murray, D.A., and Ashe, P., 1985, 'A description of the adult of *Buchonomyia thienemanni*, Fittkau and a re-assessment of the phylogenetic position of the Buchonomyiinae (Diptera, Chironomidae)', *Spixiana, Suppl:* 11: 149-160.

Murray, D.A., and Douglas, D.J., 1980, 'A checklist of the Chironomidae (Diptera) of the Killarney valley catchment area, Ireland', *In* Murray, D.A. (ed.) *Chironomidae - Ecology, Systematics, Cytology and Physiology*, Pergammon Press, Oxford. 123 137.

Nash, R., Anderson, R. and O'Connor, J.P. 1997, 'Recent additions to the list of Irish Coleoptera', *Ir. Nat. J.* 25 (9): 319-325.

Nelson, B., 1997, 'Records of aquatic Heteroptera from Northern Ireland and Co. Kerry', *Ir. Nat. J.* 25 (9): 342-343.

Ni Annrachain, O., 1972, *Studies of the Ephemeroptera in the Killarney region*, B.Sc. thesis (Unpublished) University College, Dublin

O'Connor, J.P., 1978a, '*Hydroptila tigurina* Ris new to Ireland, with notes on *Apatania wallengreni* McLachlan and *Limnephilus binotatus* Curtis (Insecta: Trichoptera)', *Ir. Nat. J.* 19 (6): 191.

O'Connor, J.P., 1978b, 'The stonefly *Capnia atra* Morton (Plecoptera, Capniidae) confirmed as an Irish species', *Entomologist's Gaz.* 29: 156-158.

O'Connor, J.P., 1981, '*Apatania auricula* (Forsslund)', *Ir. Nat. J.* 20 (7): 302.

O'Connor, J.P., 1982, '*Ithytrichia clavata* (Trichoptera:Hydroptilidae) a caddisfly new to Ireland', *Ir. Nat. J.* 20 (12): 548-549.

O'Connor, J.P., 1983, 'A record of a human-biting deer fly (*Lipoptena cervi* (L.)) from Ireland', *Entomologist's Rec. J. Var. 95: 32-33.*

O'Connor, J.P., 1986, 'Notes on *Scolopostethus puberulus* Horvath and *Limnoporus rufos-cutellatus* (Latreille) (Hemiptera) in Ireland', *Entomologist' s Rec. J. Var.* 98: 33-35.

O'Connor, J.P., and Ashe, P., 1994, 'Further records of *Drosophila repleta* Wollaston (Diptera) in Ireland', *Ir. Nat. J.* 24: 467

O'Connor, J.P.,1987, 'A review of the Irish Trichoptera', *Proc. 5th Int. Symp. on Trichoptera*: 73-77.

O'Connor, J.P., 1989, 'Notes on Irish temnostethus (Hem.-Het. Anthocoridae) in the National Museum of Ireland', *Ent. Mon. Mag.* 125: 206.

O'Connor, J.P., 1996, 'Further records of Irish Pteromalidae (Hymenoptera: Chalcidoidea), including ten species new to Ireland', *Ir. Nat. J.* 25 (7): 254-2257.

O'Connor, J.P., and Bracken, J.J., 1978, 'Notes on *Hydropsyche instabilis* (Curtis) and *H. siltalai* Dohler (Insecta: Trichoptera) in Ireland', *Ir.Nat. J.* 19: 282-283.

O'Connor, J.P., and Murphy, D., 1988, 'Some records of Irish Odonata (Insecta)', *Bull. Ir. Biogeog.* Soc.11: 35-40.

O'Connor, J.P., O'Connor, M.A., and De V. Graham, M.W.R., 1989, 'Some records of Irish Pteromalidae (Hymenoptera: Chalcidoidea) including five species new to Ireland', *Ir. Nat. J.* 23(2): 69-71.

O'Connor, J.P., O'Grady, M.F., and Bracken, J.J., 1986, 'Observations on the Corixidae (Insecta:Hemiptera) of the Killarney lakes and district', *Bull. Ir. Biogeog.* Soc. 9: 15-26

O'Connor, J.P., and Sleeman, D.P., 1987, 'A review of the Irish Hippoboscidae (Insecta: Diptera)', *Ir. Nat. J.* 22: 236-239.

O'Connor, J.P., Winter, T.G., and Good, J.A., 1991, 'A review of the Irish Scolytidae (Insecta: Coleoptera)', *Ir. Nat. J.* 23: 403-409.

O'Connor, J.P., and Wise, E.J., 1984, 'Observations on the Trichoptera of the Killarney lakes Co. Kerry, Ireland', *Ir. Fish. Invest. Series* A 24: 1-15.

O'Grady, M.F., O'Connor, J.P., and Champ, W.S.T., 1979, 'Preliminary notes on Irish lake oligochaeta', *Ir. Nat.J.* 19: 323-326.

O' Rourke, F.J., 1950, 'The distribution and general ecology of the Irish Formicidae', *Proc. R. Ir. Acad.* 52B (9): 383-410.

O'Sullivan, A., 1979, *An investigation of the localized effects of organic enrichment on benthic macroinvertebrate community structure in the littoral zone of Lough Leane,* Co.Kerry, M.Sc. thesis (Unpublished) University College, Dublin

Ottoson, J.G., and Anderson, J.M., 1983, 'Numbers, seasonality and feeding habits of insects attacking ferns in Britain: an ecological consideration', *J. Anim. Ecol.* 52: 385-406.

Pearce, E.J., and Walton, G.A., 1939, 'A contribution towards an ecological survey of the aquatic and semi-aquatic Hemiptera - Heteroptera (Waterbugs) of the British Isles', *Trans. Soc. Brit. Ent. 6: 149.*

Pollard, E., 1988, 'Temperature, rainfall, and butterfly numbers', *J. Appl. Ecol.* 25: 819-828.

Quirke, W., 1986, A study of factors influencing the distribution of macroinvertebrates in Ross bay, Lough Leane, Co. Kerry with particular reference to the effects of sewage effluent, M.Sc. thesis (Unpublished) University College, Dublin

Ragge, D.R., 1965, Grasshoppers, crickets and cockroaches of the British Isles. Warne, London.

Raymond, N., 1976, *A quantative comparison of the effects of organic enrichment on the productivity of benthic macroinvertebrate communities in the littoral zone of Lough Leane,* Co. Kerry. B.Sc. thesis (Unpublished) University College, Dublin

Rear, D., 1966, 'Lepidoptera seen on the Blasket islands and the adjoining mainland, 1965', *Ir. Nat. J.* 15: 6.

Roche, S., 1988, *An investigation of the macroinvertebrate community of the three lakes in the Killarney valley system using artificial substrates as a sampling technique.* B.Sc. thesis (Unpublished) University College Cork. .

Saunders, E., 1902, 'Hymenoptera collected by Col. Yerbury in S.W. Ireland in 1901', *Entomologist's mon. Mag.* 38: 51-5.

Sleeman, D.P., and Smiddy, P., 1994' 'Bat fleas in Ireland: a review', *Ir. Nat. J.* 24: 444 448.

Sleeman, D.P., and Smiddy, P., 1994, 'Records of fleas (Siphonaptera) from Irish mammals and birds', *Ir. Nat. J.* 24: 465-467.

Sleeman, D.P., Smiddy, P., and Moore, P., 1994, 'The fleas of Irish terrestrial mammals: a review' *Ir. Nat. J.* 25 (7): 237-248.

Smithers, C.N., and O'Connor, J.P., 1991, 'New records of Psocoptera (Insecta) (Booklice, Barklice) from Ireland, including a species previously known from New Zealand', *Ir. Nat. J.* 23: 477-486.

Speight, M.C.D., 1972, 'Ground beetles (Col. Carabidae) from the Bourn Vincent National Park', *Ir. Nat. J.* 17: 226-230.

Speight, M.C.D., 1976, 'Irish Orthoptera: Some distribution records, including the first record of *Tachycines asynamorus* Adelung (Rhaphidophoridae)', *Ir. Nat. J.* 18 (9): 272-273.

Speight, M.C.D., 1976, '*Amara montivaga* Sturm (Col., Carabidae) in Ireland', *Ent. Mon. Mag.* 111 (1337-9): 200.

Speight, M.C.D., 1978, '*Myopa curtirostris* new to Ireland and some other Irish Conopid (Diptera) records', *Ir. Nat. J.* 19 (8): 276.

Speight, M.C.D., 1980, '*Brachypalpus laphrifomis* (Diptera: Syrphidae) in Ireland, and its probable demise', *Ir. Nat. J.* 20: 70-72.

Speight, M.C.D., 1981, 'The Irish *Anasimyia* species, including a key and first records of *A. contracta* (Diptera: Syrphidae)', *Ir. Nat. J.* 21 (4): 187.

Speight, M.C.D., 1982' '*Acrocera globulus, Limnia paludicola* and *Sphaerophoria loewi:* insects new to Ireland', *Ir. Nat. J.* 20: 369-372.

Speight, M.C.D., 1983, '*Cordilura aemula* and *Microprosopa pallidicauda* new to Ireland, *Trichopalpus fraternus* confirmed as an Irish insect and other Irish records of Scathophagidae (Diptera)', *Ir. Nat. J.* 21 (4): 187.

Speight, M.C.D., 1985, 'The extinction of indigenous *Pinus sylvestris* in Ireland: Relevant faunal data', *Ir. Nat. J.* 21: 449-453.

Speight, M.C.D., 1986, 'Use 00of invertebrates, as exemplified by certain insect groups, in considering hypotheses about the history of the Irish postglacial fauna', *Occ. Pub. Ir. Biogeog. Soc.* 1: 60-66.

Speight, M.C.D., 1987, 'The Irish Asilid (Diptera) fauna', *Bull. Ir. Biogeog. Soc.* 10: 56-71.

Speight, M.C.D., 1988, 'The Irish Cerambycid fauna (Coleoptera: Cerambycidae). *Bull. Ir. Biogeog. Soc.* 11: 18-24.

Speight, M.C.D., 1989, 'Some Irish records of the genera *Glischrochilus* and *Soronia* (Coleoptera: Buprestidae)', *Bull Ir. Biogeog.* Soc. 12: 18-21.

Speight, M.C.D., 1989, 'The Irish elaterid and Bupestid fauna (Coleoptera: Elateridae and Buprestidae), *Bull. Ir. Biogeog. Soc.* 12: 31-62.

Speight, M.C.D., 1990, '*Pyropterus nigroruber* (Degeer) in Ireland (Coleoptera: Lycidae), with a key to distinguish this beetle from related European species', *Bull.. Ir. Biogeog. Soc.* 13 (2): 166-172.

Speight, M.C.D., 1991, 'The fauna of Irish sand dunes', *In* Quigley, M.B., (ed) *A guide to the sand dunes of Ireland*, 3rd. Congress European Union for Dune Conservation and Coastal management, Galway.

Speight, M.C.D., 1996a, '*Aulogastromtia anisodactyla, Lyciella stylata* and *Sapromyza zetterstedti* (Diptera; Lauxaniidae), insects new to Ireland', *Ir. Nat. J.* 25 (5): 175-176.

Speight, M.C.D., 1996b, '*Cheilosia psilophthalma* and *Odinia Boletina*: insects new to Ireland and *Sapromyza sexpunctata* confirmed as an Irish species (Diptera; Syrphidae, Odiniidae and Lauxaniidae)' *Ir. Nat. J.* 25 (5): 178-182.

Speight, M.C.D., Anderson, R., and Luff, M.L., 1982, 'An annotated list of the Irish ground beetles (Col., Carabidae + Cicindelidae)', *Bull. Ir. Biogeog. Soc.* 6: 25- 53.

Speight, M.C.D., and Chandler, P.J., 1995, '*Paragus constrictus, Pteromicra pectorosa* and *Stegana similis:* insects new to Ireland and *Stegana coleoptrata*, presence in Ireland confirmed (Diptera)', *Ir. Nat. J.* 25: 28-32.

Speight, M.C.D., Chandler, P., and Nash, R., 1975, 'Irish Syrphidae (Diptera): Notes on the species and an account of their distribution', *Proc. R. Ir. Acad.* 75B (1): 1-80.

Speight, M.C.D., and Irwin, A.G., 1978, *'Irish Paragus* (Diptera: Syrphidae) including a key to British Isles species', *Ir. Nat. J.* 19 (6): 193.

Speight, M.C.D., and Nash, R., 1993, *'Chrysotoxum cautum, Ctenophora ornata, C. Pectinicornis, Helophilus trivittatus* and *Mesembriana mystacea* (Diptera), insects new to Ireland', *Ir. Nat. J.* 24: 231-236.

Speight, M.C.D., and Williams, M. de C., 1981, *'Macrophya duodecempunctata, Nematus frenalis* and *Pamphilius gyllenhali:* Sawflies (Hymenoptera: Symphyta) new to Ireland', *Ir. Nat. J.* 20 (8): 345-347.

Speight, M.C.D., and Williams, M. de C., 1992, 'Records of 23 species of Dolichopodidae (Diptera) whose presence in Ireland requires reconformation', *Ir. Nat. J.* 24: 17-20.

Stelfox, A.W., 1927, 'A list of the Hymenoptera Aculeata of Ireland', *Proc. R. Ir. Acad.* 37B (22): 201-355.

Stelfox, A.W., 1939, 'Some additions and corrections to the list of Irish bees, wasps and ants', *Ir. Nat. J.* 7: 203-205.

Sweeney, P., 1977, *An investigation of the effects of cultural eutrophication on certain macroinvertebrate communities of Lough Leane,* Killarne, B.Sc. thesis (Unpublished), University College, Dublin

Twomey, H., 1984, The profundal macroinvertebrates of the Upper Lake, Muckross Lake, and Lough Leane, Killarney, B.A.(Mod) thesis (Unpublished) Trinity College Dublin

White, A., 1858, 'On a newly discovered moth in Ireland (*Notondonta bicolor*)', *Proc. Dubl. Nat. Hist. Soc.* 2: 137-138.

Williams. A.C., 1914, 'Early butterflies at Killarney', *Ir. Nat.* 23: 160.

Wise, E.J., 1976, 'The Ephemeroptera, Odonata, Plectoptera and Coleoptera of the Killarney lakes', *In* Bracken, J.J., and Casey, T.J., *Final Report of the Killarney Valley Lake Survey (1971-1975),* Limnological Research Unit, University College Dublin.

Wise, E.J., and O'Sullivan, A., 1980, 'Preliminary observations on the benthic macroin-vertebrate communities of Ross Bay, a polluted area of Lough Leane, s.w. Ireland', *Water Res.* 14: 1-13.

Withers, P., 1992, 'A further occurrence of *Psectra diptera* (Burmeister) (Insecta, Neuroptera) in Ireland*', Ir. Nat. J.* 24: 79

Withers, P., and O'Connor, J.P., 1992, 'A preliminary account of the Irish species of moth fly (Diptera: Psychodidae)', *Proc. R.Ir. Acad.* 92B: 61-77.

Wright, W.S., 1972, 'Report on migrant insects in Ireland for 1971', *Ir. Nat. J.* 17: 193-194.

Wright, W.S., 1973, 'Report on migrant insects in Ireland for 1972', *Ir. Nat. J.* 17: 414.

Wright, W.S., 1974, 'Report on migrant insects in Ireland for 1973', *Ir. Nat. J.* 18: 80.

Wright, W.S., 1975, 'Report on migrant insects in Ireland for 1974', *Ir. Nat. J.* 18: 251.

Wyse, L.H.B.,. 1917, *'Notondonta bicolor* in Co. Kerry', *Irish Nat.* 26: 164-165.

Yerbury, J.W., 1902, 'A list of the Diptera met with in Cork and Kerry during the summer of 1901', *Ir. Nat.* 11: 74-93.

MOLLUSCS

Adams, L.E., 1989, *'Paludestrina jenkinsi,* Smith, var. minor, nov, in south Ireland', *Ir. Nat.* 7 (8): 199.

Berrow, S., Nunn, J., Flannery, K., and Rogan, E., 1995, *'Adula simpsoni* (Marshall, 1900) recorded from a whale skull trawled up off south-west Ireland', *Ir. Nat. J.* 25 (4): 150-151.

Bishop, M.J., 1977, 'The Mollusca of acid woodland in west Cork and Kerry', *Proc. R.Ir. Acad.* 77 B (13): 227-244.

Bloomer, H.H., 1927, *'Margaritifera margaritifera;* notes on the variation of the British and Irish forms', *Proc. Malac. Soc. Lond.* 17: 208-216.

Collier, E., 1902, *'Succinea oblonga,* Co's. Cork, Kerry S. and Fermanagh', *J. Conch,* 10: 53.

Gosselin, L.A., and Bourget, E., 1989, 'The performance of an intertidal predator *Thais lapillus,* in relation to structural heterogeneity', *J. Anim. Ecol.* 58: 287-303.

Jackson, J.W., 1925, 'The distribution of *Margaritifera margaritifera* in the British Isles', *J. Conch.* 17: 195-211.

Kemp. S.W., 1905, *'Geomalacus maculosus* on Deenish Island, Co. Kerry', *Irish Nat.* 14: 262.

Lucas, B.R., 1908, *'Testacella haliotidea* and other mollusca in Co. Kerry', *Irish Nat.* 17: 22.

Lucey, J., 1995, 'The distribution of *Anodonta cygnea* (L.) and *Anodonta anatina* (L.) (Mollusca:Bivalvia) in southern Irish rivers and streams with records from other areas', *Ir. Nat. J.* 25: 1-8.

Macon, T.T., and Lund, J.W.G., 1954, 'Records from some Irish lakes: Part 1, Mollusca, Gammarus, Asellus, Ephemoptera and Heteroptera: Part 2, Phytoplankton, *Proc. R. Ir. Acad.* 56B (4): 135-158.

Minchin, D., 1985, *'Lutraria angustior* Philippi (Mollusca: Lamellibranchia) in Irish waters', *Ir. Nat. J.* 21 (10): 454-459.

Nunn, J., 1996, *'Charonia lampas* (Linnaeus, 1758) alive at Fenit Seaworld', *Ir. Nat. J.* 25 (8): 303.

O'Grady M.F., 1974, *The ecology of Potamopyrgus jenkinsi (Smith) in the Killarney lakes,* M.Sc.thesis (Unpublished) University College, Dublin

Platts, E.A., and Speight, M.C.D.,, 1988, 'The taxonomy and distribution of the Kerry Slug, *Geomalacus maculosus* Allman, 1843 (Mollusca: Arionidae) with a discussion of its status as a threatened species', *Ir. Nat. J.* 22 (10): 417-430.

Praeger, R. Ll., 1899, 'Marine shells from the Kenmare river', *Ir. Nat.* 8 (7): 164.

Rogers, T., 1892, 'On the viviparous nature of *Balea (Balea perversa)* at Killarney', *Journ. of Conch.* 7: 40.

Rogers, T., 1900, 'The eggs of the Kerry slug', *Irish Nat.* 9: 168.

Scharff, R.F., 1893, 'Note on the geographical distribution of *Geomalacus maculosus* Allm. in Ireland', *Proc. Malacol. Soc. London* 1: 17.

Scharff, R.F., 1892, 'The Irish land and freshwater mollusca', *Ir. Nat.* 1 (4): 65-67, 1 (5): 87-90, 1 (6): 105-111, 1 (7): 135-138, 1 (8): 149-153, 1 (9): 177-181.

Scharff, R.F., 1898a, 'The land Mollusca of the Great Skellig', *Ir. Nat.* 7 (1): 9-11.

Scharff, R.F., 1898b, 'The Mollusca of the Great Skellig', *Ir. Nat.* 7 (2): 49.

Scully, R.W. 1891, 'A new locality for *Geomalacus maculosus'*, *Zool.* 3 (15): 35.

Seaward, D.R., (Ed.), 1982, *Sea area atlas of the marine molluscs of Britain and Ireland,* Nature Conservancy Council, Shrewsbury.

Stelfox, A.W., 1911, 'A list of the land and freshwater mollusks of Ireland', *Proc. R. Ir. Acad.* 29B: 65-163.

Stelfox, A.W., 1915, 'A list of the land and freshwater Mollusca of the Dingle promontary', *Ir. Nat.* 24: 17-37.

Stubbs, A.G., and Adams, L.E., 1889, 'Supplementary notes on the Mollusca of south-west Ireland', *Ir. Nat.* 7 (11): 261-263.

Sykes, B.A., 1905, *The Molluscs and Brachiopods of Ballynakill and Bofin harbours, Co. Galway and of the deep water off the west and south-west coasts of Ireland,* Ann. Rep. Fish. Ireland (1902-1903), H.M.S.O., Dublin.

Tomlin, J.R. le B., 1910, 'Land and freshwater Mollusca at Cloghane, Co. Kerry', *Journ. of Conch.* 12: 77.

Went, A.E.J., 1947, 'Notes on Irish pearls', *Ir. Nat. J.* 9 (2): 41-45.

CRUSTACEANS

Hillis, J.P., 1966, 'Stone crab, *Lithodes maia* (Linn.) from Co. Kerry', *Ir. Nat. J.* 15 (6): 175-176.

Hogan, M., 1977, *Studies of the Cladoceran microfossils in short cores from Lough Leane, Killarney,* B.Sc. thesis (Unpublished) University College, Dublin

Holmes, J.M.C., 1983, 'Some amphipods (Crustacea: Podoceridae) recorded off the south-west coast of Ireland' *Ir. Nat. J.* 21 (3): 128-129.

Mercer, J.P., 1973, 'Littoral and benthic investigations on the west coast of Ireland II (Section B, Shellfish investigations, The occurrence of *Palinurus mauritanicus* Gruvel 1911 on the west coast of Ireland (Decapoda: Palinuridae)', *Proc. R. Ir. Acad.* 73B: 445-449.

Minchin, D., 1989, 'The most northerly population of the deep water crawfish *Palinurus mauritanicus* Gruvel', *Ir. Nat. J.* 23 (4): 142-145.

Minchin, D., and Holmes, J.M.C., 1987, '*Phronima sedentaria* (ForsskÜl) (Crustacea: Amphipoda) in Irish waters', *Ir. Nat. J. 22 (5): 202-203.*

O'Hanlon, R.P., and Bolger, T., 1994, 'The current status of *Arcitalitrus dorrieni* (Crustacea: Amphipoda: Talitridae) in Ireland', *Ir. Nat. J.* 24: 434-444.

O'Riordan, C. E.. 1973, 'The deep water crustacean *Paromola cuvieri* (Risso) in Irish waters', *Ir. Nat. J.* 17: 352.

O'Riordan, C.E., 1983, 'Some observations on the occurrence of *Paromola cuvieri* (Risso) (Crustacea) off the Irish coast', *Ir. Nat. J.* 21 (1): 36.

Pack Beresford, D.R., and Foster, N.H, 1911, 'The woodlice of Ireland: their distribution and classification', *Proc. R. Ir. Acad.* 29 (B): 165-190.

Pack Beresford, D.R., and Foster, N.H., 1913, 'Additions to the distributional records of woodlice in Ireland till the end of 1912', *Ir. Nat.* 22: 45-48.

Quigley, D.T.G., Flannery, K., and Holmes, J.M.C., 1994, 'First record of the crab *Chaceon (Geryon) affinis* from Irish waters', *Ir. Nat. J.* 24: 460-461.

Reynolds, J.D., 1982, 'Notes on the Irish distribution of the freshwater crayfish', *Bull. Ir. Biogeog. Soc.* 6: 18-24.

Scharff, R.F., 1899, 'Crustacea from the south-west coast of Ireland', *Ir. Nat.* 8 (3): 60.

Selbie, C.M., 1914, 'The Decapoda Reptantia off the coasts of Ireland. Part I. Palinura, Astacura and Anomura (except Paguridae)', *Sci. Invest. Fish. Brch. Ireland* 1-116.

Walshe, S., 1977, *Biological monitoring of Lough Leane with special reference to the zoo-plankton communities and related physico-chemical parameters*, B.Sc. thesis (Unpublished) University College, Dublin.

White, P., 1973, *The Cladocera of Lough Leane, Killarney, Co. Kerry*, B.Sc. thesis (Unpublished), University College, Dublin

OTHER INVERTEBRATES

Adair, F., 1974, Notes on the distribution and behaviour of the cave spider *Meta menardij* Latri in Ireland (Arancae argiopidae), *Ir. Nat. J.* 18: 40.

Barber, A.D., and Keay, A.N., 1988, *Provisional atlas of the centipedes of the British Isles,* Institute of Terrestrial Ecology, Grange-over-Sands.

Blackwall, J., 1861, *A history of the spiders of Great Britain and Ireland*, Ray Society, London.

British Myriapod Group, 1988, *Preliminary atlas of the millipedes of the British Isles*, Natural Environment Research Council, Huntingdon.

Carpenter, G.H., 1898, 'A list of the spiders of Ireland', *Proc. R. Ir. Acad.* 3 (5): 128-210.

Collins, S.P., 1980, 'Notes on the distribution and ecology of marine polyzoa from some shores in Cork and Kerry', *Scient. Proc. R. Dubl. Soc.* (A) 6: 373-83.

Conroy, J.C., 1984, 'Some comments on the species of the sub-genus Monatractides viets in Ireland, with a description of *Torrenticola (Monotractides) hibernica* Sp.Nov. (Acari, Hydrchnellae, Torrenticolidae)', *Ir. Nat. J.* 21(8): 329-34.

English, M., 1976, 'New records of millipedes from Munster, Ireland' *Ir. Nat. J.* 18 (2): 341.

Locket, G.H, Millidge, A.F. and Merrett, P., 1974, *'British spiders* 3: i-ix, 1-314. Ray Society, London.

Martyn, K.P., 1988, *Provisional atlas of the ticks (Ixodoidea) of the British Isles,* Institute of Terrestrial Ecology, Grange-over-Sands.

Mackie, D.W., 1972, 'The distribution of some Irish spiders and harvestmen', *Ir. Nat. J.* 17: 234-237.

Nichols, A.R., 1911, 'Polyzoa from the coasts of Ireland', *Scient. Invest. Fish Brch. Ire.* (1910) 1: 1-37.

Sankey, J.H.P., 1988, *Provisional atlas of The harvest-spiders (Arachnida: Opiliones) of the British Isles.* Institute of Terrestrial Ecology, Grange-over-Sands.

McCarthy, T.K., 1975, 'Observations on the distribution of the freshwater leeches (Hirudinea) in Ireland', *Proc. R. Ir. Acad.* 75B (21): 401-451.

O'Riordan, C. E., 1973, 'Notes on the distribution of *Actinauge richardi* (Marion) (Coelenterata: Actiniaria) off the Irish coast', *Ir. Nat. J.* 17: 351.

O'Riordan, C. E., 1975, 'Notes on the occurrence of *Charonia lampas* L. off the Co. Kerry coast', *Ir. Nat. J.* 18: 237.

Pack Beresford, D.R., 1909, 'A supplementary list of the spiders of Ireland', *Proc. R. Ir. Acad.* 27B: 87-118.

Pack Beresford, D.R., 1929, 'Araneida -a revision of the Irish spider list', *In* Praeger, R.L. (ed.) 'Report on recent additions of the Irish fauna and flora', *Proc. R. Ir. Acad.* 39B 1: 41-52.

Parker, J.R. 1975, 'Spiders from Inishtearaght: Blasket Islands: S.W. Ireland', *The Secretary's News Letter of the British Arachnological Society* 12: 8-9.

Parker, J.R. 1976, 'More spiders from Inishtearaght', *The Secretary's News Letter of the British Arachnological Society* 14: 7.

Petersen, A.C., 1975, 'A review of the distribution of Irish millipedes (Diplopoda)', *Proc. R. Ir. Acad.* 75B: 569-583.

Roberts, M.J., 1985, *The spiders of Great Britain and Ireland*: 1, Harley Books, Colchester.

Somerfield, P., 1988, 'New records of marine halacaridae (Acari: Prostigmata) from rocky shores around the Irish coast', *Bull. Irish. Biogeog. Soc.* 11: 6-21.

Van Helsdingen, P.J., 1996, 'The county distribution of Irish spiders, incorporating a revised catalogue of the species', *Ir. Nat. J.* Special Zoological Supplement.

Wanless, F., 1965, 'Spiders collected in Ireland during 1964', *Ir. Nat. J.* 15: 43-46.

West, A.B., 1978, '*Cittotaenia pectinata* (Cestoda: Anoplocephalidae) in a wild rabbit from Co. Kerry', *Ir. Nat. J.* 19 (7): 251.

INDEX